Now Hiring

Now Hiring

The Feminization
of Work in the United States,
1900–1995

Julia Kirk Blackwelder

TEXAS A&M UNIVERSITY PRESS
College Station

Copyright © 1997 by Julia Kirk Blackwelder

Manufactured in the United States of America

All rights reserved

First edition

04 03 02 01 00 99 98 97   5 4 3 2 1

The paper used in this book meets the minimum requirements
of the American National Standard for Permanence
of Paper for Printed Library Materials, Z39.48-1984.
Binding materials have been chosen for durability.

Library of Congress Cataloging-in-Publication Data

Blackwelder, Julia Kirk, 1943–
    Now hiring : the feminization of work in the United States, 1900–1995 / Julia
    Kirk Blackwelder.
        p.   cm.
    Includes bibliographical references and index.
    ISBN 0-89096-776-8 (cloth). — ISBN 0-89096-798-9 (paper)
        1. Women—Employment—United States—History—20th century.
    I. Title.
    HD6095.B57   1997   97-15922
    331.4'0973'0904—dc21   CIP

FOR ZILPHA

Contents

Illustrations

Tables

Preface

Contemporary backlash against working women in the United States and their rights to equity in employment generated the writing of this book. Because the backlash has so frequently perverted the historical record in defining concepts such as "family values," "traditional women," and "traditional families," I hoped to let history speak for itself. Women's latitude to choose unpaid work over market labor has steadily decreased during this century, partly as a consequence of the major changes in the content of jobs that have steadily fed employers' efforts to hire women and partly as a consequence of the public's increasing dependence on commercial goods and services. The flow of women into the labor market began far in advance of this century, and similar trends accompanied economic development throughout the world. It seems highly unlikely, then, that paid employment among women will decline significantly in the future. We in the United States have consistently struggled at some level with a conflict between idealized notions of womanhood and women's employment. It is unlikely that debate over gender roles will fade away, but long-term economic trends also suggest that backlash will not reverse women's rising rates of employment.

In researching this book I turned first to statistics on the labor force and occupations, with the U. S. Bureau of the Census serving as the primary source of data. In addition, I used secondary analyses of labor force history and of the U.S. economy in the twentieth century. Federal statistics also provided a basic outline of educational expansion and school attendance. In examining women's work experiences, I relied heavily on interviews, some of which I collected myself, but most of which were obtained from oral history collections throughout the country. The U. S. Women's Bureau, the U. S. Office of Education, the Arthur and Elizabeth Schlesinger Library, and the archives of the Girl Scouts of the U.S.A. (New York) yielded both primary and secondary sources on work and on the education and socialization of girls.

In writing this book I began with the economy itself as it has influenced hiring choices of employers and job choices of employees. I worked outward from the economy to examine the fit or lack of fit between employment opportunities and the messages about work that families, schools, girls' clubs, and women's literature directed toward women and girls, as well as the fit between hiring prospects and women's economic needs. Much of the story of women's work told here has been rescued from the past by other historians who have focused on shorter periods or on specific issues, such as women's education, feminist politics, labor protest, and legislation to protect working women. I have had to leave out much of the rich detail of these findings in an effort to present an overview and to preserve a central place for consideration of the economy itself.

Because of my focus on structural economic change and the forces that have assisted or discouraged women's occupational advancement, I have also covered somewhat different topics from those addressed in fine surveys of American women such as Alice Kessler-Harris's *Out to Work*, Glenda Riley's *Inventing the American Woman*, and Rosalind Rosenberg's *Divided Lives*. I have tried to tell a complete story while recognizing that I could not tell the whole story of women, work, and family in the twentieth century. A plethora of secondary sources have shaped my understanding of women in the twentieth century, but my research began with primary sources. My reading of documentary evidence produced detail not found elsewhere in the current literature on U.S. women and led me to some conclusions that conflict with the findings of my colleagues in women's history. For the most part, the secondary sources that contributed heavily to my overall understanding of periods, developments, and events are cited in the bibliography but not in the notes.

Many archivists and librarians provided invaluable help in my research, including but not limited to the staffs of the Schlesinger Library, the National Archives, the Southern History Collection of the University of North Carolina, and the Girl Scout Archives. I extend a very special thanks to the documents librarians of the Woodruff Library at Emory University, who tracked down obscure published and unpublished government reports where other librarians had failed.

The University of North Carolina at Charlotte Foundation funded large portions of this research. I am especially grateful to Schley Lyons, dean of the College of Arts and Sciences at UNCC, who arranged a release from my administrative duties at the university so that I would devote time to completing the first draft of this book. Carole Haber assumed the responsibilities of chairing the UNCC Department of History in my absence, and only she and I know the depth of her contribution to my work. Lisa Kannenberg generously shared materials that she gathered from the archives of the United Electrical, Radio and Machine Workers of America. Individuals who have commented on parts or all of this book at one stage or another include Sara Alpern, Cynthia Bouton, Robert Calvert, Anna Clark, Stanley Engerman, Donna Gabaccia, Nancy Hewitt, Jacqueline Jones, Harold Livesay, Martha Swain, and Louise Tilly. All have helped me to see work issues more clearly, and several have corrected errors of fact and directed me to valuable sources. I take responsibility for any errors that remain and confess to obstinate resistance in the face of a few differences of opinion with generous and thoughtful manuscript readers.

Now Hiring

Introduction

The economic and technological triumphs that thrust the United States to world dominance and lifted twentieth-century Americans into the air have coursed through the nation from its mainstreams to its backwaters, leaving little untouched. Where once daughters heading west sent news home by train, migrant daughters now communicate by phone or the Internet and occasionally fly home for a weekend visit. To have reached adulthood in the United States during this century has permitted—indeed, has required—constant adjustment and readjustment in outlook and behavior, and these adaptations have revolutionized the lives of ordinary women. Economic growth and emergent technologies have decreased the share of human capital devoted to the production of goods and have redirected labor into the creation and delivery of services, bringing an end to the industrial age. In the United States, and in economically and politically diverse settings elsewhere, the twentieth-century transition to postindustrialism has fueled the feminization of work.

Throughout the century employers increasingly sought female workers, women entered occupations that had formerly excluded them, and new jobs defined as "women's work" developed. The impact of this quiet revolution manifests itself in a single statistical statement: in 1900, one of every five American women worked for wages; by 1990, the figure had risen to three in five. The number of women in the labor market rose from 5 million at the dawn of the century to more than 56 million in its last decade. In addition, as the century progressed, these wage-earning women spent more years on the job. These two facts, taken together, mean that women's role in the national labor effort grew by a factor even greater than simple statistics suggest. A transformation so fundamental reflects shifts, gradual in pace but stark in consequence, in attitudes and structures within society. Viewed across an adequate time span, these shifts emerge clearly: in the twentieth century, for example, wage labor for women has evolved from an atypical to an anticipated behavior; the expectation of spending years at such work has crept upward from the working class to engulf middle-class women as well; married women have come to dominate this labor force, once the domain of single women; the majority of two-parent households now depend upon the wages of wife and husband both; a significant proportion of households rely primarily on women's earnings alone; in 1990 women occupy a range of occupations vastly expanded since 1900.

Changes so profound in a group of people that constitutes half the population result from multiple causes, but among them the changing twentieth-century U.S. economy dominated. Arguably the greatest engine for job creation yet known, U.S. business, and the government and labor institutions that expanded with it, not only grew rapidly but also reorganized the nature of work, thus multiplying both the number and variety of jobs. Consequently, women's wage-earning options broadened and improved over the century as, pushed by economic necessity or pulled by the opportunity for a better lifestyle or by the attraction of the job itself, women responded to emerging, task-specific labor demands.

THE WOMAN WORKER

Understanding why women work for wages has occupied the attention of economists, journalists, and government bureaucrats for much of the twentieth century. Starting from the premise that women and men differed as economic creatures, both critics of and advocates for working women believed that women behaved differently in the labor market because of childbearing and traditions of household labor. Constrained by conventions of gender and by notions of sexual difference, advocates of higher wages for women argued that the need to supplement or replace men's pay forced women to work. Employers and critics, on the other hand, often maintained that women opted to work for "pin money," or discretionary income. The latter argument, embroidered on the banner of middle-class social conventions, ignored such vicissitudes as widowhood, abandonment, divorce, agricultural and industrial depression, male unemployment, and other setbacks that had forced women—especially working-class women—into the wage labor force long before the twentieth century.[1]

The forces propelling women into the labor force persisted vigorously as the years after 1900 rolled by and often intensified under the pressure of identifiable events such as the Great Depression and World War II. Explaining the increasing presence of women, especially mothers, in the workforce by choice rather than necessity has proved more of a challenge, especially given that such a decision required surmounting social pressures that discouraged it. In 1961 economist Jacob Mincer concluded that middle-class wives entered the labor force when their prospective wages rose sufficiently to permit material improvements in household consumption.[2]

In 1970 sociologist Valerie Oppenheimer advanced the debate on women's work by establishing that women joined the workforce voluntarily as a result of shifting market demand, rather than as a consequence of changed social attitudes. When employers articulated strong demand for their services—that is, when jobs existed for them—women went out to work. Oppenheimer thus concluded that gender conventions did not keep women from the labor market and, moreover, that societal disapproval of single women's wage work did not wane until their employment had become the rule rather than the exception. Oppenheimer similarly found that married women with school-age children accepted employment when labor demand swelled in the 1940s and the 1950s, despite widespread disapproval among men and women of mothers' employment.[3]

What Oppenheimer and Mincer demonstrated for the first sixty years of the century held true into the 1990s. After 1960 employment grew more among mothers of young children than among any other segment of the population. Mothers' labor force participation expanded as demand for female labor outstripped the supply of women without child-care obligations and as wages exceeded the child-care expenses of workers in all but the lowest strata of the economy. Demand for female workers increased partly because overall job growth surpassed the supply of men entering the labor market. In addition, the female labor market expanded because structural changes in the economy fueled the rise of occupational specialties such as nursing that women had long dominated. Emerging female professions offered women, including the aspiring young Margaret Sanger, both a calling and a vehicle for occupational mobility. As the pioneering Sanger recalled later, although unable to fulfill her medical school ambitions, she "could at least make a start with nursing."[4]

THE U.S. ECONOMY

The chapters that follow here trace the twentieth-century evolution of the U.S. occupational structure and the rise in demand for female workers through the closing episodes of the Industrial Revolution and the advent of postindustrialism. This reconfiguration of the labor market trailed the shift of the leading sector, the premier driving force of the U.S. economy, from agriculture to manufacturing to service. In addition, alterations in the labor market redirected female education and transformed family structures in the United States, changes that this book also investigates.[5]

In the years between the Civil War and World War I, the United States emerged as the leading industrial power in the world. In 1900 the industrial sector, composed of manufacturing, transportation, and communication, contributed twice as much dollar value to the U.S. economy as agriculture, forestry, and fishing combined. The place of agriculture in the total Gross National Product (GNP) had declined before 1900 and continued declining thereafter, while industrial production increased its share of the GNP through the 1960s. Diminishing fertility and decreasing immigration from abroad after 1920 reduced the flow of new male workers into the labor force, while labor demand continued to climb. In periods of severe labor shortage, such as in wartime, the number of women in manufacturing, including heavy industries, rose sharply.

Industrialization made the nation wealthy and changed the nature of work itself, but manufacturing enlarged rather than eroded the nation's service needs. Producers of industrial goods depended, for example, on commercial vendors to market their wares and on financial services for credit and financial transactions, requirements that increased to keep pace with a growing population and rising buying power. Intertwined with the industrial expansion of the first half of the century, a broad range of white-collar jobs developed as the research, management, record keeping, and merchandising requirements of industry proliferated. Other services such as medicine and education also blossomed in the fertile revenues of industrialization. So rapidly did the economy's appetite for services expand that, while manufacturing continued to increase into the 1960s, the industrial age was in fact already passing. By the 1970s the service sector surpassed manufacturing in scale as service needs continued to multiply and mature manufacturing industries such as steel contracted. By the end of the 1980s services accounted for 65 percent of the national income, with proportionate widening of job opportunities for women.

Historically, gender conventions linked to patriarchy have discouraged employers from hiring women for positions in which they would supervise men. Gendered ideas of physical differences between the sexes prevented industrial managers from employing women to operate metal lathes or blast furnaces but favored their hiring in textile mills. Women presumably lacked the mental powers or the physical strength required of tool makers and steel workers, but the simultaneous operation of multiple power looms followed logically from women's traditional roles in home textile production. As the contrast between the textile and metal industries suggests, technology is gender-laden. Some technological developments incorporate and perpetuate assumptions about gender, but others may redefine them. In the twentieth century, for example, automation, while solidifying the transfer of work-process control from workers to management, simultaneously removed the rationale behind occupational segregation in many manufacturing settings. Innovations in office technology encouraged the broader employment of women in the service sector.[6]

The shift away from agriculture and manufacturing toward a service-based economy entailed a transformation of work content as sweeping as the job redefinition that had accompanied industrialization. Women emerged as the majority of the workforce in most low-level service occupations through the century, and the share of jobs available for women increased as service employment grew. Employers maintained occupational segregation through elaborate conventions of class and race as well as gender.

Women's eagerness to earn income induced them to accept employment at lower wage rates than men, and this gender gap in wages increased the incentives for employers to hire women. As Oppenheimer argued, occupational segregation by gender not only kept women in inferior positions in the economy but also ensured that employers preferred women to men in some positions. Claudia Goldin later systematically analyzed the importance of occupational segregation in preserving men's higher earnings relative to women's pay.[7]

As the service sector grew, the tasks of working women grew as varied and complex as those of working men, even though women failed to achieve employment equity with men. Middle-class women entered the labor force in ever greater numbers as white-collar jobs proliferated. Among themselves female workers replicated the class lines of working men with the accompanying income and status differences between hourly wage labor and salaried positions.

As the transformation of the twentieth-century U.S. economy unfolded and women permeated the labor force, both the dynamics and the economics of family life changed. Wage-earning wives gained more authority within marriage, but they also assumed heavier responsibilities for the financial support of their families. Rising rates of separation and divorce burdened mothers who generally sought and won custody of their children. Women's economic advances, as William Chafe and others have observed, paradoxically worsened their financial well-being.[8]

THE CHANGING CONTEXT OF WOMEN'S WORK

This book explores such repercussions of the U.S. economic transformation in the private lives as well as in the work lives of women. Class and race or ethnicity shaped women's opportunities and their expectations, and the following pages consider the interaction of the labor market and these factors in the evolving roles of working women. This study probes the evolution of the family and explores the ways in which women's emergence as paid workers reshaped other institutions of U.S. society. Popular attitudes and educational policies lagged behind labor force restructuring, and advice literature for women, school curricula, and girls' clubs often directed young people along avenues that led them away from developing the skills that maximized their employment opportunities. Slowly the labor market forced these institutions to reconcile their messages with the changing needs of employers and of workers. Racial and class prejudices constrained educational policies as well as hiring practices, and these biases proved resistant but not impenetrable to the forces of social as well as economic change.

Working women themselves gradually nudged social and educational institutions ahead, all the while reshaping their own daughters' outlook. With each generation mothers sent stronger messages to their daughters that woman's place was in the labor force. Women's expanding roles in the labor force thus edged their daughters' career expectations upward. Each generation of American girls built its dreams on the world of their mothers, as had the generations before them, dressing up in adult clothing and imagining their futures. These daydreams, as well as lessons taught at home and at school, launched children on the odyssey that led from youthful ambition to adult accomplishment. As the feminization of the workforce progressed through the century, women's destinies increasingly involved long-term wage earning, and youthful ambitions increasingly included full-time careers outside the home.

Significant changes in women's work and family lives began with the emergence of factories at the end of the eighteenth century. Both men and women assumed new responsibilities outside the home, obligations that redefined their functions within the family. In the preindustrial West women's earnings had derived from domestic service, farm products, and home manufactures. Industrialization relied heavily on the exploitation of women's skills as spinners, weavers, and needleworkers. As these functions moved from the home to the factory, the new mode of employment altered relations between men and women as well as the relationship of worker to employer. Although some differences had existed between the jobs of men and of women in cottage industries, factory production further segregated occupations by gender and narrowed the skills of both men and women. Wage labor, a component of the shift from domestic to factory production, emerged within the context of a social system that defined the world in masculine terms, fastening women to a secondary status that excluded them from economic as well as political power. Not only did women earn less than men, but factory labor for wages further diminished their abilities to produce commodities that sustained them and their families.

The industrial transformation of work occurred gradually. In the early–nineteenth-century United States, entrepreneurs lured the first generation of female factory workers away from their rural employments and into the textile mills of New England by offering comparatively high wages and paternalistic benefits. As expanding manufacturing capacity flooded consumer markets with cheap products that marginalized home production, young people of both sexes found themselves pushed from the home and pulled into the industrial labor force. As industrialization ground relentlessly on, pressures of overproduction and rapid population growth forced wages downward, while families' dependence on wages broadened. For the first generation of Massachusetts mill girls, workers of the 1820s and 1830s, wage labor had been an option, and Yankee working women did not necessarily pledge all their earnings to their parents. Money sent home might not be consumed totally by family subsistence and might be invested in the education of siblings. Working girls earned high enough wages to save dowries for married life outside the mills. By the end of the nineteenth century, however, farm labor or factory employment had become a necessity rather than a choice among poor women, and female earnings, stretched to cover the bare necessities, permitted few discretionary expenditures.[9]

As daughters entered industrial labor, the rhythm of family life remained essentially intact. Although women in their late teens and early twenties left home for wage work, their mothers and younger siblings remained at home to keep the domestic routine running smoothly. For the young women who left farms and villages here and abroad, traveling alone or with relatives to roiling cities, factories, and mills, merging there with the native-born daughters of urban immigrants in the swelling ranks of industrial labor, life assumed a different cast altogether. Unlike those left behind, women who took jobs in their teenage years developed much of their identity in the workplace. Their earnings, their working conditions, and their peers fostered goals and attitudes based more on experience than on formal instruction. Factory labor taught the merits as well as the limits of cooperation and educated women in the ways of a heterosocial world outside the household.

By the beginning of the twentieth century, toiling for wages had become a tradition among single women of the working classes, and significant numbers of wives and widows also worked for pay. Whether or not they lived at home, single working women strengthened the family as an economic unit because they generally contributed some or all of their earnings to their parents. From their youthful entry into paid labor through their adult lives, women learned to balance income requirements against the demands for unpaid labor at home. Working daughters might delay marriage to support parents and siblings; wage-earning women, married or single, might work sporadically as the care of the young or the infirm permitted.

The first two chapters of this book trace the routes that women followed into the labor force during the first two decades of this century, describe the work of wage-earning women, and examine the educational forces that molded youthful expectations of work. Subsequent chapters track chronologically the recharting of women's paths from childhood to adulthood and the modifications in work and education that trailed the economic transition to postindustrialism. The penultimate chapter outlines the impact of the feminization of paid work on the family economy. The final chapter summarizes the effects of a century of change in women's employments and delineates social and economic challenges that will confront women and families of the twenty-first century.

CHAPTER ONE

Working "Girls"
at the Turn of the Century

By 1900 the triumphant industrial economy of the United States had reconfigured the U.S. labor force and the institutions associated with it. Almost as if the pulsing currents of industrialization had turned their very skeletons of iron and steel into magnets, the cities, mills, and factories of America drew workers from near and far, from home and abroad. Women's employment levels rose as their own cash requirements mounted and as expanding consumer markets produced new jobs for women in manufacturing and commerce. As industrialization proceeded, individuals and families depended increasingly on factory-produced commodities that further inflated the need for cash income. These structural changes enticed growing numbers of women, not all of whom came from poverty, into the labor market with such effect that in 1900 five million women in the United States worked for wages and one in five U.S. workers was female.

Women seeking jobs in 1900 followed the paths of forebears who had accepted employment in a society marked by elaborate and long-standing hiring preferences based on gender, on marital status, and on ethnicity or race. This employer discrimination, generally predicated on widely shared community prejudices, protected some jobs for women but kept women out of others. Within female labor markets, class, race, and ethnicity intertwined with the strand of gender to define women's job options. These factors, as much as economic considerations, determined which jobs women could have and thus influenced their decisions about whether, when, and where to seek work.

In terms of status and job desirability, the occupational structure of the female labor force resembled a stratified pyramid, with professionals (who made up approximately 12 percent of the nonfarm female work force) at the apex, followed by clericals (5 percent), salesworkers (5 percent), and factory operatives or manual laborers (34 percent), with domestic and other service workers (44 percent), such as hotel maids, laundry workers, and the like, at the base.[1] As these percentages show, the overwhelming majority (78 percent) of wage-earning women in 1900 toiled in manufacturing or service jobs.[2] Other data on the female labor force further exhibit the interplay of economic factors with popular attitudes toward gender, class, race, and ethnicity, none more dramatically than the fact that women workers at the turn of the century earned roughly fifty cents for every dollar earned by a male. This discrepancy, though diminished over time, has persisted through the twentieth century. For most of the century the wage gap has kept independence beyond the reach of virtually all women, while making their labor an economically attractive proposition to many employers.

Whether driven by poverty or drawn by the prospect of wages and a life outside the home, working women had established a conspicuous presence by 1900. The visibility of teenaged shop girls and factory women strolling the streets of American cities on Sundays and after work drew the scrutiny of social critics such as Jane Addams, who lamented that never before in history had so many "young girls been suddenly released from the protection of the home" and allowed to roam "unattended upon city streets and . . . work under alien roofs." "For the first time," she added, "society cares more for the products they manufacture [and] for their labor power . . . than for their tender beauty, their ephemeral gaiety, [or] their immemorial ability to reaffirm the charm of existence."[3] Addams's comments reveal as much about the prevailing middle-class value system in turn-of-the-century America as they document about the overall reality of female employment.

Poor women did turn to the labor market out of necessity, and often enough toiled in the sort of brutal, sweatshop misery exposed by the death of 147 people in the Triangle Shirtwaist fire in 1911. Even in poverty, however, women and families exercised choice, and not all labor was dangerous or debilitating. Working women affirmed their "gaiety" through commercial entertainments and the occasional fashionable purchase that middle-class critics derided. In the neighborhoods of the working poor, shops catered specifically to women's whims as well as their needs, selling dressy shoes, hats, gloves, scarves, buttons, and bows, as well as workaday gear.

A minority of teenagers did work (as some still do), but their numbers were declining. The typical working "girl" at the turn of the century was a single woman whose earnings helped support her parents and siblings. Children, male or female, rarely entered the labor force until the age of sixteen, when they were considered fully grown and had most likely left school. The rare exceptions nearly always followed a close relative into the factory and worked under the watchful eyes of kin. Diane Quellette recalled, "[Mother] worked more than 20 years in United Bunting

Company. Then when I was 14 I got a job there as a doffer."[4] Even after girls had left school, families weighed their potential wage contribution to the family's welfare against their utility at home—and most often opted for the latter.

The vast majority of female workers were not girls but adults; two thirds of working women were twenty-five years of age or older, and their average age was twenty-seven. In 1900, only one in four women aged sixteen through twenty and one in three aged twenty-one through twenty-four held paid jobs. Teenage boys, by contrast, were twice as likely to work as teenage girls, and nine of ten men in their early twenties had joined the workforce. Differing role proscriptions by gender also dictated different behavior in the work life cycle. Unlike men, who once in the labor force tended to stay there until death or retirement, women frequently left, returned to unpaid household labor in marriage, motherhood, or care of aging family members, sometimes returning to work later in life.

Despite the widely held popular view that women belonged in the home, economic reality translated into a far different set of cultural values and expectations for women in large segments of the population. Race or ethnicity, factors closely linked to economic well-being, shaped a woman's options for work, education, or leisure through their impact on her family's outlook. African American women, immigrant daughters, and native-born working-class white women most certainly would have expected employment to fill some period of their lives. Middle-class girls, by contrast, did not work, and relatively few adult middle-class women earned wages in 1900 (though Jane Addams was a conspicuous exception).

MARITAL STATUS, RACE, AND WOMEN'S EMPLOYMENTS

Marital status also shaped women's options and decisions about work. At the turn of the century two of five single women, three in ten widowed or divorced women, and one in twenty married women participated in paid labor, but ethnicity and race further defined whether single, married, and widowed women worked for wages (see table 1.1). Single immigrant women, the majority of whom expected to work when they arrived in the United States, had the highest work rates of all unmarried women, with three of five of their numbers pursuing gainful occupations. Single African American women, approximately half of whom worked, ranked next in work rates among the unmarried.

Employed wives and female family heads played a significant part in the U.S. wage economy and in the support of their families. The 5.6 percent of married women who were in the labor market in 1900 accounted for 13.3 percent of the total female workforce, and African American women accounted for a disproportional share of working wives. One of every four married African American women

Beginning in the nineteenth century and continuing to the present, occupational segregation by sex provided women with employment opportunities but also suppressed female wages. Women like this turn-of-the-century shoe worker in Lynn, Massachusetts, stayed on the job in their maturity. Courtesy National Archives

TABLE I.I
Work Rates of Women* by Nationality or Race and Marital Status, 1900

	NATIVE WHITE OF NATIVE PARENTAGE	NATIVE WHITE OF FOREIGN PARENTAGE	FOREIGN-BORN WHITE	AFRICAN AMERICAN
Single	21.5	34.3	60.9	47.7
Married	3.0	3.1	3.6	26.0
Widowed	26.1	32.3	20.7	67.0
Divorced	47.5	52.9	51.4	82.2

SOURCE: *U.S. Bureau of the Census,* Twelfth Census of the United States, 1900, Statistics of Occupations *(Washington, D.C.: GPO, 1907), tables LXXVIII, ccxiv.*

* Figures are for women ten years of age and older.

labored for profit or wages, while only three in one hundred white wives pursued paid work. Abandonment, divorce, or widowhood often propelled women from the home into paid work before their children had grown to working ages. Although the death or departure of husbands forced many women to seek income, the work rates of white women in these straitened circumstances trailed far behind those of black women. Among white women, approximately 50 percent of divorcées and 25 percent of widows worked, as opposed to 80 percent of black divorcées and 70 percent of widowed African American women. Often these unfortunate women found themselves on the bottom rung of the employment ladder, and discrimination by race and ethnicity compounded the obstacles faced by women no longer married. Among the working women of 1900, 45 percent of white divorcées of native parentage and 31 percent of white widows of native stock accepted low-skilled service employments. Among black workers, 68 percent of divorcées and 63 percent of widows were service workers.[5]

At the turn of the century, native-born white workers, the majority of them single, benefited most from the range of occupational opportunities available to women, as table 1.2 suggests. Although aspiring young professional women could look to few highly visible role models in 1900, significant numbers of white women had entered the professions. Three in twenty white working women of native parentage and one in ten native-born whites of foreign parentage held professional jobs, while only three of one hundred immigrant working women and four in one hundred black female workers had secured professional positions.

The vast majority of professional women pursued the time-honored callings of teaching or nursing. By 1900 nearly three fourths of the teachers in the United States were women.[6] Most of these teachers had come from middle-class homes, but patterns changed in the new century. As normal schools, women's colleges,

TABLE 1.2
Female Occupational Sectors by Race and Nativity, 1900*

	NATIVE WHITE OF NATIVE PARENTAGE	NATIVE WHITE OF FOREIGN PARENTAGE	FOREIGN-BORN WHITE	AFRICAN AMERICAN
Agriculture	264,687	25,775	40,917	434,041
Professions	275,384	112,921	25,937	15,515
Domestic and service	535,566	325,949	456,070	634,104
Trade and transportation	223,938	193,588	59,793	3,930
Manufacturing	473,534	432,967	257,969	32,073

SOURCE: *U.S. Bureau of the Census,* Twelfth Census of the United States, 1900, Women at Work *(Washington, D.C.: GPO, 1907), table 21.*

*Figures are for female workers sixteen years of age and older.

and hospital schools of nursing proliferated at century's end, the daughters of the working poor entered the stream of occupational mobility. Those women who had trained hardest to obtain high occupational status proved the most reluctant to surrender their pursuits upon marriage. Among white female professional women of native parentage, virtually no schoolteachers were married, but more than half of all engineers, three in ten lawyers, and two in five medical doctors remained at work after marriage, a relationship between learning and persistence in professional careers that held across other female census categories as well.[7]

While teaching often raised daughters' occupational status above that of their mothers, teachers often aspired to even higher attainments. For example, Hazel Stevens, born in Bluehill, Maine, in 1896, moved as a child to Lowell, Massachusetts, where her mother found work in the mills and her father at a grocery store. Stevens had set her course for college, but financial circumstances dictated otherwise: "I would have gone to college instead of going back to normal school my second year, but my father's health simply went all to pieces. . . . So I had to go back to normal school . . . to get through and earn my living as fast as possible."[8] Not easily discouraged, Stevens later completed her bachelor's and master's degrees by attending Middlebury College during the summers.

Another Lowell resident, Elizabeth Hamblet, worked as both a teacher and a nurse. After completing her secondary training in Canada, Hamblet taught school for two years before coming to the United States. She attended the Lowell General Hospital school of nursing, where she lived in a school cottage filled with residents of Canadian heritage. Graduating in 1901, at the age of twenty-nine, Hamblet found employment in the same hospital that had trained her.[9]

In addition to poverty, race and ethnicity circumscribed women's opportunities to gain white-collar jobs. Emphasizing the importance of written or spoken

English and American manners, employers turned overwhelmingly to native-born white women in hiring office workers or sales clerks, jobs that engaged one in ten working women in 1900. White women of native parentage predominated in the preferred jobs of accountant, bookkeeper, typist, stenographer, and office clerk, while women of foreign parentage found work as shippers, packers, and sales clerks. Poverty, discrimination, and cultural values sustained demand for the services of African American and ethnic midwives. Midwives varied from women with extensive formal training to those with no schooling or apprenticeship, and midwives along this spectrum of expertise delivered most babies in immigrant and black communities in the early decades of the century.[10] Black clerical workers, as well as black teachers and black hospital nurses, found themselves effectively limited to employment in racially segregated settings, and black businesses were too few and too small to provide extensive opportunities to African American women.

In 1900 two of every five female wage earners ages sixteen years and older were household domestic workers or employees with similar jobs in hotels, boarding houses, or the like (Table 1.2). The service sector employed more African American women, immigrant women, and native-born white women of European stock than any other area of the economy. Blacks and white immigrants concentrated most heavily in domestic service, but the service sector also engaged the most native-born white women of native stock.

Most African American women who were not employed in domestic service labored on the nation's farms, largely in the South. In the South, the Midwest, and the West white women of native stock also worked in agriculture, but first- and second-generation immigrant women rarely worked in the fields. Nationally, white women of native stock held a plurality of manufacturing jobs, although manufacturing and mechanical occupations also attracted large numbers of second-generation immigrants. Immigrant whites comprised a third sizable group in the manufacturing labor force, with black women virtually excluded from manufacturing and sales jobs.

LABOR MARKETS AND MIGRATION

As the stories of Hazel Stevens and Elizabeth Hamblet suggest, the United States in 1900 was both a land of immigrants and a nation of internal migrants.[11] Not by accident did these women find themselves in the textile manufacturing center that was Lowell, Massachusetts. Thriving U.S. industries, affluent urban households, and burgeoning commercial establishments of the early twentieth century drew female job seekers from homes throughout the country as well as from Canada and Europe. Textile, shoe, and garment factories transformed wives and daughters from dependent family members into economic assets, and the migration of women to mill towns materially improved the circumstances of countless impoverished rural families before the end of World War I.

With some knowledge of the labor market, however sketchy or faulty, women, on their own or with their families, set out for U.S. towns and cities in search of work. The drawing power of the U.S. urban economy, weighed against deteriorating local conditions, determined the strength and geographic locus of wage labor's pull on women and men. Advertisements, labor agents, promotions by railway and steamship lines, and letters from friends or relatives attracted native and foreign migrants to specific towns or regions.[12] Whether women came to the United States from abroad or left their U.S. birthplaces for new homes, migration changed their work activities and transformed their roles within families, as the two following examples illustrate.

Diane Quellette, born in Quebec in 1898, lost her father to a fatal illness in 1903. As life in Canada grew increasingly precarious, Quellette's mother made the difficult decision to leave home with her three children. She brought her family to eastern Massachusetts, an area well known among French Canadians as a region dotted with textile mills and shoe factories that employed women. Driven by need and drawn by a mature industrial economy, the young widow found work at the United Bunting Company, where she remained employed for twenty years; her daughter Diane joined her at the age of fourteen.[13] With time, Diane freed herself from her mother's protection, but she, like most young working girls of her time, did not find herself adrift on the darkling sea of factory life, but rather at work in close proximity to a family member. Taken together, mother and daughter exemplify the demographic diversity of the work force in 1900 and the economic strategies that preserved family life among ordinary Americans.

The history of the Mayfield family of North Carolina offers a similar example of female labor's triumph over adversity. The Mayfields left their North Carolina farm for Durham at the end of the nineteenth century when injuries left the paterfamilias unable to do farmwork. Durham held the promise of financial stability as the four Mayfield daughters could enter the mills. With all the family's women working in textile or hosiery mills, the family not only survived but thrived without a working male householder. When the Mayfield sons reached working ages, parents and sons returned to the farm while the daughters remained behind in Durham.[14] As the examples above show, inducements to move and migration paths chosen reflected labor demands and migrants' family circumstances. The anticipated employability of women encouraged rural families to send their daughters to town, spurred southern women to move north, and encouraged single and widowed women to immigrate.

Female family heads and women on their own followed different migration routes from those of two-parent families and men alone. The propensity of women to migrate singly or to move as members of family units varied by race and by nationality, and the realities of occupational segregation dictated which areas of the economy they would enter. Single or widowed women moved primarily in search of employment, but migrant wives did not enter the labor market as rapidly as their spouses or women alone. Native-born wives frequently followed their husbands into employment outside the home, but immigrant wives overwhelmingly remained tied to the home, supplementing husbands' earnings by taking in boarders or accepting industrial homework.[15]

More than fifteen million women have immigrated to the United States in this century (see Table 1.3). In the years preceding World War I, European immigration reached an all-time high, with a majority of the newcomers traveling from eastern and southern Europe. Approximately thirteen million immigrants came to the United States from 1900 through 1914, and one third of the newcomers were women or girls. The outbreak of the war in Europe interrupted passages across the Atlantic, and federal legislation controlled immigrant arrivals thereafter.[16] From 1915 through the 1920s, nearly six million immigrants, predominantly of European origin, arrived in the United States, and more than four of ten newcomers were female. The proportion of women among newcomers continued to increase as immigration declined further during the Great Depression. Economic forces encouraged women to migrate, but culture shaped the circumstances under which women moved and the economic roles that they played in the new land.

TABLE 1.3
Female Immigrants to the United States, 1900–1988

1900–09	2,492,336	1950–59	1,341,404
1910–19	2,215,582	1960–69	1,786,441
1920–29	1,881,923	1970–79	2,299,713
1930–39	386,659	1980–89	3,224,661 *
1940–49	454,291	1990–94	2,719,447

SOURCES: *U.S. Bureau of the Census,* Historical Statistics of the United States, Colonial Times to 1970 *(Washington, D.C.: GPO, 1975), Series C 102–114; U.S. Department of Justice, 1978* Statistical Yearbook of the Immigration and Naturalization Service *(Washington, D.C.: GPO, 1978), table 10; 1984 Statistical Yearbook of the Immigration and Naturalization Service (Washington, D.C.: GPO, 1987), table I M M 4.1; 1988 Statistical Yearbook of the Immigration and Naturalization Service (Washington, D.C.: GPO, 1989), table 11; 1994 Statistical Yearbook of the Immigration and Naturalization Service (Washington, D.C.: GPO, 1996), table 12.*

*Figures for 1980–89 are estimated.

Patterns and experiences of immigration differed by nationality as well as among individuals. Economic conditions, the matchmaking customs of particular regions, and immigration regulations determined whether women came to the United States as single or as married women. Widows came to the United States in significant numbers, and wives occasionally immigrated without their husbands. Overall, married women predominated among female adults coming to the United States in the twentieth century, but among particular ethnic groups, such as the Poles and the Irish, unmarried women were in the majority.

Crop failures and political conditions in nineteenth-century Ireland caused widespread poverty, discouraged family formation, and encouraged emigration. After the famines of the 1840s and 1850s, the loss of income to women in particular and the pressure to lower fertility caused the Irish to postpone or even forego marriage. Under these circumstances single Irish women predominated among emigrants from 1885 into the twentieth century.[17] Irish women not only came to the United States in large numbers but also remained single permanently or for long periods after arriving. Irish American daughters inherited this pattern, with the eldest daughter often remaining single and responsible for her parents in their old age. Late marriage and low marriage rates among Irish and Irish American women persisted well into the twentieth century. Polish women, married or single, faced few cultural barriers to employment, and factory work provided them with bright employment prospects in the United States. In America or in their homeland, Polish women married younger than their Irish counterparts, and fewer of them remained single.[18] Marriage, then, was tied to employment and migration in specific ways for Irish women but not for their Polish counterparts.

In contrast to both the Polish and the Irish, Italian women generally came to the United States with their families because of traditional preferences for keeping women within the family circle. Single Italian male immigrants characteristically returned to their native villages to marry. Italians built ethnic enclaves in northeastern cities where men worked in construction and manufacturing and established small businesses. Custom discouraged Italian women from working outside the home, and Italian families generally forbade wives or daughters to accept domestic work in the homes of others. Women occasionally took on factory jobs but more frequently pursued homework or helped out in family businesses as need required.[19]

The occasional woman in all national groups migrated to the United States to join her betrothed, but a promise of marriage often proved no guarantee. Women who came to the United States to meet their fiancés or husbands commonly confronted the unpleasant surprise of a broken pledge. Shortly before World War I, for example, Nina Talpiniuk left her home in Croatia to come to the United States.

She immigrated to marry Jakub Dubiac, who had earlier left Croatia for Chicago. After two years in the United States, Jakub had sent Nina a steamship ticket. Obviously immune to precipitate passion, Nina deliberated for two years before setting sail. Too long, it proved, for Jakub had wed another, as Talpiniuk learned after crossing the Atlantic. Summarily released from Ellis Island, Nina boarded a train for Chicago, there to find herself adrift in a strange city, unable to communicate with most people around her. She turned to the Immigrants' League, which found her a hospital cleaning job that paid five dollars per week and room and board. What this involved in a turn-of-the-century hospital one can well imagine, but within a month Talpiniuk had relocated to a new household where she worked as a domestic.[20]

Coming to America as wives, as daughters, or as independent women, immigrant women entered an industrial society in which they found their work prospects already largely determined. Immigrants frequently knew the characteristics of local labor markets through advertisements or correspondence with family members already in this country. Drawn to ethnic enclaves by their fellow countrymen, newcomers there found friends or joined family members who initiated them into the ways of the workplace. Women adrift, like Nina Talpiniuk, might gain jobs through service agencies, but virtually all immigrants entered the workforce at the bottom of the wage scale.

Women moved independently to places with strong female labor markets, and foreign-born white women outnumbered male immigrants arriving in New England at the turn of the century. Lowell, Massachusetts, was one of many factory towns in New England that drew newcomers from abroad. Katherine Speronis, her mother, and her two sisters came to America in 1916 to work in the Lowell Mills. Her father and brother never left Greece. Sophie, a Polish widow, came to America alone after neighbors in her agricultural village raised the money for her passage. She left her young son with friends and planned to send for him once she had established herself in the land of plenty. Sophie also settled in Lowell, where she found work in the cotton mills. As the years crept by Sophie passed through difficult economic crises and never managed to save for her future. Her dreams of seeing her son dimmed gradually, and in time she lost all knowledge of him. Mary Podgorski's widowed mother also emigrated from Poland to Lowell. Mary and her mother came over in 1911, but her brother stayed behind with his grandparents. By the time Mary's mother had saved passage money for her son, he had been conscripted for military duty. After he returned from the army and married, Mary's mother gave up the idea of bringing him to the United States. She, too, never saw her son again.[21]

Through the twentieth century, immigration has strengthened the U.S. economy and enriched its culture, but internal migration has had a greater impact on the size and shape of communities than have population movements from abroad. Internal migration has been a constant feature of the American experience, but local economic conditions affected men and women differently. Women moved disproportionally to urban settings in all regions, but the Northeast particularly enticed women at the turn of the century. While U.S. women with family members in large cities might move great distances to live with those relatives, most migrant women moved initially from the countryside to a nearby town or from their native village to a city within their native region. Native-born white women of native parentage, like the Mayfield women, most often moved to a labor center near their birthplace. By the end of the nineteenth century, however, migration out of the South to the North had become a significant trend, with higher rates of migration among blacks than among whites from World War I through the 1940s.[22]

African American husbands who participated in the Great Migration from the South generally left their families behind until they had a job that allowed them to pay the family's moving expenses.[23] Lizzie and John Avery struggled to improve their circumstances and to preserve family ties despite a series of moves and separations. The Averys worked a tenant farm in Alabama in the first decade of the twentieth century. After a succession of bad years, John left the farm in search of industrial employment, while Lizzie and their daughter Sally moved in with an aunt. John's job search led him from Bessemer, Alabama, to the coal fields of West Virginia, to Cincinnati, back to mining in West Virginia, and finally to Detroit. Lizzie and Sally eventually followed John, with Lizzie adapting her routine to the local economic environment. In Cincinnati Lizzie quickly gained work as a domestic, but John could find none. The subsequent move to West Virginia proved better for John but worse for Lizzie. After a time she opened a boarding house that improved the family's welfare and gave her considerable satisfaction and pride of accomplishment. A disaster in the mine left John unemployed and Lizzie with few clients. In 1918 John went to Michigan to buy land but stayed in Detroit, where he found a factory job. Lizzie and her sister soon joined John in Detroit, where Lizzie went back to domestic work. Injuries and spells of unemployment for John left the Detroit family in poverty in the years that followed.[24]

Occupational segregation, low southern wage scales, Jim Crow laws, and the demand for domestic workers in northern cities encouraged African American women to leave their birthplaces. Black women competed effectively with European immigrants for service jobs in the North despite the persistence of racial prejudice there. The job opportunities of northeastern and mid-Atlantic cities drew local African American women into the labor market and attracted black migrants to these areas. Washington, D.C., proved an especially attractive destination be-

World War I opened new industrial employments to African American women but kept them at the bottom of the earnings ladder. These workers participated in a project to set wage scales in industry in 1919. Courtesy National Archives

cause of its large service sector and its proximity to the South. By 1900 the nation's capital had already emerged as a major employment center for women. Three fifths of the black women, one quarter of second-generation immigrants, and nearly one quarter of foreign-born white women resident in the District of Columbia were employed at the turn of the century.[25]

Jane Addams's perceptions of girls adrift in the city followed from turn-of-the-century migration and employment patterns. Whether she moved to a city from the U.S. countryside, came from abroad, or was born to urban parents, town jobs beckoned the working woman. In cities of fifty thousand persons or more, over one half of women ages sixteen through twenty years worked for wages, and nearly one half of women in their early twenties participated in the labor force. Numerically, second-generation immigrants led the urban female workforce, with immigrant and native-stock white women trailing behind. Despite the high work rates of women in large cities, the majority of the nation's working women lived in smaller urban places or in the countryside, outnumbering their counterparts in large cities by a margin of five to one. White native-stock women like the Mayfield daughters tended to migrate to small factory villages, while larger northeastern industrial centers attracted immigrants like the Speronis family. While migration out of the South distinguished African American population movements in the early twentieth century, southern towns and cities also attracted thousands of black women.[26]

WOMEN ALONE IN THE CITY

Whether they had come from near or far, women on their own faced many challenges in the cities. Regardless of race, migrant women isolated from kin networks confronted unique dangers and faced different prospects for employment than those of women with family to assist them. At each stage of the process, from the purchase of steamship tickets to application for U.S. citizenship, the immigrant might confront swindling and entrapment. While internal migrants faced fewer barriers than immigrants, all newcomers vied for suitable employment and safe housing.

Middle-class urban women campaigned to end the exploitation of migrant women and staffed a variety of agencies and services that assisted migrants in adapting to urban life. In the early twentieth century, several organizations in the nation's cities helped women alone to find safe housing or employment, with an eye toward protecting feminine virtue. Young Women's Christian Association branches and other women's clubs assisted native-born, generally white, newcomers to towns and cities. Although separate African American branches of the YWCA appeared as early as 1911, these segregated clubs had few residential facilities.[27] In Boston and elsewhere the YWCA offered some nonresident assistance to black migrants. A representative of the Cleveland YWCA Traveler's Aid Department met Cassie and Lucille Johnson, African Americans ages twelve and four years, respectively, when they arrived at Cleveland's Union Station from Florala, Alabama, on October 14, 1919, and conveyed them to the home of their mother, who had come ahead to find work.[28]

Immigrant aid societies, many representing women's ethnic or religious organizations, served particular groups of independent women. The National Council of Jewish Women, founded in 1893, assisted single Jewish women after they arrived in the United States from eastern Europe. In 1907 the council opened an office at Ellis Island to ease Jewish women's entrance into American life.[29] Although the resources of migrant aid groups were limited and aid frequently involved enduring middle-class censure and moral lessons inflicted by charity workers, the help offered often provided the margin of survival to newcomers.

Social activists like Kate Holladay Claghorn and Jane Addams enlisted public and private resources to suppress practices that deceived and endangered young women. Claghorn complained that employment agents and supervisors extorted fees for keeping workers on the job and, she wrote, "From the women workers the foreman may also claim more than a monetary reward for keeping her in a job. Instances are known in which foremen have taken advantage of their positions to force women into improper relations."[30] Although unprincipled agents occasionally harmed clients, such actions did not characterize private or public placement offices. In the early part of the century agencies that placed women workers dealt primarily in domestic service and guided women into domestic work regardless of their skills and preferences. Placement agencies misled and exploited defenseless job applicants, but they also found jobs for migrant women who had no financial resources.[31]

Claghorn, Addams, and many other politically active reformers believed that prostitution constituted the paramount threat to the well-being of migrants, and they left no stone unturned in attempts to expose the evil ways of white slavers. Claghorn claimed, "In placing women, a special abuse of the employment agencies is [to send] them to disorderly houses under the pretext of providing situations as domestic servants—an abuse concerning the immigrant woman particularly, as so great a proportion of the domestic servants are newly arrived immigrants, and as new immigrants are especially liable to be deceived, through their ignorance of the country."[32] Similarly, a 1913 Boston newspaper warned of "the discovery of white slave agents engaged in plying their trade" among striking garment workers in the city.[33] The U.S. Immigration Commission reported cases of young Chinese women who believed they were coming to the United States as picture brides but discovered that the men awaiting them were procurers for houses of prostitution rather than bridegrooms.[34]

In *A New Conscience and an Ancient Evil* Jane Addams related comparable episodes, as in the sad tale of "Little Marie from Brittany":

Marie, a French girl, [was] the daughter of a Breton stone mason, so old and poor that he was obliged to take her from her convent school at the age of twelve years. He sent her to Paris, where she became a little household drudge and nursemaid, working from six in the morning to eight at night, and for three years sending her wages, which were about a franc a day, directly to her parents in the Breton village. One afternoon, as she was buying a bottle of milk at a tiny shop, she was engaged in conversation by a young man who invited her into a *patisserie* where, after giving her some sweets, he introduced her to his friend, Monsieur Paret, who was gathering a theatrical troupe to go to America. Paret showed her pictures of several young girls gorgeously arrayed and announcements of their coming tour, and Marie felt much flattered when it was intimated that she might join this brilliant company. After several clandestine meetings to perfect the plan, she left the city with Paret and a pretty French girl to sail to America with the rest of the so-called actors. Paret escaped detection by the immigration authorities in New York through the ruse of the "Kinsella troupe," and took the girls directly to Chicago. Here they were placed in a disreputable house.[35]

The defenseless Breton maiden plucks at our sympathies, but welfare files on prostitutes and former prostitutes suggest that white slavers played a minor role in the dark industry.[36] Case files of one hundred prostitutes interviewed by a Boston welfare agency reveal many paths to the life. In the preponderance of the cases poverty had nudged women toward prostitution after lovers had abandoned them. Maisie D., "seduced at the age of 17 before leaving home," typified the women's stories. Elizabeth R. was "seduced in her native town by a married man who promised to get divorced from his wife and marry her." Other women turned to prostitution in hopes of escaping the poor working conditions and low wages of industrial work that held them in penury. Rare was the prostitute's daughter and "fast house" resident who confessed, "I was born bad, I never knew anything else, only to do as I felt like doing. My mother told me so," or the young woman who had been entrapped into prostitution.[37]

Few women coming to U.S. towns and cities fell prey to the flesh trade, but even fewer women initially found jobs that assured their financial independence, and most women relied upon cooperative living arrangements of one kind or another to stretch their meager earnings. Local conditions, such as the presence of recent immigrants and migrants, defined the residential arrangements of working women. Boarding or living in proved the only solution for many women alone. Those who had neither economic resources nor family to assist them tolerated the long hours and lack of privacy that characterized live-in domestic work. Over time the incidence of boarding and living in decreased, but the personal circumstances of women played a larger role in the decline than did women's wages. As new workers were increasingly recruited from urban families rather than from the ranks of migrants, boarding and live-in service declined. Domestic work increasingly became the lot of African American women with dependents. Employers rarely welcomed a servant's family; conversely, parents abhorred employer intervention in their family lives. African American women frequently pooled their economic resources to assist each other in moving out of live-in service.[38] To a lesser extent, increases in the real earnings of women over time allowed more and more single women to maintain their own homes or to share homes with other working women. Of working women in twenty-seven cities in 1900, 35 percent lived with their employers or boarded. Live-in employees included many hotel workers and hospital cleaners like Nina Talpiniuk, as well as household servants.

Boarders and lodgers lived in a variety of settings, including women's residences, private family homes, and commercial lodging houses. Social settlements, churches, and women's clubs all attempted to provide safe and decent living accommodations for young women. The Young Women's Christian Association and business women's homes existed in all major U.S. cities by the 1920s, but these facilities intentionally limited women's independence and were woefully inadequate to meet the tides of migrant women. With the exception of the black Phyllis Wheatley branches of the YWCA, most privately supported housing facilities for working women rejected blacks, and many accepted neither immigrants nor Hispanics. Most club-supported residences also would not accept married, widowed, or divorced women. Although less discriminatory with regard to race, ethnicity, and marital status than business women's residences, housing facilities maintained by the Salvation Army and settlement houses provided only short-term emergency housing to migrants.

Boarding houses evoked universal condemnation from welfare workers, who claimed that moral degradation was the inevitable lot of lodging women, who lacked both privacy and matronly supervision. In the cheapest boarding quarters, a woman had neither a room nor a bed to herself but shared a bed with a boarder who worked while the other slept. Social workers cited individual cases to illustrate that boarding corrupted young women, although such experiences were hardly normative. Anastazia Pastrozna, a twenty-year-old Russian immigrant, lodged in the Chicago home of a Russian couple who also rented rooms to seven Russian men. Pastrozna developed an intimate relationship with one of the boarders, Paul Stornieczik. Stornieczik left Chicago when he learned that Anastazia was carrying his child. Pastrozna entered a house of refuge for "girls" after the birth of her child and remained there until the Chicago Immigrants' League found a farm family who offered room and board for mother and child in exchange for Pastrozna's domestic labor.[39]

Separation from kin propelled women to accept live-in employment or to rent quarters in the homes of others, but lodging families were not uncommon in the early twentieth century. Live-in employees occasionally had dependents, as was the case with Anastazia Pastrozna. Among live-in employees in 1900, one third were married, widowed, or divorced women who had previous or concurrent family responsibilities. Regardless of family status, few working women of 1900 were self sufficient. Working women who maintained their own homes generally supplemented their earnings with those of children or other relatives. Of working women in twenty-seven cities in 1900, the majority were members of families that included workers other than themselves, and nearly two fifths of the families of wage-earning women included three or more workers.

As single women migrated to urban centers, boarding houses or residence with their employers provided the key to surviving on their meager earnings. The majority (60 percent) of working single African American or of white immigrant women in cities lived apart from their families. Employer preferences and migrants' needs encouraged immigrant and African American women to accept domestic work that included rooming in their employers' houses. The native-born daughters of immigrants, whose parents generally resided in cities, did not need to leave home to find work. Consequently, the daughters of immigrants could reject the residential domestic and service jobs that attracted so many immigrants and African American women. Native-born white women whose parents were American born most likely turned to boarding houses as they left their parents in the countryside and accepted urban jobs. Finding work as factory operatives, retail clerks, or office workers, native-stock white migrant women turned to group homes as did most migrant men. Once married, most working women, regardless of ethnicity, lived in their own homes or with kin, but approximately one fourth of all ever-married urban working women boarded in commercial establishments or the homes of unrelated persons.[40]

Boarding and living in were most prevalent in the fastest-growing urban areas, where housing costs were highest. Although boarding decreased in most cities between 1900 and 1920, it increased significantly in Atlanta. Joseph A. Hill of the

Census Bureau concluded that the threefold increase in the number of single, white working women that occurred in Atlanta between 1900 and 1920 explained the increase in the incidence of female boarders in the Gate City. As growth stabilized and migration declined, boarding also tended to decline. Through the twentieth century boarding declined overall for both sexes as rising real earnings permitted more families and individuals to maintain their own homes.

REGIONAL LABOR MARKETS

Women turned to boarding or living with employers out of personal necessity, but the necessity followed from women's decisions to leave home in search of work. Women's employment options did not necessarily match their expectations or ambitions, and job opportunities that labor markets presented shifted constantly as the economy evolved. The structure of local labor markets shaped women's possibilities for work as well as their residential options. In 1900 women were most likely to work for wages in the South, where women's work in agriculture persisted, and in New England. At the turn of the century, textile, garment, and shoe factories were the primary industrial employers of women, and New England remained the center of these operations. In the South the high overall work rates of women reflected the high proportion of African American women in the population. Most African American women devoted major portions of their lives to market labor, and southern racial segregation confined most nonagricultural workers to domestic service.

The broad availability of low-cost household services in the South assisted white wives and mothers in moving into the work force. Despite their small incomes, southern mill workers commonly employed domestic servants, generally African American women, who helped with child care, cooking, and cleaning.[41] Work rates for southern women, regardless of race, were undoubtedly higher than the official count, as both wives and daughters participated in agricultural production on family-operated farms.

Women's work and settlement patterns in the Northeast contrasted with the southern example largely because of the greater density of industrial centers in the region. In the textile center of Fall River, Massachusetts, nearly all adult women worked. Although few black women lived in this textile town, three quarters of them worked for wages as household servants or factory employees. Two in five immigrant women worked, three in five daughters of immigrants worked, and three in ten daughters of the native born worked. Light manufacturing in New England depended largely on female labor, and these special opportunities served as a magnet to immigrant families and especially drew women immigrating alone from Europe. The typical female worker in New England was either an immigrant herself or the daughter of an immigrant. Following closely behind New England and the South in female work rates came the Middle Atlantic region, where the same industries existed as in New England and factories also heavily staffed themselves with immigrants and the daughters of immigrants.

Within regional or local labor markets, the types of jobs available determined which family members entered the labor market. In New England cotton mills, during the first decade of the century, French Canadian women accounted for nearly half the female workforce, with English, Irish, and Polish women all outnumbering native-born female workers. Among these various ethnic groups the ages of women at work differed dramatically. Among the small group of Italian women in the mills, three fifths were under twenty-one years of age, while four fifths of Irish workers were twenty-one or older. Among other national groups in New England and among southern workers, approximately two fifths of the women were under twenty-one. Differences in the ages of the workers reflected contrasts in family work habits or needs by ethnic groups. On the other hand, virtually all immigrant mill families and the vast majority of native-born families with children ages sixteen years and older had sent the children to work.

Economic conditions occasionally compelled women with employed spouses to accept work in locations distant from their husbands' employment. After she had worked for ten years, a New York flower maker of the early twentieth century married a tailor. The couple moved to Baltimore, where the husband had found work and the cost of living was considerably lower. The birth of her children and a period of unemployment or little work in the garment industry threatened the family's welfare. The mother had located only one flower factory in Baltimore, and it paid very low wages in comparison with the New York shops. Poorly educated and unskilled in any other trade, the flower maker and her children periodically returned to New York. After some time she convinced her husband to relocate to New York so that she could retain employment. The family united there, but the high cost of living dictated that they rent a small apartment and forego running water and other conveniences they had known in Baltimore.[42]

Women migrated to factory towns to seek work in specific industries, but industries also migrated. Manufacturers readily deserted locales where they found labor costs too high. Both demographic characteristics and the occupational structure dictated which women would hold jobs in a given labor market. The runaway shop transformed the composition of the labor force in the town it deserted as well as the locale it entered.

The silk industry in New Jersey originated in the early nineteenth century and underwent major expansion during the Civil War. During the war a number of English silk manufacturers immigrated to Paterson, bringing with them both machinery and skilled English operatives. Thereafter Paterson acted as a magnet for silk workers who wanted to leave their native homelands. With the exception of dyeing and finishing workers, a sizable proportion of the immigrant workers were women, and at the turn of the century nearly four fifths of the working women of Paterson earned their wages in the silk industry. Among both men and women in the Paterson mills, about one fifth of the workers were native born. Reflecting the skill demands of the industry, the most recent arrivals did not necessarily fall to the bottom of the occupational ladder. English and Italian workers had attained the highest occupational status, with about half of their numbers holding skilled positions as weavers, warpers, and twisters-in. Italian male workers enjoyed especially high status, with four fifths of them employed as broad silk weavers. Among women, Italians also fared well, with nearly half of them employed as head silk weavers. Late in the nineteenth century Paterson manufacturers began to decentralize the least-skilled parts of their operations, throwing and spinning, to take advantage of lower labor costs in Pennsylvania and elsewhere.[43] The manufacturers of ribbons and Jacquard silks, however, remained firmly rooted in Paterson until the 1913 strike.

The high skill levels generally demanded in the Paterson mills also discouraged child labor. In the New Jersey silk mills overall, only 291 of 6,161 workers were under sixteen years of age, but in the Pennsylvania mills, child workers numbered 1,298 in a total work force of 5,247. Similarly, the lower skills demanded in Pennsylvania silk mills resulted in a work force in which both women and the native-born of both sexes were particularly prominent. In Pennsylvania 3,696 of the 5,247 workers were females of sixteen years of age or older, of whom 1,107 (30 percent) were native-born. Of the 253 men in Pennsylvania silk mills, 130, or more than half, were native born. In the New Jersey mills, female adult workers numbered 3,344 in a total workforce of 6,161, with adult males numbering 2,526, or 40 percent of New Jersey silk workers, of whom only 186 were native born.

New Jersey silk manufacturers first established throwing branches in Pennsylvania in the 1880s, and by 1895 Pennsylvania ranked second in the nation in the amount of silk spun within its borders. Captive female labor supplies in several industrial towns induced the silk mills' migration to Pennsylvania. As a Senate investigatory committee concluded in 1910, "Improved machinery had aided the throwster by increasing the production per operative, but the opportunity of moving his plant into some small community where there were unemployed women and children had meant more, for it has insured him an abundant supply of labor at a lower cost. The [anthracite] mining towns in Pennsylvania have afforded just such an opportunity."[44]

As the Pennsylvania throwing mills developed, the share of silk spinning performed by women and girls also grew. In 1908, nearly one third of female workers surveyed in the Pennsylvania throwing mills were under the age of sixteen, while only one tenth of the New Jersey workers were under sixteen. Overall in the Pennsylvania throwing mills, female workers outnumbered males ten to one as compared with a three-to-one ratio in New Jersey, and women in the New Jersey mills earned considerably more than the Pennsylvania workers, even when controlling for age.[45]

In the second decade of the twentieth century, the Pennsylvania mills faced competition from other employers of female labor. Silk Association manufacturers complained in 1906 that knitting, hosiery, and weaving mills had driven up the price of female labor close to the New Jersey rates. A manufacturers' report pronounced that Theodore Roosevelt's arbitration of the anthracite coal strike of 1904 had been a great disappointment because "Before the Roosevelt era of peace in the coal fields we occasionally had a coal scare, when suddenly help became plentiful, but prosperous times for the heads of families enabled them to keep their daughters at home."[46] The specter of labor competition that had led New Jersey manufacturers to relocate or to branch out to Pennsylvania encouraged them to move again shortly thereafter. Like cotton manufacturers, the silk industry looked southward, favoring Maryland and Virginia, not because of their proximity but because cotton textiles had developed less in those states than in the Carolinas and Georgia. One Paterson silk firm avoided competition with the cotton textile industry in North Carolina by relying on black labor when it opened a plant in Fayetteville in 1899.

In New Jersey's silk mills the majority of Italian female workers were married women, an anomaly among industrial workers generally and among Italian factory workers as well. In Pennsylvania towns, areas to which silk manufacturers had moved specifically to tap the labor pool of miners' wives and daughters, Italian women were not present in the labor force and ever-married women played a very small role in the silk mills. In the New Jersey mills approximately one in five workers was a married woman or a previously married woman, but in Pennsylvania fewer than one in twenty female workers had married.[47]

The New Jersey silk mills attracted proportionally more married women than factories elsewhere in the Northeast. The prominence of Italian wives and widows and the low representation of single Italian women in the New Jersey silk mills apparently confirms the importance of cultural imperatives to protect daughters from the world outside church and home, but other evidence undercuts this conclusion. In the New England cotton mills single Italian working women outnumbered their ever-married Italian co-workers by a ratio of two to one. Wives and ex-wives, both Italian and non-Italian, were more likely to enter the New Jersey mills because they were more highly skilled than the younger women, and the state's fine fabric industry specifically demanded highly trained workers.

With gender segregation in place in the industrial setting from its very inception, capitalists found many methods of exploiting female labor that they could not apply so readily to male workers. Central to women's roles in industry, as the Paterson cases demonstrated, lay the fact that women often comprised a captive labor supply. In locales where women did not already hold industrial jobs, manufacturers could establish low-wage women's work as long as they did not demand highly skilled workers. Once these industries had drawn in local women, employers could reduce wages below their start-up rates with minimal chances of losing their labor supply. The ideal setting for maximizing the benefits of captive female labor was a community in which one heavy industry dominated local employment and where, consequently, women had generally found no employment. Troy, New York, one of the nation's oldest and most important iron-molding centers, furnished just such a locale. The ability of the Troy iron industry to hold the male labor force served as a prime factor to induce manufacturers to invest in building a shirtmaking industry in nineteenth-century Cohoes, just across the Hudson River from Troy.[48]

The pairing of industries and the movement toward employment of family groups as opposed to individuals changed the composition of the female labor force. It also enhanced the possibilities for lowering labor costs by taking advantage of workers immobilized by family ties to other workers in the area. In female-dominated industries paired with male industries and in textile mills, particularly in the South, the environment encouraged the entrance of children and married women into the labor market. In textile mill villages, North and South, employers often made the availability of company housing conditional upon a family's furnishing the maximum number of workers to the mill.[49]

Nineteenth-century textile mills were mainly family-owned enterprises. For small-scale capitalists the mill represented heavy capital investment and a lifetime commitment. As larger corporations emerged, however, the investment in a single mill represented proportionally less of total corporate capital. Mill managers could afford to close an unprofitable location and move elsewhere. The growth in corporate size that has characterized the U.S. economy in the twentieth century proved key in generating the migration of industries seeking cheap labor, male or female. Industries that do not require heavy machinery and large factories—nonmechanized nut shelling and hand sewing are extreme examples—could freely follow the labor market. In garment making, more than in any other major industry, pockets of low labor costs have set the wage level for the entire industry because of the ease of chasing the labor market. Sewing shops tend to be small in scale, sewing machines are moved easily, and industrial relocation occurs frequently. By the early twentieth century, the textile industries, like Paterson's silk mills, and other light industries had matured and faced declining profits. When local conditions drove up the price of female labor or strikes disrupted production, employers often fled in search of more favorable environments. In moving, plant operators looked specifically for a captive and previously unexploited female labor supply to perform the unskilled and semiskilled tasks that comprised the majority of their productive processes. The decline of Paterson's silk industry replicated itself in other fields, decade upon decade, as manufacturing moved from North to South, from East to West, and finally to the Third World. The runaway shop phenomenon occurred in male labor markets as well, but employer migration especially disadvantaged married women, for whom relocation has presented the greatest difficulties.[50]

CONCLUSION

In the early twentieth century, industrial towns and cities drew women of all backgrounds. The rise or decline of industry in a given location shaped women's work patterns and their geographic movements. First- and second-generation immigrant women sought jobs in domestic service or in the factories of northeastern and mid-Atlantic states. Native-born white women of native parentage preferred the employments of smaller towns with less heterogeneous populations. African American women sought domestic work in southern and northern communities. In any case, individual women in need of work sought out city or village employers who hired others of their kind. Responding to rumors, advertisements, or letters from friends and kin, women found jobs in labor markets segregated by gender and by race or nativity.

The experiences of working women at the turn of the century set the tone for much of what followed in the U.S. economy. Employment continued to call women to towns and cities in the decades to come, newcomers to the city or to the labor force faced numerous challenges in adapting to their new environments, and economic change continually reshaped women's work. Individual earnings and family circumstances dictated women's living arrangements. Immigrant women continued to play a significant role in the labor force, although European immigration declined and female immigration from the Western Hemisphere increased. New occupations for women emerged and further expanded the demand for female workers, but occupational segregation and the gender gap in wages persisted.

Increasing numbers of parents accepted employment as a natural and desirable part of their daughters' lives, but parents' reliance on the labor of their children declined.

Educators and social reformers responded to industrialization and urbanization with a panoply of measures targeted at preparing girls for their adult responsibilities. At school, in peer groups, and at home, all girls learned gendered lessons specific to ethnic culture and social class. Decades of heavy immigration also encouraged the growth of social settlements oriented toward "Americanizing" immigrants and their children as well as the development of school curricula with a similar focus. For women and girls, "Americanization" included a strong dose of middle-class Anglo American lessons on gender and schooling in domestic tasks. Schools and social settlements prepared the daughters of the poor to shoulder paid labor in addition to domestic chores, and educational programs limited girls' job options as well as their expectations. As the twentieth century proceeded, educational institutions gradually adapted their curricula to prepare more girls for the workplace. School administrators paid careful attention to local labor demands in designing vocational programs. Thus, the labor demands of the industrial economy shaped girls' work lives long before they sought their first jobs.

CHAPTER TWO

The Education
of the Working Girl

A s the nineteenth century passed, industrialization's widening arc cast factories and shops, cities and suburbs across America's vast and fertile spaces. As this process created ever more jobs beyond farm and home, it exerted pressure on U.S. education, public and private, to reconstruct its curricula, for factories and stores, locomotives and banks, telegraphs and tenements demanded skills and disciplines different from those required on the farm. Increasingly mechanized and systematized production required literacy and numeracy even among unskilled workers. In addition, the modern economy compelled submission to industrial time discipline in which management, not the family or self-regulating artisans, decided the hours, pace, and content of work, a willingness, as one ballad laments, to "let this manufacturer use my body as a tool." In the nineteenth century, U.S. education, always sensitive to the needs of business and attuned to dictates of gender convention, had applied itself to these tasks, adding, in the latter half of the era, some measure of vocational education to teach basic mechanical skills to boys and office as well as domestic skills to girls.

As the twentieth century approached, the ramifying complexities of the industrial economy, including the rise of service businesses and the multiplication of management functions, increased the number of jobs available and the skills required to do many of them. Scientific advances had a similar impact on medicine, dentistry, and nursing. Altogether these developments demanded a workforce larger than the male population could furnish, included tasks that few men would do, and created white-collar jobs outside the factory in numbers that the middle class could not (or would not) supply. For some working-class women, these shortages offered opportunities to move up the social and occupational scale, but labor demands rarely created a bridge across traditional gender barriers.

These forces, together with sheer economic necessity among the poor, pulled and pushed increasing numbers of women out of the home and into the workforce. Nothing, however, absolved women of the fundamental domestic responsibilities of homemaking and child care; wage work became (as it often remains) an obligation added to, not substituted for, traditional female burdens. Education for women in the United States long continued to reflect middle-class attachment to the notion that women should stay at home, keeping it as a "haven in a heartless world," serve as moral bulwark against the natural depravity of men, and shield children in their innocence, a view reinforced by the arrival of many late-nineteenth- and early-twentieth-century immigrants with whose gendered traditions it coincided.

The persistence of this so-called "cult of true womanhood" in the face of contrary reality, especially among working-class women, manifested itself in education which, even as it evolved in response to shifting labor market demands, resisted training women for employments that did not transfer the domestic arts into the realm of paid employment. As the Progressive movement brought reform to the turn-of-the-century United States, it brought a new scrutiny to education, which, in the minds of some reformers, exposed the absurdity of female education based on an obsolete mythology. "If we educate girls only for . . . marriage," observed education reformer Albert Leake, "we [do] them a . . . grievous wrong."[1] "Training for homemaking," echoed vocational counselor Marguerite Dickson, "must go hand in hand with training for . . . industrial life."[2]

Leake, Dickson, and others of like mind articulated realities of the industrial United States—that most working women spent many years as wage-earners, that increasing numbers of women should anticipate such a role, and that society should prepare them accordingly. This message differed significantly from the traditional view among nineteenth-century educators who saw female employment as a temporary expedient in poor families, at best a passage between childhood and full-time motherhood. Nevertheless, assumptions about class and gender defined the goals of educational reformers as well. Industrial training programs of the late nineteenth and "progressive" vocational schools of the twentieth century educated girls for employment in the town-based sectors that hired women: domestic service, light manufacturing, and retail sales.

Most women at work between 1900 and World War I had completed their education in the 1880s and 1890s. The oldest of them had had little formal schooling, while the youngest had likely attended some secondary school. Most working women of the early twentieth century had left school by the age of fourteen, and they had done so largely at the discretion of their parents or the prompting of community conventions. Later, upon entering the labor force, these women had learned their work skills on the job; furthermore, through social interaction in the workplace, women acquired new attitudes about life as well as work.

Throughout the late nineteenth and early twentieth centuries, U.S. girls learned at home and at school to expect primary adult roles as homemakers and mothers. The day-to-day experiences of youth included other basic lessons: children of the Gilded Age in the United States grew up in households where work formed part of the daily routine for girls and for boys. Within the home girls but rarely boys helped with cleaning chores and assisted in the production, preparation, and preservation of food. Rural boys toiled in the fields alongside their fathers, where they were joined by their mothers and sisters at crucial times such as the harvest season. Urban boys generally had greater freedom than their sisters to explore the world outside the household. As long as children stayed in school, steady wage work remained unlikely. Observing their elders, however, children of both sexes came to understand that adult lives left little time for leisure. Moreover, despite the ethos of social opportunity promulgated by Horatio Alger, the reality of segregation by ethnicity, class, and region meant that Gilded Age youth had little exposure to teenagers with life options radically different from their own.

Because they left school in childhood, most working-class girls and boys did not control decisions on when and where to seek employment. Whatever their reasons for leaving school, teenage women of the laboring classes generally entered the workforce unless their labor was needed within the home. For this generation of working people, the workplace and the social environments around it, rather than the school, formed the arenas in which adult ambitions emerged. Girls' expectations of work began to change as ever greater numbers entered vocational training classes.

Educational reformers such as Albert Leake demanded that schools develop educational programs and institute vocational guidance to accommodate the real prospects of ordinary working-class girls. Teachers and administrators, Leake maintained, had misled girls about their futures and sent them off into the world unprepared for the life ahead. Leake observed that although historically "woman has always been in industry," "a traditional feeling persists that she [shouldn't] be so employed." He added: "This has accounted for a great deal of neglect in her training. We have surrounded our girls with an atmosphere of unreality, and allowed our conduct to be dictated by principles which do not square with present conditions."[3]

Leake and those who shared his views insisted that girls should train for the workplace at school and not solely in the workshop, factory, or store. Driven by Progressive reformers' realization that women spent long years as wage workers, the creation of facilities to train them for industry emerged as a serious issue. The views of Leake, Marguerite Dickson, John Dewey, and others transformed U.S. public education outside the South in the early twentieth century, and vocational reforms reached sporadically into southern schools as well. In 1912 the National Society for the Promotion of Industrial Education established a separate office for the training of women and girls. Throughout the nation public educational funds expanded and schools succeeded in drawing ever greater numbers of children into vocational training. Social settlements and girls' clubs, often hand-in-hand with the schools, also readied girls for women's jobs in a gender-segregated economy.

Although Progressive educators saw curricular reforms as the key to long-term improvement in school retention, they pushed increased school attendance as the first step; in classic American fashion, they sought to compel immediate reform through legislation. This effort succeeded so well that by the end of World War I all states had compulsory school attendance laws, and most required children to stay in school until the age of fourteen years. Through the Gilded Age and the Progressive Era school attendance grew more regular and the school year grew longer. In 1880 approximately 60 percent of white girls ages five through nineteen and 33 percent of nonwhite girls of the same ages attended school. By 1920 these figures had risen to 66 percent and 55 percent, respectively.[4] In 1880 only 2.5 percent of the nation's seventeen-year-olds had graduated from high school, but by 1920 over 16 percent of youths in their eighteenth year had received diplomas.[5] Over these same decades the average number of days that a student attended school increased from 81 to 121.[6] Higher education grew similarly: between 1880 and 1920 the number of four-year collegiate degrees conferred on women increased from 2,500 to 16,600, while male degree recipients increased from 10,400 to 32,000.[7] Despite the growth of academic high schools and colleges, few working-class women, regardless of race, enjoyed the privilege of a high school education and fewer still had access to higher education.

Teaching, clerical work, and nursing, which required formal education beyond the common school, remained the almost exclusive purview of the middle class at the outset of the century. Formal training of women for such jobs had emerged in the nineteenth century and expanded rapidly in the three decades before 1900, but very few working-class women had the secondary school training necessary to enter career training or the financial resources to further their education. Some high school training equipped girls with the basic language and arithmetic skills that record keeping required, but the modern office demanded additional abilities. Typing, telegraphy, and stenography remained the province of private business academies. Some 40,000 women studied in business schools at the turn of the century, but public education soon made strong inroads into business education.[8] Reformers introduced business courses into high schools and colleges at the end of the century, and these courses had expanded widely by 1920.[9]

The general expansion of schooling in the United States opened the eyes of some working-class girls to job possibilities beyond factory labor or unskilled service work. In the first decades of the twentieth century, some children from the working classes earned high school diplomas and the most fortunate of their numbers went on to postsecondary education. Nevertheless, the curricula and culture of twentieth-century U.S. schools at all levels guided boys and girls in directions that administrators believed suited their sex as well as their racial and class backgrounds. Public education tracked girls into specific vocational lines and reinforced assumptions of female domesticity through gender-specific instruction and through the social environments of schools and colleges. Public and private industrial training programs of the nineteenth century had laid out gendered paths for the children of the poor. Greatly enhanced funding of industrial education after the turn of the century reconfirmed occupational segregation by sex.

THE DEVELOPMENT OF FEMALE VOCATIONAL SCHOOLS

Appropriately enough, Massachusetts, home of the first large-scale female factory labor force, pioneered in vocational education in private and public settings. As early as the 1860s private philanthropy had supported the establishment of gender-specific instruction for girls in Boston's poorest neighborhoods. The Shurtleff Grammar School, serving the working classes exclusively, required girls to study sewing in its three lower grades. In 1876 the Massachusetts legislature authorized the expenditure of state funds for sewing instruction in the public schools. Educators who supported the introduction of sewing into the curriculum specifically saw the subject as a social, moral, and economic corrective in the lives of girls whose indigent mothers had failed to teach their daughters the skills of womanhood. Manifesting class attitudes still in evidence as the twentieth century wanes, these late-century middle-class reformers had concluded that maternal failure to socialize daughters stemmed from working-class mothers' dual responsibilities of wage earning and family care. Introducing sewing instruction for girls in 1878, the Worcester, Massachusetts, school committee stressed the moral value of the lessons: "Nothing adds more to the household comfort, is more indispensable to the tidiness and decency of home, than this poor despised, neglected, and among our poorest people, lost art of good hand sewing." That it might be revived and made "a reformatory power through the homes of school children," the school committee approved an expenditure of funds for such instruction.[10] Throughout the remainder of the nineteenth century, public and private domestic education for

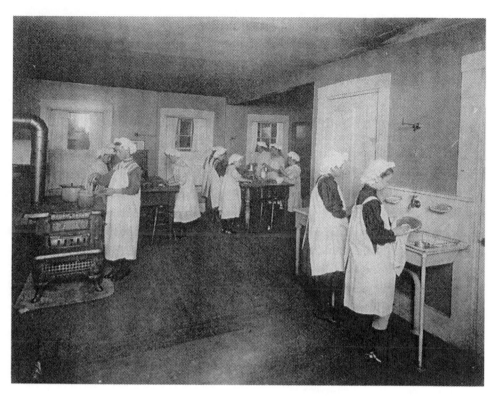

Private groups in Boston pioneered in vocational education for girls. Cooking class at Denison House, Boston, ca. 1911. Courtesy Schlesinger Library

working-class girls expanded in Massachusetts and elsewhere, adding cooking, laundering, vegetable gardening, and housekeeping to the programs as time went by.

Foreshadowing pervasive change elsewhere, Massachusetts had also established secondary trade schools before the turn of the century. These publicly or privately funded schools taught broadly defined industrial skills to the children of the working classes. By 1900 such schools worked to reduce the number of children leaving school in the early grades and guided elementary school graduates along the path to paid employment. In Roxbury, Massachusetts, for instance, the Children's Welfare League placed boys and girls "who are obliged to become wage earners" in industrial training projects.[11] The privately funded Women's Educational and Industrial Union of Boston, recognizing that women often could not afford to stay in school, recruited girls about to drop out of area trade schools by providing part-time employment and on-the-job training in their manufacturing workshops. The union program offered an attractive option because the school helped its students find full-time jobs when they completed their training. Through the nineteenth and early twentieth centuries, industrial education taught both girls and boys the discipline of the workplace, but few of the skills taught transferred directly to the employments they later gained.[12]

EXTENDING THE EDUCATIONAL EXPERIENCE

While trade school sponsors like the Women's Educational and Industrial Union strove to secure funding for program expansion, they also campaigned to improve school attendance. Both working-class parents and children at the turn of the century generally saw the completion of grammar school as an adequate education for girls. At that point, some parents sent their youthful daughters to work, but the time lag between leaving school and going to work usually extended longer for girls than for boys. Teenage girls might assume household and child care functions in support of working parents rather than seeking paid work immediately. Such home responsibilities prepared girls for their future tasks as homemakers and mothers in ways that many parents thought formal education did not.[13]

The new century brought the expansion of secondary schooling into the neighborhoods of the working classes, but many barriers to high school completion remained for the poor. Prejudices of gender, class, and race restricted educational options within the new schools, while ethnic values often precluded girls' taking advantage of the school opportunities that did exist. The definition of an appropriate education for girls varied among and within ethnic groups. Some Jewish, Irish, Italian, and Polish parents, for example, feared that too much education would make their daughters unmarriageable, while other Jews and most Poles held learning in high regard. Irish, French Canadian, and Italian Catholics often chose to send their children to church schools, but the availability of parochial education did not generally induce them to push their daughters to an education beyond basic reading, writing, and numerical skills. Polish Catholic parents, on the other hand, regularly encouraged their daughters to attend high school as long as their education took place within an ethnic parish school. Greek families also encouraged the education of their daughters and placed particular value on instruction overseen by Greek Orthodox teachers.[14]

The National Society for Industrial Education sought to garner support for practical training by demonstrating the failures of contemporary schooling. In 1914 society investigators completed a study of students enrolled in the public schools of Richmond, Virginia, which showed that whites stayed in school longer than blacks and girls longer than boys of their own race. Of 1,000 students aged 11, approximately 650 persisted to age fourteen and 450 to age fifteen. By age sixteen the majority of children, black and white, male and female, had left school. The investigators further determined that currently enrolled teenagers had failed to make satisfactory academic progress. Of 2,590 girls and boys aged thirteen and fourteen in school in the 1913–14 session, half of the white girls and boys were in grade six or below and over half of the black boys and girls were in grade five or below. The report's authors warned: "These figures indicate that large numbers of these boys and girls [will] leave school soon and go to work with an educational preparation so inadequate as to hamper them in their vocations and seriously to reduce their value to the community."[15]

Educators of the early twentieth century increasingly deplored the fact that so many children, North and South, had left school by their early teens without the basic skills to prosper in the labor market. The expansion of high schools in the Progressive Era brought secondary schooling to rural areas and urban working-class neighborhoods. The problem lay in persuading parents and children, northern and southern, rural and urban, that sticking around for secondary school would pay off for all concerned. Presuming that the future of the children in these districts lay in unskilled or semiskilled jobs in agriculture, manufacturing, commerce, and service, school administrators focused on the development of a practical curriculum that would enhance pupil retention.

EDUCATION AND THE PERPETUATION
OF GENDER CONVENTIONS

Throughout the twentieth century, as education widened geographically and attendance and retention improved, schooling remained overwhelmingly gender specific. Thus the school grew increasingly important in fixing girls' expectations of adult life. For all their commitment to reform and expansion of schools and curricula, many Progressive educators not only retained Victorian notions of female intellectual inferiority but also held fast to ethnic prejudices that discouraged rigorous academic programs in schools serving African American and immigrant children.[16]

While schools in the industrial North began to develop trade curricula for the working classes and to encourage high school completion especially among middle-class youths, southern schools remained hampered by inferior funding and a greater reliance on local as opposed to state revenues and supervision. Predominantly rural and agricultural until 1920, and fiercely committed to racially segregated education, white southerners rarely pushed for extensive or rigorous public schooling. In one-industry towns and textile mill villages, schooling depended on the largesse of factory owners and bowed to the mills' demands for child labor. Before

World War I circumstances denied high school education to all but a lucky few southern children who lived in the larger cities or whose parents paid tuition for public or private instruction. Southern parents, trapped in unskilled occupations, often disparaged the value of education in enhancing children's earning abilities; furthermore, on farms and in factory villages, families relied on the labor of children as well as that of adults.

Like poorer families of the urban North, poor southern families often focused on the short-term family benefits of sending children to work as soon as they could earn any wage. Thus parents joined employers in opposition to child labor legislation in the South. Theatis Johnson Williamson, for example, born in Sampson County, North Carolina, in 1903, began work as a cotton spinner in 1915 after her family moved from the farm to a mill village. Although Williamson's education did not end until she went to work, she and her family had always regarded schooling as a casual undertaking at best. As Williamson remembered, "I didn't go to school much, no. . . . Along then they didn't care whether you went to school or not."[17]

Shortly after the turn of the century, the educational progressivism of John Dewey, G. Stanley Hall, and others catalyzed the acceptance of vocational education and brought into the school many of the lessons of life hitherto left to parents. Indeed, Dewey's educational philosophy rested on the assumption that industrialization had robbed children of participation in the productive labor of the home, the farm, and the artisan's shop. Though no friend of child labor at home or in the factory, Dewey believed that children had formerly learned social skills, community values, and vocational competence at home, lessons that schools must now incorporate.[18]

In their reform rhetoric Progressives gave the impression of embracing gender-blind philosophy. In *Schools of To-Morrow*, for example, John and Evelyn Dewey praised the innovative school of "Mrs. [Marietta] Johnson at Fairhope, Alabama," who stressed learning by doing and the cultivation of practical skills as a basis for studying traditional academic subjects. In Johnson's school "Boys and girls alike do cooking and carpentry work, for the object of the work is not to train them for any trade or profession, but to train them to be capable, happy members of society."[19] Its southern location made Johnson's experimental institution all the more remarkable.

Elsewhere, however, the Deweys rhapsodized about educational programs that began to track boys and girls into separate vocations as early as the fourth grade. The Deweys found the Gary, Indiana, schools exemplary in their emphasis on industrial skills. They praised Gary's trade school programs in which fourth-grade girls entered the dressmaking program while their male classmates worked in the wood or metal shop. In the secondary program girls learned to apply general domestic skills to the industrial environment.

Although few public school systems in the United States had vocational courses as elaborate as the instructional programs in Gary, numerous public schools of the early twentieth century narrowed the options of all children by channeling boys into shop or agriculture and girls into home economics. In 1918 the federal government allocated one million dollars for vocational education, with state and local governments investing an additional two million in teaching trade skills. Within this year 164,000 boys and girls, approximately 8.5 percent of all public secondary school students, participated in vocational education.

Parents did not universally support vocational education. When the New York City schools attempted to implement the Gary trade school model, a group of Jewish parents protested that the curriculum would block their children's access to higher education.[20] They complained that "the girls' technical high school does about what the vocational grammar schools [do]. . . . The girls [learn] . . . to lift [housework] above drudgery by making it into a profession."[21] A praiseworthy endeavor in some respects, perhaps, but scarcely preparation for entry into college.

While the large, well-organized, and influential Jewish community in New York could make its voice heard, elsewhere the double bias against ethnic women resulted in scanty funding of educational programs for immigrants' daughters and African American girls. Public schools for African American youths stressed the teaching of domestic skills to girls and rarely encouraged them to follow a more academic program that might lead them to college or normal school. This sort of discriminatory tracking also won plaudits from the Deweys, who praised an Indianapolis school that instructed African American girls in domestic subjects and helped them transfer cooking skills to the workplace: "The girls learn to cook and serve good cheap meals, and then they sit down together and eat what they have cooked. They talk over their individual problems with the teacher and with each other, and give each other practical help. The domestic science teacher helps the girls who have some skill find work to do after school hours so that they can help their families by helping themselves; she helps pupils find steady work as they leave school and then keeps track of them, encouraging them to go on fitting themselves for better work."[22]

By the end of World War I, the Progressive emphasis on preparation for adult roles and citizenship had gained wide adoption in secondary education. As school systems translated reformers' ideas into action, however, Progressives' concerns for such things as "development of the whole person" and "engagement in learning through play" mostly fell by the wayside as the focus became more narrowly vocational. With growing percentages of children staying in school through grades eleven or twelve, schools had the opportunity not only to shape youthful values and aspirations but also to chart the occupational courses of girls and boys. Consequently, the "Americanization" of ethnic children continued and the gender tracking of students increased.

The prolongation of education through the secondary years further transferred the definition and implementation of gender roles from the home to the school. Just as class-differentiated and racially segregated school systems forged separate paths for black and white students, for working-class and middle-class pupils, most high schools tracked boys and girls into different educational paths. Adopting a pattern that came to characterize much of the South, the Atlanta Board of Education opened gender-segregated senior high schools with different curricula in 1898 and introduced gender-defined courses in the coeducational junior high schools they initiated in 1923. Girls studied less science and mathematics but took more business courses than boys. From grade seven onward girls studied home economics while boys pursued industrial arts. The teaching of physical education, endorsed by the medical community and educational reformers, provided the opportunity to instruct children in the appropriate physical ranges of male and female activities.

EDUCATION BEYOND HOME AND SCHOOL:
SOCIAL WORKERS AND SHELTERED HAVENS

Urban welfare agencies buttressed the gendered lessons of home and school. Settlement houses and the Young Women's Christian Association reached out to girls as well as adults and provided a common public space for the middle and the working classes. Although casting themselves in the roles of teachers and superiors, settlement residents and YWCA personnel also learned from their clients. Long after the establishment of the Henry Street social settlement, founder Lillian Wald remembered an impoverished family that had redirected her into a life of social advocacy. A small girl had led Wald from her nursing duty in a hospital ward to the wretched surroundings where her mother lay ill. If she could have blamed the family's condition on its own "moral unworthiness," Wald recalled, she could have found "some solace" and perhaps defended her membership in "a society which permitted such circumstances to exist." However, her "subsequent acquaintance with them revealed the fact that, miserable as their state was, they were not without ideals for the family life, and for society, of which they were so unloved and unlovely a part."[23]

Through the first half of the twentieth century, settlement houses provided an exchange place in which middle-class women learned from the working-class women and girls of settlement-house neighborhoods while trying to pass on their own skills to their clients. To that end social settlements organized classes and clubs for women and girls as well as for men and boys. While we cannot know how thoroughly clients absorbed middle-class expectations through social settlements, residents clearly hoped that the poor would emulate their manners and morals. Settlement workers sought to Americanize immigrants and to fashion democratic citizens of their children.

Lillian Wald delighted in the transformation of young immigrant wives into native-born look-alikes through the influence of Henry Street's mothers' club. Of the first mothers' club meeting Wald remembered that the women "gave no indication of any experience with social usages, for they came with untidy clothes, safety pins holding together their untidy blouses." She meant by this, of course, middle-class American "social usages," for Wald belonged to a well-to-do Jewish family of German and Polish heritage, which, like other such families, had swiftly and energetically assimilated themselves into the U.S. mainstream of language, values, and behavior. Nudged by her belief that gender transcended class, Wald deplored the tendency of the "daughters of the *shtetl*," to cling to the habits of the eastern European villages and ghettos from whence they migrated. Describing a dinner celebrating the 35th anniversary of the club's founding as "a meeting of sophisticates," Wald rejoiced that the Jewish wives of the lower East Side "no longer disfigure themselves with the *sheitel* [a wig] when they appear in public."[24]

Jane Addams noted with satisfaction that members of a Hull House woman's club succeeded in following the social action model of the General Federation of Women's Clubs. After newly found family prosperity had allowed them to move to comfortable homes away from the poor environs of Hull House, Addams's former clients engaged in the sorts of volunteer relief efforts and organizations commonly associated with middle-class women. Thus, Addams and her colleagues, despite their own career drives, applauded other women's successes in rejecting wage earning and embracing the unpaid club work of middle-class wives.[25]

Hull House, founded in 1887, organized social clubs for young people as well as adults soon after it opened. Social clubs eventually reached persons of all ages in both gender-segregated and gender-integrated activities. Hull House and other settlements sought to offer young men and women opportunities for heterosocial interaction in an environment where both middle-class social expectations and neighborhood moral values could be enforced. As Jane Addams smugly wrote: "Although more conventional customs are carefully enforced at our many parties and festivities, and while dancing classes are as highly prized for the opportunity they afford for enforcing standards as for their ostensible aim, the residents at Hull House, in their efforts to provide opportunities for clean recreation, receive most

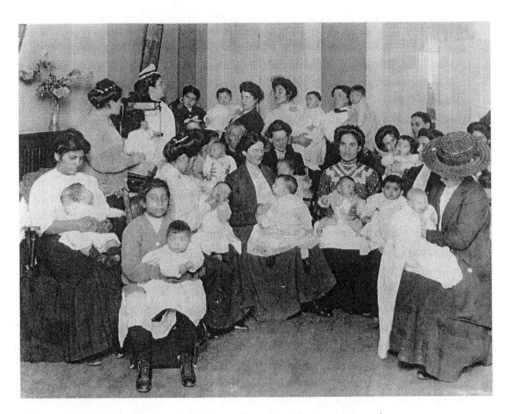

Social settlements brought middle-class and working-class women together in a variety of circumstances. Baby clinic at Denison House, Boston, ca. 1911. Courtesy Schlesinger Library

valued advice from the experienced wisdom of the older women of the neighborhood."[26] Addams and others sought to keep young women from the evils of theaters, dance clubs, and beer halls—the traditional working-class haunts—through the influence of the settlement. Although settlements succeeded in sheltering some girls from worldly amusements, other working-class youths of the 1900s flaunted convention and shaped their own recreational patterns around commercial entertainments.

While urban middle-class youths and rural children generally discovered movies and amusement parks later than did members of the working-class, educated middle-class women sought to lead and protect these sheltered offspring as well. Unlike the social settlement, rural reform organizations emerged from the leadership of public colleges, land-grant universities, and the Department of Agriculture. Faculty and graduates of agricultural colleges and schools of home economics sponsored rural clubs for girls and for boys. The 4-H program reached girls as well as boys and organized activities for farm wives sprang from girls' clubs and the home extension movement.

In 1910 a faculty member at South Carolina's Winthrop College organized the nation's first "Tomato Club."[27] Tomato Clubs, counterparts of Boys' Corn Clubs, organized rural teenage girls and set them to work growing and canning vegetables that they sold to bolster family income. The clubs, sponsored as part of the U.S. Department of Agriculture's extension program, presaged the 4-H Clubs. Through Tomato Clubs, college-educated women hoped not only to improve rural families' food supply and income but also to encourage good moral habits, sound nutrition, and the adoption of urban standards of household order and home decorating. Tomato Clubs' organizers strove to influence rural mothers through their daughters' participation. County agents saw mothers and daughters working together as a powerful weapon to safeguard families' moral standards as well to upgrade their economic habits. Once established, county extension agents used Tomato Clubs as a base for organizing the Home Demonstration Clubs that proved effective in raising family farm income in the 1930s.

TRAINING MIDDLE-CLASS GIRLS FOR WORK

Jane Addams and Lillian Wald joined a handful of other educated women of the nineteenth century in carving out new arenas of professional activity in the United States. Their careers paved the way for succeeding generations of women who, like the organizers of South Carolina Tomato Clubs, pursued careers in social work and other service occupations. The industrial economy had not only made their education possible but also created the need for their services. In the early twentieth century, colleges and universities expanded their missions to include the training of middle-class women for careers in settlement work and rural outreach projects. Middle-class women's increasing access to higher education in the first two decades of the century had broadened the cohort of women who sought to apply their schooling outside the domestic sphere.

Rising educational expectations within the middle class accompanied the growth of vocational training for the working class and the poor. In the last three decades of the nineteenth century, secondary schooling expanded greatly, but high schools remained overwhelmingly the province of the middle class. Most middle-class families expected sons to enter the workforce while still in their teenage years, thus at some point terminating their stay in secondary school. On the other hand, such families often had domestic servants to tend to the household chores, and generally did not expect their daughters to work outside the home, so middle-class girls had more years free to devote to schooling. Not surprisingly, then, rates of high school attendance and high school completion remained higher among girls than among boys.

The fact that until the end of the century high school graduates could go directly from secondary school into elementary teaching offered an additional inducement for middle-class girls to complete high school. From the mid–nineteenth century on, women steadily entered the teaching profession because teacher shortages and the desire to hold down costs had led public officials to turn increasingly to women. Educational reformer Thomas H. Galludet concluded that men would always turn away from teaching because they encountered "so many other avenues . . . to the accumulation of property, and the attaining of distinction. We must [therefore] look [to] the other sex for aid in this emergency, and do all in our power to [attract] women of the necessary qualifications to . . . common school instruction."[28]

School officials first turned to female seminaries to recruit women for teaching, but the normal school soon followed. The nation's first normal school opened in Massachusetts in 1839 exclusively to train women. Subsequently institutions to train men as well as women appeared in other northern states. The New York State Normal School in Brockport and Minnesota's Winona State Normal School opened in the 1860s. The Michigan State Normal School opened its doors to students in 1853 and graduated more than three thousand teaching candidates before the century's end. The Michigan normal school admitted female students who had reached the age of sixteen and had completed the course of instruction offered in the common schools and accepted men at the age of eighteen.[29]

While normal schools prepared both women and men for teaching, the two sexes followed somewhat different curricula as states preserved gender segregation in the teaching profession. The Michigan State curriculum of 1861–62 prescribed Latin and Greek for men but Latin and French or German for women. Students could earn a provisional common school certificate after two years of study, but the school offered two additional years of training with advanced work in languages, science, and mathematics that led to permanent certification. Women, who presumably would leave teaching when they married, had greater incentive to take the shorter course. Consequently, women prepared more frequently to teach in the lower grades while male students trained for upper school teaching, a pattern that has endured deep into the twentieth century. Women frequently entered the teaching profession at the age of eighteen, while male students had most probably reached their majority before accepting their first teaching post.

Over time, rising demand for female white-collar workers redirected both secondary and higher education for whites. Normal schools, which had become educational fixtures in the nineteenth century, expanded their offerings at the end of the century to reflect the growing demand for female clerical workers while continuing to offer advanced training in domestic tasks to the future mothers of the nation.

Most clerical training occurred at the postsecondary school level, but the study of typing, shorthand, and the like began to enter high school curricula before World War I as the demand for female clerical workers accelerated. While these classes helped prepare many for the world of work that they would soon enter, vocational education introduced and cemented class- and gender-specific content into the schools' curricula and classes. Vocational education enhanced the employability of some, but it also constrained the field of occupational choices for girls and boys while reinforcing the lesson that girls and boys functioned in separate spheres in society and in the economy.[30]

Colleges throughout the nation added commercial curricula, and in the South such public higher education usually occurred in single-sex institutions. In 1892, for example, South Carolina rechartered the Winthrop Training School as the Winthrop Normal and Industrial College to prepare white women for teaching and to offer them instruction in "stenography, typewriting, telegraphy, bookkeeping, drawing . . . art needlework, cooking, housekeeping, and such other industrial arts as may be suitable to their sex and conducive to their support and usefulness."[31] Winthrop College's curricula typified those of turn-of-the-century public institutions of higher education that prepared women for careers in teaching, office work, and homemaking. By creating such programs, state legislatures formally linked gender to career destiny; higher education often remained gender segregated until the mid–twentieth century. In time, this growing educational capacity as well as the proliferation of schools of nursing opened avenues of social mobility for women of the working class.

Nursing education advanced significantly through the establishment of hospital nursing schools such as the one that Elizabeth Hamblett attended. Bellevue Hospital in New York and Massachusetts General in Boston opened the first of these in 1873. By 1900, 432 schools of nursing had graduated more than 3,500 students. By 1920 approximately 55,000 women studied nursing at some 1,700 schools around the nation; these schools had graduated an estimated 15,000 nurses. In contrast to the grand scale of Massachusetts General and Bellevue, many of the later schools remained modest in size. For example, Dr. Charles Houston Harris established a twenty-five–bed hospital for nursing instruction in Fort Worth, Texas, in 1912.[32] Harris, the attending physicians at the hospital, and a registered nurse instructed the students.

Black colleges and black hospitals provided training for African American women to enter the nursing profession. Northern white schools had admitted a limited number of African Americans, and in the early twentieth century, a cadre of their graduates led the expansion of training at African American schools of medicine and nursing. Mirroring the gender segregation that characterized white medical education in the United States, black medical schools admitted few African American women, but emerging nursing schools trained approximately 2,000 women in the early twentieth century. Eight African American nursing programs existed by the end of the nineteenth century, and the number continued to grow through the 1920s.[33]

Although the disparity between black and white education lingered into the twentieth century, African Americans gradually narrowed the achievement gap between themselves and white youths. African American women had vastly different experiences in higher education from those of white women. Mostly educated in racially segregated institutions, black Americans in the first half of the century attended institutions less well equipped and staffed than white schools. The first private colleges for African American women trained future teachers, but they also focused on developing a moral perspective and domestic skills that would prepare graduates to assume their proper places at the center of the family circle. Similar trends marked women's training at black coeducational institutions.

Conditioned by Booker T. Washington's accommodationist self-help perspective, African American teachers of the early twentieth century warned that failure to train in the domestic arts would endanger the welfare of black families and cause African Americans to lose out to immigrants in household labor markets outside the South. In the first decade of the century, several prominent black female educators split with Washington over such issues, but the emphasis on "domestic science" persisted in public schools and in colleges such as Hampton and Tuskegee. Opportunities to study science, mathematics, and the classics long remained more limited in black institutions such as Spelman College in Atlanta than in white women's colleges.[34]

EDUCATION BEYOND HOME AND SCHOOL:
WORKMATES AND THE STREETS

Schools provided only rudimentary lessons to young women bound for the labor market. The act of going out of the home to work, like the process of migration, involved unprecedented challenges and necessitated new behaviors for both middle-class and working-class women. On the job, women learned specific job tasks by trial and error or under the tutelage of experienced workers. Women learned important lessons about the virtues and limits of their newly won autonomy. Professional women and unskilled workers of the early twentieth century often developed close ties with co-workers during breaks or after-hours activities. Professional organizations, business women's residences, and nurses' dormitories engendered friendships among women of the same profession. These contacts furnished moral support and advice in personal or professional matters. Formal and informal ties among professional women supported the development of job skills but proved less useful in providing the on-the-job assistance that one factory worker could offer to the operative working next to her.

The sisterhood of industrial labor taught women the advantages of cooperating with their peers to complete work more efficiently, to protect each other from supervisory harassment, or to protest unsatisfactory pay and working conditions. Unlike female workers isolated in domestic service or industrial homework, shop and office workers built friendships on the job and taught each other the lessons of life as well as of work. Class and other barriers, however, kept women compartmentalized. Blue-collar women on the shop floor had little contact with white-collar women in offices; individual workrooms remained highly segregated by race and ethnicity as well as sex. Working-class Irish, Polish, and Jewish parents did not see employment as compromising the welfare of their daughters, while Italian and Mexican parents worried that any activities outside the watchful eyes of relatives endangered a young woman's virtue.

The effects of employment in generating group identity and the exchange of ideas nevertheless emerged from women's earliest factory experiences, in the textile mills, shoe factories, and garment shops of the nineteenth century. In their first strike, and in literary contributions to the *Lowell Offering*, the mill girls of Lowell, Massachusetts, demonstrated the power of the workplace in inspiring both independent thought and group solidarity. While the mill girls of Lowell helped family members with their earnings, they also saved for a future that would be different from that of their mothers. As Thomas Dublin found, young women who came to the Lowell mills from surrounding farms built their own culture within the mills; the employment experience politicized them; and mill workers chose urban spouses as a result of their migration.[35]

Though the specific legacy of Lowell was lost to most twentieth-century industrial women, the daily lessons of the workplace continued, expanding as the workforce itself expanded. Through the nineteenth and twentieth centuries, employment removed young women from the limited horizons of home, church, and school and educated women on a variety of levels. Industrial workers frequently combined factory employment with night classes, and the conversations of one learning environment spilled over into the other.[36] Although women of one ethnic group typically predominated in industrial shops, immigrants also learned English on the job.

The organization of factory work and the social environment in which women labored also confirmed gender segregation. As they moved about the workplace on a daily basis, women exchanged ideas and news with sister workers who helped shape their attitudes and expectations, perhaps leading them away from the prescriptions inculcated by family. In workplaces where kin groups predominated, single girls likely squirmed under the thumb of a relative or older woman. Married women shared a culture in which family survival and family loyalty remained paramount. Young single women learned from older women, married or single, lessons that home, school, church, or synagogue had not taught. As one Italian American remembered, "You found out about sex through the shop where you worked. The mother don't tell you nothing."[37]

Where the workforce was overwhelmingly single, female work culture focused on courtship.[38] Within the emerging heterosocial society of the urban working classes of the early twentieth century, working girls forged new standards of behavior and of consumption, centering on physical appearance and leisure activities as the starlight express to romance and, hopefully, to marriage as well. Sent to work largely at the discretion of their parents, who sought to control virtually all of their daughters' earnings, single women might nevertheless see in marriage a means of escape into the domestic sphere of their own households.[39]

Young working women might also find companionship with co-workers of similar ages and situations who encouraged them to indulge in pastimes forbidden by their parents. The frequenting of beer halls, dance halls, and amusement parks surely violated gender conventions that immigrant parents expected their daughters to maintain. The sociability of work outside the home and workers' determination to enjoy their own wages undermined parents' control over their daughters. Working daughters who established complete independence from their parents repudiated their traditional familial obligations.[40] Middle-class social workers condemned such independent girls as "women adrift" who lacked the moral discipline and protection of family life.

Even when working girls retained only a small fraction of their wages, socializing on and off the job encouraged women to develop expectations different from those of their parents. Among artificial flower makers in New York factories in the early years of the century, Mary Van Kleeck found that "Practically all these flower makers who live at home turn their entire earnings into the family purse."[41] Mothers in working-class families generally managed household budgets, and even in impoverished homes the daughters often received a few coins to spend as they pleased. Although flower makers struggled at the bottom of the industrial wage scale and their families barely survived on their earnings, these factory girls nevertheless went to theaters and dance halls and shopped for notions and knickknacks, activities they had learned about at work. However limited their earnings, distinctive markets for goods and services developed around the tastes of these young female wage earners.[42]

WORKPLACE CULTURE AND LABOR REFORM

From the nineteenth century onward, working women brought their sisters and cousins into the shop with them; each generation of working women socialized the next as it entered the factory or the office. The social network of the workroom provided a basis for friendship but also for factory discipline and conversely for the mobilization of women around the issues of wages or working conditions.[43] Some nineteenth-century women, like Mary Kenney O'Sullivan, passed along not only industrial skills but vital tools and techniques of cooperative action as well. Indeed, O'Sullivan's life as an industrial worker, union organizer, and wife and mother epitomized the ways in which work and culture might optimally interact to define and redefine women's roles in the family and in the world. Born into a midwestern Irish American family in 1864 to a father who worked on the railroad and a mother who worked as a cook, Mary Kenney's parents charted a life course for her that mirrored their own. The Kenneys removed Mary from school after the fourth grade and sent her to apprentice in dressmaking. When she was fourteen years old, her father's death forced Kenney to leave her apprenticeship and seek paid employment immediately. She found work in a bookbinding shop and matured into a seasoned industrial worker who supported herself and her ailing mother before reaching her twenty-first birthday.

In the 1880s, having migrated to Chicago, Kenney joined the bookbinders' union and emerged as the first paid organizer for the American Federation of Labor. In 1894 Kenney married Boston labor activist John O'Sullivan, and from their marriage until John's death in 1902, Mary bore four children. With her husband's support and assistance at home (extraordinary for the time), she continued organizing workers. In 1903 Mary Kenney O'Sullivan's labor activities entered a new phase as she and other advocates for female workers founded the Women's Trade Union League.[44]

By whatever route a working-class Irish girl, like Mary Kenney, found her way into the permanent wage labor force, she knew that paid work would fill much of her life and that low wages or dangerous working conditions would endure as well. Like Mary Kenney, most industrial women of the late nineteenth and early twentieth centuries did not come into the labor force as sheltered young women just past adolescence. Rather, they had grown up on the job and had mastered the rules of the workplace and of worker culture before they had fully matured physically and emotionally. Kenney's youthful experience grew increasingly less common as child labor declined through the century and formal education overshadowed the workplace in fixing adolescents' expectations, but workers continued to frame workplace issues for newcomers.

In addition to the leadership of older workers, ethnic characteristics of the shop's workforce shaped women's labor consciousness and socioeconomic values and the behavior they produced. Van Kleeck found that Jewish working girls in flower making approached their work with goals that differed fundamentally from those of the Italian workers in the trade. Jews especially concerned themselves with wage levels and working conditions, whereas the Italian women focused on the quality of their workmanship and their individual earnings. Consequently, Jewish workers, who came from a culture steeped in traditions of self-preservation through community and cooperation, leaned heavily toward labor activism, while Italians did not. Van Kleeck concluded that "These differences in point of view prevent a sense of fellowship [between the two groups]: their interests as workers in the same occupation have never been realized."[45]

Van Kleeck based her conclusions on observations of a narrow sector of the female labor force in a particular place and time. Flower making reflected the pattern of seasonal labor and isolation of workers that worked against labor militancy and successful worker protest.[46] Although New York's Italian flower makers did not espouse labor militancy, Italian women in other settings emerged as prominent protesters. Italian and Jewish women predominated among the workers who struck garment shops in New York, Philadelphia, and Chicago before World War I. The environment in the woolen mills of Lawrence, Massachusetts, bred militancy among Italian workers in this era. In the Lawrence textile strike of 1912, Italian men and women led the ranks of the protesters, with Poles, Serbs, and other national groups swelling the ranks. The demonstrators brandished Italian and U.S. flags as they walked off the job, and Anna LoPizzo, an Italian American shot during the protest march, became the strike's first martyr.

Women participated in labor protests in the early twentieth century, but union membership remained low, ranging from about 3 percent of industrial workers in 1900 to 7 percent in 1920. Although female labor organizations rarely survived long, the Women's Trade Union League (WTUL) lasted over two decades and achieved remarkable success in winning long-term improvements in women's working conditions.[47] The WTUL used a mixture of tactics such as strikes and boycotts employed by male labor organizations with strategies unique for its time. It united middle-class female reformers and industrial workers in a single body, a cross-class cooperation that spelled success for the WTUL but violated the class-based organization of male unions. The WTUL also departed from the strategies of male organizations by pursuing its victories through legislation and litigation rather than relying solely on collective action, a strategy eschewed by the American Federation of Labor until 1912.

The WTUL won protective codes and enforcement of those codes based on gender conventions. Following the infamous Triangle Shirtwaist Fire of 1911, the WTUL played upon the public's outrage and its double standard of gender to obtain legal protection for women in the workplace. After completing a survey of working conditions in New York factories where women predominated, the WTUL gained stricter enforcement of fire codes in firms that employed women. The WTUL campaign for protective legislation gained ground through World War I, when, like most reform movements of the Progressive era, it lost momentum.

Although less successful than the WTUL, industry-based unions of waitresses and garment workers made some headway through strikes and collective bargaining. These unions, like the WTUL, used tactics common among male labor organizations but generally organized along gender lines rather than craft or industrial lines and embraced protective legislation along with direct action.[48]

Indifference or overt opposition from union men frequently undercut working women's struggles to improve their lot through labor organizations. During the early twentieth century the goal of a male wage that would support an entire family emerged as a powerful ideal among labor unions and their Progressive, middle-class sympathizers. As this concept of a "family wage" gained adherents among working men, tentative overtures toward gender equality in the labor movement faded among male workers. The family wage fused middle-class Progressives with working-class men in a campaign that eroded working women's social legitimacy even as economic forces pulled and thrust an ever larger share of the nation's women into the labor force. For many working-class men, the concept of the family wage embodied a protest against the diminution of manliness they felt as their wives or daughters marched off to work. Working men who had kept women at home argued that poorly paid female workers competed unfairly with male family to depress their wages.

Despite their shared opposition to long-term female labor, neither labor leaders nor Progressives expected the employment of women to disappear. Progressive leaders, particularly those grounded in the social settlement movement, worked diligently to improve working conditions for women, and organized labor encouraged their efforts. Progressive efforts at workplace reform, however, focused on gender differences and, like education reform, reinforced gender segregation in the labor force. The first battles for protective labor legislation concentrated largely on behalf of women's issues. Middle-class women and working-class women joined together in organizations such as the Women's Trade Union League to lobby for protective labor codes. Unlike male labor leaders, who usually rose through the ranks of industrial labor itself, leaders among women's groups often came from the middle class and may never have worked for wages themselves. As middle-class women raised in the mystique of Victorian gender prescriptions, labor advocates like Jane Addams appealed to sentiments about women's maternal obligations and calling. Shorter hours, the elimination of night work, and safety precautions in the workplace, as attorney Josephine Goldmark and others argued, guarded the health of mothers, future mothers, and their children. Working men could support these measures with enthusiasm. Protective legislation improved the lot of working women and kept men apart as a laboring sector whose less controlled workplaces and more demanding jobs justified wage differentials between the sexes.

Youthful workers in southern textile villages thoroughly understood the workplace by the close of adolescence; however, unions rarely succeeded in the South, and protective labor laws remained few in number and less rigorous than elsewhere in the country. Where all members of a family worked in the same factory, the "family wage" meant the earnings of all the family. Mills often combined the wages of all a family's earners in a single envelope handed to the head of household. Since labor protest by one family member endangered the jobs and the company home of all family members, youthful workers more frequently exercised their autonomy by rebelling outside the workplace. Teenaged mill workers often married against their parents' wishes. Marriage established teenagers' claims to their own company house and initiated life apart from their parents. Elopement, unlike labor protest, did not jeopardize the jobs or housing of others. Early marriage proved an attractive option in southern mill villages where family and employment so closely intertwined that boys and girls had few opportunities to know a world different from that of their parents.

Within the South, the tobacco factories proved more fertile soil than the textile industry for labor organization and protest among working women. Tobacco workers, largely African American women, received none of the employee benefits associated with southern corporate paternalism, and tobacco factories did not employ families as a unit. Consequently, employers had little to withhold from obstreperous individual workers other than the job itself. Organized protest then proved a more effective tool for dealing with management of cigarette plants than with that of textile mills in the South.[49]

EDUCATION AND UPWARD FEMALE MOBILITY

Wherever they lived and worked, uneducated women found themselves locked into poorly paid production or service jobs where they struggled as best they could for improvements in the workplace and adapted to circumstances they could not change. Poor women with access to education, on the other hand, encountered brighter work prospects. Education offered an escape for daughters of the working poor from factory or domestic work to jobs with higher social status. Some young women preferred sales jobs in shops or department stores to factory or domestic work. Although poorly paid, these jobs generally demanded some education beyond the elementary level. As public education expanded in the late nineteenth century and jobs in commerce opened to larger numbers of native-born white women, some working-class women managed to combine these circumstances to escape the factory toilers' fate.[50]

The teaching, nursing, or clerical work pursued by women like Hazel Stevens and Elizabeth Hamblett of Lowell required a level of schooling denied to most factory workers. Women like mill worker Diane Quellette could not afford the luxury of advanced education because their families had depended on their earnings from childhood. Other women, like Theatis Johnson Williamson, resided in the closed environments of mill towns that discouraged all but the most elementary educational achievements and shuffled village children from company-sponsored schools directly to the mills. Hazel Stevens herself barely escaped manual labor. Had her father's illness come only months earlier, she could not have completed training for teacher certification and might have lost her dream of a college education. Elizabeth Hamblett, like Hazel Stevens, also had the luxury of normal school training before economic need propelled her into the labor force, but Hamblett escaped the burden of providing major support for others. As an unencumbered single woman, she could enter nurse's training, live in hospital housing, and defray some of her educational costs through hospital work. By such strategies, Hamblett and thousands of other poor women attained a higher station in life than that of a factory operative.

CONCLUSION

Women at work in 1900 had learned most of their work skills at home or on the job. The majority had attended school only long enough to acquire the basic skills of reading, writing, and elementary mathematics. In the first two decades of the new century, significant changes occurred in the education of girls. As school attendance broadened and the number of years that children spent in school increased, the school emerged as a stronger agent in fitting girls for the labor market. The ever growing demand for female workers encouraged the growth of gender-specific courses preparing girls for positions as domestic servants, garment and textile workers, office workers, teachers, and nurses. Vocational programs and academic high schools existed in the late nineteenth century, but few working women had studied in these settings. Fewer still had completed studies at nursing schools, normal schools, or colleges. The structured programs of social settlements and girls' clubs helped some girls prepare for work. While hoping to imprint girls with middle-class moral values, settlement workers and club leaders prepared their charges to earn wages in urban homes and factories or to produce market goods in rural settings.

The realization that women often persisted at their jobs into their mature years prompted educators to reassess what girls learned in the classroom. Reformers such as Albert Leake stressed the importance of teaching working-class girls to anticipate spending a significant portion of their adult lives in the labor force. The most far-sighted educators reordered their instructional priorities to equip girls with skills that would maximize their earning potential in the prime years of their lives. Even after these changes, no educational program outside of celibate religious orders prepared women to choose lifelong employment over motherhood, though clearly some would. Progressive educational programs equipped girls with skills compatible with the responsibilities of motherhood rather than with job skills that might temporarily be set aside for motherhood.

The expansion of women's employment in the first twenty years of the century resulted from the maturation of the U.S. economy as industrialization entered its final phase and the postindustrial world approached. As women acquired secondary schooling and training beyond high school, they departed from the work of their mothers. The daughters of domestic workers, farm laborers, and factory girls frequently moved up to teaching, nursing, or clerical work.

The evolution of women's work roles also signaled important changes in U.S. families. As Albert Leake and Marguerite Dickson recognized, girls and women played integral roles in the economic support of working-class families and rural households. The family of the working girl of 1900 depended more heavily on the wages of men than of women, but women made significant and increasing contributions to family income. Working daughters contributed more to family income than their mothers, but these patterns too were changing as wage earning by mothers grew. Whether single, married, widowed, or divorced, women increasingly supported dependent parents and siblings as well as their own children.

Because wages provide a ready measure of individual contributions to the family economy, wage labor transformed women's understanding of their economic roles and their place in the family. The permanent nature of the wage gap has provided a constant and seemingly fixed sign of women's secondary status, but wage earning gradually enlarged women's authority within the family.[51] Although parents might control daughters' earnings, or family needs consume wives' pay, women's inability to determine the allocation of their wages did not strip them of the knowledge that their labor had individual meaning and value. In addition to the authority attached to their earning power, employment taught women to think and act both independently and cooperatively, lessons that many of them carried home. Despite their inferior earning potential, wage earning empowered women by establishing their presence as actors in the labor market, a presence that grew and strengthened as the century passed. While some women accepted inferior earnings as their lot in life, others protested them or fought to improve their station. Whether or not women's employment experiences drove them to labor protest, the workplace taught them to appreciate their own abilities and those of others as well.

Women's widening place in the U.S. labor force demanded that schools deliver more education and vocational training for girls as the century wore on. Rising educational expectations among middle-class families encouraged their daughters to pursue their schooling beyond high school, training that prepared young women to join the swelling ranks of white-collar labor in the 1920s. Schools and social service agencies responded incompletely to the needs of students and of employers as educators' biases of class, race, and gender circumscribed their curricular programs. Through the century these biases persisted and reinforced occupational segregation even as labor demand diversified and propelled educational growth and innovation. For the working class and the middle class, World War I delivered new employment opportunities that had long-term implications for women's education, female work patterns, and U.S. family life in the third decade of the century. The feminization of the U.S. labor force continued during the Jazz Age, and the composition of the female workforce altered in response to new and more complex demands.

CHAPTER THREE

Class, Mobility, and Women's Work

THE 1920S

I n the years after 1900, the world's most productive industrial economy diversified to meet the service needs of the United States's ever growing, increasingly complex, urbanized population. Consumer goods such as automobiles, electric washing machines, and radios proliferated and markets swelled as merchandisers invested in glitzy advertising and discovered selling on credit. Retailers such as Macy's and Marshall Field's and manufacturers such as General Electric and Ford devoted increasing employer hours to management and record keeping. Corporate office buildings rose to top skylines long dominated by factory smokestacks. More and bigger schools and hospitals opened to serve a population increasingly aware of the importance of education and health care.

Changing patterns of women's employment in the first three decades of the twentieth century attended the emergence and expansion of the service sector and the professions, a process that enticed increasing numbers of middle-class women into the workforce and provided upward mobility for many women of both the middle and working classes. Demographic trends also intensified labor's call to women as the total U.S. population grew more slowly than the demand for new workers, a result of declining fertility and the decrease of European immigration after the outbreak of World War I. Overall, the percentage of women working rose from one in five in 1900 to one in four by 1930.

Within this growing population of women workers, a major restructuring reflected the country's broad economic trends. White-collar employment expanded, while the number of blue-collar jobs stagnated or declined. Between 1910 and 1920, for example, the number of women holding clerical jobs tripled, while the female labor force grew by only 16 percent overall—a trend that World War I accelerated and that continued into the 1920s (see table 3.1). Women's white-collar employment diversified as the clerical, sales, and professional sectors grew. Typewriters, adding machines, and telephones reordered office work and, together with ascending standards of business record keeping, bolstered the demand for clerical workers. The new office machinery widened the call for narrowly defined office skills such as typing, stenography, and bookkeeping that required specific but short-term training. With this specialization of tasks came an overall de-skilling of clerical work accompanied by a decline in pay even as the demand for such workers rose. As often happens, these circumstances opened the door (in this case the office door) to women, who soon replaced men in the performance of many tasks.[1]

Most clerical work required one particular skill that immigrants and racial minorities often lacked—firm command of spoken and written English. Because their class advantages included a high likelihood of mastering English in secondary school, middle-class white women held a potent edge over other candidates for the most desirable new clerical positions; because the office environment appeared cleaner and more orderly than the factory, they often took them. The number of such jobs, however, greatly outnumbered middle-class recruits, which pushed the recruitment process down the social scale. Through education, working-class women, including, over time, the daughters of immigrants and eventually immi-

TABLE 3.1
Women in Selected White-Collar Occupations, 1900–1930

	1910	1920	1930
Professional service	734,752	1,017,030	1,526,234
Chemists	579	1,714	1,905
Clergy	685	1,787	3,276
College professors	2,958	10,075	20,131
Dentists	1,254	1,829	1,287
Lawyers and judges	558	1,738	3,385
Physicians, surgeons, and osteopaths	9,015	8,882	8,388
Teachers	478,027	639,241	860,278
Technical engineers	11	41	113
Trained nurses	76,508	143,664	288,737
Clerical workers	588,609	1,421,925	1,986,830
Telegraph operators	8,219	16,680	16,122
Telephone operators	88,262	178,379	235,259
Insurance agents	2,537	5,083	12,953

SOURCE: *U.S. Bureau of the Census,* Fifteenth Census of the United States: 1930, vol. V, General Report—Occupations *(Washington, D.C.: GPO, 1933), table 2.*

grants themselves, were able to obtain office jobs. Black women, however, found little office work until the Civil Rights Revolution of the 1960s.

Thus by 1930 employers had established hiring patterns that have characterized the evolution (briefly reversed during World War II) of the labor force ever since: expanding white-collar employment, stagnating or declining demand for blue-collar labor, the prospect of occupational mobility for some working-class women, and the entry of unprecedented numbers of middle-class women into the labor market. Over time these employment trends transformed the daily experiences of ordinary women, drove women's educational achievements, and reshaped U.S. family life as these labor demands emerged amid unfolding demographic patterns. The U.S. population was somewhat older in 1930 than in 1900; moreover, rising educational expectations delayed women's entry into the workforce. Over the first three decades of the century, these economic, educational, and demographic trends generated a doubling of the percentage (from 5.6 to 11.7) of married women who pursued market labor.

WORLD WAR I AND FEMALE EMPLOYMENT

Although economic circumstances as well as race limited poor women's access to the expanded number of white-collar jobs in the early decades of the century, World War I did widen the job options of blue-collar women. The Women's Land Army, civilian women who cultivated the fields in the absence of male labor, and the employment of women in tasks such as postal delivery, street car operation, and ship building opened wartime work not available to women in peacetime. Black women, hitherto broadly denied manufacturing jobs outside the tobacco industry, gained access to heavy manufacturing and to jobs in light industries such as textiles and garment manufacturing that had traditionally employed white women only. Because most women lost their wartime jobs when peace came, the number of women in manufacturing did not grow permanently as a consequence of the war. The war had nevertheless hastened a permanent shift in the distribution of work in the United States (see table 3.2) and altered the characteristics of the industrial labor force. Immigrants, whose arriving numbers fell steeply during the war, had already lost ground in manufacturing work by 1920 and declined nearly 25 percent more in the subsequent decade. In contrast, African American women managed to establish a long-term foothold on factory labor during the war.[2]

Although most women of all races lost their wartime production jobs when men returned after the armistice, 50 percent more African American women held jobs in 1920 than in 1910, and they preserved most of these gains through the 1920s. African American women, who had been largely restricted to tobacco and

TABLE 3.2
*Native-born White, Foreign-born White, and African American Women
by Selected Occupational Sector, 1910–30*

	NATIVE-BORN WHITE					
	1910		1920		1930	
	Number	Percentage	Number	Percentage	Number	Percentage
Total	4,820,918	100	5,843,783	100	7,661,508	100
Agriculture	692,843	14.4	426,797	7.3	367,228	4.8
Manufacturing	1,320,851	27.4	1,406,384	24.1	1,451,256	18.9
Trade	392,449	8.1	569,813	9.8	830,940	10.8
Professional	646,176	13.4	906,645	15.5	1,356,390	17.7
Domestic and personal	1,110,873	23.0	990,859	17.0	1,514,041	19.8
Clerical	544,770	11.3	1,322,749	22.6	1,858,914	24.3

	FOREIGN-BORN WHITE					
	1910		1920		1930	
	Number	Percentage	Number	Percentage	Number	Percentage
Total	1,222,791	100	1,118,463	100	1,156,056	100
Agriculture	57,924	4.7	39,558	3.5	26,413	2.3
Manufacturing	425,170	34.8	414,509	37.1	313,630	27.1
Trade	72,845	6.0	90,009	8.0	109,563	9.5
Professional	58,371	4.8	70,658	6.3	103,348	8.9
Domestic and personal	560,913	45.8	399,903	35.8	475,439	41.1
Clerical	40,697	3.3	90,949	8.1	114,387	9.9

	AFRICAN AMERICAN					
	1910		1920		1930	
	Number	Percentage	Number	Percentage	Number	Percentage
Total	2,013,981	100	1,571,289	100	1,840,642	100
Agriculture	1,050,710	52.2	611,810	38.9	495,284	26.9
Manufacturing	68,222	3.4	105,266	6.7	101,070	5.5
Trade	7,145	0.4	11,538	0.7	14,568	0.8
Professional	29,730	1.5	39,169	2.5	63,027	3.4
Domestic and personal	853,302	42.4	790,592	50.3	1,152,560	62.6
Clerical	3,014	.1	7,921	0.5	10,862	0.6

SOURCES: *U.S. Bureau of the Census,* Fifteenth Census of the United States: 1930, Population, Vol. V, General Report on Occupations *(Washington, D.C.: GPO, 1933), table 2.*

Agricultural labor remained a central employment among women in the first decades of the twentieth century. African American women in the cotton fields, 1928. Courtesy National Archives

food processing industries before World War I, held manufacturing jobs in the garment, chemical, woodworking, and other industries in the 1920s. By 1930 African American operatives in garment shops outnumbered women working in tobacco processing. Long-term changes in the occupational structure among African American women also reflected ongoing migration patterns that accelerated when large numbers of African American women moved northward during World War I. This migration continued through the 1920s, not least because, while black women remained excluded from most production jobs in manufacturing in the South, they had penetrated these jobs in northern locations during the war and held onto many of them thereafter.[3]

THE RISE OF THE MIDDLE-CLASS WORKING WOMAN

Changes in the occupational structure after World War I, following the expansion of postsecondary education for women, demonstrate how and, to some extent, why middle-class women entered the labor force in large numbers in the 1920s. The white-collar sector grew rapidly during the twenties as it had during the first two decades of the century, but the pattern of growth differed. The major growth in the clerical sector, work increasingly accessible to daughters of the working class, had occurred in the second decade of the century. Although the clerical sector continued to expand in the 1920s, the growth rate slowed from 142 percent to 40 percent. By the 1920s the pace of expansion in professional openings for women outstripped job creation in the clerical sector. The number of women in the professions rose by 35.4 percent during the war decade and 50.1 percent in the 1920s, but this did not constitute the only change in the professional women's workforce (see table 3.1). While thousands of women moved into the professions in the 1920s, the number of female physicians, surgeons, and dentists declined. Employment in the professions conferred benefits more alluring than income, for it affirmed women's middle-class status even though teachers, librarians, and nurses often earned less than skilled factory women. Moreover, women who attained middle-class status through work could sometimes find additional mobility by finding an even better professional job. Thus in 1923 Eva MacIntire, who had progressed by means of the educational expansion and the continuing occupational diversification of the early twentieth century, sought to improve her future prospects and increase her salary by leaving her position in the women's vocational department of Boston University for a similar position at Schraft's, a private-sector company. Clearly attuned to the benefits of professional status, MacIntire, who had first gone to work while single, had continued to work after marriage, a phenomenon increasingly evident among professional women in the 1920s.[4]

By the 1920s professional social work had joined health and education as suitable careers for middle-class women. Women trained at new and prestigious private schools of social work at Columbia University, the University of Chicago, and Atlanta University, and at public institutions for positions that coupled the traditional women's nurturing role with their political activism, newly sanctioned by the Nineteenth Amendment, ratified in 1920. Social workers donned the mantle of advocacy for women's concerns: maternal and child welfare, safeguards for working women, and consumer protection. Lobbyists for women's agendas gained a bureaucratic voice with the establishment of the federal Women's Bureau. The emergence of middle-class career women through the social settlement movement and public service agencies also fostered a new perspective within the middle class itself as middle-class women began to study themselves as well as others. Their research soon revealed that middle-class working women faced many of the same job-related frustrations as industrial women. As female social scientists identified common dilemmas facing married working women of both classes, their attitudes toward working-class mothers changed from condemnation to concern about the child care needs of working mothers.

White-collar work changed the lifestyle of middle-class women and often set them apart from the world of their mothers. Boarding houses, by serving as surrogate homes, eased the transition from childhood to adulthood for white-collar women who accepted jobs away from home but lacked the resources to live independently. In 1920, for example, Anne Jackson came to Raleigh, North Carolina, from a Georgia farm after she had accepted an editorial position with the publisher of a farm journal. Jackson moved frequently from one boarding house to another. At each residence, she made new friends, male and female, and eventually married a fellow boarder. Information about living conditions, costs, and the quality of food at boarding houses as well as the moral reputations of lodgers in these establishments circulated freely among single working people. In all her residences, Jackson felt safe and comfortable. She wrote her mother regularly and, after one move, observed that her new boarding house served outstanding food, but she also complained, "I never saw a bigger bunch of old maids." One week later she enthused, "I've met several mighty nice boys round at Mrs. Rodgers."[5]

WOMEN'S EDUCATION AND OCCUPATIONAL MOBILITY

Although middle-class women entered the workforce in large numbers in the 1920s, working-class women continued to predominate among all female wage earners. Some working-class women had marked success in entering white-collar occupations in the 1920s, as they had in the previous decade, often overcoming ethnicity and modest circumstances in the process. Clerical work, teaching, and nursing offered the most promising avenues to social mobility for working-class women of the 1920s. Compared with a liberal arts education, such training cost little and promised certain rewards. For example, Herriclia Eliades of Lowell, Massachusetts, graduated from Lowell State College in 1926 and went on to a career as a teacher. Eliades and others became self-made women of the middle class, but their working-class parents played critical roles in their upward mobility, behavior more commonly undertaken to facilitate sons' climb away from the factory floor. Eliades recalled that fellow Greeks would go to her father and say: "'Why . . . send your daughter to a higher school of learning? She will [only] learn . . . to write lovely long letters to boy friends. . . . You have lots of mills here in Lowell, send her to the mill. Let her help you with the family money situation and then she gets married.' My Dad would go home and tell this to my mother. [But] mother said no, 'Our children all are going to get a higher education because they're going to make a specialty,' like teaching as I took up."[6]

Through her own diligence, the determination of her mother, and the economic sacrifices made by both her parents, this daughter of Greek immigrants rose from the working class into the world of professional women. For most working class women, however, poverty, race, or ethnicity remained insurmountable barriers between them and middle-class status, so most women continued to toil in agriculture, in production jobs, or in domestic service jobs in homes or commercial establishments.

Poor families generally could not open the educational pathways to mobility for their daughters. The fortunate few, like Herriclia Eliades, benefited from parental encouragement to excel in school and parental willingness to defer their daughters' financial contributions until they completed their education. In a far more typical story, mill worker Narissa Hodges, unlike Herriclia Eliades, followed paths from girlhood to womanhood trod by multitudes of poor women after World War I. Hodges had hoped to escape factory work by entering nurse's training, but poverty prevented her from completing secondary school. Hodges, an Italian American born in 1914, grew up in Tewksbury, Massachusetts. Italian American families rarely encouraged professional ambitions in their daughters, and Hodges's family felt itself financially incapable of opening educational doors for Narissa. Furthermore, Hodges had laid aside her nursing dream because she believed that "at Tewksbury hospital, if you [were] Italian, you couldn't get in, no way." At age thirteen, Narissa dropped out of school and sought work to "help my folks."[7] Massachusetts had instituted compulsory school attendance by the 1920s, but Hodges got permission to work full-time by attending a "continuation school" one afternoon a week until the age of sixteen.

Hodges worked first in a retail shop but soon after signed on as a learner in the silk mills under the tutelage of a neighbor who was a seasoned weaver. In her spare time Hodges helped her father farm a small piece of land he had purchased. From the late 1920s until World War II, Hodges persisted at the mills, moving from one factory to another as wages, working conditions, or layoffs dictated. In these years she trained two of her sisters as weavers. Because of the shortage of male labor during the war, Hodges moved up to the position of weave room inspector. Later in life, after marriage, the birth of two children, and a period of self-employment, Hodges took a job as a dietary assistant in a state hospital. She had not lost her desire to be a nurse, but this was as close as she ever got to fulfilling her ambition.

The decreasing demand for agricultural laborers through the early years of the century and the dwindling market for female industrial workers after World War I disadvantaged African American women who could not move into clerical work or other white-collar service trades. Although racial segregation guaranteed a need for some black teachers and nurses, low funding for black schools and hospitals also guaranteed that proportionally fewer African American than white women would qualify to find jobs in the professions. While white-collar jobs for African Americans increased during the 1910s and the 1920s, growth in these occupations lagged far behind the expansion enjoyed by white workers. As white women ascended to white-collar jobs, they created some space for African American women in factory production. Nevertheless, white women remained the preferred workers in industry. World War I had opened many factory jobs to African American women, but they lost some of these positions during the 1920s. Black women increased their representation in clerical work, trade, and the professions between 1920 and 1930, but they remained more heavily tied to agriculture than any other group of women, and domestic work emerged as the occupation of the majority of black women.

Thus the evolution of the economy in a racially segregated society handicapped blacks while it rewarded whites. A few African American women advanced with the aid of education, but the majority confronted a dreary choice between farm labor and domestic work. As new technology and falling commodity prices forced farm workers off the land, fewer and fewer African American women retained the option of choosing field work over household labor. While white women, native-born and foreign-born, advanced their representation in the workforce and some enjoyed considerable occupational mobility, these advantages rarely accrued to African Americans. By 1930 the majority of African American women wage earners cooked, cleaned, and laundered in the homes or businesses of whites.

FEMALE MIGRATION AND IMMIGRATION

During the 1920s as before, many women chose to migrate from their home regions with the expectation that their employment options would be greater elsewhere. African American women migrating to Washington, D.C., left homes in the rural South to move in with urban family members.[8] After serving an apprenticeship in housekeeping or child care for their relatives, young women found positions in private household service through the assistance of kith or kin. Once skilled at their tasks, the women became independent workers negotiating employment terms for themselves. Friends and relations supervised the courting of young women by introducing them to appropriate prospects for marriage.

In the 1920s the migration of black women to the North continued to exceed the net migration of black men, with only the Rocky Mountain states proving more attractive to African American men than to women. The net internal migration of foreign-born women also exceeded that of immigrant men, although native-born white males were more likely to relocate than were native-born white women.

Native-born white women from all regions moved from rural areas to towns and from small towns to cities as they had in earlier decades.

Although immigration from Europe declined steeply with the advent of World War I, immigration from within the Western Hemisphere accelerated from the 1920s onward.[9] From 1915 through the 1920s, nearly six million immigrants came to the United States, and more than four of ten newcomers were female; 11 percent of all the new arrivals came from Mexico. Immigration from Mexico to the United States has, of course, reflected changing economic and political conditions in Mexico as well as economic conditions in and specific immigration policies on the part of the United States. During the 1920s, political instability and economic depression in Mexico encouraged the outmigration of thousands of poor families for whom the then-booming United States served as the destination of choice. Unlike earlier Mexican immigrants, families that arrived from the mid-1920s onward depended on the labor of wives and children as well as fathers for their survival. Traditional values dictated that young girls should be kept at home under watchful eyes of female kin, but economic circumstances pushed Mexican and Mexican American girls into the labor force before or during their teen years.[10]

Mexican and Mexican American migrant laborers and urban workers built sizable communities in Southwestern, Pacific Coast, and Midwestern towns and cities. Although Mexican American families often followed the crops together, women frequently had better employment opportunities in urban areas than in agricultural districts; consequently, wives and daughters occasionally stayed behind in the city as Mexican American men followed the dusty roads of migrant field labor. Women who stayed behind when their husbands, fathers, or brothers followed the crops took on new responsibilities in the absence of male family members, and these experiences often prepared women to migrate at a later date. Migrant work left thousands of Mexican American families in poverty and deprived of educational and health services. Even among families who escaped the migrant cycle of poverty, average incomes remained lower than among most ethnic groups.[11]

During the interwar years as before, local demographic characteristics shaped area economies and women's work options, and prejudice reinforced distinctions by race, ethnicity, and class. In the 1920s San Antonio, Texas, for instance, emerged as a low-wage market that attracted labor agents from throughout the nation. In the 1920s the New York infants' and children's wear industries reinstituted homework in locations distant from the city, a move made economical by the low weight and small bulk of the items manufactured and by the abundance of skilled handworkers in San Antonio and elsewhere in the American Southwest.[12] San Antonio, a city with original Mexican roots, has continuously attracted migrating Mexican citizens. In the early twentieth century, however, Mexican emigration swelled beyond any previous experience because of the Mexican Revolution and the severe Depression of the 1920s. Largely peasants, disproportionate numbers of the immigrants of the 1920s chose San Antonio as their destination.

In San Antonio most Mexican newcomers joined the ranks of migrant agricultural labor. The migrant workers wintered in San Antonio and frequently left wives and children behind as they worked the crops from Texas to Michigan. Like the wives and daughters of Pennsylvania miners, Mexican and Mexican American women in San Antonio comprised a captive labor force. Unlike the miners' families, however, the wages of San Antonio's Mexican American males rarely afforded the luxury of keeping women at home and out of the labor market. Furthermore, San Antonio grew so rapidly because of immigration that local wages fell to the lowest level found in any major U.S. city. Strict practices of occupational segregation by ethnicity, as well as gender, effectively closed clerical and sales jobs to Hispanics, relegating them to industrial work and domestic service.[13]

National patterns in the employment of Mexican and Mexican American women mirrored those of San Antonio, an urban center with a large garment industry. Roughly 15 percent of women of Mexican heritage worked for wages in the United States in 1930. One fifth of these worked in agriculture, two fifths in domestic work, one fifth in industrial jobs, and one tenth in trades. Consistent with their limited access to education and their victimization by ethnic discrimination, only three in one hundred Mexican or Mexican American women held professional jobs, and only another three in one hundred had found clerical positions. Women of Mexican heritage were less likely to work than African Americans and first- or second-generation European immigrants. They also had less success in entering the professions than did African American women for whom legalized segregation guaranteed some jobs in teaching and nursing. On the other hand, while few Mexican and Mexican American women got clerical jobs, Hispanics in fact encountered less discrimination in entering the clerical sector than did African American women.

MARRIED WOMEN AT WORK

Through the 1920s as before, income from boarders and lodgers carried some families through the years in which child care responsibilities kept wives homebound and the family had no children old enough to be put to work. Edith Abbott, pioneer social scientist and reformer, reported that "A . . . 1925 . . . survey of living conditions among small wage-earners in Chicago . . . showed that among Mexican and Negro households over 40 per cent had lodgers [as did] 28 percent [of] Native-born white households [and] 17 per cent of foreign born [a number reduced by the fact that] more than half of the immigrant families visited . . . were Italians [whose] neighborhoods have generally had fewer lodgers than many of the other national groups."[14] Abbott saw lodging as a system driven by the low wages of working men: "Lodging and boarders have been a means of supplementing the husband's wage ever since the modern factory system call[ed] for 'hands,' and ever since men and women migrate[d] to strange neighborhoods in search of work. The migrant worker must have a bed; and the wife of the workingman, eagerly looking . . . to make the inadequate wage of the husband and father more nearly equal to the family budget, has always welcomed the added income secured by providing beds for the homeless fellow-workers of her 'man.'"[15]

During the first thirty years of the century, the ranks of married wage earners more than doubled. African American women were the most likely of all women to remain in the labor force after they had married, but white wives entered or persisted at wage labor in ever greater numbers. Wives in factory labor disproportionally occupied the least desirable, poorest-paying positions. Occupational segregation by race or ethnicity characterized the experience of married as well as single women, but motherhood further constrained women's work choices. Mothers selected lines of work and work schedules that fit around their child-care responsibilities. While many households included lodgers, wives and widows also earned wages through industrial homework or other home jobs. For example, nearly half of all laundresses were married women and generally worked at home. African American women predominated among home laundresses, but white women with young children also took in washing and ironing. As commercial laundries expanded, many of these women lost their source of income, but home laundering persisted into the 1950s. Some women needed or preferred to stay at home and remained competitive by keeping their prices below those of commercial establishments.

Wives tied to specific geographic locations, limited by inferior education, or subject to frequent interruptions of their work schedules had the bleakest employment outlook. Under these circumstances married women usually found work as laborers, the least skilled of all industrial workers. Although farm labor had declined steadily since the late nineteenth century, agriculture remained a major source of income for women in the 1920s. In rural regions farm labor occupied the majority of married women after World War I. During the 1920s Eula Fisher operated a Washington fruit farm with her husband. Eula had primary responsibility for the apple, cherry, and pear trees, while her husband cared for the berry bushes. After the birth of her son, Eula took him into the orchard with her while she pruned the trees. When they hired extra hands for the harvest, Eula also cooked for the crew. The Fishers' earnings fluctuated widely, and they, like many other farm families, frequently sought supplementary income. After the birth of their second child, the Fishers alternated farm labor with wage work. Following the harvest, they moved in with Eula's sister in a nearby town and hired on at the packing sheds. In the winter months both Eula and her husband cut and wrapped meat at local markets.[16]

Eula Fisher's seasonal work patterns contrasted with the year-round commitments of urban working wives. Among educated town dwellers, the impact of "careerism" on women emerged clearly after World War I. Many women who had invested heavily in career training persisted on the job after they married. Noting the comparatively high proportion of married professional women, census analyst Joseph Hill concluded that for "some women, particularly those having a superior education, ambition for a career or the desire for a wider sphere of activity than the domestic hearth affords . . . leads them to follow a profession or gainful occupation after marriage."[17] Among doctors, lawyers, real estate agents or dealers, and business owners or managers, married women were overrepresented relative to their overall place in the workforce. The time and energy invested in building careers in these fields or the rewards of these jobs discouraged women from leaving them upon marriage. In contrast, married women were underrepresented among trained nurses and school teachers. Teaching and nursing also required specific education, but these professions had acquired the label of single women's jobs well before 1900. The very choice of an occupation, then, partly determined the employment cycle of women, whether or not they realized it as they entered the labor force as single women.

SINGLE WOMEN AT WORK

After 1920 employment became an expectation of single adult women of all classes coincident with the rising employment of married women. The "working daughter" gradually disappeared, not because young adult women dropped out of the labor force, but because employment took on new functions in the lives of single women. Increasingly likely to complete high school and to pursue vocational training or higher education, women began to leave school with particular vocational skills and preferences. Not all young women were career minded during their early adult years, but women left school intending to apply their vocational skills and to work until marriage and child-rearing responsibilities interrupted or terminated their employment.

Girls who trained for vocations at the secondary or postsecondary level expected to support themselves at least temporarily. They may have continued to live in their parents' homes until they married. They probably paid some or all of the costs of their upkeep at home, but they did not necessarily enter the labor force because their parents needed more money. Rather, they went out to work because they had become adults and employment confirmed the passage out of childhood. As education and vocational training increased for both girls and boys, the propensity to enter employment before the age of eighteen declined. As Narissa Hodges's example suggests, school attendance laws had not effectively eliminated children from the labor force in the 1920s, but the trend toward high school or vocational school completion gained momentum after World War I. Youthful employment persisted, but wage-earning children increasingly combined full-time schooling with part-time work. The decline of child labor reflected technological innovations that replaced much of the unskilled labor performed by young girls and women at the turn of the century, as well as a long-term rise in the real wages of adult workers.

WOMEN AS PART-TIME WORKERS

From World War I onward, seasonal jobs, part-time schedules, and flexibility of work hours facilitated youths' combining work and school and wives' pairing of market labor with domestic chores. Single women generally carried some familial responsibilities as well, but regardless of marital status, women workers followed shorter and more flexible work schedules than men did.[18] Census Bureau estimates of hours of work, based on National Industrial Board Surveys, show that the weekly hours of production workers in manufacturing industries from 1914 through 1948 were consistently fewer among women than among men although the hours of both men and women moved up and down simultaneously in response to labor demands. Women worked on average from two to six hours fewer per week than did men, and women's average work weeks varied from a high of fifty hours in 1914 to a low of thirty-three hours in 1938.

Definitions of part-time employment emerged during the Progressive and interwar years with the attempts of individual states to regulate the hours and wages of women and minors. Before World War II, part-time workers were understood to be hourly or piecework employees who regularly worked fewer than forty hours per week or salaried employees whose scheduled hours of work were fewer than the standard in their workplace. During World War I public officials and private employers turned to part-time employment as a means of drawing women and students into the workforce. After the war, displaced women workers accepted short hours from employers who did not offer a full day's work. In this situation women proffered themselves as secondary workers who arranged their personal lives and family responsibilities to accommodate employer preferences. These part-time workers of the 1920s set a precedent for further exploitation of "secondary" female workers in the decades that followed. Seasonal or periodic employment of women similarly reinforced the secondary status that female industrial and agricultural workers had long known.[19]

Even women whom employers regarded as full-time, year-round workers did not necessarily work without interruption. Flexibility of work hours had characterized the industrial workplace since the nineteenth century. Payroll records of individual firms show that the size of the labor force and length of the work week varied with seasonal labor demands, but also reveal that women generally experienced more variation in work hours than did men. For example, the payroll ledgers of the Dorchester, Massachusetts, Baker Chocolate Company from 1918 through 1928 document the divergent employment patterns of men and women. Baker, like other firms, laid off workers or shortened work weeks in slack times. Company-controlled work schedules consequently enforced some variation in the ordinary work weeks of men as well as women. New employees routinely worked fewer hours than others during their first weeks with the firm. Male workers occasionally took a day off because of illness or other constraints that kept them away from the workplace, but generally men worked a forty-eight–to–fifty–hour week with occasional overtime. Women also worked a standard forty-eight–to–fifty– hour week but commonly altered their work patterns, taking off one or two days during the week or absenting themselves weeks at a time without surrendering job security.

Jennie Wright worked in the Baker sewing room from 1918 through 1922, where she sewed various packaging and oversaw two or three other sewers. In 1918 Wright worked a full six-day schedule for a total of thirty-five weeks. She missed work during the two weeks that the plant normally shut down in August and during an additional week earlier in the year. During the other fourteen weeks, she worked anywhere from four to five days while the plant operated on a six-day schedule. Katie McDonald worked in the German chocolate room from 1920 through 1928. Though virtually a full-time worker through her years at Baker, McDonald occasionally took off one day a week in addition to the five-day weeks that the company scheduled in off-peak periods. On rare occasions she missed more than one. From October through December of 1922, McDonald completed eight weeks at the full-time schedule of forty-eight hours, one forty-hour week as scheduled by Baker, took one week off, worked three days for one week, and five days during the remaining three weeks of the quarter. McDonald adhered to this pattern except in 1919, when she worked in the cocoa picking room. During that year Katie worked virtually full-time during the first quarter of the year. For the entire second quarter she worked full-time for only three weeks and for seven weeks did not work at all. She returned to full-time work for the third quarter but worked erratically during the last quarter, completing seven full weeks, three weeks of one day each, and three weeks away from work. McDonald's 1920 advancement from picking cocoa beans to making chocolate suggests that her irregular work pattern did not handicap her in the eyes of the Baker Company. Many women at Baker exhibited intervals of short-time or erratic work, but similar patterns did not characterize male workers there.[20]

SOLIDARITY AMONG WORKING WOMEN

As before World War I, women of the 1920s continued to confront unsatisfactory workplace conditions, and the difficulties that women encountered led some to labor activism or protest and others to cooperation on the job. During the 1920s, at the age of fourteen, Mary Thompson began work in a southern textile mill. Thompson married at age fifteen and had a daughter at sixteen. Her husband left shortly after the baby came, and Mary had to return to work soon in order to support herself. Although she worked long hours and had continuous responsibility for her daughter, Mary accepted as much work at the drawing frame as she could find. Of her years in the mills, Thompson recalled that "lots of people would complain about the work, but honest to goodness, I'd rather draw in than eat when I was hungry."[21]

The opportunity to form friendships at work gave women feelings of emotional well-being, but work relationships also played an important part in workplace survival. Good relationships with co-workers helped women through hard times with their jobs or with their supervisors. Mary Thompson lost little time on the job despite an injury because fellow employees assisted her with her tasks. "One time . . . I was working there at the Slater and I fell and broke my arm. . . . I was in a cast, and I could draw all my warp [but] I couldn't . . . draw a reed. One of the women would always come and draw my reed for me, and . . . I wasn't out of work but a week."

Factory worker Mary Bailey also recalled the importance of mutual support on the shop floor. Beginning at age thirteen, Bailey worked for five years as a live-in nursemaid and later found work in a tobacco plant. She enjoyed both jobs largely because of the atmosphere of companionship and mutual support among the workers. After working in North Carolina tobacco factories almost continuously from World War I through the 1950s, she remembered that "If one person was slower, you would just carry her on too. We wouldn't report her not doing nothing."[22] Although labor organizers have long viewed southern workers in particular and working women generally as unresponsive to cries for worker solidarity, the experiences of Thompson and Bailey show that women have cooperated with each other outside of as well as within labor organizations. Women who shared work or temporarily covered the responsibilities of workers on unauthorized rest breaks expressed meaningful labor consciousness and erected a protective wall between themselves and their supervisors. For workers at the bottom of the earning scale and women who had no real employment alternatives, workers' cooperation on the job provided more help and more comfort than protest.

During the 1920s female labor activists shifted their energies from union organizing to working for the adoption of protective legislation. Reasoning that legislation would be a more encompassing and rapid approach to improving women's working conditions, club women and labor leaders built upon the successes of the WTUL in the 1910s. Rose Sneiderman, Agnes Nestor, Mary Dreier, Leonora O'Reilly, and others had all risen to prominence through the Women's Trade Union League or trade-defined unions before World War I. Mary Anderson, who began her work life in bootmaking, became the first director of the Women's Bureau in 1920. This corps of women with leadership skills and access to influential politicians set the stage for the adoption of major labor legislation in the 1920s and 1930s.[23]

PUBLIC OPINION AND WORKING MOTHERS

During the first four decades of the twentieth century, the attitudes of reform-minded working women underwent some significant changes as reflected in the studies and personal records they left behind. Male researchers lagged behind female social scientists in their acceptance of wives' employment. Both groups of researchers shared assumptions about class, race, and ethnicity that colored their results despite their intentions of objectivity. In the broadest terms, welfare studies completed before 1920 criticized working mothers because of their employment. Studies directed by professional women after 1920 condemned the conditions under which married women labored rather than castigating mothers simply for working. Despite the pressures and concerns that professional women shared with employed mothers from the working classes, they faulted the child care and housekeeping practices of the working poor. Moreover, they often worked for "protection" of blue-collar working women that they did not think they needed for themselves. Thus, while fighting to end or curtail factory night work and seeking rest periods and cleaner factory conditions to protect the health of mothers or prospective mothers, middle-class reformers of the 1920s overlooked the health dangers of the office.

Throughout the interwar years white middle-class wives defended their work rights through associations like Zonta and the Business and Professional Women's Clubs and found an important advocate in the Women's Bureau, but nearly all women justified the employment of wives and mothers solely on the basis of economic necessity. The exceptions were elite women who felt no compulsion to earn money but did not enjoy full-time domesticity. A 1920s survey of working wives who had graduated from Boston University, Simmons College, and Radcliffe College confirmed that some felt their families needed their financial support, but others chose work outside the home because of their own aspirations. A mother of six who taught music at the collegiate level explained, "I enjoy teaching music and I am not a brilliant success as a housekeeper. . . . I think perhaps the children enjoy my music more than they would enjoy me, if I had let my music slip and devoted myself mainly to housekeeping."[24]

In the first two decades of the twentieth century, advice literature began to reflect middle-class women's roles in the workforce. By the 1920s, prescriptive literature also offered some encouragement to the married woman worker. Whether their career goals emerged from conversations with peers, from individual role models, or from the experiences of higher education, small numbers of educated women of the 1920s remained in the labor force after marriage. The broad educational gains of women in the 1920s created a much larger cohort of college-educated wives than had existed in the Progressive Era. Working wives of the interwar years brought the issue of married women's employment into public forums of debate. These working wives encountered a barrage of literature on the employment of mothers, but commercial magazines generally provided little support for the mother who opted for the labor market. During the twenties the *Atlantic Monthly, Harper's Magazine*, the *Nation*, the *New Republic*, and *Survey* all published articles about working mothers.[25] *Harper's* featured articles titled "Life on the Ragged Edge" and "What about the Children?" *Atlantic Monthly* published "Homemaking and Careers," while the *New Republic* ran "Confessions of an Ex-Feminist" and articles on the difficulties faced by working wives and mothers.[26]

Amidst the controversy over mothers' work, employed mothers of the middle class spoke up for themselves. In doing so they changed the climate of opinion in which they or their peers judged wage-earning mothers, but middle-class career women set themselves apart from less affluent working mothers whose children they believed lacked proper nurture and supervision. Female researchers conducted studies of working middle-class women that implied differing standards of home care by class. In 1927 Radcliffe College graduate student Anne Byrd Kennon released the findings of her study of 243 "College Wives Who Work." Kennon's work reflected the particular approach necessitated in a survey aimed at the middle class and completed without any investigator present. Questions asking the respondent to indicate the relative filth and disorder in her home, a standard aspect of home visitors' reports on the poor, would have offended prospective partici- pants. Kennon avoided this issue and thus revealed that her standards for judging middle-class homes differed from those reflected in the surveys of working-class mothers. Of the subjects' homes Kennon could only say: "Only a few homes were visited so this study can not answer the question, 'Have these women created pleas- ant home atmospheres?' However, information was obtained about the types of houses and the amounts of assistance necessary to run the houses."[27]

Some values in middle-class culture changed more slowly than others. With clean office environments and emerging professions presenting new and respect- able opportunities for female employment, the obstacles to middle-class female employment began to erode. As habits of employment and job satisfaction began to accrue to young middle-class women, these women acquired an interest in staying at work after they married. By the 1920s the "spinster" professional woman in- creasingly worked alongside young matrons who intended to stay at work until child care responsibilities kept them at home. Working middle-class wives with young children were usually professional women who could afford to hire nan- nies. The middle-class mother who worked remained a rarity through the 1920s but had definitely made her appearance, and her presence had begun to transform the ways in which U.S. institutions prepared girls for the future.

EDUCATION AND VOCATIONAL TRAINING

Changes in the education and socialization of women during the 1920s mirrored the feminization of the labor force and the demand for better-educated female workers. Both secondary schooling and higher education enjoyed growth spurts in the 1920s. Parents and schools enlarged their efforts to prepare girls to enter the burgeoning white-collar sector. The *number* of youths of both sexes receiving high school diplomas more than doubled, and the *rate* of secondary school completion nearly doubled. Higher education underwent even more impressive growth, as nearly one quarter of all high school graduates went on to college and completed four-year degrees on the eve of the Great Depression. In the 1920s the number of bachelor's degrees awarded to women more than doubled, and women increased their share of degrees from one third to two fifths of all bachelor's and master's degrees awarded. Between 1920 and 1930 women as well as men quadrupled the number of Ph.D. degrees they completed.

Race and ethnicity guided and limited girls' ambitions and expectations, but race and ethnicity were hardly monolithic influences. Within ethnic and racial groups, attitudes toward educating daughters reflected a variety of individual needs and goals. Greek and Greek American girls growing up in Lowell, Massachusetts, in the 1920s had a broad array of educational experiences. Educational achievement reflected economic realities as well as parents' preferences. Herriclia Eliades was the first Greek American woman in Lowell to earn a baccalaureate degree. The Speronis and the Karafelis sisters, Eliades's contemporaries, were not so fortunate. Katherine Speronis emigrated to Lowell from Greece along with her mother and three sisters. Katherine and one sister went directly into the mills, while the two youngest sisters continued their schooling. Although most young women of Lowell eventually entered the textile mills, Mary Karafelis and her sister found alternative employment. Mary's mother taught her daughters to sew, and Mary's sister translated her skills into a dressmaking business and thereby escaped the factory. While in high school, the Karafelis daughters studied typing. Their father bought them a typewriter to encourage their studies, preparation that directed Mary into a long-term career in office work. As in the case of Herriclia Eliades, the Karafelis sisters followed career paths that their parents had helped to chart.[28]

African American girls' educational experiences varied as broadly as did the schooling of ethnic whites, but racial discrimination proved an especially painful barrier to the advancement of black youths. Arline Steward Yarbrough, an African American, entered school in Salt Lake City at the end of the First World War. The black community of Salt Lake was so small that racial segregation never became an issue in the public schools, but life in an overwhelmingly white neighborhood held special terrors for African American children. The journey to school proved a continuous ordeal to Yarbrough and her siblings, and teachers neglected their needs.

> We used to fight our way to school, we'd fight our way home for lunch, we'd fight our way back to school, fight our way home, and we didn't dare strike out one at a time, we'd have to go to school in pairs or more. . . . And so I learned a pretty good art of self-defense as a young girl. The teachers, of course some were better than others, but for the most part I feel their attitude was just sort of, "well she's here so I just have to put up with it." You know, never any kind of special help was offered.[29]

Yarbrough's parents sought residence in a predominantly white neighborhood partly to take advantage of superior public schools, and Yarbrough succeeded educationally despite the emotional trauma of her early school years. She completed junior high school in Salt Lake and subsequently moved to Seattle to live with an older sister after assurances that she would receive a rigorous high school education there. Yarbrough went on to Washington State College, but the Depression forced her to leave before receiving her baccalaureate degree. She then followed a clerical career that culminated in twenty-two years of civil service with the State of Washington. Yarbrough thus became one of the fortunate African American women who rose through educational training to enter white-collar jobs in the 1930s.

Regardless of race or class, all public school girls of the 1920s received gendered instructional messages from their teachers, and many attended compulsory vocational classes. Vocational education established its claims as a standard element of the secondary curriculum in the 1920s, and instruction in practical skills became part of the educational experience of almost all students by the end of World War II. Business and commercial courses proliferated, and home economics instruction expanded. Home economics teachers intensified their efforts to elevate training in homemaking to a "career" with status comparable to that of the professions. Home economics instructors prepared working-class girls for the labor market as well as homemaking, while secondary teachers urged college-bound girls to train for professional positions in dietetics, fashion, home extension, or home economics teaching.

Training in domestic arts had expanded with the introduction of vocational education in the late nineteenth century, and by the early twentieth century these skills had become a "science." The rise of the home economics movement coincided with the Progressive Era reforms inspired by Dewey, Hall, and others, and in this atmosphere, home economics instruction gained an aura of national purpose absent from earlier domestic arts programs. As potential mothers, school girls learned that they could build a stronger citizenry by raising healthy families and maintaining orderly homes. To these ends educators drew middle-class as well as working-class girls into secondary home economics instruction. Americanization continued as a basic component of programs in ethnic community schools, and home economics teachers assumed much of the responsibility for "Americanizing" foreign-born girls. Teachers strove to pass on to immigrant families their own standards of morality and home order as well as Anglo American gender values.

In the early twentieth century home economics instruction occurred in elementary school and instruction reached boys as well as girls. Instruction in the lower grades consisted of rudimentary lessons in domestic order, health, and cleanliness. In some school systems home economics instruction persisted into the junior high years as school administrators sought to "assist boys and girls in forming helpful and cooperative attitudes toward their families."[30] By the 1920s boys had been largely excluded from training as home helpers. A 1920s report on home economics education in the Swarthmore, Pennsylvania, schools stressed that junior high school "training should not be for future homemakers, but for present home members and helpers [so that] the junior high girl can, with some degree of intelligence, share home responsibilities for younger members of the family."[31]

The narrowing of home economics education to girls reflected the rise of the college-trained woman who had prepared for a gender-defined career in home economics and sought to pass on her goal to her pupils. Unlike the nineteenth-century teacher who passed on the domestic skills that she had learned through life, the "home economist" earned credentials in the "science" of household management and family care. She saw herself as heiress to the moral imperative of Catharine Beecher and the scientific orientation of Ellen Richards. She had chosen domestic science as her career, and public school teaching offered one of several employment options open to this professional person. Home economists presented young girls with an endeavor that elevated "natural," "biological" characteristics into the status of a profession. Thus home economics, like nursing, developed as a melding of a classically female calling with new, science-based, practical skills.

Proud of their self-proclaimed professional status, home economics instructors touted their profession as the ideal complement of women's higher duties as mothers. A World War I release from the Education War Service urged home economics training to prepare women "for an income-earning occupation and also for a woman's life needs."[32] Bureau of Education home economist Henrietta Calvin warned, "The returned soldier will demand that many occupations, now taken over by women, be given back to him, but at no time can he replace the woman . . . well trained in home economics."[33]

The development of vocational education in secondary schools augmented rather than replaced homemaking instruction in the upper elementary grades. In the 1920s, before universal high school attendance, the elementary school remained the place to reach the maximal audience with programs in citizenship and practical skills. One California school district of the 1920s combined these two goals in its Department of Americanization and Homemaking. Designed exclusively for girls, the Covina City program sought to redirect the child care and sewing skills that Mexican American girls learned at home toward Anglo notions of womanly citizenship and maternal leadership. Covina teacher Pearl Idella Ellis stressed the importance of teaching careful household budgeting, humble material expectations, and domestic order to twelve- to fourteen-year-old Mexican and Mexican American girls in the city's elementary schools. In a typical burst of middle-class Anglo condescension, Ellis explained the crucial role of the future wife of a sporadically employed Mexican or Mexican American laborer: "Severe strain falls on the housewife, who deals out sustenance to . . . her family from her meager and disappearing supply of foodstuffs. The crisis comes. The pangs of hunger acceler-

Home economics educators of the 1920s taught the scientific principles of food preparation to adults as well as school girls as they sought to improve family health and raise the status of homemaking. Courtesy Schlesinger Library

ate criminal tendencies. Forgery or stealing follows. The head of the family lands in jail. The rest . . . are helpless, and soon become county charges. Property owners pay . . . taxes for their maintenance. If we can teach the girls the food values and a careful system of budgeting; how to plan in prosperity for the day of no income and adversity, we shall avoid much . . . trouble . . . in the future."[34]

During the early decades of the century, home economics instruction for black children prepared girls for domestic service in private homes or commercial establishments. Confronted with the employment options of black women, African American educators endorsed curricula that prepared girls for domestic work. At the end of World War I, the home economics division of the U. S. Office of Education studied the "peculiar needs among negroes for instruction in home economics" and endorsed a racially segregated vocational agenda.[35] Although individual African American teachers such as Anna Julia Cooper encouraged individual black students to pursue higher education, they also promoted the dignity of domestic work and endorsed training in homemaking for the masses of African American girls.[36]

While home economics instruction for African American girls concentrated on basic cooking, cleaning, and sewing skills useful both at work and at home, the Office of Education in the 1920s encouraged elevating the status of white home-makers through the study of "domestic science." State educational authorities in California certified "science of the household" for one unit of laboratory science credit and "citizen-homemaking" as a social studies course to meet the state's requirements for a high diploma. A federal survey of white Mississippi mothers pointed with pride to the decisions of "older and more influential women's col-leges" to accept "home science courses" for entrance credit and reported that more than 1,000 mothers "believe that home science has cultural value, that social ben-efits to the girls and their communities are . . . indispensable to society."[37]

CONSTRUCTING FEMALE AMBITIONS

Paralleling educational curricula that prepared middle-class girls for college, the Girl Scouts emerged as a force that lifted girls' achievement ambitions. From its founding in 1912 through the 1920s, Girl Scout organizers targeted upper-middle-class white girls.[38] Throughout World War I, Girl Scouting in the United States grew slowly, reaching 8,400 in membership by 1918. World War I set the move-ment on a long-term course that emphasized individual resourcefulness, patrio-tism, and responsibility to the community. Although town based and structured around "troop" activities, the Girl Scouts also organized the Lone Scout program for middle-class rural girls. While 4-H clubs sought initially to raise the living standards of the poor, the Lone Scout program offered rural girls the opportunity to participate in a program initially defined around middle-class values embedded in citizenship, informal education, and recreation.

In the fall of 1917, the Girl Scouts initiated publication of *The Rally*, a magazine for its members. Articles and stories about home front activities during the war and the roles that Girl Scouts could play dominated the journal in its first year of publication. The August, 1918, issue was entirely devoted to "Home War Work" and included the articles "Solving Uncle Sam's Food Problem," "The Surgeon General's Little Army," "Our Own Win the War Page," and a feature titled "Sister's Vocation—The Story of a Girl Who Liked to Keep House," about a young girl who takes over the domestic responsibilities of managing and caring for a family after the mother dies. Stories such as "Sister's Vocation" became standard fare in *The Rally* and its successor, *The American Girl*.

In its publications and in troop activities, the Girl Scouts stressed the importance of women's preparedness to assume whatever role society demanded of them, fighting on the home front in times of economic or political peril as well as maintaining home and family. Scouting took on the task of assisting in the national emergency by training girls to take over child care responsibilities in the home to free adult women for civic work and paid employment. World War I scouts also joined the agricultural Land Army, working in farmers' fields and maintaining their own victory gardens, including a bean field on the Boston Common. Like their sisters in the 4-H movement, scouts learned to preserve the foods they had grown. Scouts also sewed and knitted garments for war relief. For wartime scouts, then, "domestic" skills developed alongside the survival skills of self-reliance and support of the "troop" that they learned in camping. Domesticity in scouting was not an end in itself during the war years but developed skills that aided the community as a whole, and domesticity was paired with an emphasis on mental and physical adventures that served to expand rather than narrow girls' horizons.

During the 1920s the Girl Scouts challenged girls to strike out on a nontraditional course of activities, a direction permitted by the affluence of early members and the novel employment opportunities that beckoned daughters of the upper middle class. Scouting, with its attendant outdoor or summer camp activities, stressed physical fitness, self-reliance, and nature as the building blocks of good health and strong moral values. The scouts simultaneously instilled career-related expectations and skills. The Girl Scout movement, along with its founder Juliette Gordon Low, found compatibility rather than conflict in the concurrent development of practical or vocational skills and women's roles as homemakers. Scouting fostered the idea, if not the expectation, that middle-class girls grow up to be career women as well as wives and mothers. The development of scouting in the 1920s thus paralleled the expansion of higher education for middle-class women and the movement of college graduates into careers.

Emerging during the war and under the leadership of Low, an avid fan of the airplane, Girl Scouting championed aviation from the beginning. Girl Scouts leaders encouraged their young charges to learn all they could about aviation and to take up flying if the opportunity presented itself. The achievement awards or "proficiency badges" offered in scouting during its formative years suggested the broad spectrum of skills that Low thought appropriate for girls. Badges introduced from 1913 through 1920 included Ambulance, Businesswoman, Clerk, Dairy Maid, Electrician, Flyer, Handywoman, Homemaker, Journalist, Telegraphist, and Zoologist.[39]

Jane Deeter Rippin, who served as National Director of the Girl Scouts from 1919 through 1930, continued the course that Low had charted. By the end of the 1920s, the overwhelmingly white membership of the Girl Scouts had grown to more than 200,000.[40] As scouting expanded in the 1920s, the emphasis on nontraditional careers for women continued, although the girls cumulatively earned more merit badges in homemaking skills than in adventurous or other nontraditional activities.[41] During the 1920s and 1930s, *The American Girl* regularly carried a feature about women in unusual careers and articles on camping and nature. In the January, 1930, issue, Girl Scout President Mira H. Hoffman encouraged scouts to look ahead to the years after high school: "1940! Some of you will be in college then; others will have taken up a career."[42] Although the Girl Scout of 1930 might not become a college student or career woman by 1940, Hoffman clearly intended to encourage her readers to think otherwise. Simultaneously, however, Girl Scout Leaders got reminded that "Every Girl is destined to be, in some degree, a home-maker, whether for herself or for her family."[43]

While the Girl Scout movement eventually succeeded in reaching working-class girls, the movement remained overwhelmingly upper-middle class in its membership through the 1920s. The first "campsite" of Girl Scout leaders in

Camping has remained an integral part of the Girl Scout program from its inception. San Antonio scouts prepare for a two-week outing, 1926. Courtesy Institute of Texan Cultures, the San Antonio Light *Collection*

New York City took place in the empty mansion of Edith Macy, whose husband, magnate V. Everit Macy, later provided for the establishment of the permanent Camp Edith Macy on family property at Briarcliff Manor, New York. In 1918, twenty-seven Girl Scout leaders arrived at Macy's 75th Street residence for a training program that "approximated" wilderness conditions "by sleeping on army cots and cooking over an open fire in a fireplace."[44] With the prospect that Girl Scouts could reasonably aspire to adventure, education, and the cultivation of unusual skills by virtue of their parents' wealth, scouting could encourage girls to excel in the 1920s without raising expectations that girls had no possibility of realizing.

Girl Scout leaders of the 1920s regarded the girls' club movement as an aspect of progressive education, a perspective they shared with the residents of social settlements. Through the 1920s scout executives worked with colleges throughout the nation to train troop leaders as part of educated women's leadership in social work. In 1918 the National Headquarters of the Girl Scouts offered a $500 fellowship for a year of graduate study at New York University with the understanding that "the recipient of the fellowship will devote herself to study and practical work. The practical work will be under the direction of the Community Service and Research Department of the Division of Public Affairs of NYU and the supervision of the National Headquarters of the Girl Scouts."[45]

Although the Girl Scouts focused on middle-class and upper-middle-class girls in the 1920s, the organization recognized the potential for work with the poor.[46] From 1918, when it offered the first summer training courses for potential leaders in New York City, the Girl Scouts included work in social settlements as a component of their training of college women for Girl Scout work. College women's work through the settlements quickly faded, however, and social settlements of the interwar years failed to establish scout troops among working-class girls.[47] In the 1920s the YWCA and the 4-H movement had more success than the Girl Scouts in drawing poor or working-class girls into their activities. None of these organizations had recreation as a primary purpose, but all of the groups used play activities to build physical and social skills. Recreation served as the device through which girls' clubs sought to instill moral convictions, civic values, and vocational skills and expectations in young women.

The Girl Scouts and *The Rally* continued a long tradition of activities and literature dedicated to leading girls and women along the correct path to virtuous and productive lives. Women's organizations, school committees, and commercial publishers sought to mold women's ideals and guide their behaviors through prescriptive literature. School libraries stocked fictional accounts of female success and failure, as well as non-fiction biographies of Madame Curie and Clara

Barton. Columns of advice for women filled the pages of newspapers and magazines for women, and career guidance books proliferated. Like scouting, advice literature more often reached the middle-class, but teachers and vocational counselors carried their ideals to working-class girls through the public school.

By the end of World War I, both the context and the content of advice to school girls had changed. Vocational counseling, increasingly incorporated into grammar school and high school programs, encouraged girls to view work as desirable rather than simply necessary. In a volume intended to help school personnel introduce girls to potential fields of work, Helen Hoerle and Florence Saltzberg advised young readers: "Fate seems rather hard on some girls, for it compels them to work in the world sooner than they'd wish to, to bring money home to the family. Even if you are one of the fortunate girls who is not compelled to leave school to go to work, you may be sure of one thing, that day will come when you'll feel the strong desire to have money earned in your own hands, and to have a job of your own."[48] The authors went on to explore the requirements and characteristics of more than eighty occupations for women. To the list of familiar office jobs they had added bookkeeper and accountant; to the field of professions they had added law, medicine, dentistry, and pharmacy.

THE CHANGING ROLES OF WOMEN

The feminization of the American labor force in the years from 1900 through the 1920s propelled changes in the ways in which parents and community institutions prepared girls for their adult lives. Advice literature for women and girls increasingly reflected women's concerns as wage earners. Schools assumed a larger role in training women for work, while community institutions such as the Girl Scouts gradually assumed some responsibility for socializing girls. All of these changes prompted or reflected changes in family life, but other forces also reshaped the family. Technological and political changes outside the home worked to democratize the ideals if not the realities of family life. The automobile freed families from the physical confinement of the home and increased the potential for individual independence from the family. Suffrage legitimized women's roles in the public sphere. Contemporaneously, wives' escalating economic responsibilities strengthened their authority within the household.

Among the middle class the transition away from father-supported families to the two-parent family economy began in the 1920s as wives combined employment with family care. The small number of middle-class wives who worked in the 1920s had trained for careers and, like Eva MacIntire, continued to work after marriage partly for reasons of personal fulfillment. Nevertheless, college-educated working wives viewed their employment largely in economic terms and rationalized their activity as born of necessity. Wives' wages supported husbands' further education or permitted a family to purchase a home.[49]

In middle-class families of the pre-Depression era, wives and mothers exercised markedly less economic responsibility and power than did working-class wives. As Helen and Robert Lynd documented in Muncie, Indiana, in the 1920s, middle-class wives regarded the important economic decisions affecting them as marital rather than paternal decisions, but middle-class wives rarely managed the family budget and many wives had little knowledge of family finances. The Lynds concluded that "There are a few families at the other extreme in which the husband turns over his pay check to his wife and she has entire charge of the household economy, but these are rare."[50] The Lynds observed that the increase in the number of wives who had worked or were working precipitated growing dissatisfaction with male domination of family finances. The Lynds cited female employment and the economic frustrations of working wives as causes of increasing divorce rates in Muncie.[51] Despite their claims that divorce resulted from female employment, the Lynds did not find significant differences in divorce rates between wage-earning and homebound wives when they returned to Muncie in 1935.[52]

Although sociologists perceived changing men's roles in the 1920s, they also reaffirmed that patriarchal authority remained primary in twentieth-century families. The Lynds found that middle- and working-class husbands in the 1920s as well as in the 1930s retained the power to forbid their wives to work. In addition, husbands had considerable power to influence their wives' activities by extending or withholding encouragement and by accepting or rejecting domestic chores. Nevertheless, women's roles outside the home changed constantly, and inevitably middle-class families found themselves caught up in the social and economic changes of a maturing industrial nation. In 1900, most middle-class women, married or single, did not work outside the home. By the 1920s, single middle-class women not in school expected to work and a small minority of married women of the middle classes held clerical and professional positions.

Women's magazines of the 1920s, which featured articles debating the pros and cons of mothers' employment, reflected the degree to which middle-class women's roles had changed in the early twentieth century. As the emerging controversy over the working mother showed, some familial values had changed little if at all. Although companionate marriage—that is, marriage as a partnership—had here and there emerged by the 1920s, men generally remained the primary breadwinners as well as the heads of families. Women remained responsible for the domestic routine of the home and for the care and development of children. Companionate marriage had not evolved to the point that middle-class families recognized men's roles as nurturers of children.

Research on the overall decline in fertility and family size causally linked these phenomena to rising costs of child rearing and rising expectations of living standards. In addition, as child labor declined, children no longer represented an economic asset. The articulation of new ambitions on the part of wives encouraged the practice of family limitation, and artificial means of birth control assisted couples in planning their families. Middle-class women's interests in careers or community activities encouraged some to curtail childbearing, but a preference for small families also reflected changes in educational expectations and in child rearing practices. As a middle-class wife in Muncie, Indiana, understood family commitments in 1925, "You just can't have so many children now if you want to do for them. We never thought of going to college. Our children never thought of anything else."[53] In industrial and postindustrial societies, well-being depended largely on earning power, which in turn depended increasingly on education, and ambitious parents encouraged their children's schooling.

Many nurses and schoolteachers who embarked upon their careers in the 1920s were children of working-class parents who had struggled to educate at least one of their children, often subsidizing him or her with the paid labor of siblings. As youthful employment dwindled, these kinds of family strategies no longer served. Siblings might assist each other financially, but family obligations and expectations had changed. As children entered the labor force at increasingly older ages, employment carried stronger dreams of independence from parental authority. Few children of the 1920s could support their brothers' or sisters' adolescent leisure or learning while funding their own independence.

As fertility declined the home and child care responsibilities of mothers decreased in terms of the amount of physical labor associated with housekeeping and the supervision of children. Nevertheless, smaller families and the technological revolution in housekeeping actually worked to redefine child care and home care responsibilities rather than to lessen them.[54] In the nineteenth century Catharine Beecher had envisioned and promoted efficiency, order, and cleanliness in the Christian home along with strict but loving discipline of children. In the twentieth century the inheritors of Beecher's domestic science notions moved in two directions: the home economics movement and the child-centered family movement. Both phenomena intensified the moral responsibility of wives to maintain the home at the center of their lives. Beecher had presumed that middle-class wives would maintain order in their homes through the careful supervision of servants, but the disappearance of servants from middle-class homes increased the time and energy that wives had to pour into achieving new, ever-rising standards of home and child care.

By the 1920s the servant had become not only an uncommon presence in middle-class homes but also a threat to the emotional and moral well-being of families. Advice books of the 1920s stressed the importance of child discipline but also stressed the importance of parents, particularly mothers, as the continuous and primary influences in children's lives. By the 1920s, as historian Paula Fass has written, families had become oriented toward child nurture and affectionate relationships among all family members. "Smaller families reflected a trend toward more care and solicitude for the interests of each child and in turn allowed for it."[55]

As child labor and family size decreased and as childhood lengthened, families grew more child centered. A romantic glow settled over middle-class Americans' notions of children and childhood. Parents, especially mothers, looked for joy and emotional satisfaction in the performance of simple but "traditionally American" child care tasks. Corra Mae White Harris, a Georgia mother wrote to a younger friend: "I am delighted to hear that the baby is getting along so finely. . . . Very few modern mothers can assimilate their own babies. If you do you will find him tremendously interesting. . . . A great many good mothers in times gone by have given their lives in vain so far as any recognition of the sacrifice is concerned. . . . If you are patient and never despair and keep him close to you, he will be the man you really want him to be. He'll be your pride and the shield and buckler against the shadows of old age."[56] While they extolled the rewards of motherhood, middle-class mothers like Harris, a prominent Atlanta writer, coupled the rearing of small families with employment.

Among immigrants and their children, ethnic values influenced all aspects of family life and of women's lives—education, occupational choice, social life, marriage, and life cycle. Because of immigration patterns, persons of European birth headed an unusually large share of U.S. families from 1900 through 1929. Attempts to adapt old-world values to American realities were a common feature of family life across ethnic groups. In the United States men and women sought to preserve their cultural inheritance, and religion played a major role in keeping this heritage intact. Women, seldom or never playing leading roles in church or synagogue, nevertheless bore the responsibility for maintaining a religious home. Keeping dietary laws, caring for religious objects, and preserving religious shrines in the home fell into the category of women's responsibilities, sometimes the wives', sometimes the daughters'. Immigrant mothers, whether or not they wished to work, were as heavily tied to the home by cultural factors as were native-born middle-class women, and large families further discouraged their employment outside the home.

We can see especially clearly in the first three decades of the twentieth century, when many first-generation immigrant women and their daughters passed through their childbearing years, how groups within U.S. society have varied their work and childbearing patterns. The reality that U.S. middle-class families had both lower fertility and lower female work rates than other groups argues against a link between fertility and women's employment outside the home. In the family and in the workplace, U.S. women led lives as varied as the manifold religious, racial, and ethnic origins of the nation.

Overall, poor working-class parents of the early twentieth century preferred to keep their children within the parental circle until they reached their mid-twenties so that adult children could help support the parental unit. Child labor persisted in the South longer than elsewhere, and the viability of child labor discouraged both education and youthful autonomy. Children in mill towns and on farms remained virtual wards of their elders until they married. African American girls might migrate to accept domestic work in nearby towns or follow relatives to the North, but white girls had fewer options. Occasionally young white single women left the farm and boarded near the mills that employed them, but single women away from home risked moral condemnation. For mill children or farm children, marriage marked respectable passage from under the parental roof, and mill owners used their control over housing and employment to keep children at home. In 1926, when she was fifteen years old, mill worker Mary Thompson eloped because "Back then, we thought that if we just got married, we could be free then, do as we pleased, and found out you don't ever get free in life."[57]

CONCLUSION

Throughout the first two decades of the century, the feminization of the U.S. labor force proceeded at a moderate pace. The maturation of the nation's manufacturing industries and the rapid expansion of the service sector after World War I altered labor requirements as workers' productivity increased, white-collar jobs expanded, and the demand for unskilled, youthful industrial and agricultural labor dwindled. Educators and legislators responded to the demands of the labor market by restricting the labor of children and broadening the reach of secondary and collegiate schooling. Both the nature of emerging jobs and the diminution in immigration and child labor drove up market demand for female employees.

In the transition away from blue-collar jobs and toward a white-collar economy, secondary and higher education paid off for women. Those women who failed to complete secondary school increasingly found themselves locked into factory jobs or domestic service as agricultural employment continued to decline. Education in the 1920s reinforced rather than challenged gender barriers in employment, concentrating on training women for "women's jobs." The Girl Scouts and elite women's colleges encouraged middle-class girls to reach for nontraditional goals, but their messages failed to propel a rise in the share of women who trained for male-dominated professions. On the other hand, middle-class working women strove to advance the cause of women in business and the professions and defended the work rights of married women in the popular press.

As increasing numbers of middle-class women, married or single, worked outside the home, women's career activities reshaped middle-class gender expectations. The Girl Scouts fostered female accomplishments in the public sphere, and married women defended their work rights through government agencies, through women's organizations, and in the pages of the popular press. Vocational counselors encouraged girls to train for careers, and rising levels of secondary and postsecondary school completion translated girls' ambitions into occupational accomplishments.

Structural changes in the U.S. economy prompted a metamorphosis in family life. Families would be smaller as the postindustrial age approached; the economy and personal dynamics of families would change as well. Fewer children and longer childhoods permitted increased attention to each child, and consequently emotional growth and social adjustment of children joined the older missions of good health, moral development, and discipline among parents' responsibilities. Although the concept of the child-centered family distinguished family values of the 1950s, the trend toward increasing "family time" began well before the Great Depression. The small family developed into a self-reinforcing expectation as parents reasoned that they could not lavish the emotional energy on several children that contemporary child-rearing literature advised. Costs of child rearing rose faster than overall inflation, and mothers' employment, which family planning facilitated, circled back, reducing parents' abilities to spend time with children and underscoring growing preferences for small families.

Companionate marriage emerged in the 1920s as a middle-class model of family order.[58] Companionate marriage followed logically from the earlier elevation of women in the domestic sphere, the egalitarian implications of women's suffrage, and the relative autonomy of female employment outside the home. Family values moved in a parallel fashion with women's rights in the civic sphere as middle-class women campaigned for broadened authority within the family. Middle-class wives and mothers claimed power in family governance as they contributed to family earnings and influenced public policies through civic activities and voting. After ratification of the Nineteenth Amendment, women's public roles expanded to include more organized roles in political parties and wider participation in politics and public service.

While middle-class reformers and working-class women fought to improve working conditions, middle-class wage-earning wives also waged a campaign to defend married women's work rights. Books and magazine articles advising women on occupational choices and discussing the combination of wage earning and unpaid labor appeared in abundance. Working women's advocacy of the legitimacy of their claim to jobs facilitated societal acceptance of the working wife, but expressions of support for married women's employment also reflected significant changes in women's expectations that education had encouraged. Similarly, family structure continued its slow drift away from patriarchy as women's economic roles in the family broadened. Class and ethnic differences among U.S. families persisted over time, but middle-class women moved gender expectations toward a model of shared authority as early as the 1920s.

Educational institutions had responded to strengthening markets for the labor of middle-class as well as working-class women and offered increasing support for women's career aspirations. The Girl Scouts emerged as a significant influence in shaping the expectations of upper-middle-class girls and encouraged the development of nontraditional skills while simultaneously reinforcing the importance of motherhood and domestic skills. Public schools and colleges pursued a similar course in widening offerings in home economics but also training girls and women for careers in the marketplace. Educators prepared women for larger roles in the public sphere but heightened messages about women's domestic roles in an environment that offered some encouragement for women to combine paid work with motherhood and homemaking. Class, race, and ethnicity continued to set the context for education, work, and family life, but economic realities and female employment gradually reshaped the family experiences of working-class as well as middle-class Americans during the 1920s.

Black Tuesday of 1929 dashed many women's dreams of educational achievement and occupational mobility. The ensuing Great Depression threw millions of women and men out of work, but it did not arrest the evolution of the economy. Rather the business disaster, like World War I, hastened structural changes already on the horizon. As the 1920s had foreshadowed, white-collar work continued to grow as employment in manufacturing and agriculture contracted. The transformation of the nation's labor needs rewarded educated women, while others lost out. The Depression did not halt the ascendance of the white middle-class working woman.

CHAPTER FOUR

Hard Times and White-Collar Growth

THE 1930S

On "Black Tuesday," October 29, 1929, the Great Crash struck the New York Stock Exchange, precipitating a decline in the stock price index from 432 in September, 1929, to 58 in July, 1933; worse yet, it precipitated the Great Depression, which endured for a decade, defying all attempts to end it. In fact, the definitive end of the Depression came only on December 7, 1941, when the Japanese bombing of U.S. military installations at Pearl Harbor in Hawaii quickly plunged the United States into its second global war in less than thirty years.

The Depression proved the source of lingering trauma for Americans and changed their ideas about the meaning of work. Controversies about work rights during the Depression centered on gender roles, and women paradoxically proved both winners and losers in employment by the end of the 1930s. Three economic phenomena occurred side by side in the 1930s: first, the decade-long collapse of commerce and industry shattered the lives of millions of working Americans, battering them with layoffs, short-time work, and wage cuts; second, the Great Depression did not destroy capitalism or even arrest its evolution; third, both despite and because of the economic collapse, the structural transformation of the industrial economy continued—specifically, the transition from an industrial- to a service-dominated economy continued unabated and perhaps even accelerated. Clearly, the Depression accelerated many changes long underway, even though the Crash and the ensuing Great Depression did retard technological innovation in many industries.

As the Depression tightened its grip, job competition increased across all occupational sectors because the unemployed lowered their standards for acceptable work. Some groups of workers, however, bore disproportional burdens. Overall, educated Americans fared best as public and private administrative activities expanded and grew more complex, while the number of unskilled service jobs contracted. Manufacturing cutbacks stripped production workers of their jobs, and collapsing agricultural prices and mortgage foreclosures displaced farmers and farm workers. Racial minorities and the least-skilled workers—always last hired and first fired—suffered most as employment fell. For men, especially among the working class, the Great Depression proved a traumatic, debilitating experience that left millions of them emotionally crippled.

For women, paradoxically, the same era catalyzed the expansion of occupational toeholds into significant, permanent lodgments. The number of white-collar jobs increased as the record-keeping and information-reporting requirements of the public and the private sectors grew. This process intensified despite economic stagnation because government services and intervention in the economy expanded under New Deal measures; between 1929 and 1939, federal expenditures nearly tripled and federal employment nearly doubled. By the Depression's end, the slow tide of middle-class white women's entry into the workplace had turned into a powerful flow.

The ongoing white-collar revolution propelled the feminization of the labor force despite the hard times, as demonstrated by the fact that, although women competed fiercely for office jobs, clerical workers and other white-collar women held more positions at the end of the decade than at the beginning. Thus a young Atlanta woman who wrote to an Atlanta newspaper columnist in 1936, "I am 20 years old . . . have two years of college [and] know typing, shorthand, and book-keeping, [but] after a year long search . . . have no job," manifested the discouragement and economic stress of countless other Americans. "Is something wrong with me?" she lamented, but her education and skills meant that she had far brighter prospects than millions of men and less-educated women.[1]

Trying to protect the jobs of male family heads, legislators passed laws that discriminated against the employment of married women. Section 213 of the Federal Economy Act of 1932 resulted in the firing of most wives employed by the federal government and set a precedent for the adoption of similar policies by states, municipalities, or corporations.[2] Invoking the time-honored practice of using public distress to legitimize behavior rooted in private greed, employers frequently exploited popular prejudices against married women to defend slashing their payrolls.

Family need nevertheless drove wives into the 1930s labor market even as laws and societal pressures drove many experienced female workers out of their jobs. Public insistence that employment be limited to one job per family led to discrimination that often became public policy and corporate practice. For example, in 1937 Mrs. Charles Quici of Bellafonte, Pennsylvania, wrote "President Franklin

Occupational segregation by gender and by race partially protected single white women from job losses during the Great Depression. Clerical workers, Women's Bureau, 1938. Courtesy National Archives

Delano Roosevelt": "I would like to know if I darhe work in a Silkmill at the lowest wage while my husband is working on the W. P. A. I was working but I was told to quit or pay a fine. So I quit. But . . . other wives are still working."[3] Driven from her job by the threat of fines against married women's earnings, Mrs. Quici did not understand the "sole breadwinner" guidelines under which her husband had qualified for public relief work. Such restrictions of adults' rights to work had not existed earlier in the century, and now they handicapped families that had long depended upon the earnings of two or more workers. Some wives defended their work rights in letters to politicians or the press. Many others shared Mrs. Quici's confusion, as policies on the employment of married women varied from one employer to another. In the face of such potent opposition, the fact that married and unmarried women joined the labor force in record numbers during the 1930s, a growth rate three times as great as that of the 1920s, demonstrates the overwhelming vigor of the white-collar revolution. The number of women employed increased by 4 percent during the 1930s, while male employment declined by 11 percent. Because all of this growth came in white-collar employment, working-class women, most of whom lacked the education to fill clerical and administrative jobs, in fact lost positions while middle-class women advanced against all opposition.

No matter how many women like Mrs. Quici succumbed to government policy or popular pressure to give up their jobs, the result did little or nothing to relieve male unemployment or stem the tide of rising female employment. The core of male unemployment lay in the collapsed industrial sector, and few unemployed male factory workers could qualify for jobs created by the white-collar revolution. Few blue-collar males would accept traditional women's factory work, even if offered to them, a reluctance intensified by many ethnic traditions. Unemployed Polish coal miners in Pennsylvania, for example, given the choice between the humiliation of idleness or the virtual castration of working in a garment or pocketbook factory, manifestly preferred the former.

The nature of the 1930s economy, then, presented millions of U.S. families with the reality, however repugnant, that female members of the household could find work when male members could not. Women, long habituated to accept responsibility for home and hearth, could rationalize taking on the burden of getting hold of the rent and the fuel as an involuntary but defensible extension of traditional female obligations. In the process, of course, the internal dynamics of the family realigned, often a torturous experience for all concerned. Although the laboring classes had long understood the importance of women's contributions to family income, middle-class families as well came to rely on women's earnings in the 1930s. Across the spectrum of U.S. society, the perception of work for women transmogrified from a "discretionary" source of "pin money" to grim necessity, though many women welcomed the opportunity embodied in the imperative.

As daughters, wives, and mothers, women struggled to maximize earnings so as to keep families intact despite loss of male incomes. Women who had never worked for wages and never expected to do so found themselves in bitter competition with women who had worked most of their adult lives. Married women ignited the hostility of single women, who argued that wives had no right to take jobs during hard times. Moreover, working women generally faced hostility from a public (and its pundits) who claimed that men should hold whatever jobs existed. As throughout the century, however, economic reality rather than public opinion dominated the behavior of employers and workers alike.

Federal employment programs provided some relief for unemployed working women, although the majority of public works jobs went to men. Work programs for women operated primarily in towns and cities where most women resided.

Federal and state officials recognized that some families depended on women's earnings, but emergency job projects for women seldom equipped women with marketable skills. New Deal employment projects for women, particularly those sponsored by the WPA, incorporated the assumption that domestic skills would generate income for women in the short run and in the long run would translate into improved housekeeping when these wives and widows returned to their destined roles as full-time homemakers. Despite the reality that female WPA workers provided the sole support of their families, the fiction persisted that WPA women were temporary workers. WPA work projects for women focused on food service, housekeeping, and sewing and other manufactures, a policy of developing skills that provided income in hard times and personal satisfaction and household efficiency when recovery let women retire to the home. For example, the WPA paid women to manufacture furniture from packing crates as a lesson in the economies and improvements in family life that women could achieve at home.

Women seeking certification for WPA work had to prove that their families included no able-bodied males. A widow whose son had enlisted in the Civilian Conservation Corps, for example, had no claim to federal relief employment. Even wives who convinced public or private employers of the legitimacy of their job claims had not removed all obstacles to their employment; they still had to overcome public opinion and bruised male egos.

WORKING CONDITIONS DURING THE GREAT DEPRESSION

Among the fortunate women holding jobs, pay reductions intensified the privation inherent in gender-based wage discrimination. The gender gap persisted as wages fell in most occupational sectors, although the gap narrowed as the already low full-time weekly earnings for women fell less than for men. In 1930 women earned 58 cents for every dollar earned by men, rising to 65 cents by 1935. Reflecting the comparatively strong demand for female labor in the clerical sector, as well as the absence of a historical male pay scale in this new arena, women in clerical fields earned 71 cents for every dollar earned by male clericals. The ratio in other sectors ranged from 39 cents to the dollar in the professions to 61 cents in sales work.[4]

In addition to displacing working women, the Depression exacerbated already poor employment conditions in numerous industries. Hard times not only heightened job competition but also compelled job holders to endure in low-wage positions under poor working conditions, but women did leave unsatisfactory work situations when family members or other resources gave them the option. Even when a woman's earnings played a critical role in family welfare, the emotional support of her family could stiffen her resolve to quit a job or protest her situation. Mabel Mangan, whose husband lost his position in a Depression layoff, earned 15 cents per hour in a cookie factory, the only income the couple and their children had. Mangan's husband thought conditions in the factory, where Mabel worked in hot surroundings and supervisors constantly pressured employees to speed up production, would destroy his wife's health. He encouraged her to quit despite the hard times, telling her: "You can't do this. We can't get along without you. We're in this together, we'll stay together. So [Mabel] went [to her boss] and . . . said, 'Listen lady, Lincoln freed the slaves and . . . I don't intend to go back to those days. . . . You can take your job and you know what you can do with it. . . . I got work [at] Ames Worsted. . . . From then on I was in the mills."[5]

Organized protest rarely reversed the downward slide of wages and working conditions, but thousands of female workers in the 1930s chose collective action over Mabel Mangan's form of protest. In San Antonio, one of the nation's lowest wage markets and poorest cities, employers threatened worker welfare on several

Manhattan lunch counter workers express their grievances and their views of a company owner. Woolworth Company, 1937. Courtesy National Archives

fronts. San Antonio garment workers, who had earned poor pay in the 1920s, found themselves trapped in even worse conditions during the 1930s. During the Depression wages in the garment industry sank even lower than 1920s rates, literally to pennies a day in some cases. Depression conditions generated labor protest in the Alamo City, and the International Ladies Garment Workers Union selected San Antonio as a major target for organizing activities. One company where the ILGWU found receptive workers was the Dorothy Frocks Company.[6]

In 1936 the ILGWU struck Dorothy Frocks. The company, often with the assistance of local law enforcement agencies, had numerous resources for breaking the strike. Scabs with police escorts arrived during the first days of the strike, but the forceful antagonism of pickets encouraged the company to subcontract work to another San Antonio firm. Dorothy Frocks finally ended the strike by closing the plant and opening at a new location in Dallas. With the Dallas workshop as leverage, Dorothy Frocks signed a contract with the ILGWU and reopened the San Antonio shop. Although the union survived and negotiated a contract, many jobs vanished permanently because Dorothy Frocks never returned to its prestrike employment level in the Alamo city.[7]

The Dorothy Frocks strike exemplified many instances in which female workers proved powerless or nearly powerless to influence wages or working conditions in San Antonio. The children's and infants' wear industries provide even more startling examples of the relationship between low wages for women and employers' mobility. Infants' and children's wear required more highly skilled labor than men's or women's wear. Infants' and children's garments, usually sewn entirely by hand, featured intricate embroidered or drawn designs. Employers kept this segment of the industry fluid and mobile by having the cut fabric sent from New York and parceling it out to homeworkers, thus avoiding the need for factories to assemble the garments. Women and girls chose homework over factory work because of household responsibilities and because factory labor carried some stigma, especially among Mexican American wives. Although more skilled than factory workers, the home sewers settled for lower wages because they could not or would not leave home.[8]

At the depth of the Depression, contractors warned the home sewers that they could not expect raises in the piece rates because the contractors could easily smuggle work across the Rio Grande to Mexico. Residents of border towns had comparable skills and worked even more cheaply than women in San Antonio. Manufacturers could cut their costs by sending work south, even when absorbing the occasional fine for violations of U.S. labor laws. While the most highly paid factory sewers in San Antonio earned more than 60 cents per hour, homeworkers averaged about 5 cents, reflecting the fact that labor unions either would not or could not organize homeworkers. The Fair Labor Standards Act of 1937, which established the first national minimum wage, sounded the death knell of hand sewing employments within the forty-eight states. Thereafter U.S. companies contracted for the manufacture of hand-embroidered infants' and children's garments in Puerto Rico, exempt from mainland minimum wages. Subsequently manufacturers cut costs again by further removing fine handwork to the Philippines and other Asian nations.[9]

San Antonio's laboring women hardly stood alone in their battles to secure a living wage. The protectionist tariffs of the 1920s continued and even strengthened during the 1930s, but job security and wages in private industry remained the paramount issues of the decade, as New Deal measures failed miserably in this regard. The ILGWU and other largely female unions won few victories in protecting jobs anywhere in the nation. As in the case of Dorothy Frocks, strikes usually ended in defeat or hollow gains.

Cross-gender labor cooperation proved somewhat more successful elsewhere in other industries, and here Depression-era legislation had significant impact. Empowered by the Norris–La Guardia Act and the Wagner Act, the Congress of Industrial Organizations (CIO) set out in the 1930s to organize men and women in the same locals. In the 1938 General Motors strike, union women and union wives joined forces in the Women's Brigade. Although men's and women's roles in the strike played out in separate spheres, in the years following the strike women continued in the union. Nationally, labor won few victories during the 1930s, although the CIO triumph over General Motors greatly strengthened the hand of organized labor.

The CIO set out important principles of gender and ethnic inclusiveness that boded well for shared benefits during the economic recovery of the 1940s, but practices did not always live up to ideals. Women wearied of men's refusal to consider their views or share power. Where women or a specific minority group dominated an industry or a union local, the CIO sometimes fought vigorously on their behalf and respected women's leadership, but these battles seldom produced enduring victories. Moreover, the CIO could do little to protect minority women through the 1930s, partly because so many toiled for small-scale firms like Dorothy Frocks that closed or relocated under pressures to raise wages, a strategy for which the union found no effective countermeasure.

In contrast with the misery of San Antonio's garment workers, some lucky workers found few grounds for complaint at their workplace. In such cases, a sense of well-being encouraged female autonomy, although it discouraged unionization. For instance, Martha Hughes, who left the family farm in Vermont in the 1930s, found work as a tube maker at General Electric in Schenectady, New York. Despite some ethnic hostility among workers in the Schenectady plant, women co-operated on the job, and friendships developed among the Irish, German, Polish, Italian, and Yankee women in GE's female workforce. Hughes made friends with several workers, friendships that formed a basis for her social life outside of work.[10]

Hughes's wages supported an independent lifestyle, and her economic self-reliance influenced her decision not to marry. For most of her working life, employment conditions at GE reinforced Hughes's pride in her craft and the workplace bred collegiality with co-workers and supervisors. From her earliest days at General Electric Hughes felt that the company and its supervisors took a genuine interest in employees' welfare. The feeling of expressed personal interest that supervisors engendered among their employees—one aspect of the welfare capitalism practiced by General Electric in the 1930s—often generated intense company loyalty.

DEPRESSION, MIGRATION, AND IMMIGRATION

Martha Hughes participated in the chain migration that had shuffled women into the labor force for more than a century, but she belonged to a dwindling band of women on the move during the 1930s. Hard times discouraged immigration and internal migration. From the Depression through World War II, immigration fell to the lowest levels of the century; from 1930 through 1945 fewer than one million persons immigrated. After the onset of the Great Depression, the gender balance among immigrants shifted further. From 1930 through the early 1970s more than half of all immigrants were women.

Because authors such as John Steinbeck and photographers like Walker Evans created powerful portraits of homeless, migrant Americans forced onto the roads by U.S. agriculture's collapse, the Depression acquired an enduring aura of a people on the move. In fact, fewer Americans moved during the Depression than before it. Farmers in the South and in the Dust Bowl West—the sources of such compelling images—deserted agriculture in great numbers, but poverty kept most of them from moving far. Overall, migrating Americans of the 1930s moved shorter distances than the internal migrants of the 1920s. During periods of heavy interstate migration, men had outnumbered migrant women, but the Depression upset this balance. Though the total number of migrants in the 1930s declined, the ratio of women to men reversed; among whites, twice as many women as men moved to U.S. cities in search of employment or support. Thus the Depression underscored the disproportionate draw that urban economies exercised on women.[11]

THE WORKING WIFE'S DEFENSE

The Depression caught wives in a dilemma. Just when their participation in the world outside the home had enlarged women's claims to authority within it, economic conditions further eroded husbands' confidence in their authority as heads of household. Employed men as well as unemployed men saw their earnings decline and their self-esteem collapse as their ability to provide for their families diminished. Working wives encountered public pressure to terminate their employment as men and single women claimed superior need. Although the suffrage amendment and legal reforms had recently opened the public sphere to women, journalists, lawmakers, and private citizens repeatedly and emphatically reminded wives in no uncertain terms that their status outside the home was secondary, that they belonged at home, and that husbands bore ultimate responsibility for sustaining families.

Employed wives had their defenders, although the popular press generally condemned them. Married workers' campaigns to claim their job rights in the 1920s had not entirely fallen on deaf ears. A 1936 *American Mercury* article, for example, endorsed the right of married middle-class women to work regardless of their husbands' employment status, embracing the women's sentiment that "old-fashioned domestic life would stifle their mentality."[12] The *Mercury* author, Frank Hopkins, avoided the two-wage issue in recounting his wife's emotional response to prejudice against married women's employment. When he asked her if she should resign her teaching position to make way for a man, Mrs. Hopkins simply answered "Baloney!" Other journalists endorsed married women's rights by confining their discussions to women with unemployed husbands. *Good Housekeeping* praised "The New Amazons—women of thirty-five, forty, forty-five—[who] have come forward and assisted family after family in the fight against destitution and despair. When Father's job at the bank folded, Mother made . . . her [hobby] into a business. While Dad [held out] for a job with pay large enough to meet the family expenses, Mother . . . took what work she could find."[13]

By contrast, the Atlanta *Daily World*, an African American newspaper, recognized the necessity of wives' employment during hard times but overlooked the long history of black women's work. Warning that the displacement of black male workers by whites during the Depression had brought the African American community to the brink of disaster, the *World* lamented that male unemployment had driven black homemakers into the labor force: "The depression has caused an amazing number of . . . house-wives to be the bread-winners in their families. The close of the depression, no doubt, will swing the pendulum back and will force man power back [to work], giving woman the opportunity to keep house and rear her children properly."[14]

Through the Depression Eleanor Roosevelt spoke and wrote widely (and ambiguously) on women's issues. She spoke with the authority of an educated and experienced social activist, but her role as First Lady led her to tiptoe around federal policy controversies. Section 213 of the Economy Act of 1932 prohibited the federal employment of both partners in a marriage, and wives rather than husbands usually surrendered their jobs when the law took effect. In response to letters protesting Section 213, Roosevelt merely noted that "Government salaries are at best small." She maintained that most "married women . . . working in factories and shops and in lower-paid office positions or in domestic service" did so only because they had to if their families were to "exist at all." She defended married female workers who "direct or create work" for others. With regard to the two-worker issue, Roosevelt conceded the necessity of spreading employment, but also insisted that wholesale dismissals of married women would not benefit the nation.[15]

In the campaign against married women's employment, women as well as men charged that hiring wives took jobs away from male family heads. Single women thought their job claims superior to married women's and frequently condemned working wives. Thus when San Antonio clerical worker May Eckles, a single woman, learned of the termination of wives in her office, she entered her thoughts in a personal diary: "Well all the married women are missing this morning and I ain't sorry, for I certainly am not in favor of married women working unless they have to, there are too many unmarried ones without jobs."[16] Eckles lived with her unmarried sister, who also worked, but she never acknowledged the irony of her antagonism toward dual-earner married couples.

Some corporations did not eliminate married women's work altogether but fired those wives who could not convincingly demonstrate that family survival depended on their earnings. Esther Moore, an ex-employee of the General Electric Company in Erie, Pennsylvania, sought help from Women's Bureau Chief Mary Anderson: "I now have been notified that my services are no longer required, even after 23 years of efficient service, simply because I am married, even though my husband is not working."[17] The Women's Bureau asked General Electric in Erie to clarify its position on married women. The Erie plant's general manager responded that the company did employ married women but might ask a wife to resign if, in their view, she did not need to work and if her work record indicated "no special efficiency."[18] The company's explanation did not address Moore's claim that when she protested her termination on the grounds that her husband was unemployed, a supervisor told her the company could not afford to investigate such claims. Throughout the Depression countless women echoed Moore's complaint, many writing to public officials or prominent personalities. Legions of wives joined Mrs. Charles Quici in writing to Eleanor or Franklin Roosevelt to complain of the hardships caused by discrimination against married women and employers' inconsistent policies toward wives.

Married women in business and the professions generally defended the work rights of married women, but not all of them did. A Depression-era contributor to *The Zontian*, the magazine of the professionally oriented Zonta Clubs, argued that some working wives led happier and healthier home lives than full-time homemakers and that highly skilled women improved society and the economy through the contribution of their knowledge to business and industry. However, an opposing article in the same issue, while acknowledging the necessity of wifely employment in the nation's poorest households, warned that mothers' employment caused child neglect and depressed male wages.[19]

GROWTH OF MARRIED WOMEN'S EMPLOYMENT

Despite the array of policies and attitudes discriminating against working wives, more married women held jobs in 1940 than in 1930. Wives' growing commitment to wage labor in the 1930s fit the earlier trend and set the stage for women's work during World War II. Gathering momentum in the prosperous 1920s, married women's participation in the labor force continued to climb after the onset of the Depression and in fact reached its most rapid rate of growth thereafter. In *Middletown* and *Middletown in Transition*, Helen and Staughton Lynd studied social change in predominantly white Muncie, Indiana, in the 1920s and 1930s. The Lynds chose Muncie on the basis of two primary concerns: "(1) that the city be as representative as possible of contemporary American life, and (2) that it be at the same time compact and homogeneous enough to be manageable in such a total-situation study."[20] Thus, the Lynds selected a setting of modest size dominated by a native white population of modest means.

The Lynds found that the lowest-paid husbands among their participants were the most likely to have working wives and that the Depression had softened husbands' opposition to wives' employment.[21] Despite the implied threat to their positions as household heads and despite the legislation and propaganda intended to drive wives from the Depression labor force, husbands in Muncie more willingly saw their wives off to work in the 1930s than in the 1920s. The Lynds' findings underscored the importance of occupational segregation and of sectoral change in the economy in husbands' acceptance of wives' employment. The employment of women, both married and single, had expanded in occupations with minimal competition between men and women, jobs such as clerical worker and schoolteacher. Simultaneously, women's hourly wage employment in factories had declined as manufacturers substituted machines or "stronger," more productive male workers, while retaining poorly paid female pieceworkers for some jobs. Single women could not subsist on the low earnings of piecework and left manufacturing. Married women, whom the Lynds regarded as supplemental workers and thus able to settle for lower incomes, had replaced the single workers. As more married women had gone out to work, working and lower-middle-class husbands had accommodated themselves to the idea; moreover, consumer expectations, rising since the 1920s, reinforced the acceptance of wifely employment as a source of income in the 1930s.[22]

Two additional factors (not mentioned by the Lynds) may have contributed to the increasing acceptance of wives' employment in Muncie. First, the Lynds resurveyed Muncie in 1935, when many believed that economic recovery had begun. The panic of 1930–33 had passed; the downturn of 1937–38 had not yet developed. Meanwhile, Section 213 of the Federal Economy Act of 1932, together with the policies of public and private employers, had effectively institutionalized discrimination against married women. The adoption of discriminatory hiring codes that appeared to protect male jobs dampened the issue of married women's competition with male workers. Although women continued to lose jobs if they married or if their unemployed spouses found jobs, the wholesale dismissal of married women had occurred before 1935. The debate over married women's employment remained alive in 1935, but discussion focused on removing rather than instituting the marriage bar.[23] Second, husbands may well have understood that their own wives, who were not truck drivers, welders, or engineers, did not compete with men, while clinging to the notion that married women in general took jobs that otherwise went to men or single women.

THE IMPACT OF ETHNIC AND RACIAL DISCRIMINATION

As the controversy over married women's employment shows, the Depression did not affect all segments of the population in the same way. It hit some sectors of the economy harder than others and inflicted higher unemployment on some groups than on others. Comparing the employment and the unemployment patterns of black and white women between 1930 and 1940, for example, exposes the less than random character of layoffs and firings. Overall, white women's job prospects improved despite the Depression, while those of African American women declined.

African American women have always been the most likely of U.S. women to be wage earners, but their labor force participation has fluctuated with market conditions. During the 1930s structural economic change and the business depression exacerbated the twin evils of restricted education and discrimination in hiring and promotion and crippled black working women. Between 1930 and 1940, while the black female population increased by 500,000 (9 percent), the black female labor force shrank from 1,840,642 to 1,720,994 (5 percent), as African American women, discouraged by high unemployment, either stopped looking for jobs or never entered the labor force at all (see table 4.1). In contrast, white women continued to enter the labor market; between 1930 and 1940, as the white female population increased by 4,000,000 (8 percent), the white female labor force increased from 8,817,564 to 10,327,866 (17 percent). Better educated than their mothers, young white women of the 1930s flocked to the expanding clerical sector. African American women found themselves forced out of the labor force even as white women found jobs or sought them, and the unemployment rates of black women—always higher than among white women—rose to new levels.

The Depression also accelerated the movement of the occupational structure away from agriculture and household service, a development that hit African Americans especially hard. As agricultural employment declined sharply during the thirties, women moved into all other sectors of the economy. While black women shared in this occupational transition, they turned primarily to domestic work as farm jobs declined. Structural changes during the Depression expanded clerical and other occupations that generally paid better than farmwork, but African American women, blocked from a fair share of these new job sectors, found their concentration in menial labor increasing while it decreased among whites. By 1940, nearly 70 percent of African American working women sought or held jobs as servants, charwomen, and the like.

For a select few African American women, those who held high school diplo-

TABLE 4.1
Black and White Women (Employed or Seeking Work) by Occupation, 1930 and 1940

	BLACK		WHITE	
	1930	1940	1930	1940
Professions	63,027	69,469	1,459,738	1,448,571
Sales and clerical workers	25,430	24,616	3,192,340	3,355,001
Manufacturing and mechanical				
pursuits	101,070	137,772	1,765,568	2,325,051
Service	1,152,560	1,196,501	2,006,065	2,327,796
Agriculture	495,284	256,695	393,650	228,778
All other	3,271	35,741	194	642,669
Total	1,840,642	1,720,794	8,817,564	10,327,866

SOURCES: *U.S. Bureau of the Census,* U.S. Census of Population, 1930: The Labor Force, General Report *(Washington D.C.: GPO, 1933), table 2; U.S. Bureau of the Census,* U.S. Census of Population, 1940: The Labor Force *(Washington, D.C.: GPO, 1943), table 62.*

mas or postsecondary certificates or degrees, the Depression brought significant occupational advancement. More black women filled positions as clerical workers, trained nurses, and teachers in 1940 than in 1930, but the numbers remained minuscule compared with those of whites (see table 4.1). While these attainments signified important upward mobility for those who achieved them, racial discrimination continued to lock the vast majority of African American women in the least remunerative jobs or out of work altogether. The intensification of black women's occupational segregation contributed heavily to their high unemployment and declining participation in the labor force; furthermore, the disproportional poverty of African Americans and other minority groups increased the likelihood of their remaining captives of local labor markets.

The disadvantaged position of immigrant as well as nonwhite women shows clearly in the changes in female work patterns that took place between the turn of the century and World War II. Native-born white women, partly as a consequence of the curtailment of immigration, made strides in the labor market, while other women lost out. In 1900, 15 percent of native-born white women worked; in 1940, near the end of the Great Depression, their participation had risen to 24 percent. In contrast, the labor force participation of immigrant whites declined slightly from 19 percent to 17 percent, while black female work rates dropped sharply from 41 percent in 1900 to 33.5 percent in 1940.[24]

THE DECLINE OF CHILD LABOR

In addition to driving African Americans from the workforce, the Depression accelerated the exit of children from industrial labor. The trend toward longer schooling and decreasing employment of children, well established by the end of World War I and reinforced by child labor legislation of the 1920s, reached deeper into the youthful population of the 1930s. Despite weak and sporadic enforcement of child labor laws, a number of developments during the Depression encouraged employers to abandon child labor and move toward a workforce of individuals sixteen years of age and older. The declining agricultural sector employed fewer children as well as fewer women. In 1930 African American children led the ranks of youthful workers, with 20.3 percent of black boys and 12.0 percent of black girls ten through fifteen years of age working, but these ranks dwindled as part of the overall contraction of child labor. These workers resided almost exclusively in the South, where a market of agricultural workers remained, although it had contracted through earlier decades.[25] Nationally, the expansion of clerical and sales work relative to agriculture and manufacturing narrowed job opportunities for youthful workers of all races.

The Depression effectively terminated child labor because of public demands to protect jobs for adults. The National Youth Administration created programs to employ youthful girls and boys, but certification for these jobs required evidence that a family included neither an able-bodied adult male head or a self-supporting female head. NYA jobs for girls brought little compensation and centered on arts and crafts projects that did not compete with work programs for adult women.

The Fair Labor Standards Act of 1937 included a minimum wage that removed the major incentive to hire youngsters. Older teenage workers also lost jobs as compulsory school attendance policies broadened and the FLSA took effect. Between 1900 and 1940 the reported work rates of youths of the ages sixteen through nineteen years fell from 62 percent to 34.7 percent.[26] The decline of child labor reflected social pressures before and during the Depression, but it also reflected earlier and contemporaneous changes in the workplace that disadvantaged younger workers. As manufacturing grew more mechanized and the pace of work increased in industrial settings, child labor could not perform the requisite tasks. The most rapidly growing employment areas for women required social maturity or specific educational qualifications beyond elementary school. Merchandisers perceived very young workers as ill-suited to convince adult shoppers of the good taste or utility of consumer purchases.[27] Not until the youth market exploded with post–World War II prosperity would a teenaged clerk find a role behind the boutique or department store sales counter. Women's places within the sales sector underwent additional changes that required mature workers. Increasingly, women in sales work found jobs as agents rather than clerks—that is, in jobs that required detailed product knowledge and personal poise. Young girls also had little preparation to compete for clerical jobs that demanded specific training in secondary or postsecondary environments. While adolescents could still find jobs as bus girls, stock clerks, and the like, jobs that required education and maturity expanded while juvenile employment opportunities in agriculture and manufacturing contracted.

The Depression intensified pressures to eliminate youthful employment, but restrictions on child labor also mirrored changes in familial values that had developed since the turn of the century. Middle-class critics of child labor argued that industrial work stunted children's health and growth. Labor unions asserted that child labor undercut the male living wage. Children earned less by far than adult family members, and the sum total of children's earnings within the family declined as fertility fell. Parents in all social classes watched educational thresholds for employment rise to the point that failure to complete secondary school severely handicapped children; parents who themselves felt that they had suffered from educational deficiencies often determined to avoid the same fate for their children. For example, Ruby Haynes and her husband sustained a family of five through the Depression on two hundred dollars of annual cash income and the produce and livestock of their small Georgia farm. Their son repeatedly asked to leave school to get a job in town and help the family. Ruby, adamant, threatened and cajoled until he relented because she believed her own failure to complete grammar school had damaged her ability to provide for her family.[28]

SECTORAL ECONOMIC CHANGE AND WOMEN'S EDUCATION

The decline of child labor and a growing commitment to education also reflected significant changes in the kinds of work that employers demanded. During the Depression the white-collar sector, an area in which the uneducated and the very young could not compete, continued to expand as the service needs of the economy grew despite hard times. Employment in clerical work, increasingly dominated by women, rose faster than any other occupational category within the white-collar sector (see table 4.2). The growth of female employment in clerical work and in the professions had begun to reshape girls' schooling in earlier decades, but the trend toward preparation for white-collar work intensified in the 1930s.

Employers acted on their ethnic and racial prejudices and overwhelmingly hired native-born white women for white-collar positions. Partly because of the virtual elimination of immigration in the 1930s, white newcomers presented few challenges to employers' hiring practices during the Depression, and bans against hiring blacks in white businesses remained intact. Although census data suggest that white women lost professional jobs in the 1930s, the aggregate figures create a false impression. While women did leave entertainment and the arts during the Depression, they advanced in medicine, teaching, and social work. Regardless of race, women held more jobs in teaching, nursing, and social work at the end of the 1930s than at the outset because laws and habits of segregation protected African American teachers and nurses from white competition. Thus for both African American and white women, investments in secondary and postsecondary schooling paid off through the Depression.

Although many elderly Americans recall that hard times interfered with their schooling in the 1930s, male and female education actually advanced during the Depression. The near elimination of child labor during the 1930s removed a major obstacle to youths' school completion, and accordingly school retention improved and higher education expanded. Total high school completion rates increased from 30 percent in 1930 to 63 percent at the end of the 1950s, and girls continued to be more likely to finish high school than boys.[29] The disparity be-

TABLE 4.2

Occupational Distribution (in Percentages) of Working Women Ages
Fourteen Years and Older, 1900–1989

1900	1910	1920	1930	1940	1950	1960	1970	1980	1989*
Professional, technical, and kindred workers									
8.2	9.6	11.7	13.8	12.8	12.2	12.5	15.2	13.6	18.1
Managers, officials, and proprietors									
1.4	2.0	2.2	.7	3.3	4.3	.6	3.5	7.2	11.5
Clerical and kindred workers									
4.0	9.2	18.7	20.9	21.5	27.4	29.1	34.2	33.6	27.0
Sales workers									
4.3	5.1	6.3	6.8	7.4	8.6	7.8	7.3	11.3	13.1
Craftsmen, foremen, and kindred workers									
1.4	1.4	1.2	1.0	1.1	.5	1.2	1.8	2.4	2.2
Operatives and kindred workers									
23.8	22.9	20.2	17.4	19.5	20.0	16.2	14.9	10.1	8.8
Laborers									
2.6	1.4	2.3	1.5	1.1	0.9	0.6	1.0	2.0	.5
Private household workers									
28.7	24.0	15.7	17.8	18.1	8.9	7.9	3.8	1.3	1.6
Service workers (not household)									
6.7	8.4	8.1	9.7	11.3	12.6	13.5	16.5	17.8	16.1
Farmers and farm managers									
5.8	3.7	3.2	.4	1.2	0.7	0.5	0.2	0.3	0.4
Farm laborers									
13.1	12.0	10.3	6.0	2.8	2.9	1.2	0.6	0.6	0.7

SOURCES: *U.S. Bureau of the Census,* Historical Statistics of the United States, *Part 1, table D 182–232;* Statistical Abstract of the United States, 1985 *(Washington D.C.: GPO, 1984), table 673; 1991 (Washington, D.C.: GPO, 1991), table 652.*

*1989 figures based on employed persons.

tween the educational achievements of black and white children remained, but African Americans narrowed the gap as their parents continued to encourage their daughters' school achievement despite the Depression. For example, Anna Graves's parents sent her from their home in Seguin, Texas, to live with kin in San Antonio and finish high school because Seguin had no black high school.[30]

Although Depression conditions encouraged young people to remain in school longer, the effects at the postsecondary level differed by gender. Proportionally, women made smaller gains during the Depression, and their achievements at the post–high school level declined relative to men's. Although youths' difficulties finding employment encouraged school attendance during the Depression, the economic contraction also required that families manage their economic resources carefully. In making hard choices for their children, both middle-class and working-class families tended to place the higher education of their sons above that of their daughters. Postsecondary education cost more than high school, and parents generally offered stronger encouragement and support for sons than for daughters to attend college.[31] Women consequently enjoyed smaller gains in undergraduate education and lost ground to men in completing graduate degrees.

African American women had vastly different experiences in higher education from those of white women. Whether public or private, racially segregated African American colleges had less financial backing than white institutions, and few blacks gained entrance to white universities. The first private colleges for African American women trained future teachers and focused on developing a moral perspective and domestic skills. Originally designed to equip graduates to take their proper places at the center of the family circle, these programs persisted through the Depression. Similar trends marked women's training at black coeducational institutions. Opportunities to study higher-level instruction in science, mathematics, and the classics remained much more limited in black institutions such as Spelman College in Atlanta than in white women's colleges. Nonetheless, African American women made sizable educational strides through the 1930s; by 1940 the rate of college completion was higher for black women than for black men.[32]

During the 1930s, both segregated and integrated schools enlarged their home economics curricula. As home economics instruction expanded, it increasingly associated itself with the responsibilities of women as wives and mothers and further distanced itself from women's employment prospects. The 1931 report of the U.S. Department of Education's Home Economics Division pointed to a rising divorce rate during the 1920s and charged that "Home influences responsible for creating . . . a less stable home environment are the recent World War; the changed economic and social status of women; and the 'machine age.'"[33] The report offered home economics instruction as a remedy for the forces destroying family life. Nonetheless, the message that woman's true vocation could be turned to profit in times of adversity never fully disappeared.

Southern schools continued an emphasis on preparing African American girls for dual responsibilities as paid household workers and agents for social uplift within their families. The Alabama State Board of Education published and adopted a Tuskegee home economics program for the instruction of African American girls in their seventh year through the tenth and final year of school. The Tuskegee authors presumed that "Students enrolled in the homemaking classes are seeking to become better homemakers and better wage earners." Home economics teachers not only worked to raise the standard of living in students' families but also to prepare girls for immediate service careers because "Many girls living in small town and urban centers hold jobs in homes and restaurants while they are still in school." Tuskeegee urged teachers to "Talk with each girl personally and get her interested in what she can do to improve her home" but warned against plans that girls could not accomplish because "Most of their homes as well as their modes of living are very simple." The second-year program included the collection of sacks to be sewn into garments. The Tuskegee manual stressed the importance of girls' learning to work well within the family and suggested that joint programs with the agriculture faculty would "help the boys and men to have a better understanding of what is being done in the home and make them feel more willing to share its responsibilities" while agricultural instruction for girls would enhance women's homemaking skills.[34]

The economic setbacks of the 1930s influenced the tone and the activities of the Girl Scouts and brought the movement into closer coincidence with the teaching of home economics. National Girl Scout headquarters spread its training resources by concentrating on correspondence courses for leaders, courses that trained nearly 1,000 women from 1938 through 1939. Programmatically, scouting turned toward activities with practical applications. The Depression left most upper-middle-class families with less disposable income and made expensive activities like boating and aviation unaffordable to most families in the 1930s. In its attempts to meet the needs of a broader spectrum of girls, the Girl Scouts de-emphasized personal ambition and emphasized nonmonetary contributions that girls could make to the welfare of their families and communities. Girl Scout literature of the 1930s featured gardening, food preservation, and handicrafts while continuing its earlier attention to camping skills. Girls Scouts participated in volunteer relief efforts in addition to traditional community service projects such as assisting in hospitals. Girl Scout cookie sales had begun in the 1920s when girls held bake sales of their own products, but the difficulties that scouts encountered in paying their dues during the Depression escalated the cookie campaign. In 1936 the Scouts contracted with a commercial bakery to produce cookies, and sales reached 2,000,000 boxes annually by the end of the decade. The Depression also prompted the Girl Scouts to expand their programs for handicapped girls to include the financially needy.[35]

FAMILY STRATEGIES IN HARD TIMES

As home economists' and Girls Scouts' activities suggest, the Depression refocused many women's attentions on careful home and resource management. After the

African American children routinely attended poorly funded schools. West San Antonio Heights School, ca. 1936. Institute of Texan Cultures. Courtesy Delores Linton

1920s, focusing on homemaking as a uniquely feminine vehicle for raising the U.S. standard of living, home economists reoriented their mission to meet the national emergency. The Depression energized home economists into viewing the economic collapse as a challenge to women to protect their families through recycling clothing and durables and by preparing satisfying low-budget meals.

In an effort to document the successes of college training in home economics, the American Home Economics Association (AHEA) sponsored a study of the family lives and responsibilities of college-educated mothers in two-parent households. First undertaken in 1927, the study continued in 1933 as the AHEA resurveyed its subjects to assess the impact the Depression had on their family lives. It found that despite the high unemployment, mortgage foreclosures, and bank failures of the 1930s, most U.S. families survived the Depression intact and a small proportion effectively did not suffer at all. The AHEA study of upper-income families found a segment of the U.S. population that did not radically alter its lifestyle during the 1930s. This conclusion foreshadowed the Lynds' later observation that upper-middle-class families had a much better chance than working- and lower-middle-class families passing through the 1930s without serious hardship.[36]

Family incomes of this elite group of respondents had fallen decidedly between 1927 and 1933, but a concomitant drop in the cost of basic necessities had mitigated the effects of declining profits and wages. Half of the families had lost between $700 and $1,200 in income while one tenth had gained an equal amount over the six-year interval between the studies. Only 15 of the 331 fathers had been unemployed at any time during these years. Four fifths of the families had annual incomes of more than $1,200 in 1933, and few of the respondents in 1933 found family finances a greater source of distress in 1933 than in 1927. On the contrary, more families owned vacation homes in 1933 than in 1927.

While most mothers claimed that they had fewer economic resources in 1933 than previously, not all agreed that the downturn had hurt their families. Mothers reported that economizing on recreational expenditures had strengthened marital and parent-child relations and that reduced circumstances had improved the family's sense of values. The home economics graduates remained highly active in social, cultural, and civic activities outside the home. The majority of them attended church, participated in parent activities at their children's schools, and took part in social or cultural activities outside their homes. Few of the mothers admitted to having no activities outside the home.

Despite the benefits that women said they had reaped from their education, only half of the mothers interviewed in 1933 had found homemaking a satisfying occupational choice. Fifteen percent of the women held paying jobs and another 30 percent would have preferred employment to full-time homemaking. Between

1927 and 1933, these women's husbands also had grown more supportive of wives' employment. In 1927, 29 percent of fathers declared themselves unwilling to see their wives work under any foreseeable circumstances, but by 1933 the adamantine had fallen to 15 percent.[37]

The growing array of relatively well paying jobs for white women, as well as widespread employment among their husbands, pulled and pushed wives into the labor force despite social censure. Fertility, long declining, pitched downward during the early 1930s, reaching an unprecedented low of 18.4 births per 1,000 women in 1933.[38] Childlessness among married women, especially black women, had increased since the late nineteenth century and crested in the 1930s. Women born from 1905 through 1909 were most likely to remain childless, with 20 percent of married white women and 28.5 percent of married black women never bearing children.[39] Women in this age cohort passed through their prime childbearing years in the 1920s and the 1930s. Economic conditions in the 1930s depressed fertility, but women's work experience and their career aspirations also stimulated fertility control. By the late 1930s the birthrate had begun to climb, but the long-term trend continued downward. Once the World War II baby boom ended, the birthrate dropped again and fell below Depression decade levels in the 1970s.[40]

In the Depression and the years that followed, the U.S. population aged as young people postponed marriage, the birthrate remained low, and life expectancy increased. The Depression discouraged women from establishing independent households, but the incidence of female household headship among whites nevertheless rose during the 1930s, partly because wives generally outlived their husbands and the gap between male and female life spans continued to widen. Although divorce rates fell in the early 1930s as families banded together to cope with bad times, the Depression did not increase the stability of U.S. families. Indeed, toward the end of the Depression, and doubtless because of the stress it had inflicted, divorce rates rose and further increased the number of women heading households.

Declining fertility and the low earnings of children offered additional incentives for families to yield to public pressures to end child labor. Smaller family size also meant that mothers' child care obligations contracted temporally, easing the movement of mothers into market labor. While child care responsibilities proved less an impediment to wage earning among African American than white women, the high level of childlessness among both racial groups also helped married women commit to employment in the 1930s.

The Depression intensified the importance of the family as an economic unit. Like the anonymous twenty-year-old who turned to a newspaper columnist for advice, many adult children searching for their first jobs felt the urgency of the

search compounded by the pressures of family need. A 1939 study
Cleveland, Ohio, revealed that 97 percent of working sons and 98 pe
ing daughters paid some of their families' expenses.[41] Hard times oft
family unity but in the process increased stress among husbands a
among grown children unable to strike out on their own. Despite the incentive to
pool their resources, the stresses of family life, complicated by unemployment,
ultimately drove thousands of married couples apart, often as soon as recovery
made divorce affordable. Thus while the Depression reduced divorce in the short
term, encouraging families to band together to survive hard times, subsequent
events showed that couples who married under the uncertain economic conditions of the 1930s faced elevated risks that their marriages would end in divorce.[42]

Some couples ultimately divorced because one or both partners could not adapt
to changes that the Depression forced in family structure. The stress of coping
with wage reductions, male unemployment, or the loss of a wife's job forced married couples to interact with each other in unprecedented ways. Sociologist Glen
Elder found that children growing up during the Depression saw their mothers
emerge as stronger figures within the household, as fathers' fortunes declined even
though the children continued to acknowledge their fathers as household heads.[43]
The Lynds found that husbands of the 1930s accepted wives' employment as a
mandatory concession in the face of economic hardship, rather than a choice made
by the wife or the couple.[44] Overall, then, the Depression accelerated rather than
retarded changes in family structure and in the family economy, as wives and
mothers replaced sons and daughters as family earners.

Working-class families embodied a broad spectrum of familial values and often had a ferocious struggle to survive the Depression. Increased marital stress
related to reduced earnings and unemployment besieged virtually all working-
class families in the Depression, but families at the bottom of the ladder in the
1920s entered the Depression with fewer resources. Already living on the edge in
the 1920s, the 1930s exacerbated the problems of the poor, as the health statistics
of the 1920s and the 1930s show all too plainly.[45] Death rates from pellagra, scurvy,
tuberculosis, and gastrointestinal diseases and parasites stalked the poor and particularly ravaged blacks, southern whites, and Mexicans or Mexican Americans
in the 1920s.

High fertility and high infant mortality marked family life among working-
class Mexican Americans, and high adult mortality produced disproportionate
numbers of Mexican American orphans. Mexican American families faced the
added stress of "repatriation" during the Depression, as thousands of persons of
Mexican heritage, including many born in the United States, "voluntarily" returned to Mexico at the expense of the public or unidentified "benefactors." The

epeated use of deportation threats to silence labor protests of Mexican American men and women during the 1930s underscores the "voluntary" nature of repatriation.[46]

African American and Mexican American families faced discrimination in receiving public assistance as white relief agents rationalized that black and brown Americans deserved less than "Anglos" and had in any case learned to live on less than other Americans. Because of the unique burdens of poverty among African Americans and Mexican Americans in the Depression, wives and mothers in these families faced handicaps not generally shared by majority women.

Overall by 1930, U.S. families depended less upon children's wages than they had in 1900, but the transition to a family economy of adult workers only had barely begun among minority families. Opportunities for young blacks and Mexican Americans to help support their families contracted mightily during the Depression, while adult minority women failed to benefit from the expansion in the service sector that rewarded Anglo women, married or single. The white farmwife whose family lost its farm in the Depression might take on an office or a waitress job in a nearby town in the South, the Midwest, or the West in the 1930s, but the black wife whose family lost its rural home had less chance of finding a town job in the 1930s than she would have had in the 1920s. Mexican American wives from migrant families or families in the *barrios* of Chicago, San Antonio, or Los Angeles similarly saw their employment options disappear along with those of their husbands and children.

Families of all ethnic backgrounds frequently turned to relatives for assistance during the Depression, but African American and Mexican American families especially relied on kin networks. San Antonio resident Beatrice Clay has described a pattern of neighborhood and family cooperation that helped her family and other African Americans survive the Depression in the Alamo City. Relatives moved in with each other to economize on housing; neighbors shared commodities as some had greater access to one product or another. Clay held a job in a department store where she could purchase clothing cheaply at season's end. She helped clothe her neighbors as well as her family; others in turn assisted her with food and friendship.[47] Such strategies helped families of all kinds survive, all across the United States.

Public and private assistance improved the lot of minority Americans during the 1930s, even though the majority population enjoyed greater benefits. The health of minority families improved as the Depression focused the nation's attention on the needs of the poor, needs largely ignored in the 1920s. The New Deal brought decent housing to some African Americans and Mexican Americans through the WPA and other agencies, even though Anglos enjoyed larger benefits from the federal government. The same result obtained from other federal job programs for men, women, and young people. Public and private medical clinics opened during the Depression and, along with public and private food assistance, these programs ameliorated the suffering of the nation's minority and majority populations. Between 1929 and 1940 public funding and private charitable funding of health care increased from $712 million to $938 million.[48]

Improvements in diet and in medical care allowed the average life span of Americans to continue to rise during the 1930s as it had through the first decades of the century, but whites continued to live longer than nonwhites, and during the Depression the mortality rate of whites declined three times as much as that of nonwhites. As life expectancy rose, not only did women outlive men, but the average number of years by which they outlived men increased, and the trend persisted after the 1930s. White women alive in 1930 had a life expectancy of 63.5 years, 3.8 years longer than white men. By 1960 white women's life expectancy had risen to 74.1 years with a probability of living 6.7 years longer than white men. Among nonwhites, life expectancy remained consistently lower, 49.2 years for women in 1930 and 66.3 years in 1960. The differences between the sexes for nonwhites was 1.9 years in 1930 and 5.2 years in 1960.[49] For all married women, then, the number of years by which they survived their first husband tended to increase, but women were widowed increasingly later in life as the life spans of people in the United States grew longer. Racial differences in mortality persisted, however, and nonwhite women continued to assume responsibilities of household headship at younger ages than white wives by virtue of the shorter life expectancies of black than of white men.

CONCLUSION

Among all but the wealthiest people in the United States, the 1930s marked an especially important turning point in family history as economic conditions depressed male employment, drove children from the labor force, and broadened the responsibilities of women of all races. The Great Depression reinforced the trend toward smaller families and further eroded the weary institution of patriarchy in the United States. The lengthening of the life span and the widening disparity between male and female life expectancy also recast women's economic needs.

By the end of the 1930s, Hitler's war in Europe had stimulated a modest economic recovery in the United States, and the country's entrance into the war after Pearl Harbor would soon summon its women to full participation in the labor force. Despite the apparent discontinuity between economic depression and the war emergency, the 1930s had well prepared the U.S. workforce to staff the wartime economy. Wives, whom labor analysts regarded as the principal reserve army of U.S. workers, had gradually increased their employment rates during the 1930s. The decline in fertility during the Depression freed more women to pursue market labor without assuming the double burden of employment and child care. Women honed their home management skills during the trying times of the Depression, and these abilities served them well in coping with wartime shortages. The long-term trend toward the empowerment of women within the family and in the public sphere helped military wives and other women function as household heads. Because of the increase in school completion during the Depression, the nation went to war with a better-educated workforce than it had during the 1920s. Women had not only broadened their schooling, but also increasingly learned to expect paid labor to hold a central place in their adult lives.

Manufacturers had largely eliminated their reliance on children who would have ill suited security-bound, fast-paced, and highly mechanized war industries. Wartime demands recalled minority as well as majority women to employment, but long-term patterns of ethnic and racial discrimination did not give way to full and equal treatment of African Americans, Hispanics, or other minorities. The war carried new challenges and opportunities for women, introducing many to novel occupations and unprecedented high wage levels. The structural transformation of the economy that had proceeded despite the Depression continued through the war, enlarging white-collar work and moving the nation further down the path toward full-time, long-term employment for most adult women.

CHAPTER FIVE

Women Answer
the War Call

THE 1940S

T he Second World War called women to new tasks and challenges at home
and in the labor force as they replaced military husbands and brothers in
the civilian economy and accepted supportive roles in the armed forces; for
many it proved the most profound experience of their lives. In historical perspective, World War II emerges as a conflict over empires—building, preserving, con-
quering, or destroying them—and a war about genocide. For most Americans,
however—especially those who did not actually fight in it—the war served as a
clumsy, traumatic, but crushingly effective economic mechanism that ended the
misery and uncertainty of the Great Depression. By July of 1945, the size of the
overwhelmingly male armed forces had reached 12.3 million persons, individuals
who otherwise might have staffed the nation's offices, factories, and farms. World
War II mobilized more women, especially married women, than had ever previously worked for wages and kept them at defense-related jobs for a longer period
of time than had World War I.

The United States met wartime demands by tapping new labor markets and
achieving higher productivity through managerial and technological innovations.
Both the reach for a broader labor pool and the structural changes in production
rewarded women's talents and efforts. Experienced female production workers in
industry and agriculture had their choice of jobs, and the white-collar labor force
grew more rapidly than it had during the Depression. Women's wages reached
unprecedented levels, although the gender gap in pay persisted. Some of women's
wartime employment advances proved temporary, but the war so profoundly altered labor demands and women's expectations that women entered the workforce
in even greater numbers after the war.

In the early 1940s the female labor force grew by 6.5 million women, a gain of more than 46 percent, but 4.6 million of these women had left the labor market by February of 1946. Although employment of married women increased dramatically during the war and in the Cold War era that soon followed, the rise in married women's work rates was part of a trend stretching back to the turn of the century. The war years marked an important stage in that trend, however, as working wives outnumbered single working women for the first time in 1944. Although war-end firings briefly reversed the phenomenon, married women again led the ranks of female workers in 1947, and they maintained their lead in the decades to come.[1]

Faced with the crisis of a global war, the U.S. public's opposition to the employment of married women swiftly reversed itself, approving, even applauding behavior that it had condemned only weeks before. The federal government, which had used traditional "family values" as a framework for New Deal legislation, pivoted equally nimbly. The War Manpower Commission proclaimed that: "Barriers against the employment of women with young children should not be set up by employers. The decision as to gainful employment should in all cases be an individual decision made by the woman herself in light of the particular conditions prevailing in her home."[2]

WOMEN ANSWER THE CALL

World War II redirected and accelerated occupational changes among women in addition to increasing their labor force participation. Although more protracted and more costly than United States participation in World War I, the Second World War carried similar consequences for women. During both wars female work rates increased as new occupations in manufacturing and public service opened to women and as agriculture called them to the fields. The Women's Land Army, organized by the Department of Agriculture in April, 1943, recruited three quarters of a million nonfarm women into food production in 1944.[3] The incentive to switch from almost any "woman's job" (including some "professional" positions) into manufacturing proved irresistible to millions of women who gladly traded low-paying jobs in restaurants or laundries for production work that doubled their income.[4]

Wives at work in 1941 were the most likely to remain at work through 1944, though they often shifted to better-paid jobs, but millions of housewives who had never earned wages leapt at the chance to add welding or machine tooling to their responsibilities as homemakers. For example, Gene Dickson recalled: "On December 7 last I gave my house a fine cleaning, washed up the dinner dishes and went to work in an airplane factory, night shift, along with thousands of other housewives like myself."[5]

Although most mothers of young children remained at home through the war, enough of them followed the siren song of wages to make day care a continuous concern for working mothers during the war. Despite the need for child care, employer-funded and government-sponsored day care centers failed to fill to capacity.[6] Mothers, often regarding the centers as dumping grounds for the poor, preferred to engage relatives or sitters for child care.[7] With their own wages, often supplemented by husbands' incomes, they could afford to hire the help.[8] Defense workers' demand for help at home tripled the average yearly earnings of domestic workers from $540 to $1,411, while teachers' wages rose only 31 percent, and manufacturing pay 75 percent.

Lurline Bates, for one, heeded the call of patriotism and economic opportunity. Bates, a Spartanburg, South Carolina, schoolteacher and mother of grown children, left teaching to work in a textile mill early in the war. Although women had traditionally provided the bulk of the textile workforce, the shortage of men allowed women to move up in the industry. Bates accepted mill employment partly because she believed that her contribution to clothing the troops supported her soldier son, but she found the job itself more satisfying than teaching school. During her training as a winder fixer, a position previously restricted to men, she earned more than she had as a teacher with twenty years of experience.[9]

Civilian employment constituted most working women's contributions to the war effort, but women also performed significant service in the armed services in a variety of support capacities (although none performed combat duty). Nurses, pilots, and others risked death or capture despite their noncombatant status. Eighty-three female officers became prisoners of war, all but a few of whom spent thirty-seven months in Japanese prison camps in the Philippines.[10] Women enlisted in all branches of the military, with the largest number in the Women's Army Corps (WAC). The only exception to total gender segregation in the services was the acceptance of a small number of female physicians in the medical service of the army and navy. Because the military refused to accept female pilots, who performed critical roles ferrying planes within the United States and abroad, the War Department formed the Women's Auxiliary Ferrying Squadron (WAFS) and the Women Airforce Service Pilots (WASP) as civilian units. While women worked as cooks, mechanics, and clerks, the largest single occupation was nursing, with nearly one third of all employed trained nurses being military employees.[11]

Women also served at home and abroad as United Services Organization (USO) and Red Cross officers. Anne McCaughey served as Red Cross attaché to the army's 50th General Hospital. Along with medical personnel, McCaughey landed on Utah Beach on July 16, 1944. The tent hospital to which she was attached lay a half mile from a bridge under German attack and only five miles from the front lines.

World War II created upward mobility for women in industries, such as textiles, in which women had long constituted a majority of workers. Mrs. V. Scott Rogers, Pepperell Manufacturing Co., 1944. Robert Yarnall Richie photograph, courtesy National Archives

McCaughey confided her anxieties in the pages of her diary: "And what does one think about as one lies in one's small army cot in one's cozy sleeping bag during bombing and strafing and anti-aircraft fire? One says, 'Dear God, let this one pass over' and one falls asleep again very quickly."[12] Although segregated by race as well as gender, African American women also entered the military as support staff during the war. The navy refused black women until 1944, but the army accepted as soon as the Women's Auxiliary Army Corps legislation passed. Within the army black women suffered occupational discrimination. Commanding officers initially assigned them overwhelmingly to kitchen or laundry work, and they never achieved equal representation with white women in military office jobs.[13]

Among women outside as well as inside military service, World War II stimulated female migration. Some women followed husbands or sweethearts who moved to military bases or civilian jobs. Many more, identifying new options in distant places, independently answered the labor call of expanding industries. For example, Rhoda Pratt Hanson and her young children moved from the West Coast to New York City shortly after her husband left for the war. Hanson hoped to find work there as a writer, and she quickly worked up from free-lance writing to a full-time position.

Millions of U.S. women like Hanson relocated during the war. They faced severe housing shortages in all labor centers. As the population of some towns and cities multiplied, women found lodging in rooming houses, the YWCA, hotels, and hastily converted garages and warehouses.[14] The population of Mobile, Alabama, for example, doubled in the early 1940s as migrants arrived from the rural South following news of defense contracts awarded to the Gulf city employers.[15] In Mobile, as elsewhere in the South, whites constituted most of the new arrivals; black southerners knew they would do better elsewhere. In the San Francisco Bay area recent migrants made up the vast majority of new female workers who swelled the wartime workforce, and African Americans figured prominently among them.[16]

Just as the war encouraged women to move to distant towns and cities, the emergency temporarily discouraged educational achievement as women responded to the needs of the wartime economy. Intense demand for workers in all fields encouraged women as well as men to forego schooling in favor of immediate if temporary employment. Temporarily reversing the twentieth century trend, male secondary school completion declined as youths left school for defense jobs or for the military, and, at the height of the war, fewer girls graduated as well. Girls as well as boys found jobs without completing their secondary education. Many rural high schools had only eleven grades; youths graduated from these schools at sixteen or seventeen and went directly into the labor force.

The war also had a dramatic effect on college enrollment by both men and women. In 1940, 77,000 women and 110,000 men completed undergraduate degrees, but by 1944 the number of female graduates had fallen to 70,000, and the number of male graduates had plummeted to 56,000.[17] By 1947 males had returned to prewar patterns, but women did not regain their prewar attendance rate until 1956.[18] The ravenous appetite of the wartime labor market forced employers to suspend the minimal educational requirements of some occupations. Women found jobs for which they would not have qualified in the 1930s, and consequently some chose immediate employment over higher education. El Marie Nelson, for instance, graduated from Central High School in Monette, Arkansas, in 1941. In 1943, after three tries, she managed to pass a teacher certification examination for a temporary certificate that let her teach the first three grades of elementary school. She began teaching at age eighteen in the same district in which she had been a pupil.[19] Her lack of college training, however, prevented her permanent certification, and she left teaching at twenty, shortly after marrying.

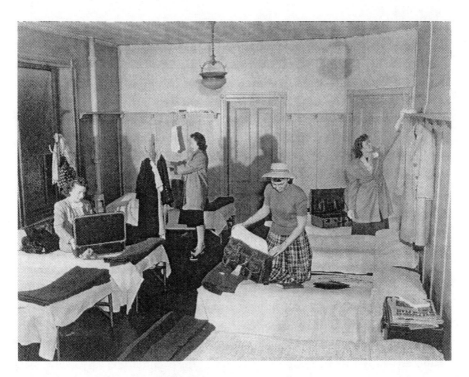

Women's organizations like the YWCA offered temporary housing to women who had come to the city to work during the wartime job boom, but most of these facilities reserved space for whites only. Emergency Dormitory at Berkely Street Residence, Boston YWCA, ca. 1942. Courtesy Schlesinger Library

CROSSING GENDER BOUNDARIES, CHALLENGING RACIAL DIVIDES

The war fractured traditional gender barriers not only in war industries, but also in pursuits that served the public's needs. Women made a thrilling if temporary entry into professional baseball. The General Electric Company sponsored radio broadcasts by an "all girl" orchestra. Rose Kaminski trained as a crane operator at a Wisconsin ordnance plant after finding a neighbor to care for her young daughter.[20] Although she had no idea what the job required, Kaminski chose crane operation because her father had done it. She found the work daunting at first, but she persevered. Within days she had learned enough to operate on her own and worked until terminated in favor of a returning veteran, whereupon she returned temporarily to the home.

World War II stimulated black as well as other women to return to the labor market as the discouraging conditions of the Depression receded. Although black women joined the female labor force at the same rate as whites, unemployment among African American women remained higher as racial discrimination persisted. Moreover, black women frequently found skilled production jobs closed to them, so that while World War II did prove a significant opportunity for African American women, much of this happened because white women vacated service jobs for better-paying work. Some African American women did find new positions in federal employment, in nursing, and in teaching. White women dominated the best industrial jobs, but black women won some wartime production jobs, and small numbers of them desegregated industrial workplaces.

The San Francisco economy proved a microcosm of this process. In San Francisco as elsewhere, discrimination had driven black women from the labor force as job competition crested in the 1930s, but the labor shortage of the 1940s weakened employers' abilities to discriminate against racial or ethnic minorities. Blocked from high-paid production jobs in the Bay Area shipyards until 1944, black women had nevertheless found production jobs in lower-paying industries such as food canning, jobs previously not open to them.[21]

Camping skills gained a civil defense connotation in wartime. San Antonio Scouts roasting hot dogs "to develop self-reliance in the event of a bombing," June 18, 1942. Courtesy Institute of Texan Cultures, the San Antonio Light *Collection*

Whether from patriotism or the incentive of high wages, white women sometimes accepted jobs in shops employing racial minorities, something they had rarely done during the Depression. Even in the North and West, however, defense contractors mostly retained segregation and embedded racial stereotyping in their allocation of tasks. San Francisco area shipyards employed black women largely in outdoor work, while they selected Chinese American women for indoor electrical work involving a myriad of small parts.[22] With the experience of their ethnic group in garment sweat shops, Chinese Americans appeared to their employers to be especially suited to the close work in electrical assembling, while some black trainees never found jobs in the crafts for which they had trained.

Both the nature of economic growth in the South during the war and the enduring rigidity of racial segregation dictated that whites of the region would benefit much more from the war boom than would blacks who remained there. In the North and the West some black women eventually joined Hispanic and Anglo workers on assembly lines, but the South proved intractable throughout the war. African American women who stayed in the South frequently had to settle for moving from household labor into similar service jobs in commercial establishments or government, while white women moved into higher-paying production jobs. A few black women, like Anna Graves, found white-collar jobs within federal agencies.[23] Graves broke the race barrier at San Antonio's Kelly Air Force Base when she was hired as the first African American civilian clerical worker. Graves welcomed the job opportunity, but fellow employees shunned her and made her work life lonely at best. In Greenville, Mississippi, black women took jobs previously held by men at the local wood veneer plant.[24] Although the South generally enjoyed stronger economic growth than the North in the 1940s, the unyielding barriers that southern blacks faced channeled them from the southern countryside into northern cities.

North Carolina, for example, entered World War II with an economy heavily based in agriculture, textiles, and furniture manufacturing. The war brought investments in shipbuilding and munitions, temporary gains at best. The establishment or expansion of military bases in North Carolina and the rest of the South proved a longer-range investment than defense manufacturing, but the war also increased investments in such traditional North Carolina industries as textiles and agriculture. All these investments benefited people who had held property at the end of the Depression, among whom whites predominated overwhelmingly. Investments in industry and agriculture boosted property values and promoted equipment purchases that replaced hand labor. The war increased cigarette consumption, and tobacco output, the state's leading agricultural activity, tripled. Cotton production, which had lagged far behind tobacco, increased five-fold. Other agricultural commodities quadrupled in output. The growth meant boom time for land-owners, but it squeezed tenant farmers between rising production costs and declining labor needs as mechanization advanced. Between 1940 and 1949 the average value of an acre of farmland increased from $138 to $341, further narrowing the prospects for tenants to become landowners. Tenants consequently left agriculture for urban jobs; many blacks sought work in the North, and their families often followed, their departure encouraged by a continuing decline in the North Carolina market for household workers during and after the war.

Meanwhile, white women in the Tar Heel state gained supervisory and craft positions during the war, and some managed to hold onto them after it. More women held production jobs in furniture, textiles, and garment manufacturing in 1950 than they had in 1940; other women continued to enjoy the benefits of a growing market for clerical workers after the war. Altogether, the number of white women holding jobs in North Carolina increased 50 percent during the 1940s, while African American women held only 6 percent more. In Georgia, race distinctions proved even stronger than in North Carolina. African American women in Georgia actually lost jobs during the 1940s, while white female employment rose by 55 percent, twice the rate of male job growth. The evolving female labor market in the wartime South had thus continued to disadvantage black women and to encourage their exodus from the state.

While racial discrimination persisted nationwide, black women nevertheless made substantial advances outside the South, paving the way for greater progress in decades to come by cracking during the war racial barriers that were not fully restored in peacetime. For example, while the war generally decreased school completion, the shortage of male teachers and heightened demand for medical care opened unprecedented opportunities for black women to train for and work in teaching and nursing. Outside the South, schools and hospitals accomplished a modest amount of racial integration in staffing.[25]

WOMEN AND ORGANIZED LABOR IN WARTIME

Regardless of race, the war also increased women's participation in the labor movement; from 1939 through 1943 women increased their membership in organized labor from 800,000 to more than 3,000,000.[26] Many women, like Bette Murphy, first encountered unions through their war-related employments. Before World War II, Bette Murphy had pursued traditionally female occupations, which had not exposed her to organized labor: first supporting herself and her child as a waitress, then as a nursemaid and single parent. Miserable as a live-in domestic, Murphy took a job in the aircraft industry when the wartime recruitment of women began. Of her life as a young mother Murphy recalled, "I didn't really want to work. I wanted to raise my child."[27] Having accepted the inevitability (not the desirability) of working, she decided to make as much money as possible.

At Douglas aircraft, although the company suggested that she work in the dispensary, Murphy asked to be a riveter. She found riveting demanding and exhausting work, but regular raises and promotions convinced her she had made the right choice. As Murphy realized that other employers provided overtime pay and benefits that Douglas did not, and as she recognized the power that male supervisors exercised over young women at Douglas, Murphy began to work secretly for unionization of the plant, arguing that a union would protect female workers and win better compensation for all. Bette Murphy was one of the fortunate few female workers who held on to jobs in heavy industry after World War II. As a union member and as an elected union representative, Murphy fought during the 1940s and early 1950s for benefits such as day care.

Historian Sherna Gluck has chronicled Bette Murphy's story in *Rosie the Riveter;* other chapters in her collection of Los Angeles–area war workers' life stories show that among these women orientations to the labor movement varied. In contrast to Murphy and her allies, who felt that women had to band together and fight their own battles, other defense workers had no interest in unions or resented the union shop where it existed. Mern Freige "didn't like the union, didn't want to spend money on it," "didn't join." Also in contrast with Murphy, Freige stated, "I'd rather work with a man being a leadman. . . . I never like to work under a woman."[28] Addie Srangeland, like Murphy, didn't want to work but had to support her family after her divorce in 1938. Although she also needed to maximize her income, Srangeland opposed the unionization of Douglas. She worked through a strike at the plant and did not join the union until she was forced to. Although both Srangeland and Murphy might theoretically have benefited equally from participation in a labor union, Srangeland's family situation discouraged her support of the union, while Murphy's encouraged it. Murphy's father took care of her daughter, but Srangeland had no family assistance with her children; when she accepted work in the defense industry in 1942, Srangeland had to put her children in an orphanage. One year later she brought them home, but she had to leave them alone while she worked the graveyard shift. Constantly worried about her children, she had neither the time nor the emotional energy for extensive activities outside of work.[29] Moreover, Srangeland had also concluded that the union did not really work on behalf of women; she believed that at least one shop steward had opposed raises for women.

In fact, men's wages did remain higher than women's during the war, partly because organized labor worked to protect male workers from female competition, but largely because industry observed discriminatory pay standards. Male labor leaders claimed that hiring women for positions formerly filled by men would lower the wage scale and eventually drive men out of their civilian jobs. Where wartime exigencies demanded that women fill "men's jobs," organized labor argued for equal wages so that women would not undercut men in the labor market. As sociologist Ruth Milkman has shown, the United Electrical Workers (UE) got Westinghouse and General Electric to agree not to employ women if men could be found to fill defense jobs. When they could not, Westinghouse agreed to pay women the same wage as male co-workers.[30] Despite such promises, both Westinghouse and GE paid different rates to women and men for similar tasks, leading the War Labor Board to cite the two for sex discrimination in 1945.[31]

WOMEN'S WORK AND WOMEN'S ROLES: WARTIME EXPERIENCES AND POSTWAR DESTINY

Even though the war failed to narrow the gender gap in wages and many working women looked forward to full-time homemaking at war's end, women's war work changed the occupational structure permanently, and it changed women's assessment of their own abilities. Women's Bureau Director Mary Anderson summarized the impact of wartime occupational mobility, observing that most women, single or married, worked from necessity and that wartime opportunities had redefined women's individual expectations:

> Charlotte Currier finds work as a flame cutter in a Maine shipyard much harder than her prewar job in a shoe factory, but the better pay has given her a real boost in caring for her invalid mother. Mrs. Olsoni, a garment worker in New York City, happily married to a bricklayer, has always needed a job—what with so much unemployment in the building trades. Sixty-year-old Mrs. Scoville has worked in a South Carolina textile mill since she was 16 and expects to go on until she's 65. After five years of unemployment Mary Simmons at 50 is very happy as a tool-room attendant in an Illinois shop and prays she'll not lose out again. Margaret Murphy, a 39-year-old widow with a boy in the service, likes her job as a railroad ticket-seller much more than her old occupation as a cafeteria cashier.[32]

Despite the marriage bar against women in the military, civilian labor demands redirected propaganda about the places of wives and mothers in the economy. The outbreak of World War II tempered criticism of wifely employment. Indeed, what the press had lately condemned as dangerous to the health of marriage and children it now trumpeted as "patriotic duty."[33] During the early years of World War II, the War Manpower Commission urged women to do their patriotic duty and support their brothers, husbands, and sweethearts by working in defense industries. The popular press, from *Life* magazine to the *New York Times* glamorized Rosie the Riveter.[34] As demand for female workers surged in the early forties, new voices encouraged mothers to punch the time clock in offices and factories. The stark contrast between the propaganda of a nation at war and that of a nation at peace helped to create the perception that the late forties and the fifties constituted a unique era of domesticity.[35] As William Chafe and Eleanor Straub have pointed out, however, the working mother of World War II garnered disapproval as well as praise. The U.S. Children's Bureau, prominent American women, some women's magazines, and the religious press all warned of the perils facing the nation's children as their mothers went off to work.[36] Despite appeals for female workers, Hollywood films and popular magazines repeatedly stressed the centrality of domesticity in women's lives and the responsibility of wives to build their activities around the emotional needs of their husbands.[37]

Wartime romanticization of women's future roles as homemaking consumers encouraged patience in the face of wartime separations and shortages and helped build markets for postwar products. Advertisements and articles praising female productivity in defense industries also emphasized that women would soon return home after the war and that defense industries would quickly return to manufacturing the consumer products that women wanted. Women's magazines stressed that peace would bring a cornucopia of products for civilian consumption and that wartime technological research would result in new and better homes, appliances, and furnishings. A 1943 advertisement in *Woman's Home Companion* praised the Kalamazoo Stove and Furnace Company, which operated "three great plants producing for war" but had continued developing "new stoves and furnaces of striking modern design" for the homes of tomorrow.[38]

As expectations of peace rose in 1944, women's magazines and prominent Americans, including Eleanor Roosevelt and Margaret Mead, reminded the nation that women really wanted to settle down at home to look after their families.[39] Hardly a blissful stay-a-home mom herself, Mead assured traditionalists that "far from wanting to get out of the home, during the years when they are needed in it, more women want, if possible, to devote themselves to their homes and their children."[40] *Ladies' Home Journal* columnist Dorothy Thompson speculated that full employment and high wages after the war would induce wives to scurry back to the kitchen because "The life of the working woman, if she be a mother, is no such bonanza as to tempt her to continue if she is not driven to it. . . . The ideal of every normal woman is to find the right husband, bear and rear

Replace
Fulfilment
as work
col patriotz
duty w/
Stuff
the stuff
for
Patriotism
↓
Consumer's
republic ?
&

Mother takes her proper place in a U.S. Information Agency photograph of 1949. The Shelby Smith Family. Courtesy National Archives

his children, and make with his earnings, for him and for them a cozy, gay, happy home."[41]

Wartime propaganda thus conveyed the message that women's work roles in the defense economy would end with the war, and by the end of 1944 women appeared to have heeded this message. Although wartime female employment actually crested in 1945, in its 1944 Labor Day issue, *Time* magazine reported that "Women workers are fading from the labor market in increasing numbers."[42] *Time* cited newly released data from the Office of War Information documenting the failure of recently discharged women to apply for other jobs, perhaps because they found alternative jobs less desirable, or perhaps because they had already done their patriotic duty and wanted to return to home and family.[43]

In 1944 *Newsweek* magazine collected a number of short essays by leaders in government, labor, and business that speculated on roles women would play in the economy after the war. Women's Bureau Director Mary Anderson warned, "Those postwar planners who casually dismiss the problems of women workers on the basis that 'they will return to the home' after the war, show a deplorable lack of realism."[44] Representatives of the business community, including national Chamber of Commerce president Eric Johnson, argued that civilian needs and the United States's role in rebuilding the world after the war would demand the continuing employment of women. (In this and other such supportive statements from businessmen and their camp followers, altruism perhaps occasionally flickered; more likely, the war had taught business that women could do many jobs traditionally thought to require men—and would do them for less money.) These experts did not see women as inherently unsuited to industrial occupations, but only the women among them emphasized the importance of protecting women's occupational advances and entry into nontraditional jobs after the war ended. New Jersey Congresswoman Mary T. Norton announced her intention to introduce an equal-pay-for-equal-work bill in the Congress. In a paper presented at an annual meeting of the American Economic Association, equal rights advocate Rebekah Greathouse confidently predicted that a constitutional amendment providing women with equal rights would go to the states for ratification before the war's end.[45] On the whole the essays articulated views similar to Anderson's position, but male writers insisted that "when all is said and done, probably the majority of American women will always find their deepest satisfaction and the best use of their talents in taking care of their families and making the American home the best place in the world in which to live."[46]

In the face of the intense 1944 domestication campaign, carried out largely in the popular press, and continued optimism that the war would soon end, the recruitment of married women slackened; however, despite this downturn in married women's employment, World War II had created an important and permanent shift in the thinking of at least some public officials. During the war, the employment of women in the war effort had been coordinated through the Women's Advisory Committee (WAC) of the War Manpower Commission. The WAC expended little effort fighting for protection of women's work rights during the war, but, when victory appeared imminent, the committee urged that women not be penalized during demobilization. The WAC urged public planners to view women as permanent workers and supported funding of family care programs. The War Manpower Commission and the Department of Labor adopted the perspective of the WAC and sought to protect the jobs of married women.

The war had altered some employers' assessments of women's abilities and energized the Women's Bureau's efforts to protect married women's work rights. In 1946 the bureau prepared a statement stressing the necessity of mothers' staying on the job after the war.[47] Based on a 1945 survey of working mothers in the District of Columbia, the bureau reported that 85 percent of the mothers expected to continue their employment indefinitely. Wives of veterans stated that the high cost of living coupled with the obstacles to the immediate and satisfactory employment of their husbands would keep them at work. Nearly a third of the women were widowed or divorced mothers.

The Women's Bureau had completed a more extensive survey of working women from 1944 through 1945 in which it found that, among women in ten different war production areas, 75 percent intended to keep working after the war. The bureau argued that its research had documented "the imperative need for serious consideration of the postwar employment problems of women workers. . . . We can neither escape the fact that women need to work or deny them the right to a job."[48] In an article outlining married women's efforts to protect their jobs, *Business Week* endorsed the bureau's conclusions and publicized government support for the inclusion of maternity leave in union contracts.[49]

In the months after V-E Day, the Women's Bureau had sought actively to defend the work rights of married women. In July of 1945 it issued a statement defending the job rights of married women and filed it in support of members of an upstate New York local telephone workers' union who brought a case before the National War Labor Board. The workers protested discriminatory policies that would terminate married women once their employers concluded that the wartime labor shortage had eased. The Women's Bureau statement described the movement of married women into the labor force as part of a permanent transformation of the workforce and not simply a response to an emergency: "Women workers . . . constitute a significant and constantly increasing proportion of the labor force. The proportion of married women to single women in the labor force and in the population generally has . . . gradually increas[ed] since the beginning of the century. The long-time trend toward the increasing employment of women was accelerated by the war, and part of the increase will be permanent."[50]

Although the War Manpower Commission and other public agencies defended the work rights of married women, these groups did not represent the opinions of most labor unions or the Congress. Despite a 1944 statement defending women's rights to work, Harry Truman as president did not fight for the protection of working women. Large corporations instituted blanket firings of married women in 1946.[51] In addition to such wholesale firings, employers often reclassified the jobs of the women they retained in order to justify lower pay. Demobilization in fact meant an end to most of the new positions occupied by women during the war, but the shift in perspective among even a handful of bureaucrats, scholars, and journalists meant that the attitude toward the employment of wives and especially of mothers would never return to its post–World War I configuration.[52]

Although for some women the war, like the Great Depression, altered the daily rhythm of their lives only slightly, for many life had changed irreversibly. Seemingly temporary economic and social changes associated with the war transformed the lives of many U.S. women permanently, altering their roles in the family and in the economy. The declaration of war on Japan encouraged some young couples to rush into marriage before the war separated them. Marriages rose noticeably in 1941 and 1942 and crested in 1946 as men and women reunited after the war. The war subjected many couples to unbearable stress. Divorce rates climbed steadily through the war, peaking in 1946 with eighteen divorces for every one thousand women, a record unequalled through the 1960s. Although a majority of fathers remained at home through the war, millions of women bade sons and husbands good-bye, not knowing if or when they might return. Military wives faced childbirth and child rearing alone and assumed primary responsibility for family decisions, including day-to-day financial matters. War widows, grieving over their losses, confronted new economic responsibilities.

While the efforts of businesses and the War Manpower Commission to recruit married women had lured many into the labor force, most mothers in fact remained at home. Working mothers faced a struggle to provide care for their children while satisfying their employers' demands, but mothers at home faced challenges as well. While the war restored prosperity overall, in the short run it forced many wives and mothers to continue to cope with many of the difficulties they had confronted during the Depression. Full employment had returned suddenly after a discouraging economic downturn in the late 1930s, but men who left well-paying white-collar or production jobs for military service suffered a sharp reduction in earnings that translated into hardship for their dependents. Hand-me-down clothing remained the order of the day as it had been in the 1930s, partly because frugal habits did not disappear, but largely because of the scarcity, high cost, and low quality of wartime consumer goods. Adults' and children's winter coats made the rounds of family and neighborhood. Mothers patched poorly made children's shoes, waiting for the next ration coupons to arrive. Subsistence gardens of the Depression became the "victory gardens" of the war. Housewives fed their families "oleomargarine" or made their own butter because butter fell under rationing but cream did not. Neighbors shared transportation to save precious gas coupons and families planned activities to which they could walk.

The wartime experiences of Mae Belk, a young mother, typified the difficulties faced by military dependents. For Belk, living conditions during the 1940s proved as difficult as the hard times of the Depression. In 1940 Mae, a chemist in her hometown of Richmond, Virginia, surrendered her job to marry Ford Belk, a co-worker. The chemical firm that employed Mae had a standing policy against the employment of married couples, and there was never any question about which partner would resign. The young couple timed their January wedding carefully. Mae's firm paid substantial annual bonuses based on corporate profits, and bonus checks were issued at the end of December. The two bonus checks that the couple had earned would allow them to purchase their own home.[53]

Within weeks after the wedding, Mae found that she was pregnant. Her daughter Lee was born ten days before the attack on Pearl Harbor. Ford entered the army in 1943, received a desk job, and was never posted abroad. Although Mae had little worry over her husband's safety, a cozy family life in their honeymoon cottage was not to be. Fearful that the United States might lose the war and that the Axis powers might seize private property in the United States, Mae and Ford sold their bungalow, a decision they would regret in the postwar housing shortage. Mae, now pregnant again, felt she had no option but to move in with her parents.

Three months after Ford left for the service, Mae delivered twins. The responsibilities of caring for two newborns with an older child still in diapers increased Mae's dependence on her parents. Although Mae had skills in high demand in war industries, employment remained out of the question because of her child care responsibilities. During the years that Ford served in the military, Mae kept close ties with other young mothers and found their companionship a great comfort. One neighbor always accompanied her when she took her children to the pediatrician, a task Mae could not manage on her own. Although Mae appreciated her parents' help and support, her loss of privacy and authority at home taxed her daily.

Mae and her children remained under her parents' roof through the war, and the entire family lived in the parental home for nine months after Ford returned from the service late in 1946. Overjoyed to be reunited, Mae and Ford found it difficult to manage the stress of their overcrowded living conditions and the interference of Mae's parents in their daily lives. Although their postwar home was neither as large nor as well built as their honeymoon bungalow, the Belks were relieved when they finally moved into their own home. Both the purchases that the Belks had deferred during the war and the high cost of living in the postwar United States ultimately propelled Mae Belk back into the labor force. In 1948, when the twins entered kindergarten, Mae accepted a teaching job at her children's school.

POSTWAR ADJUSTMENTS

For families in which the G.I. (and the marriage) survived, the end of the war brought a "return to normalcy" in family living. What the Depression and war had taken away in terms of the independent living of married couples and families with young children, the prosperity and building boom of the late 1940s and the 1950s restored. From a high of 8.7 percent in 1947, the share of married couples who did not maintain their own households fell to 2.4 percent by 1960. However, marriage and family life had undergone permanent changes in the Depression and the war, changes that emerged in the postwar era in the form of confusion about gender roles and relationships between parents and children.

Regardless of their employment status, World War II changed the daily lives of most adult women, and the Allied victory portended changes of equal magnitude. World War II had ushered in an especially unusual time for working mothers, bringing high wages, making jobs easy to find, and eroding the rule of occupational segregation. These circumstances raised women's expectations of income and job satisfaction. As the war wound down, married women protested termination of their employment because they needed the income or because in employment they had found a measure of self-satisfaction or self-worth. Trying to protect the progress that they had made, wives encountered opposition from men and from single working women, all of whom resented their competition in the labor market. However, married women had some success in countering discrimination within organized labor.

At the 1947 convention of the United Electrical, Radio and Machine Workers, Springfield, Massachusetts, Local 202 unsuccessfully introduced a resolution to set aside UE's seniority rules to give preference to single women over married women in hiring and retention.[54] Less than a year later, the single female employees of a Westinghouse Electric plant in Sharon, Pennsylvania, supported management's decision not to hire or to continue the employment of married women unless their husbands were in the armed forces or disabled. Further, marriage would cost any single female worker her job unless she qualified for employment because of her husband's military status or disability. The leadership of Local 617 of the United Electrical, Radio and Machine Workers, which represented the Sharon employees, caved in to pressures from single women and accepted the new policy.[55] However, after the married women retained legal counsel and protested to the Department of Labor, UE President Albert Fitzgerald told the local that discrimination against married women violated the union's constitution, which led to a restoration of their seniority.[56] By December, the local reported that all of the women fired because of their marital status had had their seniority restored.[57] The UE, one of the more radical organizations in the CIO, subsequently defended equal employment opportunities and conditions in a 1950 handbook for members.[58]

The opposition of single female electrical workers to the continued employment of their married sisters constituted but one of a variety of hostile attitudes toward full-time maternal employment just after the war. Despite many women's intentions to remain at work, pressures to drive mothers out of the labor force surfaced in the termination of public support for day care. The Women's Bureau and the *Washington Post* fought the elimination of the federally funded District of Columbia day care program by the 1949 Congress, but to no avail.[59] In New York, state funds also kept war era public centers open until 1948. The Child Care Center Parents' Association of New York City campaigned extensively for the long-range funding of the city's ninety-one publicly assisted centers. Although lobbying at the state level proved fruitless in the face of Governor Thomas E. Dewey's fierce opposition, the association won continuation of local funds; by the end of the 1940s city leaders had made up much of the shortfall. Mayor William O'Dwyer requested $2,984,000 in city funds for day care in 1949, an increase of more than $600,000 over the previous year. By the end of the decade six additional centers joined the ninety-one that had operated during the war.[60] A few other cities maintained public assistance for child care after World War II, but the majority of the wartime centers had closed by 1948.[61] Governments' opposition to continuing day care subsidies mirrored the attitudes of employers after the war. Although the Women's Bureau and other groups had found some employers willing to hire wives and mothers, evidence of discrimination against married women persisted. A 1950 meeting chaired by Hazel Gabbard of the Office of Education learned that the percentage of employed "working age" wives had risen from 15 percent in 1940 to 24 percent in 1949. Ninety percent of employers surveyed by the federal government had no formal policy regarding the employment of married women, but the responses showed discrimination against married women "more pronounced among salaried than hourly workers."[62] In addition, although marriage no longer kept women from employment in most areas, motherhood barred them from many jobs. The report concluded that about one third of the firms surveyed fired salaried female employees who became pregnant; therefore, the committee concluded that "a considerable area of social protection [is] needed for employed married women and working mothers."

Women who managed to retain industrial jobs after the war felt understandably insecure about their positions. In 1950, for example, the Women's Bureau attempted to survey the financial responsibilities of union women. The bureau's field representative in Cleveland, Ohio, reported: "Women took the questionnaires but would not return them. Apparently [they believe] there is considerable antagonism toward women—especially married women—and the women did not want to fill out [questionnaires] fearing that in some way [the information] would be used against them."[63] Those who did respond commonly complained of the public's failure to understand that wives worked for the survival of themselves and their families, a valid claim frequently enough, but often only part of the story. For example, Maria Fierro, who had worked most of her married life, got a production job at Douglas Aircraft during the war. She left in 1945, shortly before the birth of her fifth child, and shortly before the war-end layoffs. She soon decided to go back to work but had to settle for less-desirable jobs until the end of the 1940s, when the boom in civilian aviation led Douglas to recall some wartime workers. Fierro gladly returned, and she stayed at Douglas until she retired in 1976. Fierro worked to support her children, and frequently worked overtime at better wages than she could earn elsewhere, but she also "loved" her job. After returning to Douglas, she enjoyed promotions and the responsibility of supervising other workers, most of them male.[64]

Female veterans fared little better than working wives during demobilization. While ticker-tape parades and public praise greeted returning male veterans after V-J Day, the military mustered out women with little pomp or circumstance. Marjorie Peto, who served as chief nurse for the 2nd General Hospital in England and France, found the nurses in her charge abandoned by the military when they returned from Normandy in 1945. The nurses arrived at Fort Dix for discharge to find that the base had made no provisions for housing women. The base billeting officer suggested that Peto send her nurses home and have them return the next day for discharge. Pointing out that the women didn't live in New Jersey, Peto inquired why the women could not stay in the base's barracks. The officer replied, "That space is . . . reserved for troops from overseas!" Peto's explanation that the service women had themselves returned from overseas duty had no effect, so the nurses spent their last night in the military "squatting" on base or in hotel space rented with their own money.[65] Charity Adams Earley, an African American who rose from second lieutenant to colonel in the WAC, concluded in her autobiography that "The trailblazing by the women who served in the military during World War II has been virtually ignored and forgotten. That is why I have written my story."[66]

Although the public and the Veterans' Administration ignored the implications of the stresses that beset military women during the war, and their contributions went largely unheralded until the 1980s, military service did permanently alter the opportunities and status of U.S. women. Early in the war, Congress passed legislation creating the Women's Army Auxiliary Corps (WAAC). Like the nurse corps, WAACs were attached to the military but not fully part of it. Months later Congress authorized the Women's Naval Reserve (WAVES) and the Coast Guard Reserves (SPARS) and finally the Women Marine Reserves (WMRs). Each of these organizations, in contrast to the WAACs, granted women parallel ranks, pay, and benefits as male soldiers and sailors received. Subsequent legislation replaced the WAAC with the Women's Army Corps (WAC), a military branch that carried full military status and the same benefits that men in the army enjoyed. By the war's end over 300,000 women had served in the military. By the end of the 1940s, women had gained a permanent place in military service, with only the Coast Guard terminating female enlistments. Congress passed the Army-Navy Nurse Act in 1947, legislation that gave nurses permanent status in these two branches of the military. In 1948, further legislation ended the tenuous status of women in the military and merged the women's services with the regular and reserve army, navy, air force, and marines. While women remained separated from men and restricted to noncombatant roles, these laws guaranteed their long-term access to military service.[67]

PEACETIME RESURGENCE OF WOMEN INTO THE WORKPLACE

Although wholesale dismissals of women from high-paying industrial jobs occurred in 1946, most women workers could not afford to stay home long. Single women and women heads of households obviously had to support themselves, but working wives and their families also depended heavily on women's earnings, even after their husbands rejoined the workforce. Civilian jobs paid better than the military, and male wages continued to rise after the war, but living costs also rose substantially as inflation gripped the postwar economy. The wages of male and female production workers continued to grow from 1946 through the end of the decade, but the hourly pay of women rose at half the rate of males'. Living costs, which rose 28 percent during the war, increased by 34 percent in the five years immediately after it.

Despite the layoff of female defense workers in 1946, employers wanting to hire women in the postwar era soon confronted a shortage of "traditional" workers, single women between the ages of sixteen and twenty-four. The drop in fertility during the Depression, coupled with a sharp decline in age at first marriage, severely diminished the cohort of young single women entering the labor market. Employers thus had to rely more heavily on married women of all ages, especially wives without children and women whose children had reached their teenage years. As the nation's principal "reserve" supply of labor, married women now entered the postwar labor market as they had in the early 1940s. Women "retiring" at the war's end did not stay home long. By 1947 the female labor force had resumed growing, and the work rates of married women in 1947 exceeded those of 1944. By 1948 married women outnumbered single women in the labor force.[68] Through the late 1940s and the 1950s, the place of single women in the labor force declined as they married, left the workforce, or postponed employment in favor of education. As the employment of women continued expanding after 1947, maternal employment registered the greatest gains, as women with children at home increasingly participated in the employment trend.

Rose Kaminski left her crane operator's job at the end of the war when her husband returned from the service and reentered the civilian economy. The young family soon welcomed a second child, but three years later Kaminski called her former boss to ask if Hanischfeger still hired women on the shop floor. Brought back temporarily to replace an injured employee, she stayed on the job for nearly three decades. Kaminski's work history typifies a multitude of stories about temporary opportunities that opened to women during the war and the variety of their experiences after it. Most women left or lost positions in heavy industry after V-E Day, but many eventually found their way back. As in Kaminski's case, reemployment often hinged on a fortuitous confluence of circumstances that produced temporary rehiring offers, some of which became permanent.[69]

Rhoda Pratt Hanson also wanted to keep working after the war. Hanson had looked for a wartime job in New York partly because her husband's wartime absence had left her feeling isolated from the world. By moving east she found success and personal satisfaction as a journalist. Hanson, her family, and her employer all expected that her job would end when her husband came home from the service, but she knew that a return to full-time housekeeping in the West would never again satisfy her. Before 1946 ended she had found part-time newspaper work that fulfilled her twin needs to continue her career and spend more time with her family. Hanson and Kaminski exemplify the multitude of women who had found gratification in wartime jobs and later found ways to perpetuate that satisfaction in peacetime.[70]

CONCLUSION

How had the war changed women? Overall, the number of women employed grew 30 percent during the 1940s, a rate far greater than the slow growth of the 1930s but lower than the expansion to come in the 1950s. During the conflict, the majority of single women worked as they always had, and most mothers of very young children stayed home as usual, though hundreds of thousands of them did not. Among the nearly eight million working women, both civilian and military employees found new respect for their abilities. While some war workers gladly returned to the home after the war, most did not. Women—often reluctantly—lost skilled blue-collar and white-collar jobs at the war's end; as ever, married women continued to face hostility and discrimination in employment. The gender gap in wages did not narrow during the war decade, but working women, black and white, enjoyed higher wages relative to their own history and substantially improved their occupational status through the 1940s. In terms of occupational change, the 1940s brought a marked shift of women into nontraditional production jobs, nontraditional professions, and supervisory positions.

For women like Rose Kaminski and Rhoda Pratt Hanson, the war permanently improved their occupational status, even though they lost their wartime jobs. Between 1940 and 1950 the number of women employed as craftspersons increased from 70,800 to 167,589, a growth of nearly 140 percent; the number of forewomen rose from 43,215 to 67,955 (57 percent). The number of employed female operatives in metals and machinery manufacturing increased from 175,246 to 331,140 (89 percent). In the professions nontraditional jobs grew along with some traditional sectors that women had long dominated: female physicians and surgeons from 7,608 to 11,714 (54 percent), lawyers and judges from 4,187 to 6,256 (50 percent), college presidents or professors from 19,884 to 28,907 (45 percent). In all these sectors—the professions, managers and proprietors, crafts, and factory operatives—male employment growth rates lagged behind the advances of women.

Once they found new positions after the war-end layoffs, most working women returned to the labor force. African American women who had moved into production jobs or military service resented restriction of their opportunities after the war. White women similarly resented their downward occupational slide after the war, but for white women the postwar restrictions proved less intense and more short-term. For both black and white women, the war had opened doors to new expectations and new job possibilities.

While most women suffered occupational demotion at the war's end, all did not. African American women who had secured new professional jobs during the war largely succeeded in holding on to them after the war. The experiences of whites and blacks who worked together during World War II changed the viewpoints of some forever. Male and female African Americans, having proved their abilities during the war, acquired ambition and self-confidence that energized the civil rights campaign to come. By war's end, some African American women had gained entry to civil service jobs outside menial service work, and the integration of the armed services soon followed. Black women lost many of their production jobs after the war, but federal civil employment remained an important shelter against their return to agriculture or household service.[71]

White women had also clearly progressed during the war. Their loss of production and supervisory positions after the war did not reduce them to their prewar status. Levels of female employment, white and black, rose again less than a year after 1945 layoffs but did not surpass the wartime high of 19,570,000 until 1956.[72]

Signs of recovery and the threat of war after 1939 increased marriage rates and created an economic environment that brought additional single and married women into the workplace. Economic and political changes encouraged marriage among couples who had postponed it during the Depression. The proportion of women marrying in their teens rose during the war and remained high in the decade after it. The war had prompted hastily scheduled weddings as troop departure notices appeared, but in the long run, the prosperity of the war and the years thereafter continued to encourage marriages of young adults confident of their abilities to earn and establish lives apart from the households of their parents. Veterans' benefits would ease the transition of soldiers from the military to independent civilian householders.

Because World War II lasted longer than World War I and because the second conflict involved more mothers in paid labor, World War II presented unique logistical problems and spurred debates about family life. By dramatizing the problems of working mothers, many women felt World War II had legitimized sex-typed labor issues such as day care. In the postwar years union women pressed these issues within local and national organizations. In response, men condemned day care and maternity leave as "special interests" of the female minority; as a result, the issues of women's role in organized labor languished.

Both the child care problems and the highly emotional debate over child welfare during the war provided propaganda for the attack on working mothers at the war's end. The wartime experience deeply colored postwar literature on U.S. family life while simultaneously creating expectations of continued employment for many mothers who had answered the emergency call.

In their actions and in the controversy that they provoked, the working wife and the working mother of the first half of the century paved the way for those who came after. Women workers in World War II played an especially significant role in shifting women's status because they cracked occupational barriers and because they attracted widespread attention from public, press, and government while on the job. Despite the difficulties in balancing job and home responsibilities, World War II had clearly accelerated the feminization of the U.S. labor force and increased employment among married women. As more and more married women went to work during the 1950s, employers tried to duck child care issues, while women tried to use part-time employment as a way of combining child care with wage work. Without the protective cover of wartime propaganda, the working mother of the 1950s found herself caught between economic reality and the neo-domestic mythology of the decade.

CHAPTER SIX

Aftershock

THE 1950S

*Korea wars
+ Cold wars
stimulated of return
to workforce.*

T he decade of the 1950s reaffirmed the nation's faith in capitalism as prosperity reigned, living standards soared, and American women streamed
into the labor force. Government spending for the Korean War and the
Cold War stimulated expansion, and growing families fueled the consumer market. By 1950 the Gross National Product (GNP) exceeded wartime production
and, despite brief downturns, the GNP doubled during the decade of the fifties.
The 1950s made clear that the labor force changes that had accompanied World
War II had made a long-term rather than temporary impact on women's place in
the labor force. Labor demand called women of all ages, regardless of family status, to the ranks of paid workers. Young adult women of the 1950s, women in
their twenties and thirties, had grown up amidst depression and war, when wage
labor had been the rule rather than the exception for single women. The Depression and World War II had drawn many of their mothers or other female relatives
into the labor force. If they remained single or became widowed or divorced, they
would have had to work. In light of their own experiences during World War II or
the behaviors of wives around them, they could have foreseen paid work as a normal activity for mothers living in stable marriages. Plentiful job opportunities
existed in the fifties, but counter pressures discouraged wives' employment.

WORK AND MOTHERHOOD IN THE 1950S

The American family emerged as a centerpiece of Cold War propaganda, an icon
of television serials, and the primary target of consumer marketing. Employers
increased their efforts to lure mothers into the labor force while psychologists and

advice columnists warned parents of the need for full-time attention to child nurture. Television idealized middle-class motherhood in the characters of June Cleaver, Harriet Nelson, and others. Real estate developers and manufacturers of home furnishings and appliances courted the housewife and reasserted the importance of feminine domesticity. Consumer advertising had a double-edged impact, however. Moving to the suburbs and buying televisions and food freezers cost more than most husbands could afford. Consumer desires thus propelled mothers to supplement the family income. Offered the added incentive of flexible schedules by eager employers, more and more mothers marched off to work during the 1950s, as economic forces—not for the first time—overcame the messages of popular culture.

While working wives had fought to justify and protect their places in the labor force during the 1920s and 1930s, their efforts intensified in the 1950s, and working mothers found new allies in government and industry. More than in any other decade, the 1950s enveloped women in culture wars over the meaning of motherhood, culminating in a redefinition of middle-class women's obligations to their children. In wartime, women had clear missions: keep the home fires burning and build weapons for their men at the front. The Cold War, however, spun a more subtle mandate. Fascists had attacked democracy with troops and armaments, but communism first and foremost battled for the human mind. Countering communism clearly required military preparedness, but economic strength, technological superiority, and moral purity forged the true weapons of the Cold War. In a decade following twenty years of slow population growth, the resulting shortage of male workers meant that economic expansion required women's labor. The scientific and technological struggle between capitalism and communism required that the best minds, male and female, focus on the hard sciences and on production skills. But technology alone could not win the war against communism; capitalist democracies had to demonstrate their capacity to produce a morally superior society. The resulting campaign to protect and proclaim America's moral righteousness focused on the family as the smallest, most basic social unit.

As the traditional center of home life and as moral tutor to her children, the mother of the 1950s found her role newly scrutinized. How could conscientious motherhood coexist with the necessity for bringing women to new levels of participation and leadership in the economy? Employers and bureaucrats thought they had the answer in a redefinition of maternal obligation, a redefinition that included providing for as well as protecting children, a redefinition that ultimately prevailed. Beginning in the 1950s middle-class women took on employment as an extension rather than an abdication of their parental responsibilities. While debates over the virtues of mothers' employment continued, behaviors had changed permanently. Both the work rates and the time that mothers spent outside the home could continue to grow through the second half of the century relatively unhampered by moral opposition.

While mothers marched off to work—indeed by the very act of marching off to work—they affirmed their devotion to family life. Postwar family values focused on monogamy, child nurture, and material comfort. The trend toward the mother-dominated, child-centered home gathered an added moral imprimatur with the publication of Benjamin Spock's *Baby and Child Care* in 1946. Spock moved away from an earlier presumption that dictated order and strict discipline from birth, to a view that infants required constant care and immediate gratification. In Spock's view, only a mother could provide the loving attention and emotional security that young children needed.

CRACKS IN THE IMAGE

Not long after *Baby and Child Care* appeared, mothers began to write to Spock of their guilt and frustrations, telling him that child care demanded too much of them, and of their sense that they had failed as mothers. Conflicting emotions—frustration and boredom if they stayed at home, guilt if they went out to work (subsequently dubbed the "feminine mystique" by Betty Friedan)—beset millions of wives and mothers in the 1950s. These feelings followed directly from the heightened maternal expectations of the post–World War II environment. The publication of Alfred Kinsey's *Sexual Behavior in the Human Male* in 1948 and *Sexual Behavior in the Human Female* in 1953 alerted U.S. readers to empirical evidence, regardless of flaws in Kinsey's studies, that a significant minority of men participated in homosexual encounters and that women engaged in premarital sexual intercourse. Kinsey's findings reinforced fears that wartime disruption had encouraged a breakdown in sexual morality, as was suggested in popular novels and films like *The Hucksters*, *The Man in the Grey Flannel Suit*, and *From Here to Eternity*.

Americans of the 1950s focused intently on family partly because, after decades of depression and war, marriage rates and fertility rose sharply as couples realized goals long out of reach. Federal assistance to families in the form of mortgage assistance, veterans' benefits, and other programs encouraged economic investment in child rearing.[1] As David Reisman argued, postwar employers and middle-class society extolled the virtues of cooperative or "other directed" behaviors that maximized the accomplishment of group goals.[2] The democratic family presumably functioned in this environment as the basic unit of cooperation, a setting in which all members learned to respect the needs of others and accepted responsibility for the well-being of all. In addition, politicians, educators, and the clergy of the 1950s popularized the family as the base line of defense against communism. The decision of the United States Information Agency to gather photos of Americans engaging in family work and play activities demonstrates the centrality of the "traditional" family in Cold War propaganda. Nevertheless, public agencies did not mount a single-minded campaign to keep wives and mothers out of the workforce. For example, in 1953 Wesley Day, an employment counselor with the Connecticut State Employment Service, reported that "It is now accepted that most wives are working wives. . . . Comparatively few girls getting married today figure on leaving their work." Entering the long debate over the causes of youthful deviance, Day added, "I definitely do not associate juvenile delinquency with mothers who go out to work. Women are not going to stop working."[3]

In the popular mind, in a manner somewhat similar to the sanctification of republican motherhood after the American Revolution, postwar Americans looked to the family not only to teach moral values, but also to teach the virtues of democracy and the obligation of civic responsibility. The burdens of teaching the family ethics of the 1950s fell disproportionately on women, but the decade also held fathers to new standards of assistance and cooperation within the family. At the same time, government and business expected women to make up the shortfall in the labor force, and economic realities increasingly pushed them out the door and into the laboring ranks.

The United States's emergence from the war as the leading nation in the world economy foreshadowed what sociologists Steven Mintz and Susan Kellogg later described tongue-in-cheek as "The Golden Age" of family life.[4] While postwar consumerism and a renewed emphasis on the family as a source of emotional well-being introduced new stresses in the lives of mothers and fathers, the same postwar decade brought unprecedented prosperity to U.S. families generally. On the basis of income, more families than ever before or since could reasonably expect to attain a middle-class lifestyle. In this respect, the fifteen years following World War II did represent a Golden Age in the United States. Economically and socially, African Americans especially benefited from the prosperity of the postwar era. Although white wage earners continued to have consistently higher incomes than African Americans, black family income rose from the Depression through the 1950s, increasing at a faster pace than white income and growing particularly rapidly during the 1940s and 1950s. The prosperity of the postwar years permitted African Americans to reaffirm patterns of family life that had characterized black America before the 1920s. Marriage rates and fertility increased, and the share of black families headed by women declined somewhat. The fifties, however, proved a brief interlude indeed for black families, as female family headship resumed its climb by the end of the decade and rose sharply thereafter, a pattern repeated in other ethnic groups as well.

STRUCTURE OF THE FEMALE LABOR FORCE

The economic growth that brought prosperity to U.S. families also demonstrated that some of women's wartime occupational gains had proven permanent rather than temporary. Women had continued to gain jobs in nursing, teaching, and clerical work during the war, and growth in these areas persisted through coming decades (see table 6.1). The expanding market for social workers, librarians, and other traditionally female professional pursuits also contributed to the expansion of the white-collar sector in the postwar United States. The growth of nonprofessional service enterprises such as food service and beauty shops also drew increasing numbers of women into the labor force. In a temporary reversal of a long-term

TABLE 6.1
Change in Selected Occupations in the United States, 1940–60
(Numbers of Workers in Thousands and Percent Increase over Decade)*

	1940	1950	INCREASE	1960	INCREASE
Occupational gains					
Social and welfare workers	not reported	77		98	27.3%
Librarians	39	56	43.6%	85	51.8%
Nurses	377	483	28.1%	630	30.4%
Teachers	1,086	1,133	4.3%	1,684	48.6%
Medical and dental technicians	not reported	78		141	80.8%
Dieticians	not reported	23		27	17.4%
Buyers and department heads, store	74	145	95.9%	238	64.1%
Clerical and kindred workers	4,982	7,132	43.2%	9,617	34.8%
Salesworkers	3,450	4,026	16.7%	4,801	19.3%
Service workers	3,657	4,524	23.7%	5,765	27.4%
Factory operatives	9,518	11,754	23.5%	12,846	9.3%
Occupational losses					
Dressmakers and seamstresses	172	147		124	
Private household workers	2,412	1,492		1,825	
Total workers in all occupations	51,742	59,230	14.5%	67,990	14.8%
Total female workers	12,754	16,507	31.3%	22,304	35.1%

SOURCE: *U.S. Bureau of the Census,* Historical Statistics of the United States, Colonial Times to 1970, *Bicentennial edition (Washington, D.C.: GPO, 1975), tables D 182–232 and D 233–682.*

*Total number of workers in each occupation counts men and women together.

decline in household service, the number of domestic workers increased during the 1950s as housewives or working mothers sought help with their domestic responsibilities.

The expansion of clerical work provided nearly two million new jobs to women between 1950 and 1960, and the broadening service sector yielded an additional million. These jobs came primarily in occupations that women had long dominated or in which they already had strong representation. Nursing and public school teaching jobs increased by more than 400,000. Clearly, the major growth for women came in traditional areas, but signs of occupational change also appeared. Women's enrollments in nursing school declined nearly 50 percent while the number of professional women increased by 40 percent. Women entered a variety of nontraditional professions such as drafting and engineering in significant numbers, but their rates of growth fell far below those of men, indicating a relative decline in status. Overall, women's growth at the upper levels of the occupational structure reflected general economic expansion rather than female occu-

Although few women retained wartime jobs after 1947, all occupational gains were not erased with the peace. Taxi drivers, 1950. Courtesy National Archives

pational mobility. Among blue-collar workers, however, a very different pattern of women's occupational gains emerged.

The number of women employed in blue-collar jobs increased little, but women moved into some new occupational areas at higher rates than men. Women lost positions in declining industries such as commercial laundries, dressmaking, and textiles—industries that they had long dominated—and craft positions in heavy industry that they had held since World War II. On the other hand, women posted gains in many nontraditional crafts and industries, acquiring jobs as assemblers, bakers, bus drivers, surveyors' assistants, delivery persons, power station operators, welders, aircraft parts makers, and in other production occupations. During the 1950s women came to dominate craft and lower-level jobs in the printing industry as automation de-skilled work in the industry. In effect, women gained positions in blue-collar jobs as market demands drew men into higher-paying areas, or as demand in rapidly growing areas such as the aircraft industry outstripped the supply of qualified men. Although immigration resumed after World War II, the numbers of newcomers remained well below pre–World War I levels, and U.S.-born women retained some industrial jobs through the decade.

Although racial prejudices persisted in the 1950s, African American women preserved some of their wartime gains in employment and made notable advances in some occupations (see table 6.2). Women lost production jobs after the war; nevertheless, female representation in heavy industry and in supervisory or craft positions remained much stronger in the 1950s than in the 1920s or 1930s. African American women lost proportionally more craft and durable goods production jobs in the 1950s than their white co-workers, but they also made some long-term progress. Racial barriers remained strong in the 1950s, a reality that occupationally advantaged some black women but disadvantaged others.

Although racial segregation persisted within the broad area of professional and commercial services, African American women advanced faster than white women in some fields during the 1950s. The Civil Rights Revolution of the 1960s ultimately played a major role in broadening African American women's employment options, but World War II served as an important prelude to the changes that occurred after 1960. African American women had entered clerical positions in large numbers during the war and retained stronger representation in these areas than they had had in the 1920s or the 1930s. The number of black women employed in clerical jobs increased nearly 150 percent during the 1950s, while the number of white clerical workers increased by less than 50 percent. The number of black women employed in teaching grew slightly more during the decade than the number of white teachers; the number of professional black nurses increased 127 percent while that of professional white nurses increased by 31 percent. The

TABLE 6.2

Selected Occupations of White and African American Women
Employed in 1940, 1950, and 1960

	AFRICAN AMERICAN		
	1940	1950	1960
Professions	65,888	104,278	175,308
Teachers	50,112	67,857	99,779
Professional nurses	6,680	14,871	33,752
Social workers	1,692	4,454	8,683
Managers and proprietors	10.914	24,557	24,757
Clerical	13,145	74,255	181,678
Sales	7,620	25,492	36,083
Crafts	2,374	11,629	15,877
Operatives	96,190	274,000	310,233
Metal and machinery	495	12,384	8,017
Household	917,942	773,590	88,206
Nonhousehold service	159,805	351,856	519,823
Farm	189,549	139,657	69,495
Total employed	1,542,273	1,869,956	2,455,140

	WHITE		
	1940	1950	1960
Professions	1,402,246	1,830,440	2,556,332
Teachers	725,968	766,466	1,089,791
Professional nurses	341,162	447,358	585,528
Social workers	43,081	54,308	66,734
Managers and proprietors	411,277	650,386	749,372
Clerical	2,360,450	4,208,510	6,068,735
Sales	771,960	1,302,089	1,615,420
Crafts	103,994	223,496	234,788
Operatives	1,942,245	2,734,283	2,919,243
Metal and machinery	174,731	320,474	359,632
Household	1,045,726	554,859	763,859
Nonhousehold service	1,098,040	1,556,458	2,302,557
Farm	115,572	302,892	167,420
Total employed	9,563,583	13,794,932	18,548,577

SOURCES: *U.S. Bureau of the Census,* Sixteenth Census of the United States, 1940: The Labor Force *(Washington, D.C.: GPO, 1943), table 62; U.S. Bureau of the Census,* Seventeenth Census of the United States, 1950: Population *(Washington, D.C.: GPO, 1952), table 128; U.S. Bureau of the Census,* Eighteenth Census of the United States, 1960: United States Summary *(Washington, D.C.: GPO, 1964), table 205.*

decade of the 1950s, then, provided significant occupational mobility for black women, while large numbers of white women went to work but made little progress up the occupational ladder.

WORKING MOTHERS

The rising work rates of married women in the post–World War II era encompassed women at all stages of the life cycle. During the Cold War years as before, mothers were most likely to seek employment after their children had completed secondary school, and more mothers of school-age children worked than mothers of infants and toddlers. Nevertheless, female work rates increased among women with children at home as well as among mothers of older children, and by 1960 the work rates of women with school-age children had surpassed the labor force commitments of wives with no minor children (see chapter 7, table 7.3). Although the climb in maternal employment accelerated after 1947, the rise in fact extended a long-term trend in the work rates of married women.

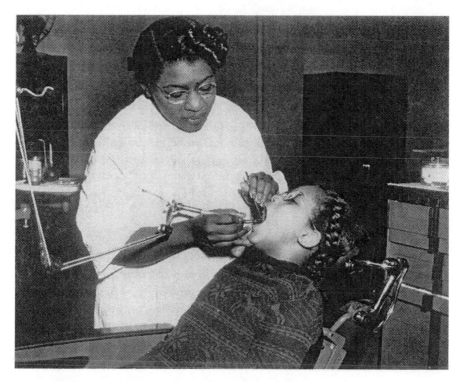

African American professional women faced little competition in their work through the 1950s, but segregation severely restricted their opportunities to gain professional skills. African American dentist, 1950. Courtesy National Archives

Consumer desires and personal ambitions moved mothers like Mae Belk (see chapter 5) to rejoin the labor force after World War II. The war had hastened the way toward the democratic and egalitarian family life suggested by the concept of "companionate marriage" and demonstrated by the changes in Ford and Mae Belk's marriage as they settled into a two-earner pattern of responsibilities during the 1950s. When a friend in the superintendent's office learned that Mae had a teaching job and that the family had moved to the suburbs, she urged Mae to apply for a job teaching chemistry at the high school near the Belks' new home. In 1951 Mae started a long-term career as a chemistry teacher. She stayed home for two years after the birth of her fourth and last child. She had planned on a three-year absence, but like millions of other U.S. women, she loved her job; when a position at the high school suddenly opened, she went back to teaching because she feared the opportunity might not come again.[5]

Returning to teaching in 1955, Mae remained with the Richmond public schools until she retired in 1989 at the age of seventy. Mae had always aspired to a career as a physician, a plan shattered by her parents' straitened economic circumstances during the Depression. Although she had kept the dream alive, a medical career exceeded her grasp, as the family depended on her earnings as well as her attentions. She eventually accepted that a doctorate in science education would be more compatible with her established career and with her family circumstances. Balancing the demands of home and work, Mae squeezed further education into the summer months, receiving a master's degree, a sixth-year certificate, and finally her doctorate in 1986. Mae's demanding life required Ford's cooperation and assistance with home and family, the aid of Ford's mother, who sat for the youngest child, and the assignment of many household chores to the older children.

WORKING WIVES: A DUAL ROLE AND A NATIONAL NECESSITY

By 1950 the idea of part-time employment had also become highly attractive to U.S. housewives. In publishing the results of its eighty-eighth readers' poll, *Woman's Home Companion* announced that "keeping house full time is still the number one job choice of modern women."[6] Yet 10 percent of the two thousand *Companion* readers polled in 1950 reported that they would like to have full-time jobs, and an additional 36 percent described part-time employment and part-time housekeeping as their ideal situation. One reader responded that wives who held jobs outside the home seemed happier than women like herself who had chosen the domestic sphere.

Middle-class prescriptions had long conflicted with the real lives of wage-earning women, and, as the *Companion* poll revealed, a significant share of white middle-class women preferred employment outside the home. The U.S. popular press participated in the debate over women's roles outside the home during and after the war. The debate, which carried into the 1960s, revealed confusion about women's roles, but it also offered encouragement to career-minded women as women's magazines broadened their perspectives on domesticity. In 1962 and 1963 *Ladies' Home Journal, McCall's,* and *Mademoiselle* all published portions of *The Feminine Mystique,* Betty Friedan's influential attack on the mind-numbing hold of domestic obligations on the energies of middle-class homemakers.

During the 1950s additional publications had taken issue with the domestication literature of the era. In 1952 the Public Affairs Committee, a nonprofit educational organization, published *Working Wives,* by Stella Applebaum. Applebaum began by arguing that the vast majority of working women totally or partially supported other persons. She offered mothers practical counsel on making decisions about employment and in dealing with the logistical and emotional difficulties of balancing home and employment obligations. Lillian M. Gilbreth, a professional woman and the working mother immortalized in *Cheaper by the Dozen,* wrote a brief introductory note to Applebaum's pamphlet. Gilbreth's perspective suggests the degree to which the debate over the employment of mothers had shifted from the issue of whether to work to the issue of employment conditions. Gilbreth advised:

> Industry has the responsibility, not only of doing away with discrimination against women, but of affording them special privileges such as maternity leave and part-time jobs—if women with home responsibilities are to give satisfactory service and lead satisfying lives. The working wife and mother, carrying two jobs either through necessity or choice, can be best helped by family approval, community understanding and assistance, and guidance in finding and developing her skills. Given such help, she is proving she can be an asset and not a liability in every relationship of life. It's everyone's job to see that our sons and daughters are brought up to realize this and accept it.[7]

A 1952 Women's Bureau publication substantiated Applebaum's views by documenting the roles of working women in family support. The bureau found that, regardless of marital status, the vast majority of the working women surveyed provided some economic support to members of their immediate or extended families.[8] Subsequently, the Women's Bureau assured the public that "mothers [can] often . . . meet their children's emotional needs more fully if they can devote some time in the day to wholly outside experiences and achievements, either in paid employment or in some community service or creative activity."[9] Once the defender of the mother who worked only out of necessity, the bureau had begun also to defend mothers who worked for wages by choice. The imperative of economic necessity no longer constituted the sole defense of the working mother.

In *The Feminine Mystique*, Betty Friedan argued that, while full-time home-making stultified wives of the 1950s, working mothers suffered severe distress over their abandonment of home and family and guilt over their enjoyment of employment.[10] Sociological studies of the 1950s confirm that many women felt the dilemma of the "feminine mystique" but warn against generalizing from Friedan's narrow analysis. Survey data reveal that middle-class women from the 1950s onward often regarded work as a personal as well as an economic enhancement in their lives. Social scientist Alfreda Iglehart studied the effects of employment on the self-concepts and aspirations of wives and mothers of the 1950s and of the 1970s. Iglehart based her analysis on 1957 and 1976 national surveys of "sources of well-being and discontent" conducted by the Survey Research Center of the University of Michigan.[11] Iglehart argues that, although some wives had always worked out of necessity, until the 1970s women overwhelmingly rejected notions of combining marriage and employment because their elders and peers so instructed them and they themselves believed that the two would inevitably conflict. Working wives and mothers not only would bring unhappiness upon themselves but might also inflict harm on their loved ones. These norms, Iglehart asserts, dominated during the 1950s when the march of married women into the workforce was accelerating. She, like Friedan, hypothesized that during the 1950s working wives and mothers experienced deep conflict over their dual roles. Married women who remained at home, Iglehart concluded, had greater chances of being happy and satisfied women than did working wives.

In contrast to the findings of either Friedan or Iglehart, sociologist Mirra Komarovsky located different expectations and sentiments in the world of working-class white women. In her classic 1962 study *Blue-Collar Marriage*, Komarovsky found that working-class wives thought they should stay at home with the children and that most preferred to remain there even after children had begun school.[12] Komarovsky concluded, however, that working-class wives felt more comfortable with their roles in the home and in the workplace than did middle-class women. Working-class wives whom Komarovsky interviewed did not feel that housewifery lacked prestige as did Friedan's Smith College classmates.[13] On the other hand, the "blue-collar" women felt less ambivalence about entering the labor force than did Friedan herself in the 1950s. A minority of working-class women found the continuous care of young children taxing and did not feel guilty about wanting to work simply "to get out of the house." Approximately one third of the women interviewed wanted to hold a job although they preferred part-time to full-time work.

Among the employed white, native-born, working-class wives whom Komarovsky studied, attitudes about employment followed from the particular pressures and rewards that employment brought the women. Wives whose jobs left them exhausted and who performed virtually all the family's household tasks felt highly dissatisfied with their lot. Women who did not feel overworked by combining employment with domestic responsibilities enjoyed their dual lives. Working wives believed that employment enhanced their power within marriage, and they enjoyed their improved status.[14]

Iglehart and Komarovsky might have asked somewhat different questions if they had studied mothers' employment of the 1950s in the context of long-term labor force trends.[15] Among working-class women maternal wage earning had long been accepted as a necessity for some, a reality that did not warrant guilt or extensive debate. Komarovsky came to unfounded conclusions about the universality of home-bound assumptions among the working class, but the middle-class also shared the domestic ideal less widely than scholars would have us believe. By 1950 the long-term trend of employment among wives, despite Depression-style or war-end propaganda, had made itself abundantly clear. The work rates of married women—including working mothers—had steadily increased for half a century.

The working mother had come to stay, in the words of the Women's Bureau, "likely [as] a permanent part of our economy."[16] In 1954 the bureau targeted high school girls for career advisement. Urging them to plan for long-term employment, Alice K. Leopold, director of the Women's Bureau, declared: "Prepare for both a job and marriage! You are right in thinking you will probably marry. Most girls now in high school or vocational school can expect to marry. . . . The chances are you will [work]—before marriage and perhaps for a few years afterward. Nowadays, more and more married women continue with their jobs or return to work when their children are old enough."[17]

The Women's Bureau, historically devoted to defending women's right to work, had numerous allies in its view that mothers had become an indispensable part of the paid labor force. In 1952 representatives of government agencies, colleges and universities, and social service agencies met in New York at a conference on "Women in the Defense Decade." The published proceedings of the conference reflected consensus among the participants on the necessity of women's acceptance of triple roles: mother, wage earner, citizen. Motherhood must remain woman's primary role because the United States could not retain its sacred familial values and children could not grow into healthy adults and good citizens without intensive maternal nurture. However, the conferees also maintained that women could not devote themselves exclusively to motherhood. Producing consumer goods that kept the nation strong and happy, ensuring a rising standard of living for U.S.

families, and preventing the United States from falling behind the productivity levels that communist countries might achieve—all these things required an active female presence in the labor market. Women not currently engaged in wage earning formed the backbone of the volunteer army of good citizens, individuals whose social conscience protected democracy by keeping watch on and providing leadership for the nation's schools, churches, children's clubs, and social welfare agencies.

The 1952 conference reflected a growing body of opinion that the U.S. economy and its democratic institutions depended not only upon an acceptance of the working life, but also on increasing the movement of wives out of the home and into the realm of public activities. Eclipsing some of the earlier issues in the debate over wives' employment, the Cold War had created a sense of alarm that the United States might lose out in critical defense industries. A speaker at a University of Pittsburgh convocation queried his audience "whether we can afford the loss of our womanpower. Again the facts are simple. Look at the competition. In the Soviet Union 35 percent of all the faculties in higher education are made up of women. The majority of physicians and surgeons are women."[18]

Proponents also argued that the broadening of maternal employment would stimulate economic growth at the same time that it strengthened the nation's defense system. In 1951, economic analyst Eliot Janeway asserted that the United States could meet the challenge of the Korean War only with an economy that encouraged consumption along with defense production. For Janeway, wives played key roles as consumers in a strong economy, and their consumption paved the way for their return to the labor force as needed: "What better guarantee of . . . inflation control than a high-earning civilian labor force obligated to pay off debt. . . . And don't forget that if Rosie the Welder [comes] out of the kitchen again, she will need a dishwasher and a washing machine and a vacuum cleaner to leave behind her, and she will need a car to get her to work."[19]

The sudden turn away from domestication propaganda of public agencies and women's magazines of the late 1940s reflected the collapse of near-hysteria over the possible economic effects of peace. Because the armed forces did not contract permanently after World War II, instead rebuilding in the wake of the Cold War and the Korean War, and because many veterans chose higher education over immediate employment, the dreaded flood of the labor market and the return of the Great Depression did not occur. A severe housing shortage and other pent-up demands stimulated the consumer economy, creating additional jobs in the civilian sector. By the 1950s labor specialists acknowledged what demographers had earlier recognized; in the 1950s the country had entered a decade of labor shortage.

The need for new workers forced analysts to emphasize the possibilities of employing those married women who had not traditionally worked, married women in families above the poverty line. At the 1957 meeting of the National Manpower Council, Howard Kaltenborn succinctly stated the necessity of recruiting married women into the labor force, maintaining: "These older women, as a group, constitute the least effectively utilized sector of our working population. [We] will [have] to employ them in increasing numbers in business, industry, and government in order to meet the nation's manpower needs and to insure the continued prosperity and growth of our national economy."[20]

Thus by the late 1950s, despite the persistence of domestication literature, the working mother had become an indispensable employee. During the 1950s new service jobs appeared at a rapid rate as demographic, technological, and managerial changes continued to transform the structure of the U.S. economy. Demand for teachers, nurses, and clerical workers mushroomed, and the laws of occupational segregation dictated that women fill these jobs. In addition, before the end of the 1950s many employers adjusted their earlier notions of women's roles in order to fill "women's jobs." In the process, employers modified earlier views of the female life cycle in order to redefine hiring criteria. Whereas factory and office managers in the early decades had preferred single women in their mid- to late teens, the second half of the century brought a decided preference for mature women. Employers found older women less likely to quit than younger employees. Employers had in fact accepted the assertion of Stella Applebaum and others that the life cycle of working women had changed from earlier times. Whereas Applebaum assumed men worked continuously from adulthood through old age, women's "first work life begins when [they finish] their formal education. . . . They usually marry early and work for a year or two after marriage. . . . They give up their jobs . . . to have their families. Then when [in] their middle thirties, or even their forties or fifties, they are ready to go back to work."[21]

In 1957, a U.S. Department of Labor analyst predicted that the "typical woman" of 1965 would follow this life cycle.[22] Numerous surveys of employers conducted during the 1950s confirmed the willingness of businesses to hire mothers. Some employers acknowledged a preference for hiring older women rather than young, single women because they thought older women more stable and reliable employees. Some employers declaimed that mothers should remain at home even though their own employment practices indicated that they believed otherwise.[23] Whether or not an employer preferred to hire mature women, the demographics of the female population dictated that the labor pool of 1950 would be older than in 1900. Changes in the population structure caused the average age of women workers to increase and the place of single women to decline, regardless of other pressures operating to effect this same transformation. The Women's Bureau responded to the realities of labor supply and demand by publishing *Training Mature Women for Employment.*[24]

A 1957 Columbia University conference on married female workers confirmed that educators, social policy analysts, and employers had recognized changes in the composition of the female labor force. James P. Mitchell of the U.S. Labor Department clung to traditional notions that the first responsibility of mothers (but not of fathers) remained the care of home and children. Even so, Mitchell felt uncomfortable about his position: "I think the fundamental job of the American woman remains what I consider . . . the most difficult of all jobs: being a good wife, a homemaker, a mother. She is only secondarily an economic provider. I am sure that to many ears that must sound either old-fashioned or heretical, but I sincerely believe it."[25] On the other hand, Mitchell believed that mothers should have the opportunity to work and that more women would have to enter the labor market to prevent erosion in U.S. living standards. Mitchell's suggested resolution: an increase in employers' allocation of jobs to part-time workers.

RECRUITING WIVES AND MOTHERS

The intense demand for educated female workers put special pressure on women of the middle classes, the group most entangled in the "feminine mystique." Employers, as Secretary Mitchell suggested, had to redefine their hiring expectations to draw middle-class wives into the labor force. In the 1950s labor analysts proposed part-time work as the answer to filling the nation's current and projected labor need. Howard Kaltenborn argued that part-time jobs had already attracted "many older women" who otherwise would not have sought employment. Kaltenborn's advocacy of part-time employment for housewives was rooted in more than current and projected labor demands; he argued that employers could lay off housewives during slack periods as they always laid off the most recently hired workers. Since women, as "secondary" workers, worked only for family extras or for self-satisfaction (or so Kaltenborn myopically saw it), their layoff would not result in serious injury to family well-being. Furthermore, Kaltenborn concluded, "secondary" workers rarely seek other positions during a layoff and consequently could be reemployed when the employer's labor need resumed.[26]

Because the National Manpower Council regarded women as the only population group to whom employers could turn to fill a projected long-term labor shortage, it proposed an agenda for government and private agencies to sell young women on the feasibility of combining marriage and employment. The council also sought to encourage women to develop high skill levels for manufacturing, technical, and professional occupations. It concluded that a shortage of skilled female workers to meet current and future demands would ensue unless society encouraged women as fully as men to develop their intellectual potential into practical knowledge. Such encouragement would begin with secondary schooling, but employers would also have to alter radically their policies and attitudes. The council recommended that unions and employers abolish gender discrimination in hiring, training, and promotion; conduct experiments with part-time and flexible work schedules; and implement equal pay for equal work.[27] Although the Manpower Council saw itself as looking ahead to the eventual loosening of the bonds of occupational segregation that had strengthened during the 1950s, its endorsement of part-time employment in fact only reinforced the notion of dual labor markets.

Employers learned that part-time work, an arrangement that minimized their labor costs, enticed married women out of the home, and thus during the 1950s, employers and educators presented part-time maternal employment as being complementary to homemaking and child care. In 1950 the majority of women in the labor force worked fewer than fifty weeks per year or fewer than thirty-five hours per week, and part-time employment grew especially rapidly after 1953.[28] Mothers who chose employment during the 1950s responded to their yen for productive activity outside the home, to the need to support their families, or to rising consumer expectations. As observers noted, unfortunate was the wife who had to work, but far worse the family that could not afford the perceived necessities for the home.[29]

The part-time solution helped undermine the shaky support for publicly assisted day care that had existed during the war. The absence of support for publicly or privately funded day care during the 1950s helped maintain the illusion that postwar society had not compromised the nation's traditional familial ideals. However, the absence of adequate child care helped confine working mothers to dead-end, part-time jobs. Women may have found satisfaction in such employment, but the lack of security and advancement opportunity in most part-time jobs also reinforced occupational segregation and the gender gap in wages. As part-time jobs have typically carried few if any fringe benefits, the increased allocation of work to part-time employees cut industry's labor costs at the expense of working wives.

PART-TIME WORK

Government agencies and employers touted part-time jobs as the optimal compromise, thus playing off of rather than violating the gender-based propaganda of the 1950s. In the 1940s the Census Bureau began collecting statistics on part-time employment on a regular basis, thus providing useful indicators of the proportion of employed women who worked fewer than thirty-five hours per week.

Researchers who began studying part-time work in the 1940s and the 1950s started with the assumption that such work had long characterized female employment and had historically accompanied women's participation in agriculture, sales work, domestic service, and piecework done in the home. Intermittent statistics from the 1920s and 1930s demonstrated not only a rising trend in part-time employment but also a positive correlation between increasing part-time work and female employment. In 1943 the Women's Bureau reported that part-time employment of women did not develop in wartime. In fact, "stores, restaurants . . . laundries and certain other service establishments have long employ[ed] women either for short daily hours or for the busiest part of the week, thus adjusting the size of the labor force to meet daily and weekly fluctuations in public demand."[30] The bureau later reported that one in five women engaged in paid labor between 1947 and 1950 worked part-time and that agriculture, sales, domestic work, and other service jobs provided the main employment for such labor.[31]

Depression-era surveys and censuses as well as reports on part-time labor published in *Current Population Reports* demonstrate that such employment reflected structural changes in the U.S. economy in addition to increasing dependence on women workers, particularly married women. As farm labor and domestic service declined in importance, part-time employment became increasingly associated with the broad area of service occupations from white- to pink- to blue-collar jobs that increasingly characterized women's full-time employments as well. The expansion of service trades, from college teaching to fast-food sales, created new markets for women who sought or who would accept part-time work. In 1940 fewer than one fifth of all employed women worked part-time, but by 1980 that fraction had nearly doubled.[32]

In a 1949–50 study of 3,385 firms, the Women's Bureau found that part-time employment characterized a distinctive stage of the life cycle of women. Typically part-time workers had married, had children of school age or older, and had previous employment experience related to their current employment. By mid-century, optimal conditions existed to launch the rapid expansion of part-time employment among women by melding a long and newly energized tradition of socialization limiting women's career aspirations and the growing trend toward part-time female employment into an appeal to working-class and middle-class mothers.[33]

As early as 1943, the Women's Bureau had defined specific part-time jobs as especially suited to housewives, finding "much of the work in stores and public service industries . . . particularly appropriate for part-time employment of women homemakers. Women are used to sorting, washing, and ironing clothes, serving food, trading across a counter, making change."[34] In studying women's part-time jobs less than a decade later, however, the bureau found that the majority of part-time positions held by women involved specific skills for which women had trained at an earlier stage of their lives, not commercialized versions of the housewife's traditional chores. Most part-time positions required at least a high school diploma; moreover, employers who expected employees to begin productive work immediately would not invest in extensive training for their part-time hires. The Census Bureau began the systematic collection of data on part-time workers in 1946.[35] At that time roughly 8 percent of all wage earners regularly worked fewer than thirty-five hours per week and women outnumbered men among such employees. Women comprised the majority of part-time workers, but twice as many women as men among them reported that they both preferred and could accept full-time jobs.[36] Part-time employment, male and female, rose through the late 1940s until, by 1950, 24 percent of working women and 11 percent of working men put in fewer than thirty-five hours per week.[37] Then, through the 1950s the share of men and women working part-time remained essentially constant, fluctuating with labor demand, but more women than men worked part-time by choice. Among women twenty years and older, part-time employment climbed slightly until 1970 and declined thereafter.[38]

Although mothers more often than other women had short-term or part-time schedules, the 1950s also brought an increase in full-time, long-term employment among married women. Some jobs, such as school teaching, required a stable, full-time labor force for optimal performance. Part-time work could not meet the needs of single mothers or of the Mae Belks who entered the labor force to build a decent life for themselves and their families. The goals and problems of full-time working mothers differed dramatically from those of women who fitted wage earning around their domestic lives; full-time working mothers faced child-care dilemmas not shared by part-time workers. Full-time working women expected improvements in wages and in their positions as they persisted in their jobs; as men passed them by, their frustrations mounted.

The new definition of the female life cycle that Stella Applebaum and others discovered constituted an additional barrier to career advancement for women. Although educators and labor analysts encouraged technical training for women, advanced education seemed a poor investment as long as women seemed likely to take long absences from the workforce and to restrict themselves to part-time employment during much of their adult life.

THE FEMININE MYSTIQUE

In contrast with its historical image as a decade in which social pressures confined women to domestic tasks more tightly than in the past, the 1950s in fact presented

War brides faced a new land and a new culture without the help of ethnic communities. Korean war bride Mrs. Diana Carbaugh at home with her mother-in-law, 1951. Courtesy National Archives

a new array of choices for women that may well have fueled the very anxieties and discontent that Betty Friedan identified. By the 1950s, the public debate on maternal employment had shifted from whether or not mothers should work to the issue of appropriate conditions for their employment. Cold War fears that the United States would lose out to technological and economic advances in the East—intensified by the Russian orbiting of the satellite "Sputnik" in 1957—created a sense of urgency regarding efforts to increase women's skills and economic productivity. The sense that the "feminine mystique" had imprisoned women—especially middle-class women—in their own or others' expectations of wholly domestic roles emerged forcefully in the writings of Betty Friedan. Friedan analyzed and summarized what many had felt in the 1950s. The reality that the cries of dissatisfaction came from the middle class reflected more than the propensity of middle-class women to articulate their feelings. Pressures to conform to the "feminine mystique" weighed more heavily on middle-class women than among others at the very same time that the expanding service sector created greater demands for middle-class women's skills. Middle-class women often married employers and supervisors who regarded working women, even their wives, as their inferiors—hardly a prescription for marital harmony. In addition, as Komarovsky's and others' studies of middle- and working-class women revealed, middle-class women of the 1950s had assimilated expectations of community service not shared by the working classes. Working would compromise or abrogate civic responsibilities; even Cold War warriors encouraged women to move from volunteer to paid employment, or a combination of the two. Women of the middle classes were especially likely to be salaried employees who got fired if they became pregnant, a message that undercut other policies sustaining maternal employment.

On the other hand, economic and sociopolitical forces encouraged middle-class women to pursue market labor. In a period of labor shortage and of Cold War hysteria over the communist menace within and without, advocates of married women's employment emphasized that women held the key to preserving a way of life based on the unique American blend of prosperity, technological excellence, strong nuclear families, and democratic ideals. These same spokespersons warned that women who isolated themselves within the domestic sphere imperiled the safety of all they loved. Educators who viewed both volunteer civic service and paid employment as strengthening and enriching motherhood contributed a crucial element to the redefinition of women's roles. Civic service such as membership on school committees, participation in political campaigns, and fundraising for nonprofit organizations had gradually drawn middle-class women out of the home through the first half of the twentieth century. By the 1950s civic roles for women had become as consistent with role proscriptions as cultural and charitable activities had seemed in earlier decades. In stressing the similar value of compensated and volunteer labors outside the home, educators offered middle-class wives free choice in selecting one option over the other and in moving easily from unpaid to paid work. The association of employment with volunteer work construed wage earning as consistent with women's primary obligations to family.

The support for employment that women of all classes found in testimonial literature and in isolated corporate policies and federal programs of the 1950s signaled a significant shift away from the views of the two previous decades. As in the upswing in married women's employment in the 1920s, some of the new support for working wives and mothers in the 1950s came from women who had entered the labor market before or during the war and declined to retire to the home once the "emergency" had passed or they had married.

The 1950s and 1960s were decades of transition in which mothers moved gradually from homebound work roles to a combination of market labor and unpaid domestic labor. To the extent that wives worked part-time and pursued "traditional" occupations in these decades, they affirmed the myth of the "feminine mystique" while simultaneously moving full-time domesticity farther from the reality of women's lives. In addition, the trend toward the increased allocation of work in "women's" occupations into part-time jobs further ghettoized the working woman by reinforcing her low pay and poor working conditions. The Cold War consensus on part-time maternal employment left the full-time, long-term working mother isolated from the support and resources she needed at a time when the number of such women working was increasing. Although part-time work may have lured additional wives into the labor market as employers of the 1950s had hoped, after 1970 family needs as well as labor demand minimized the place of part-time earning, while wives' full-time employment continued to grow.

THE ROLE OF EDUCATION: CONTINUITY, CHANGE, AND DEBATE

Part-time work had expanded in the 1950s partly in deference to loudly touted gender role prescriptions of the 1950s and partly as an accommodation to mothers' desires to fit wage earning around domestic activities. Girls of the 1950s lived in a world in which the dual pressures of mothers' lives steadily increased, but educational and socialization practices failed to adapt successfully to the pressures besieging women. Girls of the 1950s passed through an era in which education, associational activities, changing gender behaviors, and their own families delivered conflicting messages about women's roles. Until the 1960s, most teachers shared expectations that women's primary roles in life would be those of mother and homemaker although the work experiences of female educators suggested otherwise. Home economics instruction expanded into the 1950s, maximizing girls' exposure to the field just as a new debate erupted over the broadening of women's education. Postwar employers, Cold War bureaucrats, and minority and women's rights leaders all challenged older assumptions about women's places in society and in the economy. Although the future direction of women's education remained unclear in the 1950s, the decades-long expansion of secondary and collegiate programs specifically designed to "track" women into domesticity or secondary roles in the economy ended by 1960.

Changes in educational patterns after 1960 confirm the critical nature of the educational debate of the 1950s and the lagging impact of women's economic behaviors. By the 1960s generational differences among U.S. women appeared in their labor force behaviors. Wives without children under the age of eighteen years —largely older women who had never accepted employment, especially full-time, as a desirable life option—tended not to work. By contrast, two in five wives with school-age children held jobs. Women's work rates had risen from 29 percent to 34.5 percent during the decade of the 1950s after slow growth through the first half of the century.

Educators and counselors of the 1960s saw clear signs that work rates would continue to climb and family formation would end women's working lives. Counselors and teachers began to encourage girls to train for a wide range of careers. The share of women completing high school, completing junior college, and completing baccalaureate degrees rose steadily through the 1950s.[39] Although white women went further in school than black women, African American women's relative success in raising their level of educational achievement equaled white women's during those years. They achieved this continued improvement even though, despite the Supreme Court's *Brown vs. the Board of Education* ruling against school segregation, most African American children of the 1950s and 1960s still sat in segregated classrooms.[40] Although desegregation progressed through the 1970s, inner-city schools in which minorities predominated suffered from neglect and underfunding. Even where school integration appeared to succeed, minority children often found themselves resegregated into vocational or general education tracks less frequently followed by Anglo children. Minority girls especially confronted an educational environment that discouraged school completion and crippled their hopes and prospects for employment.[41]

In the postwar United States, secondary schools continued to perform crucial roles in educating girls not bound for college to occupy secondary positions in the economy and to anticipate full-time motherhood. By the early postwar era, home economics for girls and shop for boys had become an expected part of the high school experience. In 1949 roughly half of all high school girls enrolled in home economics courses. Southern schools persisted in efforts to reshape nutritional habits and family values in African American homes through public instruction in home economics. In their efforts to mold maternal moral values, some African American home economics teachers explicitly lectured girls on religion, often encouraging girls to place religion at the center of home life.[42]

The expansion of gender-oriented instruction in commercial subjects also continued in the postwar years and increasingly tracked young women into clerical occupations. As the 1950s began a quarter of the nation's secondary pupils studied industrial subjects; another quarter studied typing or an alternative subject related to clerical occupations. By the 1950s home economics, typing, bookkeeping, and business mathematics comprised the curricular core for high school girls not preparing for college or for specialized trades such as cosmetology. Home economics and business subjects completed an educational package that prepared girls for a few years on the job followed by full-time motherhood. By the 1950s thousands of young women left high school annually and entered clerical work without seriously considering alternative careers. A Boston clerical worker of the 1970s observed:

> In my house you didn't [expect to] work in shops. You went to school and worked in an office, and you considered yourself better than people in the shops. My father worked in an office, but it wasn't my father that had these ideas, it was my mother. . . . Her family was immigrants from the old country, and a woman's role in her time was you were taken out of school and you [went to work]. A woman didn't have any function other than to be a wife and have babies. What [would] she want to go to school for? So when [mother] was 13 she was put in a mill, and it crushed her because she had all A's in school. And when she had her own kids, [they weren't] going . . . [to] work in a mill. . . . She insisted that we . . . go to high school, which was fortunate because if she hadn't I don't know where the hell I'd be.[43]

The emergence of commercial and business curricula in high schools of the 1920s had answered the rising demand for female clerical workers after World War I and had attracted girls hoping to avoid the factory. Parents and young adults of the 1940s continued to view the office as preferable to industrial work. Working-class and middle-class parents, still likely to regard female employment as a temporary phase preceding marriage and child rearing, often reinforced the advice of school administrators who channeled girls into business courses. The narrowing of girls' options through business curricula persisted after World War II. In studying a group of working-class Italian American women from Rhode Island, for example, historian Sharon Hartman Strom found that nearly all had pursued secondary clerical training at the urging of teachers and school counselors.[44] A Boston legal secretary of the 1970s explained: "I always thought that I would be a secretary, because of social and parental conditioning. I thought it was all I could hope to attain since I was going to marry and have babies. It wasn't necessary to go to college, so I could always work as a secretary until I met a man."[45]

Strom's interview subjects typified the millions of young female high school graduates who entered the postwar clerical labor market or the service trades without considering other options. While business and home economics teachers reached unprecedented numbers of adolescent girls in the 1950s, education critics scrutinized the content of education and recommended changes that would modify both the goals and the curricula of girls' schooling.

Labor market analysts and federal bureaucrats of the 1950s, cognizant of the nation's dependence on female labor, urged restructuring of girls' secondary education to encourage goals beyond homemaking and clerical work. Educators sought to include more girls in college preparatory courses and to train women for technical careers and the professions. The National Manpower Council, a Columbia University think-tank funded by the Ford Foundation, complained in the mid-fifties that most high school girls were preparing largely for a rapidly disappearing life cycle. Girls were underrepresented in college preparatory courses and overly concentrated in business or other vocational subjects that limited their future options. In 1957 the Manpower Council criticized both the instructional and advisory programs of secondary schools for their failure to acquaint girls with the probability that motherhood would not permanently end their working lives. The publication of the Manpower Council's recommendations coincided with the launching of *Sputnik*. Shortly thereafter, critics of U.S. secondary education demanded a more rigorous high school curriculum, especially in math and science, for girls as well as boys.[46]

The recommendations of the National Manpower Council emerged in an environment of ongoing Cold War debate over secondary and higher education for women in the United States. While educators agreed that capitalism and democracy battled for survival in the 1950s, they disagreed on woman's place in the war. Female educators from leading liberal arts institutions, as well as business leaders, emphasized the importance of training women in science and technology, while home economics educators doggedly continued to stress the importance of training women as skilled managers of the home and moral guardians and nurturers of the family. Many of these issues came to the fore at the 1951 "Conference on Women in the Defense Decade" sponsored by the American Council on Education.

On recommendation of Althea K. Hottel, dean of women at the University of Pennsylvania, and other leaders in women's education, the council formed the Commission on the Education of Women, a body that worked to expand programs for women in science and mathematics as well as in the liberal arts. Surprisingly, the debate did not pit public institutions against private ones; in fact, the female home economics faculties of many land grant institutions aligned with representatives of conservative women's colleges to push an educational agenda that conflicted with the goals of Althea Hottel and like-minded reformers. Both sides agreed that college-educated wives and mothers would spend increasingly longer periods of their lives working as the century progressed, but they differed as to what constituted the best education for the future awaiting the American woman. Home economics educator Mildred Morgenroth advised her peers: "Adolescent girls need [help] to see that they can combine marriage, children, and work life; being educated to understand the needs of babies and of young children for their mothers' care. To be a successful woman a mother must [prepare] to pick up and lay down work outside the home as the needs of her husband and children [require]."[47]

Cold War propaganda emphasized the family as the critical unit of a democratic society. To that end some educators began to stress the importance of home economics or "family education" for college men as well as college women, but they had little luck recruiting male students into these classes. In a 1959 brochure describing the Earlham College Program in Family Relations, college president Landrum Bolling explained that "Through this new educational enterprise Earlham College seeks to awaken in both men and women a genuine concern for the establishment of sound homes and families."[48]

The 1950s debate on higher education for women spilled over into government bureaucracies and the popular press. Several monographs, including Lynn White's *Educating our Daughters*, Kate Hevner Mueller's *Educating Women for a Changing World*, and the published reports of the American Council on Education and the National Manpower Council kept the debate alive but failed to achieve a resolution.

Although educators disagreed about the appropriate courses of study for women in higher education, consensus endured on the necessity of a double standard for male and female students residing on college campuses. In predominantly white and in African American institutions of higher education, parietal policies restricting the behaviors and activities of women remained in place through most of the 1960s. Women, but not men, faced discipline and possible expulsion if they failed to observe dormitory curfews. Colleges and universities regulated the dress of students and dictated the circumstances under which women might leave campus. As Anne Moody remembered, African American Natchez College in Mississippi enforced particularly harsh behavioral codes for women although "[t]he boys weren't too upset over campus rules because they could go anywhere without permission, spend the night off campus, and do just about anything else except openly tamper with the girls on campus. And most of the boys had no desire to mess with the campus girls because they had three or four girls in the city."[49] Anne and her companions rankled at the deferential treatment demanded by staff members and the insistence that a college matron accompany women on their scheduled shopping trips to town. At Tougaloo College, also in Mississippi, Moody enjoyed a less repressive atmosphere and the opportunity to participate in a campus NAACP chapter, an opportunity that led her later to challenge racial barriers in Mississippi.

THE GIRL SCOUTS: MISSING THE BOAT AND THE PLANE

Like educational institutions of the 1950s, the Girl Scouts fell under the spell of Cold War rhetoric on female domesticity. Scout executives extracted messages from women's roles in World War II that led them to scale back rather than heighten girls' ambitions. The advent of commercial aviation, the absence of a role for the woman "sailor" in World War II or commercial seafaring, and the relegation of female pilots to ferrying operations during the war showed that women could not compete with men in these fields. In professional areas such as the law, *The American Girl* had consistently encouraged women to challenge gender barriers, but the magazine warned readers that real prejudice against women existed in these areas, and scouting leaders did not encourage women to challenge gender divisions that they viewed as inflexible.[50]

Despite its long history of encouraging women in aviation, the Wing Scout Manual of 1949 advised, "Piloting airliners for commercial air transport companies is strictly a man's job. You might, however, look into the possibility of flying with a smaller passenger or cargo line."[51] Wing Scouts also learned that they might find commercial aviation prospects as airline stewardesses. Scouting took a pronounced turn toward a conventional "feminine" tone in the 1940s as changes in the Wing Scouting program indicate. Ironically, the Girl Scouts obtained ownership of their first aircraft in 1945 through a gift from the Piper Company.[52]

A history of scouting published in 1947 revealed dramatic changes in images of scouting. Scouting publications of the 1920s and 1930s had included photos of girls involved with domestic chores, but camping activities and other outdoor scenes predominated. *Citizens in Action*, a 1947 history touting scouts' place in the community, featured girls of all ages in home kitchen scenes that did not predominate in earlier publications.[53] The turn toward femininity intensified during the 1950s as membership in scouting grew by leaps and bounds and the resources devoted to leader training failed to keep pace with the movement's growth.

A rising birth rate and better economic times at the close of the 1930s fed the expansion of scouting and other youth activities in the 1950s. The Girl Scouts grew as they reached across class and racial lines, as well as into the rising population of Anglo middle-class girls. Changing theories of child rearing, which included a new emphasis on the influence of peer groups on children's behavior,

Although the Girl Scouts of the U.S.A. disavowed segregation, the organization of racially integrated troops proved difficult. African American Senior Girl Scouts from Washington, D.C., Troop 492 are pictured here with their leader and the white members of a Long Island, New York, troop, ca. 1955. Renie photograph, courtesy Girl Scouts of the U.S.A. Archives, New York

encouraged scouting but also changed its direction. Revisions to the Girl Scout Handbook in 1953 and 1954, as well as features in *The American Girl* and *The Girl Scout Leader* turned away from their earlier emphasis on adventure and individual achievement and refocused on the social adjustment and domestic skills components of scouting.[54]

Revisions to the scouting program in the early 1950s changed requirements for earning "badges" of accomplishment to include more required group activities. The 1955 *Girl Scout Leader's Guide* noted that some activities required individual accomplishment but warned the adult leader to watch out for "about any troop member who spends a great deal of time doing Scout work by herself. Social adjustments can be difficult at this age, and a girl may be tempted to substitute the 'success' measured by rapid earning of merit badges for the 'success' measured by being able to get along happily with girls and boys in school, troop, and other social situations."[55]

The Girl Scouts underscored the importance of preparing girls for motherhood and homemaking at precisely the time that full-time homemaking began to decline precipitously among U.S. women. Although continuing to include the development of skills that had career applicability, scouting de-emphasized them. The 1955 guide for troop leaders deleted references to broadly based skills in its declaration of purpose: "The Girl Scout organization is dedicated to helping girls develop as happy, resourceful individuals willing to share their abilities as citizens in their homes, their communities, their country, and the world."[56] Scouting, which had consistently maintained the importance of civic duty, especially stressed citizenship amidst the Cold War climate that had similarly affected adult women. In a 1954 article in *The Girl Scout Leader*, Lillian Gilbreth touted "Girl Scouting— One Answer to Communism."[57]

In a radical departure from its earlier assertions that girls would best develop into self-sufficient and skilled adults in gender-segregated activities, scouting leaders of the 1950s grew concerned with guiding girls toward comfortable interaction with boys. A 1950 feature in the *Leader* advised that "Training in good sportsmanship, thoughtfulness, and team work, already gained in Girl Scouting, is a good background for the development of a charming manner with the opposite sex."[58] Officials at scouting's national headquarters in New York increasingly saw early adolescence as years during which scouting could help girls develop good dating habits, habits that would reflect strong moral values and convey an attractive personality. In the mid-1950s, the Girl Scouts commissioned a survey of high school girls that included questions regarding gender values, sexual behavior, and sexual identity as well as career, educational, and family aspirations.[59] Generally concerned about a youth culture that might lead innocent girls toward adolescent promiscuity or other "maladjusted" behaviors, scouting executives hoped to use the survey findings as a guide in encouraging girls toward a successful adjustment to a heterosocial world marked by moral order.

Although the Girl Scouts did attract minority membership during the 1950s, organizing across economic or racial lines proved a formidable challenge. The segregated nature of American life, permeating church membership, school attendance, and residential patterns, dictated pervasive segregation in children's play activities as well. Regardless of their race, scouts of the 1950s headed down blind paths as their leaders prepared them to be sociable and well-mannered wives and mothers but failed to offer guidance that would facilitate their success in the world of work that awaited most of them.

CONCLUSION

The 1950s delivered mixed blessings to U.S. women. Although World War II, the emerging Cold War, and the Korean War propelled married women into the labor force, these phenomena did not transform women's work patterns as thoroughly as the economic and social changes that came after 1960. Nevertheless, the flow of wives into the labor force through the early 1950s signaled the major changes to come. Workforce participation grew, especially among married women, but many new jobs were part-time positions that fastened women more securely into secondary positions in the labor force. Women made progress in entering the professions, but they advanced almost exclusively in female-dominated occupations such as teaching. As women increased their numbers in blue-collar jobs, female membership in labor unions also rose, but women failed to gain a distinctive voice in the labor movement. Agencies that educated and socialized girls of the 1950s failed to heed the winds of change in the economy despite the advice of economists, labor analysts, and educational reformers. Public schools and the Girl Scouts bent instead to the voices of the feminine mystique and compounded the difficulties that their charges faced in their adult lives.

Despite the overwhelming signs that women's status did not improve during the 1950s, the feminization of the labor force had continued. Because white wives' employment conflicted with the strong emphasis on domesticity in middle-class culture, in contemporary programs of vocational education and in girls' clubs, women's work drove the debate on gender roles in the 1950s. In succeeding decades the conflicts between girlhood training and adult realities, and between domestic responsibilities and the demands of the workplace, would evolve into major social issues. The emergence of a service-oriented economy, rising consumer expectations, inflation, and the broadening acceptance of paid work for all women fueled a steep rise in wives' work rates after 1960, with the employment of mothers showing the sharpest increase. As their contributions to the economy grew further in the 1960s and 1970s, women increasingly articulated their needs and forced broad issues of gender into the political arena. In these decades schools would adapt more successfully to the feminization of the labor force and girls' clubs would struggle to find a program relevant to the nation's youth.

CHAPTER SEVEN

Changing Course
THE 1960S AND 1970S

The prosperity of the 1950s gave way to even greater economic growth that drew growing numbers of women into the labor force. The feminization of work progressed as labor demand mounted and both low-status and high-status service occupations grew. The 1960s and 1970s brought a critical and enduring shift in the lives of women and their families as the wage-earning mother became the rule rather than the exception in the United States. What had begun as a part-time or "empty-nest" commitment to the labor market for a minority of mothers in the 1950s had become a full-time experience for most mothers by the end of the 1970s. Legal tools for achieving desegregation in employment emerged in the 1960s, but the new body of law had little effect on most women's earnings or their jobs until the 1970s. During the sixties the continuing structural transformation of the economy and the demand for female labor had broader impact than civil rights law on women's everyday lives. In the 1970s the law and public policy opened unprecedented professional opportunities for women, but not all women climbed the income ladder. Through these decades of economic expansion, the gender gap in wages persisted and profound changes in family structure increased the economic responsibilities of most women.

DECADES OF STRUCTURAL CHANGE

During the 1960s the number of women in the workforce grew from twenty-three million to well over thirty-one million, and female labor force participation increased from 37.7 percent to 43.3 percent. Women had entered the labor force in the 1950s partly because the wage gap had narrowed significantly since the 1930s, but women of the 1960s did not make substantial progress in earnings relative to men. Women's expectations had changed through World War II and the 1950s. Subsequently, employers did not need to devise new strategies to lure married women into the job force. More women entered the workforce as defense spending, population growth, innovations in consumer goods, and new techniques in marketing powered the economy. Total employment grew even more during the 1970s than during the seemingly expansive 1960s, and women continued to benefit more than men from economic growth. Both female and male employment grew at higher rates—44 percent for women and 17 percent for men—than in the 1960s, when the growth rates were 37 percent and 9 percent, respectively.

Women coming into the labor force in the sixties represented the leading edge of the baby boom. Women born in 1942, before the baby boom had begun but after the Depression had lifted, turned 18 in 1960. Unlike their mothers or the working women of the fifties, these young women had no memory of the Depression and few if any memories of World War II. They grew up in the darkest days of the Cold War and "neo-domesticity," when girls had been encouraged to excel in school but to remain feminine at all times. Whether cultural or economic conditions shaped their behaviors, their work lives differed in significant ways from those of women ten years their senior. Women who came of age in the 1960s married younger but had fewer children than the cohort one decade older. They were more likely to combine child rearing with paid labor and spent more of their lives in the labor force than older women.

During the sixties the greatest numerical growth in female employment occurred in clerical work as it had in the fifties, but the craft, professional, and management sectors expanded at even greater rates than during the previous decade. As the electronics industry blossomed, women's employment in manufacturing grew more than any other area of work. Economic expansion in female-dominated industries, rather than the erosion of gender barriers, accounted for women's advance into production work.

WHITE-COLLAR, "PINK-COLLAR" ASCENDANCY

The dynamic of structural economic evolution drove occupational changes that highlighted distinctions between the skilled and the unskilled, the highly educated and the less educated. The female white-collar ghetto of clerical work continued to grow, as occupational segregation in rapidly growing white-collar areas, including low-level or "pink-collar" pursuits such as clerical work, multiplied women's chances of finding a job. The occupational term "pink-collar" emerged in the 1960s to separate low-level white-collar positions from better-paying service jobs. While nonmanual and typically housed in office environments, the skills demanded for pink-collar jobs do not require collegiate educational training, and the positions hold little opportunity for advancement. By the 1950s women held nearly exclusive domain over low-level office jobs, and "pink-collar" describes the gendered allocation of the work as well as its inferiority to other white-collar occupations. Approximately a third of working women in the 1960s pursued clerical occupations (see table 7.1) as they had during the 1950s. Clerical jobs increased at a slower rate than professional positions. In addition, women gained more supervisory jobs than they had held in previous decades.

Within the professions the areas of greatest growth remained the traditionally female occupations of teaching, nursing, and librarianship. Mae Belk's daughter Lee (see chap. 4) left the South at the end of the 1950s to attend a private women's college. Like many other young women of her generation, Lee migrated—first to further her education, then to find a job—and never returned to her birthplace to live. In concert with most college women of her cohort, Lee chose work in a traditional field, elementary education. Elementary and secondary teaching, nursing, medical and dental support services such as nutrition and dental hygiene, vocational and personal counseling, and library work accounted for three fourths

TABLE 7.1
Employed Women by Occupational Category, 1960 and 1970

	1960	1970
Total	21,172,301	28,929,845
Professional and technical	2,753,052	4,550,584
Managers and administrators	779,701	1,055,381
Sales workers	1,661,113	2,141,600
Clerical workers	6,291,420	10,105,818
Craftspersons	252,515	521,147
Operatives	3,255,949	4,014,993
Transport operators	—	132,052
Laborers	109,746	284,300
Farmers	118,100	70,772
Farm workers	242,885	153,301
Service workers	2,846,289	4,790,043
Household workers	1,664,763	1,109,584
Occupation not reported	1,196,768	—

SOURCES: *U.S. Bureau of the Census,* U.S. Census of Population, 1960, United States Summary *(Washington, D.C.: GPO, 1964), table 202; U.S. Bureau of the Census,* U.S. Census of Population, 1970, Detailed Characteristics, United States Summary *(Washington, D.C.: GPO, 1972), table 223.*

of all professional women, but women had also made some headway in medicine, engineering, the law, and other well-remunerated professions during the 1960s. Women did not win these jobs, which required specific collegiate or postcollegiate training, with the assistance of civil rights legislation or litigation. Rather, they succeeded by getting into professional training in programs with specific (although frequently veiled) gender quotas, and by the willingness of some employers to employ women in these professions. Although the 1964 Civil Rights Act had outlawed employment discrimination based on race and gender, gender quotas in education had not yet been challenged effectively, and enforcement of the law lagged behind its adoption. Women who entered law, medicine, dentistry, or veterinary medicine before 1970 did so despite discrimination based on gender. At the time of the 1970 census, sample data revealed that about 20,000 women held jobs in engineering, 13,000 as lawyers or judges, and nearly 26,000 as physicians or dentists. By 1970 women had clearly succeeded better in entering some "male" professions than others; one physician out of ten was a woman, but only one in twenty veterinarians was a woman.[1]

While middle-class mothers increased their commitment to full-time employment during the 1960s and 1970s, not all felt comfortable with the choice. Many young adult women of the 1960s grew up with the assumptions of the 1950s that only single women and married women without children worked for wages. Unlike those of earlier periods, women of the 1960s no longer saw social class as a distinction between wives who worked outside the home and those who did not. During the 1940s and 1950s, wives without child care responsibilities participated in paid labor regardless of social class, and mothers frequently returned to the labor market after raising their children. The expansion of part-time work made the part-time working mother of school-age children a common phenomenon; Betty Friedan herself had worked part-time. Friedan published *The Feminine Mystique* in 1963, based on her study of a survey of Smith College graduates of her generation. *The Feminine Mystique* ignited a new wave of feminism in the late 1960s, but considerable attitudinal change had occurred in advance of the book's release. Portions of *The Feminine Mystique* had earlier appeared in *Ladies' Home Journal, McCall's Magazine,* and *Mademoiselle.* While *Mademoiselle* targeted young and single middle-class women and *McCall's* and the *Journal* aimed to reach married women, all three periodicals had long stressed traditional feminine roles and offered advice on cooking and housekeeping. By printing Friedan's essays, women's magazines signaled that social change had reached the middle-class mainstream. Readers' concerns stretched far beyond beauty and domesticity, the twin preoccupations of these popular magazines during the 1950s. Friedan belonged to the cohort of women who came of age in the 1940s and raised their children in the 1950s. The angst of middle-class mothers who worked part-time after their children entered school belonged largely in the 1950s, but full-time wage earning still troubled many middle-class mothers in the 1960s, and women's magazines began to address their concerns.

By the early 1960s substantial numbers of middle-class and working-class mothers of infants and toddlers had accepted full-time employment. Women who had grown up in families with mothers at home during their early childhood years might combine raising their own children with working for wages. Women who married and bore children in the 1960s brought the baby boom to an end. Fertility continued to rise until 1965 and declined thereafter. The average age of brides at first marriage had declined into the 1950s, reaching a low of 20.1 years in 1956 and climbing again thereafter. Mothers of the sixties faced a greater likelihood of divorce than their mothers had. For women of all races and all classes, the 1960s brought a very different world and clearly demonstrated that economic forces had fundamentally changed the daily rhythm of women's lives and the life cycle itself.

The 1960s began with the conservative Cold War assumptions about women's roles that had disturbed Betty Friedan, but labor demand and consumer needs continued to accelerate the feminization of work. By the end of the 1970s legislation and feminist leadership had redefined women's opportunities and expectations. President John F. Kennedy created the Presidential Commission on the Status of Women (PCSW) in 1961, but his leadership did not mark the advent of a new feminism. Rather, the PCSW confirmed the Women's Bureau's success in publicizing the economic roles of women and the rise of the working mother, as refracted through the maternalist prism that had colored bureau activities since its founding. The PCSW endorsed the broadening of women's political and property rights but regarded the states rather than the federal government as the primary agents of change. The President hoped the commission would confirm U.S. women as mothers first and wage workers second. In fact, his liberal image to the contrary notwithstanding, Kennedy embraced and extended the Eisenhower Cold War perspective that mother-centered American families symbolized the nation's moral superiority over its communist rivals. Eleanor Roosevelt chaired the commission, and her maternalist outlook reflected the tone of commission hearings.

Women's Bureau chief Esther Peterson, a moving force on the PCSW, reinforced the Cold War sanctification of full-time motherhood and maintained a protectionist perspective on women's work rights until court rulings invalidated special protections for women in the mid-1960s.[2] Peterson played the central role in drafting a PCSW report that recommended the abolition of laws limiting married women's property rights and imposing civil disabilities on married and single women. The commission recommended, however, that states rather than the federal government should take the initiative to improve the legal status of women. The commission did not induce changes in the law and had little impact on public policy. The PCSW urged the broader employment of women in federal agencies, a call that President Lyndon Johnson hoped to satisfy by appointing a few women to visible positions in his administration. Esther Peterson, among others, opposed Johnson's endorsement of the inclusion of gender in Title VII, the section forbidding racial discrimination in employment, of the 1964 Civil Rights Bill. Peterson argued (wrongly, as it turned out) that adding women to Title VII would, as congressional opponents hoped, sink the entire civil rights bill; she maintained that race should take precedence over gender.

Both the Equal Pay Act of 1963 and the 1964 Civil Rights Act expanded women's claims to equal rights in the labor market. The laws passed largely through the efforts of African American civil rights leaders. Few opponents or proponents of the legislation foresaw the passion with which women would pursue their new legal rights. Convinced that the White House would not move to enforce the clauses outlawing gender discrimination, concerned women formed the National Organization for Women (NOW) in 1966. Other organizations, such as the Women's Equity Action League (WEAL) and the National Women's Political Caucus (NWPC), soon followed. These groups worked during the 1970s for full compliance with existing federal law as well as for the Equal Rights Amendment.[3] Feminists' campaign for women's economic and legal rights culminated in passage of a ban on gender discrimination in education through Title IX of the Higher Education Act and won congressional approval of the Equal Rights Amendment in 1972.

Empowered by the law, blue-collar and white-collar working women brought legal suits that abolished discriminatory pay in some settings, opened all-male workplaces to women, and laid the groundwork for the broadly conceived "affirmative action" plans that followed. Well before the founding of the National Organization for Women, women had begun to present cases under Title VII. By July of 1965, the Equal Employment Opportunity Commission had received forty-eight complaints of which women had filed nine; through the following three months women brought an additional 143 cases before the commission.[4]

BLUE-COLLAR BLUES

Although women overall enjoyed unprecedented economic gains in the 1960s and 1970s, not all women bettered their circumstances. Millions of working women found themselves locked in low-wage jobs because they lacked the education to escape menial work in manufacturing or service industries. While highly trained women worked their way up the income ladder in the 1970s, poorly educated women found that the American dream had eluded them and that working conditions had deteriorated. Textile workers of the seventies voiced the familiar complaints of earlier generations of mill workers. Supervisors pressed employees to "speed up" machinery and "stretch out" the number of machines that they tended. Although some women remained relatively satisfied with their employment in the mills, few workers wanted their daughters to follow them there. Textile workers interviewed in North Carolina reported that the increased pace of work had heightened mental stress, raised noise levels, and, above all, destroyed the atmosphere of conversation and mutual support that had once made mill work tolerable. Although some factory and office workers like Mary Thompson genuinely enjoyed the work itself (see chap. 3), most working women found the pleasure of employment in the camaraderie of the workplace, and when employers, for whatever reason, destroyed the social context of women's labor, workers grew dissatisfied. Mounting production pressures and increasing supervisory harassment alienated some North Carolina mill workers, eventually driving them to accept positions outside the mills that offered substantially better workplace conditions, despite lower pay.[5]

Through the century demeaning working conditions have persisted in female workplaces. Women have consistently suffered sexual harassment and have filled society's least desirable jobs. Female workers have felt devalued by the unpleasantness of their tasks as well as their low wages. Blue-collar and low-level service workers of the 1970s found that the Women's Liberation Movement and equal opportunity legislation had left their lot in the workplace unchanged, and their sense of being passed over for promotions heightened their resentment over poor working conditions. Service workers understood their inferior situation to be the consequence of men's preeminence in the economy. As one nursing home employee summarized her position, "No man is gonna wipe people's butts."[6]

Lower-level white-collar workers shared many of the frustrations that factory and service workers experienced. Clerical workers thought of themselves as middle-class employees, and their frustrations partly reflected feelings that their status entitled them to better working conditions and better wages than they had secured. A Massachusetts office employee remembered that she had looked forward to a secretarial job because her high school business teacher had repeatedly promised that her training would lead to high pay, but her actual experience as a legal secretary had fallen far short of her adolescent expectations. Burdened with a heavy, repetitive workload, she commanded little respect from her employers and her income had failed to rise substantially over time.[7]

Most office workers understood that their low pay and occupational segregation resulted from familial and peer pressure, as well as educational specialization that had prepared them to choose "women's jobs" that did not require extensive education, and that they would leave after finding the right man to marry.[8] To the extent that women accepted the occupational choices their educational backgrounds dictated, they focused their attention on improving the circumstances of their employment. As the realities of the workplace usually fell short of their expectations, women in factory jobs and pink-collar positions returned to labor unions to fight for better conditions and to stretch the limits of the gender-segregated labor markets in which they found themselves.

WOMEN "PUSH THE ENVELOPE"

Whether women developed a distinctive labor consciousness through long-term experience on the job or through the influences of the Civil Rights and Women's Liberation movements, working women of the 1970s expressed and acted upon perceptions that employers exploited and discriminated against female employees. The Women's Liberation Movement provided working women, regardless of class, with a rhetoric and a conceptual framework to press their issues within the labor movement and within the political arena. The Women's Liberation Movement recast "maternity" leave and child care issues as family or human concerns and not as exclusively female issues. Such rhetoric helped lift women from a separate sphere, from the status of a minority special-interest group. The equal rights rhetoric allowed blue-collar and pink-collar women to press their claims for occupational advancement and for equity on the job, but they realized far smaller gains than those of college-educated women.

Women's limited success in entering nontraditional professional careers in the 1960s partly reflected the encouragement that some girls received in high school. For example, as Cold War fears of a talent gap between the United States and the Soviet Union reshaped secondary education at the end of the 1950s, high school teachers identified Ellen Ross as a student with strong abilities in science and mathematics; consequently, she began advanced classes in these subjects in the tenth grade. After her graduation in 1961, Ross entered Barnard College to pursue a degree in mathematics. While attending Barnard Ellen met Columbia liberal arts major Robert Cooper, whom she married one month after receiving her bachelor's degree. The young couple settled in Robert's hometown of Nashville, where he found work in a local business. To that point, life had gone more or less according to Ellen's expectations. Her college-educated mother and most of her mother's friends had been full-time housewives during their child-rearing years. While Ellen placed her husband's career ahead of her own and expected to stay home with her preschool children, she also planned to work before her children arrived.[9]

In Nashville Ellen began her job hunt with little notion of the kind of work she wanted or the length of time she would work before having a child. "The first question I was asked by employers was whether or not I planned to have children," Ellen recalled. "That convinced me that, if I ever wanted to have a real career, I would have to have my kids first and then start looking for jobs again." Ross interviewed in a number of fields before accepting the only position offered, a job teaching secondary mathematics. Four months after starting her teaching job and seven months after marrying, Ellen delighted in the discovery that she was pregnant with her first child.

In the late 1960s Ross made the decision to return to school in pursuit of a doctorate. Unrestrained by law or public policy, university admissions counselors advised her against entering a graduate program, reminding her of her obligations to her husband and child. Undeterred, Ellen persisted and completed her doctorate in the early seventies. In the job market after graduation, Ellen met similar discouragement, landing temporary or part-time work until receiving her first tenure-track academic job offer seven years later.

Title IX of the Higher Education Act of 1972 empowered women to break gender barriers in undergraduate, graduate, and professional training, but cases such as Ellen Ross's show that some colleges and secondary schools, however reluctantly, had already responded to changes in the female labor market. Educational programs of the 1960s demonstrated that school administrators had accepted the necessity of training women for jobs all across the occupational spectrum, but that they had failed to follow through on the heightened expectations of female achievement. Both the campus climate for women and girls and the content of female instruction changed after 1960. During the 1960s and afterward, changes in educational practices, consistent with the earlier urging of the National Manpower Council and the Commission on the Higher Education of Women, encouraged women to aim high in their educational aspirations and to train for a broad range of careers. Women's participation in higher education grew until women comprised the majority of college students by 1981.

Both the Civil Rights Movement and the Women's Movement influenced the education and socialization of the nation's children after 1960. Court-ordered desegregation and civil rights legislation, measures for which Anne Moody and her contemporaries had fought, created broader opportunities for women and minorities in higher education, if not at lower levels.

In the 1960s women began to reject the educational paths chosen by high school and college women of the 1950s. Numerically women's enrollments in collegiate and secondary home economics courses rose gradually into the 1970s, but their enrollments in other fields rose more swiftly, and thus the place of home economics training in women's education declined. Although not heavily recruited into science, mathematics, and advanced technical studies, women's persistence in higher education and their dwindling interest in home economics opened to them broader career possibilities than those enjoyed by women who had followed the narrow prescriptions of the immediate postwar years.[10] Federal assistance to higher education funded the collegiate and graduate careers of some women in the 1960s, although men were the primary beneficiaries of grants and fellowships. Colleges and graduate schools continued to discriminate against women in admissions and in the award of financial aid until Title IX of the 1972 Higher Education Act took effect in 1975. Women nevertheless increased their representation among the holders of master's and doctoral degrees during the 1960s and 1970s. In the 1960s and 1970s women advanced relative to men in all fields of learning except home economics. Women's enrollments in postgraduate education rose sharply during the 1970s. Educational barriers against women remained after 1975, but amendments to the Higher Education Act through the 1970s helped women achieve their goals, including a larger place in intercollegiate athletics. By 1980 women earned more than two fifths of all master's degrees awarded and approximately one fourth of all law degrees, medical degrees, and doctorates.

Despite the changes in U.S. higher education and the impact of the civil rights movement on the public schools, many of the lessons that girls learned in elementary school and in the upper grades remained consistent with the secondary status that had earlier been ascribed to women. Institutional racism and sexism continued to shape the messages of the schoolroom, and feminists did not thoroughly question the gender assumptions of educational institutions until the 1970s.[11] In 1973 the National Vocational Guidance Association conducted a ten-day conference on the development of career aspirations and skills among girls and women. Unlike similar conferences of earlier decades, the 1973 conference explored the psychological, social, and educational barriers against women's career advancement in a world that had consistently limited women's options.

William C. Bingham of the Rutgers University Graduate School of Education reported that numerous studies of male and female job applicant pools revealed that the vast majority of young women had no particular work-related

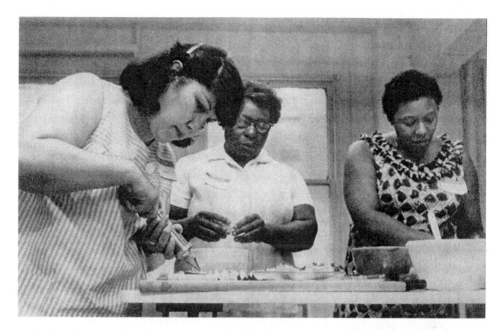

Despite educational and economic trends, federal assistance continued to support female training in domestic work into the 1960s. New York City maid trainees, 1968. Courtesy National Archives

interests, while more than four fifths of the males had specific vocational preferences.

> Boys have always known that they would [work] in adulthood, so planning for occupation[s] has caused no conflict. They have expected for most of their lives [to] have to [make] an occupational choice at the appropriate time. [Much] of their developmental experience has reinforced that expectation. Girls, on the other hand, through reinforcement of a basic conflict, have been indirectly influenced to avoid deciding: [for women], to decide on employment is to experience guilt for not selecting homemaking and motherhood; to decide on homemaking is to sacrifice opportunities for personal fulfillment and seek [it] only through husband and children. In many cases, the decision about employment is simply postponed.[12]

Having thus summarized the dilemma of the "feminine mystique," Bingham recommended minimizing sex segregation in education, that educators use consciousness-raising exercises among girls, and that female counselors realize their own potential as role models.

By the early 1970s advocates of women's career advancement had identified socialization and education as formidable obstacles, but they had not found effective corrective measures. Feminists of the 1970s and 1980s not only condemned separatism and sexist content in curricula but also criticized the power differential between men and women in educational institutions. The public school, as well as the university, taught by example that subservience characterized the role of women, while the role of men embodied—even defined—the exercise of power. One 1970s critic of public education observed that "As changes in economics, technology, and longevity [bring] more women into the job market, it is incumbent upon the schools to take cognizance." The author complained that "women almost always lack decent preparation for their new roles in the labor force" and castigated public education for teaching gender discrimination through the example of the school itself, in which women dominate teaching jobs overall but are less likely to be high school teachers than lower school teachers and much less likely to be administrators.[13]

GIRL SCOUTS IN THE SIXTIES AND SEVENTIES

Just as schools attempted to adapt to women's needs as long-term, full-time workers, the Girl Scouts eventually recognized that girls' needs had changed as their long-term prospects of wage earning increased, but scouting lagged behind formal education in adapting to economic and social change. As girls' leisure interests turned increasingly to athletics and commercial entertainment, the programs of the 1950s lost appeal as well as relevance. Working mothers had less time to devote to leading youth activities, and the recruitment of scout leaders proved more difficult than it had formerly.

By the end of the 1960s recruitment of inner-city and other working-class girls took on a new urgency in scouting. Middle-class youths of both sexes had demonstrated less interest in single-sex activities than their predecessors. As a national YWCA study concluded, "Many single sex agencies, including the YWCA, have felt the need to involve members of the opposite sex in order to build youth programs for their own constituency."[14] Girl Scouting as well as Boy Scouting had to change in order to survive. By the 1970s the Girl Scouts had jettisoned its heavy emphasis on homemaking and tried to adapt to women's changing roles. The Girl Scouts dropped much of its paramilitary ritual and experimented with updated uniforms and less formal troop structures. Despite wrestling with all of these challenges, the Girls Scouts failed to enlist girls as successfully as it had in the 1950s.

Girls Scouts and Boys Scouts failed to grow with the population, but they maintained steady enrollments through the 1960s. After 1970 the actual number of youths participating in Girl or Boy Scouting declined. The decline reflected both the drop in births beginning in the 1960s and the reality that scouting had lost touch with children's needs and with the schedules of working parents. As membership fell and many Girl Scout camps closed their doors forever, the Girl Scout movement increased its efforts to better girls' and women's lives through advocacy and political action. In the 1970s Girl Scouts joined feminist groups in supporting the enforcement of Title IX of the Higher Education Act.[15]

A NEW FEMALE OUTLOOK AND NEW FEMALE PROGRESS

By the end of the 1970s, girls' expectations of adult life had changed from those of earlier generations. A 1980 *Seventeen Magazine* survey documented significant changes in female socialization. The majority of a random sample of girls ages thirteen through nineteen aspired to and expected an education beyond high school. "According to *Seventeen's* poll of the girls not yet in college, nearly three quarters plan to attend. Their main reasons: to prepare for a high-paying job. Less than 10 percent admit they look forward to college in order to meet a husband; and only 1 percent say they'll be going simply because their parents want them to."[16] *Seventeen's* respondents planned to combine employment and child rearing in their adult years. "The surveyed girls are not Susy-Stay-at-Homes: 87 percent say they will probably work after marriage, and well over half plan to work after having children."[17] Author Judy Galen concluded that "Times are clearly changing." The teenagers surveyed did not believe that a single earner could maintain an acceptable standard of living for a growing family. This cohort of girls moved into their teen years in a different environment than the cohort only ten years their elder. Full-time working mothers had become commonplace by the 1970s, and women had achieved much more visibility in high-status jobs than had their counterparts of the 1960s.

For teenage girls, as for Ellen Ross and her contemporaries, the 1970s marked a clear turning point. Rapid growth produced jobs for women in all sectors of the economy (see tables 7.1 and 8.1). Growth slowed in the service sector, but women doubled their representation in craft-level positions. The number of female factory operatives grew modestly while the employment of male operatives stagnated. Highly educated women experienced real occupational mobility relative to men, which they had not experienced during the 1960s. Men enjoyed job growth in the management, technical, and professional areas, but with much smaller gains than those that women experienced. Law and public policy assisted women in their battles for occupational and wage equity during the seventies, but the economy rather than the law provided the major boost to women's earnings as white-collar jobs grew especially fast. Women advanced most noticeably in management and administration, with the number of positions held by women tripling from one million to three million. The conversion to a postindustrial economy accelerated during the 1970s, and the transition strengthened the market in traditional areas of professional and paraprofessional activity such as teaching, nursing, librarianship, counseling, and welfare work, which continued to account for two thirds of all professional women. However, equal-opportunity policies and increasing demand for professional workers delivered marked occupational diversification for women of the 1970s. More clearly than ever before, education defined women's chances of economic advancement.

By the 1970s, women's rates of college and graduate school completion were rising faster than men's, and they increasingly reaped appropriate rewards. The postindustrial age had arrived, and educated women benefited from the change both in upward occupational mobility and in the total number of jobs held. The number of women employed in management or professional positions swelled by 60 percent, nearly one and one half times the overall growth in female employment. The number of women in law multiplied nearly five-fold, that of women scientists and engineers more than doubled, and the number of women in dentistry, veterinary medicine, and medicine increased 65 percent. On the other hand, for less-educated Americans, male and female, the public and commercial service sector rapidly emerged as a low-wage ghetto, replacing unskilled labor in household service, agriculture, commerce, and manufacturing.

Educated women of the 1970s moved ahead through the skills acquired in advanced training and the avenues opened by legislation, litigation, and executive order. The law evolved in response to pressures brought largely by white women in white-collar occupations who had confronted invisible barriers as they sought to enter fields in which labor demand existed but school gender quotas or employer policies retarded women's progress. These women grew up in the 1940s, 1950s, and 1960s. The older among them had worked through the 1950s and experienced discrimination in the workplace. As the younger women passed from early childhood through adolescence, they watched their own mothers and their friends' mothers return to the labor force. They themselves expected to work while single and did not presume that motherhood would keep them homebound. Whether or not working women involved themselves in the Civil Rights Movement, the campaign for African Americans' rights to equal education and employment served to remind them of their own disabilities and fueled their resolve to improve their own chances in society.[18]

Through the 1960s and the 1970s African American women secured important educational and employment gains along with white women, but racial discrimination did not disappear. The occupational segregation of African American women, despite migration and World War II labor demands, remained largely intact through the 1950s. Both the earnings and the occupational status of black women continued to lag behind those of whites, although black women moved into the managerial, professional, manufacturing, and clerical sectors after 1960. As new occupational opportunities opened, African American women's labor force participation returned to pre-Depression levels. Teaching, nursing, and social work

TABLE 7.2

Occupational Distribution (in Percentages) of Spanish-Origin and Non-Hispanic White, Black, Asian, and Pacific Island Women in the Labor Force, 1980

	SPANISH ORIGIN	NOT OF SPANISH ORIGIN		ASIAN & PACIFIC ISLANDERS
		WHITE	BLACK	
Total number:	2,399,665	35,877,051	5,182,629	787,596
Percent in:				
Executive, administrative, and managerial occupations	4.6	7.7	4.4	7.4
Professions	7.2	14.3	11.0	15.8
Physicians	0.1	0.1	0.1	1.4
Registered nurses	1.0	3.0	1.7	5.2
Teachers, except postsecondary	3.1	6.2	5.5	3.5
Technical, sales, and clerical	37.4	46.9	34.0	39.4
Technicians	2.0	3.0	3.1	4.6
Sales representatives and supervisors	1.7	3.3	0.1	2.4
Sales clerks	7.5	8.9	5.3	6.9
Clerical workers and supervisors	26.1	31.7	24.6	25.4
Service occupations	20.3	16.3	28.6	17.1
Household workers	2.3	0.8	4.7	1.0
Farming, forestry, and fishing	2.3	1.0	.6	1.0
Precision workers	3.9	2.2	.3	.6
Operatives and laborers	22.7	10.9	16.7	14.7

SOURCE: *U.S. Bureau of the Census*, U.S. Census of Population, 1980, General Social and Economic Characteristics, United States Summary *(Washington: D.C., GPO 1983), table 1.*

were white-collar occupations in which appropriately trained black women could reasonably hope to find stable employment and financial security in the decades after 1960. Beginning in the 1960s civil rights legislation improved the occupational opportunities of African Americans (see table 7.2). With a stronger record of college attendance and college completion than black men in the postwar era, black women found themselves better situated than their brothers to win positions in government and business.

Despite the occupational gains of African American women after 1960, relative newcomers to the U.S. labor market secured significantly higher occupational status than black women. Hispanic women, with lower overall educational achievements than black women, had more success than African Americans in finding sales and clerical jobs. By 1980 Asian women, many of them first- or second-generation immigrants, had achieved higher representation in the professional sector than any other groups of female workers. Racial discrimination against African American women also persisted in the sales sector as other groups moved ahead. Hispanic and Asian women particularly succeeded in entering sales occupations, jobs that required little or no postsecondary education but involved extensive contact with the public. The specifics of these shifting patterns of employment suggest that black women may have been turned away because of employers' racial and ethnic preferences.

After World War II women did not gain re-entry into male-dominated skilled craft occupations in significant numbers until the equal-opportunity training programs of the 1970s. Even in the 1970s women did not enter traditionally male craft occupations as quickly as they flooded traditional female jobs. Nevertheless, the female lineperson or welder of the 1970s provided an important symbol of changing women's lives. Interview data on women entering overwhelmingly male blue-collar occupations in the 1970s reveal that they followed paths and had job experiences markedly different from those of women entering nontraditional professions during the same years. While college women planned careers in specific fields and secured those positions with credentials that carried some authority, blue-collar women came to their jobs by circuitous paths and received most of their training on the job.

Women entering the crafts in the 1970s displayed a broad spectrum of educational backgrounds, from women who had qualified for employment through a G.E.D. certificate to women who had completed college but eschewed white-collar jobs. Women who had come to the skilled crafts after a series of unskilled jobs or from a lower-class background found greater satisfaction in their employment than did women who had moved down from middle-class status into blue-collar jobs. Black women, who generally had more previous work experience than white women, and who previously had no other job choices outside service and low-skilled factory jobs, took particular pride in their achievements.[19]

DECLINE OF PATRIARCHY AND THE TRADITIONAL FAMILY

U.S. women of all races lived through dramatic changes as the economy feminized at a rapid pace; these changes included the further erosion of vestiges of patriarchy. In the years from the Great Depression through the 1950s, family life in two-parent households had moved away from patriarchy and toward companionate marriage and egalitarianism, but the transformation of family governance remained far from complete by 1960.[20] Sociological studies of families of the 1960s and 1970s do show, however, that husbands and wives were more likely than not to share decision making regarding child rearing, housing choices, and family spending. Shared responsibilities and egalitarianism described the ideal two-parent family, but significant gender differences persisted as women continued to perform the larger share of household and child care activities.[21] The burden of domestic responsibilities in two-worker households generated stress between husbands and wives, thus increasing the likelihood that marriages would fail. While wage earning enhanced women's autonomy, most women had nevertheless not achieved economic independence by 1980.

During the sixties and seventies women's inferior earnings presented ever greater challenges as divorce rates rose and extramarital fertility increased. The decline of close relations among members of extended families further complicated women's efforts to cope with child rearing on their own, and traditional dependence on kin networks among some ethnic groups eroded during the Cold War era. Sociologist Herbert Gans's study of Boston Italians, for example, demonstrated that middle-class status and suburban housing patterns eroded traditional ethnic behaviors.[22] While African American families continued to depend heavily upon grandmothers and aunts for child care, many black mothers turned more and more to acquaintances for assistance as migration separated kin groups.[23]

In the years since 1960, sociologists, psychologists, and public policy makers have focused on two related family issues that have alarmed them: female-headed families and the feminization of poverty. The Cold War consensus of the 1950s and 1960s included a high level of confidence in the efficacy of public spending and education as weapons against poverty. As public welfare expenditures expanded, however, both Great Society liberals and New Right conservatives began to brood about the idea that welfare might breed poverty and dependency. Sociological writings such as Oscar Lewis's studies of Latin America encouraged the perception that a "culture of poverty" reproduces economic failure from one generation to the next. Concern with the faults of the poor continues the historic tradition of regarding poverty as deviance. From the colonial period forward, officials of the state and the church have traditionally asked what wrongs people have done that made them poor, while assuming that hard work and virtue sufficiently explain affluence. In the twentieth century sociological and psychological theories replaced religion and sin as explanations of poverty, but assumptions about the personal inadequacies of the poor remained central.[24]

In a monograph examining changes in the household structures of whites and blacks in the United States from 1960 through the late 1970s, sociologist Suzanne Bianchi examined the impact of rapidly rising rates of divorce and changing rates of remarriage on family life. These changes put children at increasingly greater risk of growing up outside a family unit consisting of two parents and the children born of that union, as well as increasing the incidence of female-headed households. Additional changes in family formation reflected a sharp reversal of behaviors exhibited in the immediate postwar years. In the mid-1960s age at first marriage began to climb after declining in the 1940s and 1950s. Overall fertility declined from a peak in 1957, although fertility outside of marriage began to rise. The general prosperity of the 1960s and 1970s, coupled with the absence of a housing shortage, permitted baby boomers to enjoy a period of independent living between leaving school and marriage. Widowed persons similarly had greater opportunity to live independently than in previous decades. A trend toward independent living had appeared earlier in the century, but the increase in single-person households accelerated after 1960. Increasing longevity, escalating divorce rates, and a rise in the age at first marriage after the 1960s caused "perhaps the most significant change in household composition in recent decades."[25]

Female-headed families have always suffered disproportionately from poverty, but in the past, patriarchal presumptions cast women in the role of "deserving" poor. Our long history of female wage earning and the presumed attachment of mothers' pensions to widowed family heads cast a stigma of moral failure on the impoverished single or divorced woman with children; nevertheless, Great Society programs sought to aid the families of the poor. As divorce vied with widowhood as the leading cause of female family headship, the law demanded that ex-husbands assume increasing legal responsibilities for the support of female-headed families—an obligation often unfulfilled. Meanwhile, the public's sense of responsibility to unmarried mothers declined.

Although the majority of female family heads were not black, critics and analysts of public policy focused their attentions on the disproportionate rate of family headship among African American women and the history of poverty among blacks in the United States. The work of Robert Coles, Michael Harrington, and others on nonblack as well as black poverty diversified the hitherto single-minded study of poverty as a predicament peculiarly related to an African American "subculture," but the preoccupation with race and charges of an African American "family pathology" persisted.[26]

In fact, sometime between 1920 and 1970—for whatever reasons—marital instability and female headship came to characterize African American family life, and a dramatic rise in black female family headship began in the late 1950s. Similar but more slowly developing trends emerged in nonblack families, suggesting that contemporary socioeconomic conditions rather than black (or any other) culture explain the transition, but the debate over the black family obscured rather than clarified the rising trend of female family headship among all women. The family experiences of African American women heading families generally differed dramatically from those of white women. Consistent with their inferior economic position, more African American women had to work than white female family heads; more of their children had to work than white children in families without fathers. Proportionally fewer African American than white female family heads eventually escaped poverty. Nevertheless, the majority of poor women heading families in the decades to come would be of non-African heritage.

EMPLOYMENT AND THE CHANGING FEMALE LIFE CYCLE

The rising work rates of married women in the post–World War II era encompassed women at all stages of the life cycle. During the Cold War years as before, mothers tended more to seek employment after their children had completed secondary school, and mothers of school-age children tended more to get jobs than the mothers of infants and toddlers (see table 7.3). Nevertheless, female work rates increased among women with children at home, as well as among the mothers of schoolchildren. As noted before, although the climb in maternal employment

TABLE 7.3
Work Rates (in Percentages) of Married Women by Ages of Children, 1960–89

	CHILDREN UNDER 6 YEARS	CHILDREN 6–18 YEARS	NO CHILDREN
1960	18.6	39.0	34.7
1970	30.0	49.2	42.2
1980	45.1	61.7	46.0
1989	58.4	73.2	50.5

SOURCE: *U.S. Bureau of the Census,* Statistical Abstract of the United States, 1991 *(Washington, D.C.: GPO, 1991), table 643.*

accelerated after 1947, it constituted an extension of a long-term upward trend in the work rates of married women.

In addition to a strong labor market, demographic and social changes of the 1960s and 1970s further encouraged women's movement out of the home and into the labor force. A return of Malthusian fears of a population explosion followed the postwar baby boom, but advances in reproductive technology—particularly "the pill"—during the 1960s increased women's abilities to control fertility, and population growth soon slowed. Between 1965 and the mid-1970s, fertility declined temporarily to zero population growth. The mean age at which women entered first marriages climbed from a low of 20.1 years in 1956 to 23.7 years by 1988. Consequently, most women were older at the birth of their first child than their mothers had been and younger when their last pregnancy occurred. These demographic changes meant that the time before women became parents lengthened and the years devoted to child rearing decreased. Consequently, mothers of the 1960s and the 1970s had a longer period to establish their careers before childbearing than women of the immediate postwar era, and they could devote a longer span of time to employment after their children had grown.

However, changes in fertility patterns did not deliver increased freedom from family responsibilities for women. After declining in the 1950s, the share of women heading families resumed its climb in the 1960s. Before 1960 single and widowed women without dependent children primarily accounted for the rise in the share of households headed by women. After 1960, however, divorce and childbirth outside of marriage began to drive up female household headship dramatically.[27]

Female household headship has in fact risen consistently since the Great Depression. Women headed fourteen in one hundred U.S. households in 1930; by 1980 the figure had doubled. Until the 1950s, however, twentieth-century young women had remained less likely to head households than they had been in the nineteenth century (see table 7.4); however, extramarital pregnancies as well as divorce increased sharply after 1960, and the gap between the lifespans of men and women widened. These factors, together with increased spousal abandonment and the rising age of first marriage, have expanded the likelihood that women between the ages of fifteen and twenty-four and women in their prime working and child-rearing years, ages twenty-five through forty-four, will spend several years as family heads.

RISING SATISFACTION, LINGERING PANGS OF GUILT

Although two of every five married mothers of young children and more than half of wives with school-age children worked in the mid-1970s, many of these moth-

TABLE 7.4

	TOTAL	UNDER AGE 25		AGES 25–34		AGES 35–44		AGES 45–54		55 AND OVER	
		No.	%	No.	%	No.	%	No.	%	No.	%
1890	1,833	59	3.2	230	12.5	378	21.1	466	25.4	691	37.7
1930	3,793	120	3.2	371	9.8	685	18.1	862	22.7	1,794	46.1
1940	5,269	113	2.1	470	8.9	879	16.7	1,144	21.7	2,663	50.5
1950	6,389	164	2.6	541	8.5	935	14.6	1,264	19.8	3,486	54.6
1960	9,151	330	3.6	803	8.8	1,227	13.4	1,607	17.6	5,184	56.6
1970	13,287	820	6.2	1,324	10.5	1,401	10.5	1,959	14.7	7,782	58.6

		AGES 15–24		AGES 25–44		AGES 45–64		AGES 65 AND OVER			
		No.	%	No.	%	No.	%	No.	%	No.	%
1983	24,668	2,061	8.4	8,463	34.3	6,198	25.1	7,946	32.2		
1989*	26,010	—	8.5	—	51.9	—	26.0	—	13.6		

SOURCES: *U.S. Bureau of the Census,* Historical Statistics of the United States, Colonial Times to 1970, *Series A 320–324;* U.S. Census of Population, 1980, U.S. Summary, *table 121;* Statistical Abstract of the United States, 1985 *(Washington, D.C.: GPO, 1984), table 58; 1991, table 60.*

*1989 percent distribution by age is for families rather than households.

ers still wrestled with lingering guilt about their absence from the home. The 1960s protests of women like Betty Friedan and earlier campaigns by working mothers had not resolved the role conflicts that many wage-earning mothers experienced in the 1970s. New women's magazines like *Ms.* and *Working Woman* offered advice and encouragement to the working mother, but the real problems of juggling family needs with employment responsibilities had grown no easier. The dilemma of the working mother stemmed partly from the nation's refusal to mandate child day care at local, state, or federal levels.

From the Cold War forward, legislators' views of American family life conflicted with the reality that labor shortages and economic need pulled and pushed mothers into the labor force. As women's labor force participation increased after the Johnson presidency, the Republican White House and conservative religious and political pressure groups reasserted a nostalgic and flawed view of American family life. Conservative preachers, conservative political groups such as the Congressional Club, and Presidents Nixon, Reagan, and Bush all called for a return to "traditional" family values. Although politicians feared lecturing mothers on their obligation to stay home, the religious right felt no such compunction, as its opposition to publicly funded day care clearly reflected.

In the face of the inadequacy of affordable day care and continued public rhetoric undermining working mothers' confidence, working mothers of the 1970s turned to each other for support and for advice as they had done in the past. A "handbook" for working mothers published in 1977 addressed the issue of guilt before turning to advice on the emotional, career, and logistical issues confronting working mothers. The author, Niki Scott, reached a not overwhelmingly affirmative conclusion about the situation of the working mother: "Perhaps you'll learn . . . that some of your guilt is unwarranted; that though . . . guilt in working mothers is nearly universal, most women do not 'do it all'—they just do the best they can; that children are not quite as vulnerable as we might think, given a chance to develop; and that you are not alone."[28] After conducting her own research and consulting an employment counselor for women, Scott advised mothers contemplating a return to work to take time to explore all their options. She suggested that the preemployment process might include further education even though "Most women reentering the job market [do] so because of immediate necessity."[29] Scott also advised mothers to consider the pros and cons of part-time employment as the Women's Bureau had done since the 1950s.

By the end of the 1970s, for-profit day care facilities had expanded somewhat, but publicly supported programs had not advanced substantially. By the end of the 1980s, corporately sponsored day care for the children of employees had begun to appear, but these programs also fell far short of the overall demand for child care. Educators, peer groups, and counselors also succeeded marginally in altering the work expectations of a minority of girls, but a 1981 study revealed that female college students remained overwhelmingly enrolled in courses that led to traditionally female occupations, and that girls who did not aspire to careers in the professions had even more limited aspirations for employment in nontraditional occupations.

Throughout the postwar period women's expectations continued to differ by race or ethnicity as well as by class. Black and Hispanic girls expected a longer and more continuous attachment to wage earning than did non-Hispanic white girls, while Anglo girls more frequently expected to hold part-time as opposed to full-time jobs.[30] Betty Friedan had earlier argued that full-time housewives felt vaguely dissatisfied with their lot but that working mothers suffered severe and specific distress over their abandonment of home and family.[31] While working-class mothers often shared middle-class women's preferences for remaining at home with their children, working-class women accepted market labor without the pervasive burden of guilt that Friedan ascribed to middle-class wage earners.

Alfreda Iglehart's study of the effects of employment on the self-concepts and aspirations of wives and mothers of the 1950s and of the 1970s (see chap. 6) had concluded that in the 1950s housewives had a better chance at happiness than did working wives. By the 1970s, however, Iglehart believed that norms had shifted. Working wives of the 1970s had real commitment to their employment, despite some lingering guilt pangs, and had found greater happiness than their stay-at-home sisters because society now accepted the combination of employment and marriage or motherhood.

The much higher percentage of women who preferred employment in 1976 compared with that in 1957 seemed to confirm Iglehart's conclusions about the fifties. However, the survey that she utilized also documented that working wives of the fifties had felt largely content with their choice of employment. Wives more often cited economic need as their reason for working in 1957 than in the later survey, but ego satisfaction also supplied a significant employment motivation in 1957. Together the surveys suggested that, in 1957 as well as in 1976, working wives had better self-images and were happier than full-time homemakers. The data suggest that the proscriptions of the 1950s may in fact have caused more psychological distress among wives who remained at home than among those who entered the labor market.

Postwar attitudinal shifts reflected the depreciation in the value of wives' housework following from the increasing expectation that married women would engage in wage work. Simultaneously, the women's movement condemned housework as exploitative because it functions as unpaid or poorly paid labor. These developments encouraged dissatisfaction among housewives because "Even for women who do not agree with the movement's rhetoric, this [denunciation] of housework directs their attention to the negative aspects of [it]."[32] Although Iglehart somehow concluded that satisfaction with housework had not declined substantially during the two decades between the surveys, the results actually suggest significant attitudinal change. Among women who did not work, positive satisfaction in household labor declined from 68 percent of the women in 1957 to 58 percent in 1976. Iglehart also found that working mothers' confidence in their parenting had improved over these years.

By the 1970s changes in the labor force patterns of U.S. women had not only caught the attention of educators but also captured the interest of a variety of researchers. This interest in the ways in which the lives of U.S. women had changed resulted in the 1967 initiation of the National Longitudinal Surveys (NLS) of Labor Market Experience among women ages thirty to forty-four years of age. The study, directed by sociologist Lois Banfill Shaw, surveyed women eight times over an eleven-year period. A 1983 publication based on the survey reported that working wives had reduced the poverty level of two-parent households by 50 percent. On the other hand, the study confirmed historian Carl Degler's claim that women's market labor conflicted with family life. Degler's conclusion seemingly contradicts evidence of superior income levels in intact families with working mothers but comports with the fact that wives with relatively higher earnings did seem to have more discretion in terminating unhappy marriages.

Like later studies of family dissolution among the poor, the Shaw study demonstrated that white and nonwhite working wives whose marriages ended in divorce had higher earnings and more education than women whose marriages had ended through widowing or separation. In addition, white mothers who had worked while their children were young were much more likely to work into middle age than other middle-aged white mothers.[33] Black women, on the whole always less likely to remain at home with their children, have experienced less change in this regard as long-term employment commitments have historically been more common among them.[34] A follow-up publication from the NLS data revealed that middle-aged women employed over a fifteen-year span had failed to gain positions of equal authority with those of men who had similar education and work backgrounds.

The Shaw publications highlighted the degree to which the employment of middle-aged wives extended the utilization of traditional "women's roles" in service occupations from cleaning to teaching.[35] Blue-collar working mothers of the 1970s, like their counterparts in earlier decades, experienced less emotional conflict between employment and domestic obligations than did middle-class women. At home blue-collar wives received more help from husbands than did middle-class working women. Although blue-collar women often wished they had more time to spend with their children, the advantages that their earnings brought to family well-being easily outweighed any benefit that might have come from their full-time presence in the home. This class difference had persisted despite the reality that working-class wives typically had fewer household conveniences than did their middle-class counterparts.[36]

FEMALE MIGRATION IN THE SIXTIES AND SEVENTIES

Through the 1960s and 1970s women sought to advance themselves economically by moving to new locations as their mothers had also done. Internal migration trends of the 1970s differed markedly from those of the first half of the century when the cities of the Northeast and Midwest drew both immigrants and migrants to work in factories, private homes, shops, and offices. At the time of the 1980 federal census, the Northeast and the Midwest showed a combined net loss of over three million residents over a five-year period while the South and the Midwest had absorbed comparable gains. South Atlantic and southwestern states except Texas and Florida generally lost population during the 1960s, but during the 1970s and 1980s the rise of Sunbelt industries reversed the trend of outmigration from southern and mountain states while the Northeast and the Midwest continued to lose population. Internal migration outpaced immigration in the sixties and seventies as it had previously. Although race dictated significant differences in the prospects they faced, black and white women fleeing southern poverty followed similar routes and shared similar disappointments. For example, at the end of the 1950s, Wyoming Wilson moved to Cincinnati from eastern Kentucky after her husband died in a mining accident. As a child she had moved from one coal mine to another with her family and had, herself, helped haul coal from the mines. While still in her teens, she married a man thirty years her senior and lived in constant fear of the mine disaster that eventually took his life. After finding work as a waitress, Wilson brought her five children to Cincinnati from their grandmother's Kentucky home. Wilson compared urban congestion and the closeness of city apartments to "living in jail."[37] The family inhabited a rat-infested slum and endured the jeers of city folks who ridiculed their rural look and manner. Ten years after moving to Cincinnati's "Over the Rhine" neighborhood, Wilson had moved from restaurant to factory employment, but she failed to rescue her family from poverty or from the ghetto surroundings where she lived and worked with other Appalachian migrants. Although women like Wyoming Wilson migrated without friends or relatives to assist and encourage them, most followed paths already charted by their acquaintances; among black and white southern women who moved to Cleveland in the 1960s, nine of ten had relatives or friends who had earlier established residence in the city.[38]

Like Wyoming Wilson, women migrating to the United States from abroad faced difficult challenges in adapting to their new surroundings. By the 1960s immigration had resumed turn-of-the century numerical levels, although immigration remained far smaller proportionally than in the early twentieth century. Latin American and Asian immigration surged, constituting a third wave of movement to this country since the beginning of the Industrial Revolution.[39] More than 1.6 million persons entered the United States from Asia in the 1970s, a population of roughly equal size with the sum of immigration from the Western Hemisphere during those years. Female immigrants outnumbered male newcomers in the 1960s, an imbalance that equalized by 1980.

The majority of the immigrants of the 1960s lacked the combination of formal training and English language facility that white-collar jobs demanded. Rather than displacing native-born white workers, as the immigrants of the nineteenth century had done, these new immigrants took jobs that white Americans left as their education expanded and white-collar opportunities broadened. In the 1970s and the 1980s, public schools again addressed the challenge of rising numbers of foreign-born students, many of them shunted into segregated classes for non--English speakers. For girls and for boys, separate programs often meant different content from the lessons of native-born children, just as earlier curricula had tracked working-class youths away from college preparatory work.

The new migrants, like those of the early twentieth century, struggled to preserve the gender roles and familial values of their homelands, but migration demanded significant shifts in the work roles and family responsibilities of women. The dislocation of immigration strained marriages, as men accustomed to being family heads faced the humiliation of unemployment and the necessity of their wives' accepting menial work. For example, when the Bolanos family fled Cuba for Florida in the 1960s, Mrs. Bolanos, an educated woman, eagerly accepted a job cleaning motel rooms after three months of looking had failed to secure a job for herself or her husband. Mr. Bolanos fought to keep his self-respect intact during the intervening months until he also found work.[40] This pattern repeated itself among thousands of Cuban refugees who fled the Castro regime.

Hispanic parents also strove to maintain their cultural emphases on close familial supervision of daughters' daily activities and social lives.[41] In *How the Garcia Girls Lost Their Accents*, a highly autobiographical novel of Dominican sisters' coming of age in New York City in the 1960s, Julia Alvarez recounts her parents' decision to protect their daughters' innocence and values. Expecting a protective environment in the home of kin in the Dominican Republic, the parents sent the girls back to Hispaniola during their summer school holidays. Too late, the parents discovered that young Dominicans do not universally observe the values of their elders and that schooling in the United States had already rooted the attitudes of U.S. teenagers far too deeply in their daughters for a Dominican summer to extract.

Immigration from Latin America and from Asia held the attention of the public during the 1960s and thereafter, but small numbers of immigrants continued to arrive from Europe. In the recent past Irish women still fled dim marriage and employment prospects in Ireland for a better chance in the United States. Although negligible in number compared with those of earlier periods, recent migrants bear striking similarities to Erin's daughters of yesteryear (see chap. 1). Ann Gilvary, for example, came from Ireland to New York in 1968 through the sponsorship of an aunt and uncle in the Bronx. Only seventeen, Gilvary left her parents' relatively prosperous farm because "everybody knew my brother would get that."[42] One of her sisters had already come to the United States, and the two remaining sisters followed after Ann. Like millions of lasses before her, Gilvary accepted a position as a live-in domestic. She saved money despite her meager earnings of $50 a week. She visited Ireland regularly and during one trip became engaged, but the romance soon soured, the engagement ended, and Ann returned to New York. In

New York she enrolled in cosmetology school and began earning enough to "pretty much do as I please." The end of the 1970s found Ann still single and content with her independent lifestyle, continuing a pattern in which Irish and Irish American women disproportionally chose the single life.

CONCLUSION

The 1960s and 1970s were years of radical change in women's lives, and these changes had economic origins or carried serious economic implications for women and children. Labor demand drew women into the workforce, and economic need compelled increasing numbers of women to find jobs. Rising living costs induced women to work for wages regardless of their family status. By the 1960s the data collected by the Bureau of Labor Statistics and the Bureau of the Census plainly revealed that families with working wives and working husbands had higher incomes than husband-supported families. The sharp rise in the number of women heading families also meant that fewer and fewer women could choose to remain at home with their minor children. Women's economic responsibilities mounted steadily, but women made little progress in narrowing the gender gap in wages. Well-educated women achieved remarkable upward occupational and economic mobility during these decades, but the vast majority of female workers occupied poorly paying jobs in clerical or service work or in manufacturing. Some members of racial and ethnic minorities advanced into the upper reaches of the occupational structure along with Anglo women, but Hispanic and African American women did not reap the full benefits of women's upward mobility.

Rising divorce rates outpaced female occupational mobility, and the share of U.S. families headed by women rose more sharply than women's overall employment. While female-headed families have always been disproportionally poor, the "feminization of poverty" occurred during the sixties and seventies as divorce and extramarital fertility increased. Women with college educations weathered the social and economic shifts well, as they always had. Compared with less-educated women, they had higher earnings, a better chance of raising their children in a two-parent household, and superior prospects for collecting child support in the event of divorce.

Women who had only high school education or had left high school before graduation did not fare well through the economic and social changes of the sixties and seventies. Their employment opportunities widened, but more jobs did not mean better jobs. Semiskilled and unskilled women's wages rose alongside those of male service and industrial workers, but living costs often rose faster than their earnings, and their responsibilities for child support often exceeded their earning power. Less-educated women faced higher odds of becoming family heads than their better-educated counterparts and had less chance of collecting child support from absent fathers. For the Wyoming Wilsons of the nation, the 1960s and 1970s proved hard times indeed. Women's Liberation did not reach them. Class remained the major determinant of the quality of life for women, as it had in 1900. During the 1970s, though all women advanced economically relative to men, poverty persisted among female-headed families.

During the 1960s, as white-collar women increasingly pressed for equality in the workplace, the equal rights agenda gained ground through legislation while many older protectionist regulations, advocated and largely won by maternalist social reformers, fell by the wayside or expanded to include men as well as women. During these two decades a concept of equal rights won out over the protectionist agenda that working women and their reformist allies had pursued in the early twentieth century. The passage of equal-opportunity legislation ultimately helped women compete more effectively with men in the workforce, but the victories of the equal rights philosophy opened the door for social and economic conservatives to attack the premise of mothers' pensions, upon which public welfare or aid to dependent children rested. With Ronald Reagan's election in 1980, the social agenda of Lyndon Johnson's Great Society came to an end.

Women worked to end racial segregation and broaden the civil rights of African Americans, demonstrated for "peace and love" and against the war in Vietnam, and journeyed to Haight-Ashbury. Women's experiences in the civil rights, student, and peace movements of the 1960s fueled the Women's Liberation Movement of the 1970s, just as abolitionism had encouraged the women's rights campaigns of the nineteenth century. Anne Moody and a multitude of other black women have testified movingly to their participation in the civil rights movement and the ways in which that activism transformed their own lives, thus connecting the rights movement directly to the birth of feminism. Records of sixties activism and protest inform our understanding of Women's Liberation, but focus on female activists of the 1960s has overshadowed the importance of the 1960s as a turning point in the lives of ordinary women, changing their expectations in ways in which the social unrest of the era played but a minor role.

CHAPTER EIGHT

Wins and Losses
THE 1980S AND 1990S

T he economic forces driving the feminization of the labor force created ever more job opportunities for women as the end of the century approached, but women reached executive positions—when they reached them—largely because political forces extracted affirmative action policies from government and corporations. Affirmative action created opportunities for educated women like Marcelite Harris, the first African American woman to rise to the rank of Brigadier General in the United States Air Force, to reach positions and status closed to their mothers.[1] Although these women benefited from affirmative action, they also proved their merits on the job, as had the defense workers of World War II. Nevertheless, neither affirmative action nor the overall growth of the service sector protected women against the boom and bust cycle of the eighties. The gap between the rich and the poor widened during the last decades of the century, and working women, from food service workers to teachers, saw their real earnings decline while the most fortunate women strode up the income ladder.

Although women made great educational strides during the 1980s, not even college training insulated them from the employment crisis of the late 1980s and early 1990s. Those women who graduated without a specific, marketable skill found themselves especially vulnerable. The employment difficulties of Mae Belk's granddaughter and Lee Belk's daughter Holly illustrate this problem. After receiving her B.A. degree from Syracuse University in May of 1991, Holly left for Boston to look for work. "Yes," she remembered, "I was happy to be graduating, but I didn't know what to do next. I didn't have a job and I was scared."[2] And rightly so, as it turned out: after weeks of searching she accepted a job clerking in a retail shop, but her employer laid her off two months later because of declining sales. Part-time, then full-time employment at an insurance agency soon followed; however, corporate "downsizing" hit the company and Holly was among the first to go. After four more months of unemployment, she found work in the accounting department of a small media firm. This job also ended within the year as the company sold off its major assets. Discouraged by serial layoffs, Belk retreated to Richmond. After a three-month job search, she again settled for retail work. Her new job paid less than her position at the media firm and carried no health or retirement benefits. Belk left this job after four months and signed on with a temporary help agency, a move that led to a "full-time, temporary" position with a communications firm and finally to a permanent job with higher pay after more than a year as a temporary worker. "All I have ever done is look for jobs," Belk concluded of her life since college.

In addition to the recession that confronted working women, feminization of the labor force in the 1980s and 1990s continued to deliver the mixed basket of job possibilities that had taken shape during the 1960s and 1970s. The postindustrial economy created new jobs almost exclusively in service positions. For women and for men, well-paid production jobs declined, while the demand for unskilled service workers climbed. The number of mid-level management jobs drifted, but affirmative action policies and educational progress helped women like Marcelite Harris swim against the tide and move ahead through the recession and thereafter.

As the end of the century approached, some women reaped new economic rewards, despite the vagaries of the economy, and approached parity with men in ways not apparent in the 1960s and 1970s. The wage gap between men and women narrowed, some wage-earning wives achieved income parity with their husbands, and women's ascent of the career ladder continued. Gender discrimination continued and barred women from most of the highest positions in government or industry, but women established executive-level representation in virtually every occupation. The decades of the 1980s and 1990s demonstrated not only that affirmative action policies could succeed but also that, once given the opportunity, women's abilities could lift them to the top of their chosen professions despite "downsizing" in public and private sectors.

In contrast to the most highly trained workers, women in low-level white-collar occupations and in service or manufacturing work saw their well-being erode rather than advance during the 1980s. Corporate restructuring and stagnant wages during these years wreaked havoc in the lives of working-class women. Many lost production jobs, and those who managed to keep their jobs saw their real earnings decline along with those of women in clerical and service jobs. Whatever its causes, the downsizing of industry during the 1980s and 1990s exacerbated the maldistribution of income and wealth. Like working men, working women got poorer while the upper strata of women enjoyed large economic gains. The least educated women had more difficulty finding employment, especially full-time, permanent jobs. The economic distance between the classes increased and contributed to the growth of poverty among female-headed families.

The 1980s brought women closer to male levels of labor force participation than ever before. By 1993 women's labor force participation had risen to 58 percent while men's participation had declined to 75 percent. In contrast with earlier decades, most women no longer expected to leave the labor force during their child-bearing years. Maternity leave became a standard expectation of permanent employees, and the majority of women did not plan to stay home with their pre-school children. Some whose incomes would not cover the costs of child care, as well as some middle-income women tired of working, followed the postpartum path of countless female wage earners in the past—back into the home. Despite state and federal attempts to suppress homework, home manufacturing and service work had persisted. In fact, the craft movement of the 1970s and the ongoing development of computer-based communication systems fueled a resurgence in homework, and in the 1980s the federal government rescinded its ban on it.[3] Most working mothers, however, still left home in the morning and returned in the evening.

The majority of girls growing up in the 1980s had working mothers who had held jobs regularly since leaving school. Girls' clubs and the public schools prepared girls better than in the past to compete across the occupational spectrum, but neither institution had fully eradicated long habits of discouraging girls from achieving their full potential. In 1992 the American Association of University Women (AAUW) released the findings of a study of gender bias in the public schools.[4] AAUW researchers found that boys and girls began school with roughly equal skills. Yet boys completed high school with educational achievements that exceeded girls, especially in the fields of science and mathematics. Teachers' expectations and advice, instructional materials, testing instruments, and sexual harassment of girls by boys all worked to lower girls' self-esteem and educational accomplishments, researchers concluded.

CHANGING PATTERNS IN EDUCATION AND TRAINING

Despite the difficulties that girls encountered in the classroom, women continued to distance themselves from men in postsecondary schooling through the 1980s and early 1990s. Women's enrollments in institutions of higher education had surpassed male attendance in the 1970s, and in the 1980s women outnumbered men in graduate programs, trends expected to accelerate through the remainder of the century. In the 1970s and 1980s undergraduate and graduate women deserted nursing schools and colleges of education as they identified other career possibilities and federal law assisted them in realizing their ambitions. Women's representation in business, engineering, and science programs grew steadily. Women outnumbered men receiving either bachelor's or master's degrees by 1982. Between 1980 and 1995 women increased their share of medical, dental, veterinary, and law degrees from 24 percent to 37 percent and their share of doctorates from 30 percent to 42 percent. Race and ethnicity continued to be significant indicators of gender difference in educational behaviors. African American women pursued higher education in much greater numbers than black men, while whites and Hispanics moved closer to parity in enrollments by gender. Among Asian Americans, men continued to attend colleges or universities in greater numbers than women.

The Girl Scouts, like the public schools, strove to adapt to women's evolving place in the economy, but the organization faced many obstacles to serving girls effectively. When Frances Hesselbein rose to the executive directorship of the Girl Scouts in 1976, she inherited an organization struggling to redefine its organizational methods, to reach its audience, and to recruit volunteer leadership. Hesselbein found that "Mothers were going to work in record numbers, making scout leaders an endangered species. Fewer girls were joining, more were dropping out. The Boy Scouts were rumored to be thinking about opening their ranks to girls."[5] As commercial amusements increasingly captured the energies of adolescents, the Girl Scouts and other clubs enlisted new audiences by turning to younger children. Late in the 1980s Hesselbein successfully initiated the Daisy Girl Scouts for five-year-olds. Also designing membership drives that targeted minorities, Hesselbein succeeded in the 1980s in bringing Hispanic, African American, and Native American girls into the Scouts and raising total participation in scouting from one in eleven girls in the United States to one in nine. Minority membership rose to 15 percent of all Scouts, and nonwhites filled one fourth of the policymaking posts in the organization.

The late strengthening of scouting reflected success in recruiting very young girls and minority girls, but scouting had also learned to offer a program that more nearly matched girls' real interests and prospects than had the program of the 1960s. Scouting in the 1980s emphasized recreation and civic leadership but also turned to activities that led girls of all backgrounds to educational accomplishments and expectations linked to highly skilled jobs. Despite the conservative orientation of many volunteer and paid Scout workers, Hesselbein brought girls information and activities that engaged their interest. By 1990 merit awards for mathematical and computer skills had replaced homemaking badges as the most popular scout undertakings, and the Girl Scouts had published advice literature on adolescent sexuality. The career ideals of the 1920s had returned, but now these ideals fit girls' need to prepare for long-term employment. Scouting expanded through Hesselbein's leadership, but the halcyon days of the 1950s did not return as other pastimes drew girls away from girls' clubs, and mothers' volunteerism continued to decline under the pressures of home and work.[6]

THE RISE OF AFFIRMATIVE ACTION

While schools and girls' clubs scrambled to prepare children for the world of work, market demands and political action changed the environments in which women labored. Universities began to implement affirmative action admissions policies in the 1970s, and public and some private employers developed affirmative action hiring plans. In the first court tests of affirmative action, litigation revealed the pitfalls of efforts to comply with the Civil Rights Act or the Higher Education Act. In the 1978 case of *Regents of the University of California v. Bakke,* the United States Supreme Court held that racial quotas, even if intended to advance the education of underrepresented racial groups, violated the Constitution. In the following year, however, the court upheld the constitutionality of a racial quota for acceptance into an apprenticeship program in the case of *United Steelworkers of America v. Weber*. Court cases challenging affirmative action proliferated in the 1980s; the Supreme Court first ruled in a gender-related case in 1987. In this case, *Johnson v. Transportation Agency,* the court upheld the selection of a woman over Paul Johnson for a position despite the fact that Johnson had scored higher in the interview process than the woman appointed. The court ruled the selection consistent with the law because the screening process had found both applicants qualified, and women were underrepresented in that job category. Through the 1980s and into the 1990s, federal courts upheld many affirmative action plans but disallowed others. As new appointments to the Supreme Court moved rulings in a more conservative direction, more and more affirmative action plans fell. Recently, California's 1995 revocation of its affirmative action higher education admissions program suggested strongly that legislated affirmative action might not outlive the twentieth century.[7]

For the decade of the 1980s, when public agencies and some private employers rigorously pursued affirmative action hires, women and racial minorities successfully advanced occupationally. Responding to a suit against the University of Minnesota for discrimination against female employees, the university adopted an affirmative action plan in 1980. Between 1979 and 1989, women increased their representation from 26 percent to 54 percent in the administration, from 28 to 30 percent of tenure-track faculty, and from 14 to 17 percent of tenured faculty. The plan thus had a marginal impact on the status of women faculty but greatly assisted women administrators.[8]

Women also advanced significantly faster and more broadly within the ranks of private employers who adopted affirmative action plans. By the 1980s, equal-opportunity legislation and affirmative action policies had existed long enough to have some impact on the occupational structure. In the decade of the 1980s, women's employment grew at more than twice the rate of men's. To what extent this resulted from affirmative action resists definitive measurement, but patterns of occupational expansion provide some clues about the sources of women's changing occupational status.

Within the broad sector of managerial and professional pursuits, women's status clearly advanced during the 1980s (see table 8.1). Women lost proportionally more semiskilled factory jobs than men, but women showed strong growth in precision production or craft positions, while men's representation in these areas

Legislation, affirmative action, and employer needs interacted to promote women in engineering fields in the last two decades of the century. Petroleum engineer, Houston. Houston Post *photograph, courtesy Houston Metropolitan Research Center, Houston Public Library*

TABLE 8.1
Occupational Groupings of Employed Persons by Gender for 1980 and 1990

	WOMEN			MEN		
	1980	1990	% CHANGE	1980	1990	% CHANGE
Total	41,634,665	52,976,623	27.2	56,004,690	62,976,623	12.0
Managers and Professionals	8,954,843	14,752,659	64.7	13,196,805	15,780,923	19.6
Executives	3,070,247	5,993,163	95.2	7,063,304	8,234,753	16.6
Engineers	63,158	151,962	140.6	1,318,937	1,520,597	15.3
Lawyers and judges	74,037			455,642		
Natural scientists	60,361	399,299	561.6	246,934	929,118	276.3
Doctors, dentists, veterinarians	75,115	171,791	128.7	568,601	697,752	22.7
Nurses, therapists, etc.	1,458,622	2,163,863	48.3	236,784	318,690	34.6
Teachers, etc.	2,919,028	3,997,806	37.0	1,558,296	1,715,785	10.1
Technical, sales, and office	18,971,458	23,120,191	21.9	13,598,207	10,622,048	28.0
Clerical	12,997,076	14,569,944	12.1	3,854,322	4,256,533	10.4
Service	404,269	449,506	11.2	20,406,989	1,939,998	− 19.4
Crafts	997,950	1,235,327	26.3	11,616,225	11,862,636	2.1
Operatives	4,874,300	4,489,431	− 7.9	12,985,043	12,706,901	− 2.1

SOURCES: *U.S. Bureau of the Census,* U.S. Census of Population, 1980, General Social and Economic Characteristics, United States Summary *(Washington, D.C.: GPO, 1983), table* 1; 1990 Census, Equal Opportunity File *(Washington, D.C.: GPO, 1993.)*

stagnated. In the upper reaches of the occupational structure, managerial and professional positions, female employment grew three times as much as male. The largest such gains for women occurred at levels and in fields that men continued to dominate: executive-level management, engineering, medicine, natural science, and the law. In professions in which male control of education and hiring had clearly disadvantaged women in the past, women now made remarkable progress. In 1990 women held between two times and five times as many of these jobs as they had in 1980, enjoying much higher growth there than they experienced in managerial and professional pursuits overall.

Although women remained much more underrepresented in male blue-collar bastions than in the professions, affirmative action also delivered some gains for women seeking jobs as plumbers, electricians, fire fighters, and the like. In both the professional sectors and in the crafts, women's numerical gains continued to be much larger in jobs such as teaching, nursing, and dressmaking that women have long dominated, but women's advances into male jobs increased their earning power as well as their occupational status. Doctors and lawyers continued to earn more than teachers and nurses; plumbers and electricians had higher incomes than dressmakers. The overall gender gap in wages narrowed in the 1980s through the combination of women's status and the stagnation of male workers' wages, especially in blue-collar jobs.

These developments clearly show that despite the passage of Title IX, the gender-equity section, of the 1972 Higher Education Act, women of all races made slow progress in gaining access to highly male-dominated professions and virtually no progress in entering high-level management positions in the private sector until corporations developed "voluntary" affirmative action policies in the 1980s. On the other hand, relaxation or disappearance of gender and racial barriers in higher education and graduate and professional training had, by the 1980s, resulted in significant entry of white and minority women into the professions (see table 8.2). Asian Americans, generally not targeted by affirmative action policies, benefited most from women's wider access to professional training; white women followed closely behind. African American and Hispanic women had less success entering medicine and veterinary medicine than non-Hispanic whites and Asians. On the other hand, African American women have benefited most from the hiring of women in mid- to high-level public-sector administrative positions. Within the private sector African American women scored heavy advances in sales positions, but white women had the greatest success in gaining the generally more lucrative management jobs.

The contrast between women's advances in public versus private employments highlights the successes and failures of affirmative action programs. The growth of new occupations also provides additional clues about the role of affirmative action in improving women's employment opportunities. Women have long dominated the medical field overall because of their strong hold on nursing, medical technology and therapy, and less-skilled jobs in home and hospital care. As new medical specialties have emerged with status between that of medical doctors and nurses, women have competed with men more effectively than in traditional male occupations, but they have not predominated. For example, approximately equal numbers of men and women worked as physician's assistants in 1990 despite women's overrepresentation in other medical support jobs. As members of a new profession, physician's assistants have no history of gender bias, and consequently affirmative action guidelines have not applied to training or hiring in the field. Pharmacy, an old profession with occupational status similar to that of physician's assistant, remained predominantly male in 1990; however, women had much greater relative success becoming professional pharmacists than becoming physicians. At

TABLE 8.2

Employed Women by Occupational Grouping and Race or Ethnicity, 1990 *

	HISPANIC	WHITE	BLACK	ASIAN/PACIFIC ISLANDERS
Executive and managerial	290,938	5,165,841	499,587	179,300
Professions	357,467	7,452,498	815,695	269,089
Technical workers	102,091	1,590,073	232,189	83,958
Administrative support (including clerical)	982,739	12,125,043	1,663,394	356,083
Technical workers	102,091	1,590,073	232,189	83,958
Sales workers	468,358	5,726,154	655,224	202,083
Craft workers	142,710	948,709	158,390	67,455
Operatives	493,093	2,176,492	599,509	150,422
Service workers	802,822	6,185,729	1,460,372	245,824
Protective service	21,915	223,737	77,367	3,879
Household service	124,499	255,625	138,071	12,394
Transportation	29,395	387,462	77,409	4,199
Farming, fishing	85,007	380,584	27,812	9,388
Laborers	127,570	722,137	152,681	26,330
Totals	4,028,604	43,340,084	6,648,700	1,610,417

SOURCE: *U.S. Bureau of the Census,* 1990 Census, Equal Employment Opportunity File *(Washington, D.C.: GPO, 1993).*

*Count of Hispanic women includes women of all races; counts of women of white, black, Asian, or Pacific heritage exclude women of Hispanic origin; women of all other races not included in table.

the last census, women constituted one in three practicing pharmacists, but only one in five physicians.

FAMILY LIFE AND FEMALE LIFE CYCLES

Over the past two decades, the ongoing feminization of the economy has contin-ued to shape women's family life, as had been true earlier. Whether or not women's commitments to education and work caused them to postpone marriage, the female life cycle changed markedly in the second half of the century. During the 1980s births and divorces generally held steady, and the rate of increase in extramarital fertility slowed.

By 1980, second or subsequent marriages accounted for 17 percent of the nation's couples. Americans' increasing tendency to divorce, remarry, and have more children has reintroduced the stepfamily as a prominent form and reshaped the life cycles of many women. Women who bear children in more than one marriage have them farther apart than do mothers who marry only once. Divorce, remarriage, and the resumption of childbearing may extend the years of child rearing by as much as fifteen years, reversing the earlier trend toward fewer years of childbearing. Such extensions of women's childbearing years exacerbate the difficulties of balancing wage work against domestic duties for these mothers.

In the 1990s, as in earlier periods, families differed significantly by race and class. Although working- and middle-class Americans share many values, the differing economic realities of the poor and the affluent continue to dictate differing family strategies in the present day as in the past. Working-class families, with fewer resources than their middle-class counterparts, can less indulge the individual desires of family members and must focus strongly on maintaining a cohesive family unit. Working-class wives, whether employed or not, confront greater pressure than middle-class women to protect the family's welfare through sensible money management.

Sociologist Lillian Rubin's interviews with white working-class families in the 1970s and again in the 1990s indicate substantial changes in husbands' and wives' attitudes over the last twenty years. Rubin's findings demonstrate both the impact of employment on women's self concepts and the ways in which female work patterns have reshaped two-parent family experiences. As manufacturing jobs have dwindled and male wages have stagnated, women's earnings have become increasingly important to working-class families. Although husbands and wives of the early 1970s had described wives' earnings as discretionary, couples in the 1990s no longer believed this. The working wives continued to see their husbands as the primary breadwinners and to regard themselves as wives and mothers first and wage-earners second. On the other hand, most of Rubin's subjects "endorse[d] the principle of equal pay without the equivocation and ambivalence with which their counterparts greeted the idea two decades earlier."[9] These contemporary husbands and wives agreed that heavier demands on women's time obligated men to perform more chores around the house, but actual practices had not changed much over the two decades. The increase in wives' commitment to work since the 1970s had, however, increased stress within marriages. Husbands and wives both found themselves with less leisure than in the 1970s. The increase in the number of couples who stagger work hours so that one works while the other stays at home has decreased couples' opportunities for conversation and for sex.

Egalitarian governance, common in poor two-parent African American households, remained rare in poor white families, with either the mother or father making most decisions in two-parent households.[10] Matriarchal structures also exist in some two-parent working-class families, black and white.[11] Among the poor, members of the extended family may remain strongly linked with one another through their economic interdependence. Poor white as well as poor African American families depend upon kin for child care as they search for or adjust to new employments. From the mid-twentieth century onward, women have headed at least half of poor families, not only because female-headed households are overwhelmingly poor, but also because of especially high marital instability among the poor.[12] Poor mothers typically focus more on the welfare of their children than on the marital relationship. Husbands characteristically suffer feelings of inadequacy about their roles as providers. Wives' resentments over the necessity to work and anxieties about the family's economic difficulties reinforce husbands' sense of failure, often leading to clinical depression and domestic violence. While more prosperous working wives of the working and the middle classes may gain personal fulfillment in their employment, poor wives rarely express satisfaction in their wage-earning situations; and, while sociologists continue to study the internal dynamics of family life, politicians remain more concerned with family structure as it correlates with dependence on public assistance.[13]

POVERTY, GENDER, AND RACE: REALITY AND MYTH

Concern about welfare dependency has permeated the political mood of the 1990s, perhaps because single mothers and women who have never worked may remain on public assistance for up to ten years, which calls special attention to these women and obscures the fact that roughly half of all recipients stay on welfare less than two years.[14] The marginal employment of young men, welfare policies that discriminate against two-parent households, and the decline in the real earnings of low-wage workers since the 1970s have raised the barriers to fathers' support of their children. Rising rates of adolescent pregnancy among nonblacks, failure to ensure adequate availability of job training, and the cost of day care have further contributed to the feminization of poverty and the difficulties of single mothers getting off the welfare rolls.

In fact, in the contemporary United States, the majority of poor women with dependent children are poor because the fathers of their children do not or cannot provide adequate support for them. Some fathers have never assumed financial responsibility for their children; others have abandoned wives and children or divorced their wives and failed to meet their child support obligations.

Whatever the cause, an increase in female-headed households and the poverty associated with them—always greater than in two-parent or male-headed families—resulted. Although widely published family statistics show female headship growing more rapidly among nonblack than black families, sociologists and public officials have continued to focus on the difficulties faced by children in households headed by African American women. In 1986 Marian Wright Edelman, head of the Children's Defense Fund, delivered the W. E. B. DuBois Lectures at Harvard University. Edelman prefaced her remarks by explaining her hope for "greater policy emphasis on preventing the poverty that makes children our poorest Americans."[15] While noting teenage pregnancy declining among blacks while rising among whites in the 1980s, Edelman pointed to a thirty-year increase in extramarital fertility among blacks that would "guarantee the poverty of many black children for the foreseeable future."[16] Edelman recognized significant differences between the prospects of black and white children within female-headed households: "Whether black or white, young women under the age of twenty-five who head families with children are very likely to be poor. The poverty rates in 1983 were 85.2 percent for young black female-headed families and 72.1 percent for young white female-headed families. But black female-headed families are much more likely to stay poor. In female-headed families with older mothers, aged twenty-five to forty-four, there is a twenty percentage-point gap between black and white poverty rates."[17] This gap was even greater among older female family heads.

Edelman cited additional factors that contribute to low marriage rates among African Americans. High death rates, incarceration, and military service among men all play a greater role in discouraging marriage among blacks than among whites, and white men are much less likely to remain single than black men even when these factors are taken into account. African American marriage rates have declined parallel to the declining employment prospects of young black males. Edelman concluded that "There is more than a correlation between declining black male employment and declining marriage rates among young blacks. There is cause and effect."[18] In the final analysis, poverty prevents many African Americans from marrying, and the high level of poverty into which African American children are born severely restricts their opportunities to thrive.

Throughout the twentieth century, African American women remained more likely than other women to head families. In the contemporary period especially, the vicissitudes of nonblack families have demonstrated that family structure reflects economic conditions more than cultural preferences. Working women have accumulated greater authority within the family. Since employment rates have consistently continued to be higher among black than among white wives, wage earning, more than cultural factors associated with race, explains the higher incidence of matriarchal patterns among black than among nonblack two-parent households.

As women assume the responsibilities of heading households, matriarchy follows, but egalitarianism and maternal authority also increase as women enlarge their roles in the support of two-parent households. The factors that have caused female household headship to rise affected African Americans more heavily than others, but all population groups participated in the rise in female headship. From 1960 through 1976 the proportion of U.S. households with children under the age of eighteen years and headed by women rose from 46 percent to 54 percent among blacks and from 21 percent to 23 percent among whites.

Since 1970 the overall problem of poverty has grown in this country as the real value of the minimum wage declined. Census Bureau estimates indicate that a full-time, year-round worker in the 1960s and the 1970s, earning the minimum wage could support two dependents at or near the poverty level. From 1970 onward, however, inflation cut the real value of the minimum wage much faster than legislation raised it. By the mid-1980s full-time earnings at the minimum wage equaled only about three fourths of the poverty level for a family of three.[19] Since many female heads of household earn the minimum wage or little more, poverty in the United States has become increasingly characterized by membership in a female-headed household; poverty has become "feminized," as evidenced by the fact that, by the mid-1980s, one in five children lived in a female-headed family and one in four children could expect to spend some time on welfare.[20]

The post–baby boom drop in fertility, the rise in extramarital fertility, the increase in age at first marriage, the rise in divorce rates until the end of the 1980s, the decline in remarriage in the 1970s, and increasing life expectancy reflected this transformation of the female life cycle. Women of the 1990s live or will live long periods alone or largely in the company of other women in shared housing or retirement and nursing facilities. The nature of family life itself has changed as child rearing less frequently involves the continuous presence of fathers. Women, especially African Americans and Anglos, give comparatively few years to motherhood with the smaller families that have characterized twentieth-century fertility patterns. Even among the Hispanic and Asian national groups, where large families have persisted, less of the life span is devoted to childrearing as life spans have increased.

MIGRATION AND IMMIGRATION

During the 1980s and 1990s women continued to migrate into the United States and within the country in search of work. Immigration from Asia and Latin America continued to grow. By the 1980s more than 8 percent of Americans annually completed a residential move beyond a local area, many of them migrating from "Rust Belt" to "Sun Belt."[21] Between 1900 and 1990 the proportion of native-born Americans residing in the region of their birth declined from more than 90 percent to less than 80 percent.[22]

In the 1980s and the 1990s the native-born unemployed swelled the migrant ranks. In the case of U.S. families, as in the case of refugees, wives often found jobs more easily than husbands because of the numerous unskilled, minimum-wage jobs available for women in the service sector. The Hubert Taylor family exemplified a growing number of U.S. families in the 1980s and 1990s who tried to survive on the low wages of a working wife. Hubert Taylor's layoff forced the family from its home. A *Parade Magazine* reporter wrote: "Being uprooted, unemployed, and a 'house husband' without a house is humiliating to Hubert Taylor. He has always been the family provider. He works hard at sustaining himself on Deborah's out-look that they are lucky to be together and healthy. But the climb gets steeper."[23]

WORKING WOMEN'S STATUS IN THE 1990S

As we approach the twenty-first century, three of five adult women work, and the Census Bureau projects that the female work rate will continue to climb through the year 2000. In contrast, four of five men are in the workforce, but the male presence continues its slight but long-term decline. More than half of all wives work and just over two thirds (as opposed to well over nine tenths of working husbands) hold full-time jobs. As throughout the century, divorced women re-main the most workers, followed (in order) by single women, separated women, and wives. Black women remain the most persistent wage workers, but white women have nearly closed the gap. Hispanic women have made the greatest pro-portional gains in labor force participation since World War II, but they remain somewhat less likely to work than other women.

As women have broadened their hold on the labor market in the late twentieth century, they have increased their domination of some occupational areas and have come to predominate in others. Overall, in the managerial and professional sec-tor, currently the largest job category in the U.S. occupational structure, women make up as much of the workforce as men but have failed to achieve parity in executive positions and in most professions requiring extensive graduate training. Women dominate heavily in the technical, sales, and clerical sectors, as well as in service jobs, but remain severely underrepresented in craft and technical areas and in semiskilled production jobs. Forty percent of female wage earners hold jobs in clerical, sales, or low-skilled technical areas; 30 percent work at managerial or pro-fessional pursuits; 15 percent are in the service sector; and all other jobs combined account for the remaining 15 percent of working women.

Throughout the century the occupational structure gradually moved away from labor-intensive agriculture and manufacturing and toward a variety of service jobs, from unskilled areas such as food service to highly skilled professional pursuits such as medicine. Long-term expansion in pink-collar and white-collar jobs encouraged employers to hire women and encouraged women to accept jobs just as the availability of male workers diminished because of declines in immigration and fertility.

Although women made immense strides in broadening their work commitments and in entering new occupations, many occupational gender barriers still stand. All along the spectrum of work, from trash collector to chief executive officer of Fortune 500 companies, gender inequities persist relatively undisturbed, but ironically women have had more success in entering medicine and the law than in entering many of the less-skilled sectors that men dominate. Some occupational segregation undoubtedly reflects women's as well as men's preferences, and virtually no occupational sectors exist in which women have not made some gains since 1960. Nevertheless, occupational differentiation by gender remains the rule.

Occupational segregation served both as the key that opened the doors to women seeking places of employment and as the lock that barred them from economic mobility. As economic historian Claudia Goldin has demonstrated, the "gender gap" has extremely complex roots, but occupational segregation has consistently coincided with women's low earnings.[24] Women have earned between fifty and seventy cents for every dollar earned by men through most of the century. Goldin's findings, based on the most complete historical statistics to date on the gap between the full-time earnings of women and men, do however offer some rays of hope to wage-earning women. During the years from 1890 to 1930, working women improved their earnings from forty-six cents to fifty-six cents for every dollar earned by men (see table 8.3). Although women made little or no relative progress in earnings from 1950 to 1980, actually losing ground in the late 1950s, the wage gap began to narrow noticeably after 1980. Wage data compiled by the Bureau of Labor Statistics document a narrowing of the gender differential in hourly wages between 1979 and 1987 and lead to conclusions similar to Goldin's.[25] Labor economists Michael Horrigan and James Markey estimated that the disparity moved from 63.7 cents in 1979 to 69.4 cents in 1987. Currently women earn approximately 70 cents for every dollar that men receive. In the long term, then, women's positions as paid workers have improved considerably. In a period of a hundred years, women have eliminated half of the wage gap, making particularly impressive progress after the early 1980s, when the gap decreased from approximately 40 cents to 30 cents; nevertheless, the gap remains large, and not much smaller than in the 1930s.[26]

Goldin credits women's employment gains largely to recent educational ad-

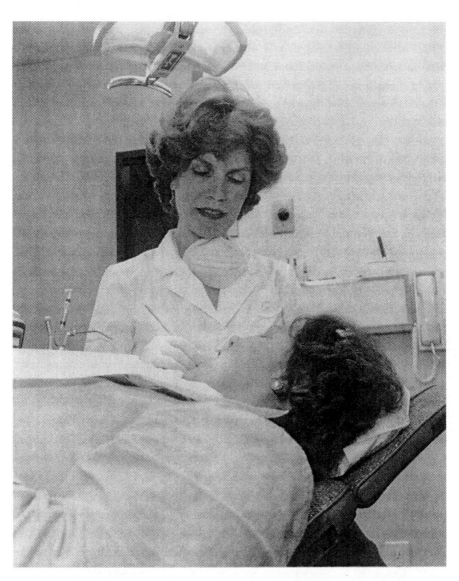

Legislation of the 1960s and the 1970s paved the way for increasing numbers of women of the 1980s to enter professional careers such as dentistry, but the vast majority of women working in medicine remained in support jobs that men shunned. Houston Post photograph, courtesy Houston Metropolitan Research Center, Houston Public Library vances that permitted significant erosion of occupational segregation.[27] From the 1960s onward, elected officials increasingly recognized the depth and the extent of discriminatory employment practices and took steps to encourage equity for women and for minorities. The 1963 Equal Pay Act, the 1964 Civil Rights Act, and the 1972 Equal Opportunity Act targeted discrimination in pay and in hiring. Initial steps in compliance, however, took time, and the earlier lack of equal access to apprenticeships, job training programs, and postgraduate education handicapped both women and minorities. By the 1980s, many of these educational barriers had fallen, and small numbers of women and minorities moved into high-level positions.

CONCLUSION

During the 1980s and 1990s, the long-term gender transformation of paid work proceeded. While the largest numbers of women continued to earn their livings in occupations dominated by women, as they had throughout the century and before, the bonds of occupational segregation loosened. In contrast with earlier decades, affirmative action policies and equal rights legislation assisted women in gaining access to positions that feminization of the labor force had not opened to them.

Although women remained far from wage parity and job equity with men as the century neared its end, the majority of adult women worked, and women, given the chance to excel, had achieved unprecedented status in business, the professions, and public service. The recession of the 1980s and early 1990s spelled hard times for women like Holly Belk, but employed women nevertheless contin-

TABLE 8.3
Cents Earned by Women for Every Dollar Earned by Men, 1983–93
Based on Weekly Median Earnings of Full-Time Workers

	1983	1985	1990	1993
All jobs	66.7	68.2	71.8	76.9
Managers and professionals	69.2	68.4	69.9	73.3
Technical, sales, and support	64.2	64.1	66.9	70.4
Service	67.8	68.0	71.9	74.0
Crafts	66.2	65.7	64.8	67.3
Operatives	66.2	66.5	69.3	72.2
Farm, forestry, and fishing	84.5	85.6	82.1	88.3

SOURCE: *U.S. Bureau of the Census,* Statistical Abstract of the United States, 1995 *(Washington, D.C.: GPO, 1995), table 631.*

ued to advance relative to men. The gender gap in wages had narrowed since the 1970s, although stagnating male wages made women's gains partly chimerical. Women and girls had also moved ahead educationally, especially in preparing for male-dominated professions, even though they failed to reach educational parity with men. Secondary schools, girls' clubs, and magazines exhorted women to aspire to and train for careers traditionally dominated by men. Minority women as well as Anglos participated in the educational and employment gains of the period.

The feminization of work delivered handsome rewards to women of the 1980s and 1990s but also swelled the ranks of low-wage or moderately paid service workers. The majority of U.S. women remained caught in traditional jobs. For them, daily life might very well have grown more difficult than it had been for their mothers. As wage earners or as unpaid workers in the home, women have always played a central role in maintaining families, but structural changes in the economy recast the rhythm of family life as many productive functions moved beyond the household. Women's responsibilities for supporting families climbed consistently through the century, and married women supplanted wage-earning daughters in the family economy. Women of the late twentieth century were more likely to head families than women of the 1950s. Consequently, mothers of the 1990s carried heavier and more diverse burdens than those that many of their mothers or grandmothers had known.

CHAPTER NINE

Families and Working Women, 1900–1995

As we have seen, the decades of the twentieth century have witnessed the intensifying involvement of women in the U.S. labor force. Pushed by economic necessity and by ambition, pulled by the continuously expanding demand of the evolving U.S. economy, the flow of women into gainful labor, inside the home or out, has swelled through war and peace, prosperity and depression. This feminization of the labor force has shown no signs, even in the late twentieth century, of abating.

In many ways, this greater involvement of women in work stems from the ongoing expansion and transformation of the U.S. economy from its agricultural origins, through industrialization, into its late-twentieth-century service-based, postindustrial configuration. Women's involvement, however, has had distinct dimensions of its own, not all of them congruent with short-term economic conditions, nor neatly dovetailing into standard historical periodicity; nor, most emphatically, does the story of working women in the twentieth century parallel that of working men, with only physiology to distinguish the casts.

Aside from the differing occupational makeup of male and female labor forces, the trend of involvement has run in opposite directions in the twentieth century—up for women, slowly down for men. Moreover, while one can speak—and historians most often do speak—of men's work as though they engaged in it as free agents, unattached and unanchored, free to follow whim, instinct, opportunity, women's work has almost always had a family context. The late twentieth century has seen the emergence—and a greater public awareness—of many women, some independent, but most of them wives or mothers, pursuing their own careers for their own reasons, reasons often related to but not dictated by family considerations. U.S. society has always had a leavening of such career women, but overwhelmingly society, and women themselves, have framed women's work as a family-related activity.[1] To understand the feminization of the U.S. labor force, therefore, requires elaboration of its relationship to the economic well-being of the American family.

In agriculture, home-based work, and work outside the home, wives and mothers have shared in the support of families, and adult women's contributions to family income increased dramatically as the century progressed. In 1900, thirty-eight of every one hundred families depended partly or wholly on the paid labor of women. By 1980 the majority of U.S. households (fifty-eight in one hundred) included a working woman. These figures by themselves understate the growth in female responsibility for family support, as over time women's earnings relative to men's wages have increased somewhat. More importantly, the percentage of men working and the financial contribution of men to family support have declined as women's contributions have increased (see table 9.1). In 1890, every 100 U.S. households had 167 working males, but by 1980 that number had declined to 78 per 100. Both the decline in child and youth labor and the increasing number of years spent in retirement reduced the overall economic contributions of men to households in the United States. In terms of persons contributing to family support, men accounted for 83 percent of family workers in 1890, women for 17 percent. By 1980 men accounted for 57 percent, women for 43 percent. Changes in the family economy through the twentieth century also reflect important trends in family size and composition. The birth of fewer children would have translated into a decline in youths' contributions to the family economy even if child labor had not ended in this century. Thus the decline in fertility certainly made it easier for mothers to enter the labor force while simultaneously upping the market demand for their labor. The decline in age at first marriage through the mid-1960s both encouraged paid labor among wives and decreased the available pool of single working women.

WOMEN AND FAMILY SUPPORT STRATEGIES

From the nineteenth century onward, working-class families in the United States have depended on the wages of more than one family member, and women's roles in generating the family's earnings have grown continuously. Impoverished two-parent families and female-headed families derived a variety of strategies for maximizing family income. Parents determined which family members entered the labor market based on the composition of the local labor market as well as the sex and ages of children. Wives with child care responsibilities had few options other than homework for generating income. Teenage daughters, on the other hand, could be taken from school and sent to factories. Some daughters, like Lottie Lemke, worked alongside their mothers in industry. Lemke recalled, "I was [almost] 14 years old when [Father] left home and we never saw him again. . . . My mother didn't believe in a good education. . . . The day I was 14 [I] had to go to work and earn some money."[2] Other young girls assisted their mothers in the industrial homework system studied by social scientist Mary Van Kleeck.

Industrial capitalism gave employers arbitrary power over the wages on which twentieth-century women and men have depended primarily to support themselves and their families. The powerlessness of individual workers to demand higher pay led to effective labor organization in many industries, but it also recast the family economy. As wage labor came to constitute the basis of family income and individual workers had little ability to control the price of their labor, families increasingly looked to the employment of multiple members of the family to improve their material well-being. The market labor of women and children replaced home production as the major means of supplementing or replacing the income

TABLE 9.1
U.S. Households and Wage Earning by Sex, 1890–1989

	NUMBER OF HOUSEHOLDS	MALE WORKERS*		FEMALE WORKERS*	
		NUMBER	NUMBER PER HOUSEHOLD	NUMBER	NUMBER PER HOUSEHOLD
1890	11,255,000	18,821,100	1.67	3,914,600	.35
1900	14,064,000	23,753,800	1.69	5,319,400	.38
1910	30,091,600	—	—	8,075,800	—
1920	21,826,000	33,064,700	1.51	8,549,500	.39
1930	26,983,000	38,077,800	1.41	10,752,100	.40
1940	31,680,000	37,511,900	1.18	12,113,400	.38
1950	38,429,000	43,678,300	1.14	16,522,600	.43
1960	47,868,000	47,103,000	.99	22,222,000	.46
1970	56,248,000	51,502,000	.92	30,547,000	.54
1980	78,910,000	61,453,000	.78	45,487,000	.58
1990	93,347,000	68,234,000	.73	56,554,000	.61

SOURCES: *U.S. Bureau of the Census,* Historical Statistics of the United States, Colonial Times to 1970, *Part 1, Series A 320–334, Series D 29–41;* U.S. Census of Population, 1990, General Social and Economic Characteristics, U.S. Summary *(Washington, D.C.: GPO, 1993), tables 121 and 131;* Statistical Abstract of the United States, 1985 *(Washington, D.C.: GPO, 1984), table 58; 1992 (Washington, D.C.: GPO, 1992), tables 62 and 612.*

*Includes workers ages 10 years and older for 1890–1950, 14 years and older for 1960, 16 years and older for 1970–89.

of male household heads. Changes in the wage-earning roles of individual family members over time reflected fluctuations in the fortunes and economic expectations of individual families as well as the evolving structure of the labor market.

In 1900 mothers, sons, and daughters as well as fathers played critical roles in generating families' income. Although most Americans in the early twentieth century accepted the male-headed, single-worker family as an ideal form, most U.S. households also required the earnings of more than one worker. As the economy matured through the century, changes in the demand for labor and rising consumer expectations dictated that families alter their strategies for family support. Consequently, the composition of this economic unit remained in continuous flux over the course of the century. Working wives largely replaced working daughters in the economy of the household, but this generalization obscures rather than explains the complexity of change in the lives of women and their families. Both single and married women played larger and longer roles in paid labor over the course of the century, and U.S. families grew more dependent upon women's wages. Men spent increasing portions of their work lives as household heads rather than working sons because both the age of marriage and youthful male employment declined through the 1950s.

In the long run adult workers replaced working children in the labor force, and a rise in real earnings allowed children to establish their own households at increasingly younger ages. Simultaneously fertility and family size were declining. As the century progressed the nation came closer to the supposed ideal of a nation of households headed by one working adult, but more and more of these households consisted of individuals rather than families, and women headed a growing share of these households. In the late twentieth century high rates of extramarital fertility would further increase the likelihood that women would head families with young children.

In 1900 two persons in every U.S. household labored for profits or wages (see table 9.1). Male wage earners, as household heads or as sons, outnumbered working women nearly five to one, and their share of family support was also larger because of their superior earning power. Although men headed most households, women carried the principal responsibilities in over 16 percent of the nation's households. As family size and child labor declined, the average number of workers per family also declined. From the 1900 high of 201 workers for every 100 families in the nation, kin support units declined to 136 workers for every 100 families in 1980. The 1930s marked an especially important turning point in family history as economic conditions depressed male employment and drove children from the labor force. When full employment returned in the 1940s and thereafter, youthful workers never again played the family support roles they had filled earlier in the

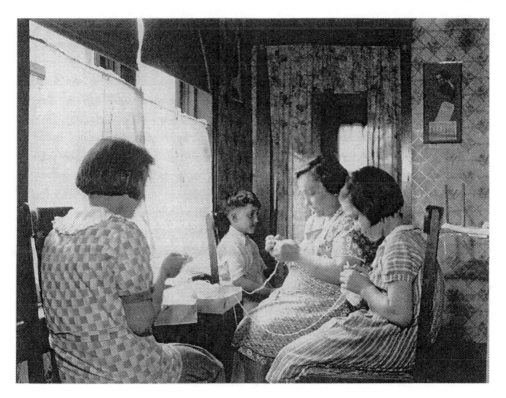

Family members often worked side by side to meet their income needs, but work re-mained highly segregated by gender even so. Industrial homework continued through the Great Depression, frequently involving daughters but not sons in needlework. Mrs. Covitto and family, 1936. Courtesy National Archives

century. Adults of the 1950s left the parental household at younger ages than had their forebears, and at this stage in their lives children contributed little or noth-ing to the support of their parents.

Cultural values and ethnic traditions heavily influenced the ways in which fami-lies defined the economic roles of their members. Through World War I, the Vic-torian domestic ideal of the nuclear family supported entirely by a working father was a reality only for the minority of Americans who were middle class. Working-class men and women did not necessarily subscribe to middle-class notions that husbands "brought home the bacon" while other family members remained at home or at school. Florie Hamm, a North Carolina textile worker, went to work at age fourteen. She had dropped out of school at age ten because she did not care to continue and her parents saw no reason to keep her at school. After Florie had been at home for four years, her mother suggested that it was time for her to enter the mill. Florie, her sisters, her brother, and her father all gave their wages to her mother, who managed the household and gave each member of the family some spending money.[3]

Whether or not parents preferred that their children complete secondary schooling, circumstances often dictated otherwise. Among the cotton mill families studied by Senate investigators in 1910, 90 percent of the families with children ages fourteen years and older had sent their children to work. Among female-headed mill families, children provided the majority of family income. Overall, poor families acted to maximize immediate earnings, but preferences for keeping mothers at home and sons at school frequently forced daughters to assume wage earning burdens before their teenage years or while in their early teens. Historians Louise Tilly and Joan Scott demonstrated that economically productive activity among daughters in Western societies was consistent with the historical experience of the poor from the preindustrial period through the nineteenth century. Of preindustrial societies Tilly and Scott argued that "Daughters in lower class families were early socialized to assume family and work responsibilities. . . . These were the cultural values held by families who sent their daughters out to work in the early stages of industrialization."[4] During the early twentieth century both economic need and the lives of their neighbors reinforced the expectations of working-class families that their daughters would contribute to family income. Young girls in working-class families expected to become wage earners before they completed high school.[5]

Some teenage workers found joy in the advantages that their wages procured for other family members. An artificial flower maker whose meager wages had helped send her brother through medical school told a welfare investigator, "When he graduated, I cried all day and was as happy as though I had graduated myself. I often say to my mother that we treat my brother as if he were a king, but I can't help it."[6] Other working girls took no pleasure in turning over all their wages to their parents, and many regretted the necessity of leaving school. Nonetheless, working-class girls and boys had grown up to expect teenage employment, and they generally resigned themselves to this abrupt termination of childhood. Southerner Edna Hargett's experience mirrored that of countless other women in a variety of industrial settings in early-twentieth-century America. Edna Pearl Charlotte Johnson Yandell Hargett was born in Rock Hill, South Carolina, in 1906. As the child of a mill family, Hargett understood her destiny at an early age. At school she learned that "Whenever a mill child got sixteen, they had to go in the mill and the others didn't. We knew that was the way of life we had to expect."[7]

Other young workers resented their sacrifices. In *Twenty Years at Hull House* Jane Addams recounted the complaints of working sons and daughters about the burdens of employment and the necessity of surrendering their earnings to their parents. Marcella, a German American girl whose mother claimed all of her earnings, turned to petty theft to relieve her misery. Desperate to provide a new shirtwaist for a special occasion, Marcella stole a few yards of fabric from a customer in the shop where she worked. Addams, who learned of Marcella's plight after her employer pressed legal charges, maintained that parents' driving their children to help feed and clothe the family was a principal cause of juvenile delinquency.[8]

As young women entered the labor market in the twentieth century, they gained a measure of autonomy, but they did not secure their independence. Rather, they shouldered financial responsibilities, responsibilities that stretched beyond the duties of a child to a parent or a parent to a child. Married women generally worked wholly to support their families, and single women bore substantial and long-term financial obligations. A 1920 survey of shoe workers in Manchester, New Hampshire, confirmed that married and single factory girls, regardless of their expectations, frequently worked many years to assist their families. Virtually all of the wives deposited their total earnings in the family kitty, and 60 percent of working daughters did likewise. One tenth of the 307 daughters in the shoe industry had been at work for a decade or more and had contributed all of their earnings to family support. Working daughters gave a larger share of their earnings to family support than did unmarried sons, but children rarely retained all of their wages as long as they remained at home. Reliance upon maturing or grown children characterized turn-of-the-century working-class families. Children continued to support their parents through the Great Depression, but few working daughters or sons of the 1930s were minor children. A 1939 study of workers in a number of industries in Cleveland, Ohio, showed that only 3 percent of working sons and 2 percent of working daughters paid none of the family's expenses.[9] At least for the first half of the century, working women rarely escaped the claims of kin upon some portion of their earnings. Labor unions, reformers, and government bureaucrats completed more than 200 studies of working women and their dependents between 1880 and 1950. On the basis of these surveys, Women's Bureau analyst Mary-Elizabeth Pidgeon concluded that "fewer than 1 woman in 10 gives none of her earnings to her family."[10]

Daughters did not escape all financial duties to their parents and siblings by marrying or moving out on their own. Some daughters stayed at work after marriage and continued to help their parents. Maiden women, regardless of age, could be expected to contribute regularly to the support of their parents and to meet financial emergencies in the extended family. Throughout the twentieth century single working women of all ages have carried substantial responsibilities for supporting their parents or other relatives.[11] A Depression-era survey of single women who taught in rural schools revealed that nearly two thirds were supporting relatives who did not live with them. On the basis of studies of electrical workers and women in business and the professions conducted from 1937 through 1945, Pidgeon concluded:

> Women who live apart from their families often are a substantial mainstay in the support of relatives. In the more usual case this takes the form of regular contributions [from] their salaries to these persons. In other instances women living apart send lump sums to take care of special needs and unusual emergencies, such as doctor's bills, funeral expenses, school tuition, or the purchase of necessary clothing. Often, they contribute to the support of elderly parents without income, or to the general support of the worker's family at home. They may assist sons and daughters, either adults unable to support themselves, or as often was the case during the war, minor children cared for elsewhere while the mother was employed. They may help to support brothers and sisters, or nieces and nephews, the children of a widowed sister or sister-in-law. All these patterns are frequently found in the lives of women workers.[12]

As Pidgeon's study verified, working women did not necessarily withdraw from the labor market after marriage. Similarly, the fact that a family included working daughters did not always mean that mothers would refrain from income-producing activities. Wage-earning mothers preferred the jobs or workplaces that fit their need to balance employment with child care. Before World War I, African American wives predominated in the Chesapeake Oyster Company plants, and they frequently brought their children to the packing sheds with them. Occasionally white mothers brought their young children into textile mills as well, but homework predominated among working mothers, black or white, from the turn of the century through the Great Depression. Taking in laundry, accepting boarders and lodgers, or pursuing industrial homework allowed mothers to earn income and care for their children. Industrial homework exploited women in poverty, but mothers often found poorly paid manufacturing tasks their only options. As Mary Van Kleeck concluded:

> It is indeed the increasing necessity that the wives of wage-earning men should become wage-earners which is fostering the growth of the homework system. In 99 or 10 out of 11 of the households visited, the mother was a home worker, sometimes alone and sometimes with other members of the family. In only nine, or about eight percent of the cases, had she been a flower maker before her marriage—a fact indicating that she turned to this

work not because she knew how to do it but because under the present order of industry it seemed to be her only resource.[13]

Census takers frequently failed to count industrial home workers or women who took in laundry or boarders as gainful workers. Consequently, there are few guides other than the scattered accounts of welfare investigators for assessing the roles of these activities in the family economy. Edith Abbott, who surveyed Chicago immigrant households in the early twentieth century, concluded that many women who took in boarders hid this information from census takers because they feared that public health agencies would interfere with their activities. Enumerators also excluded housewives who let out a single room or bed in their homes. U.S. Census data show that the number of female boarding and lodging housekeepers crested in 1910 at an official count of 142,000 and declined thereafter to fewer than 7,000 by 1970.

Several studies of working women before World War II demonstrate the importance of lodgers in the family economy. Homebound wives might combine industrial homework or taking in laundry with maintaining boarders and lodgers. Among one hundred Bridgeport, Connecticut, home workers questioned by Senate investigators in 1910, twenty-two also rented rooms or beds.[14] Welfare investigator Gwendolyn Hughes found female family heads who maintained their own homes more likely than other working women to have relatives or nonrelated persons boarding with them. In Hughes's preliminary 1918 survey of 10,782 working-class households in Philadelphia, she verified that a quarter of the households included boarders or lodgers. More than two fifths of the 713 households headed by women included them. Although the absence of husbands from the household would seem likely to have encouraged women to take in boarders, in fact, nonworking wives with absent husbands took in boarders more often than did working wives. Lodgers, especially members of the extended family, also assisted working mothers with child and home care. Among the households of female family heads whom Hughes studied, lodgers were most likely to be female relatives who contributed services as well as money to the household. Among foreign-born women in particular, two families often combined into a single household to permit both mothers to work by taking turns at home.

Hughes also found a number of other arrangements that allowed mothers to balance work and home responsibilities:

The lodgers in the homes of wage earning mothers sometimes live in the household on practically the same footing as members of the family (44 cases), but more frequently they merely sleep in the house (57 cases). The large number of persons who sleep in the household but do not eat with the family is largely due to arrangements which prevail in the homes of many foreign-born women. The working mother sub-lets a room of her house to another family. The mother of the second family takes care of the working mother's children during the day and helps with the housework. As compensation she and her family live practically rent-free in the household, and sometimes she is paid an additional sum for her services.[15]

In lodging households housewives not only cooked and cleaned for roomers but also bore responsibility for preserving the integrity of the family with strangers in their midst. Over the years many social workers agreed with Abbott's conclusion that "[k]eeping lodgers means a great deal of additional work for the overburdened wife and mother, who has a constant excuse for not maintaining a satisfactory standard of cleanliness. But most serious of all evil consequences, it also means a sacrifice of privacy, for in many cases the lodgers sleep in the same rooms with some member or members of the family."[16]

Progressive Era social workers cited immigrants as the source of the supposed "lodger evil," a perspective that informed the social surveys of the time. The Dillingham Commission, a U.S. Senate committee studying immigration, found higher lodging rates among native-born African American families in cities than among urban immigrant families. White families of native-born stock took in boarders less often than immigrant households, and second-generation immigrant families less often than immigrants. The incidence of boarding varied widely among ethnic groups. For example, native-born whites took in boarders more frequently than German, Moravian, Bohemian, and Syrian immigrant households.[17] The Dillingham data suggest that lodging helped immigrants and their families cope with the transition to new lives in the United States.

MOTHERS WORKING OUTSIDE THE HOME

Taking in lodgers permitted immigrant or native-born mothers of young children to supplement family income, but work outside the home proved more attractive over time, and the transition had gotten well underway by World War I. Before entering the labor market, through homework or an outside job, women with working husbands assayed the economic circumstances of their families; if they lived on the margin, a small change in conditions could force them into wage work. In her Philadelphia survey, Gwendolyn Hughes interviewed seventy-seven working wives with employed husbands living at home. These wives looked for jobs when inflation outpaced male wage increases. As World War I neared an end, mothers turned to paid labor because "the [amount] of income which . . . the mother [thinks] the needs of her family [require] has moved up with the increased cost of living and the decrease in real wages."[18]

The inability of the poor to accumulate savings made these families especially sensitive to changes in the cost of living. Among the 272 working mothers (married, widowed, and divorced or separated) about whom Hughes had gathered data, only 49 reported that they had gotten jobs because they wanted to work. Married women who reported that they worked out of necessity reported much lower family savings than wives who professed to have chosen employment voluntarily.

In her study Hughes found that only a minority of children of working mothers worked themselves. In a total of 280 working-class households with currently or recently employed mothers, only 70 included one or more wage-earning children. Among both whites and African Americans, Hughes found families in which both mothers and children participated in wage labor the exception rather than the rule. In 1930 mothers and their children earned wages in only one in ten male-headed African American families but one in four families headed by a woman. For native-born white families the comparable figures were fewer than one in ten, whether headed by a man or a woman. Among foreign-born white families, both mothers and their children worked in approximately three in twenty male-headed families and two in five female-headed families.[19]

FAMILY WORK UNITS

Small family-owned businesses, garment sweatshops, and textile mills employed family groups. Family units of production persisted throughout the twentieth century in small "mom and pop" businesses. President Richard Nixon laid claim to apple-pie roots in romanticizing his parents' Whittier, California, grocery store in which both parents worked and the children helped out after school. In settings such as this, wives might put in more than forty hours per week without being counted officially as workers. Families also operated manufacturing units. Garment shops and other sewing establishments have long persisted as a feature of U.S. capitalism because of the low capitalization required to operate them. Many of the nation's sweatshops began with entrepreneurs exploiting members of their own family.

Elvira Adorno's family of needleworkers, for example, nurtured the hopes and suffered the despairs of many twentieth-century immigrants from the turn of the century through the 1990s. At the close of the nineteenth century, Elvira Adorno's father decided to flee the poverty of his native Italy. Adorno bid farewell to his wife and children and set out for America. Soon after his arrival, Adorno found a job in the New York garment district and eventually saved enough to bring his family from Italy. The reunion of husband and wife provided Mr. Adorno with the opportunity to embark on a business venture: "My mother did very fine work in embroidery and crocheting, being especially expert at designs and filigree. Father reasoned that he could exploit this talent with all those different Italian organizations and clubs which constantly need[ed] regalia and banners by going into business and supplying them."[20] Mr. Adorno began "his" flag company in the family apartment. Mrs. Adorno worked night and day without violating traditional Italian strictures that confined wives and mothers to the home. Elvira recalled, "My mother helped my father in his business (she was the only embroideress he had). She would get up after he had fallen asleep and pick up where she had left off, finishing orders on the flags. These were not simply flags but were made of a beautiful double silk material that my father imported from France. Because there was no central heating my mother caught pleurisy and died leaving my father with four children."[21]   ·

Family work units also figured prominently in the economy of the U.S. South, and this pattern discouraged the education and upward mobility of farm and mill children. Until World War II, southern textile mills drew their workers from family-operated farms or from existing mill villages. Unlike farming in other areas of the country, the family remained the unit of agricultural production in the South until the war because of the tenacious hold of the tenant and share systems there. In most rural southern families, white or black, all able-bodied adults and children worked together to pay their debt to the furnishing merchant and to produce the nonmarket goods that provided subsistence. White families found some sense of security and felt some sense of privilege when mill overseers lured them, but not their black neighbors, away from the farm, with its constant fear that "the crop would not make" or the bottom would fall out of the cotton or tobacco market.

The corporate paternalism of southern textile production initially eased families' transition from agriculture, but paternalism and the absence of viable economic alternatives sealed southern laborers into low-wage jobs. As historian Jacquelyn Hall and her colleagues discovered, mill workers found identity and comfort in the notion of the mill community as a family. Senate investigators who condemned southern paternalism puzzled, "It seems that the people accept it as for their best interests."[22] Although nuclear families never composed production units in the mill and entire families rarely worked alongside each other, the mill "family" protected all its members on and off the job. Southern mill villages resembled tenant farms in that the mill provided a house for each family and space to continue the subsistence food production that typified the family farm. In ex-

While corporate nurseries were the exception, some manufacturers offered day care to retain the services of mothers. Bibb Manufacturing Co., Macon, Georgia, 1927. Courtesy National Archives

change, the family furnished a specified number of laborers to the mill rather than to the farm, preferring low wages but predictable wages to speculating on "shares" of future crops. The mill gained a hold on families not simply by providing homes and community amenities, but also by extending credit to employees much as the furnishing merchant had done in the agricultural setting. Southern mills allowed many families to retain traditional ties with the land well into the twentieth century. Land-owning farmers occasionally stayed behind as other family members marched off to the mill, but such arrangements dwindled in number as small farms deteriorated.

The successes of southern mill owners in adapting notions of family production to an industrial setting appeared clearly in the distinctive demographic characteristics of labor forces in southern as opposed to northern textile mills. In its study of cotton mill workers in 1907 and 1908, the Senate investigating committee found workers as young as seven years in southern mills, but none below the age of ten in New England mills. Child labor played a larger role in southern mills, with 7.5 percent of workers under sixteen, than in the New England mills, with only 3.6 percent. Nearly half (46 percent) of the southern mills' workers were male, but only a third of New England's were male. Because southern workers negotiated with the mill as a family unit (that is, to provide a given number of workers) rather than as individuals, children's labor could substitute for maternal employment. Although southern mill supervisors often encouraged mothers to work by allowing them time off to nurse infants or to prepare meals, working mothers figured more prominently in New England mills than in the South, where fewer than a fifth of mill family mothers worked for wages.

Northern mills in the twentieth century had abandoned most aspects of the paternalism that had marked their early years. Martha Doherty, born in Lowell, Massachusetts, in 1904, was one of nine children. Her mother persisted as a weaver at the Boott Mill despite her heavy domestic chores and responsibilities. Martha's mother worked under her husband's supervision, a familial work relationship that let her leave the mill for short periods when nursing an infant. While young, the Doherty children stayed at one of Lowell's private day nurseries.[23]

FEMALE FAMILY HEADS

The sharp rise in divorce rates since World War II as well as the increase in extra-marital fertility has focused attention on the plight of the female-headed household. With approximately two fifths of all female-headed households currently subsisting below the poverty line, the "feminization of poverty" emerged as a major social and political issue of the 1980s. While widowing and abandonment previously played larger roles in thrusting women into headship positions, the female family head has in fact persisted from the earliest days of the Republic. Occasionally, family headship has catapulted women toward exceptional accomplishments. Harriet Beecher Stowe, for example, labored long hours at commercial writing because she had to support her children. However, Stowe emerged from a family of deep social conscience and considerable influence and had the advantage of the best education available to antebellum women. Most female family heads have lacked the advantages and the options of Harriet Beecher Stowe and have had few family resources to assist in the transition from dependent wife to family provider.

The dilemmas confronting women heads of households have changed little over time. As historian Christine Stansell has demonstrated, the emergence of low-paid wage labor for women during the Industrial Revolution kept widows and abandoned wives in poverty, but it also kept them clear of the previously inevitable march to the almshouse and the emotional and physical deterioration that accompanied institutional residence.[24] The emergence of women's work also decreased the likelihood that mothers would lose their children to other relatives or social welfare institutions should their spouses die or desert them. Nevertheless, the constant struggle to maintain her children and to keep the family intact has characterized the life of the breadwinning mother in the twentieth-century United States.

Gwendolyn Hughes's 1918 findings coincide with a Women's Bureau study of 1950 and Carol Stack's 1960s investigation of female headship in a black neighborhood of Chicago. In a preliminary survey of more than 10,000 households, Hughes found 14 percent of all families headed by widows or abandoned mothers. The vast majority of these female family heads worked, and 55 percent of all working mothers headed families. Overall, Hughes found that 173 working mothers had entered wage labor because their husbands had abandoned them, while 164 working mothers headed households because their husbands had no job. Slightly more than a third of the mothers heading families had had to return to work within five years of their marriage; more than three fourths of them were under the age of 35.[25]

The economic realities that confronted the family heads whom Hughes studied often meant that mothers could not maintain their own homes. Of 728 working mothers, 328 lived with their husbands and nearly all of them lived in homes rented or owned by their families. Of the 400 widowed, divorced, or abandoned women, a fourth boarded their families in other households. Among the mothers least likely to maintain their own homes—divorcées or abandoned wives—52 of 164 boarded. Hughes reported that boarding mothers often resided in the homes of others "more or less on [condition of] good behavior."[26] Crying children or poor housekeeping habits might land these mother-headed families in the streets. Female family heads who did maintain their own homes were more likely than other working women to have relatives or unrelated people living or boarding with them.[27]

Methods for coping with the multiple responsibilities of headship, wage earning, and mothering existed, but inevitably some mothers failed to sustain all of these roles. Children lived away from their mothers in 106 of 728 families that Gwendolyn Hughes studied. The majority of the absent children were fifteen years or older and dependent on their own resources. One fifth of the younger children languished in orphanages, but most lived with relatives. A few mothers boarded their children in the homes of others at a cost of between $2.50 and $5.00 per week.[28]

Joseph Hill's census analysis of working women, based on 1920 federal returns for eleven cities, determined that fifteen percent of female earners provided the sole support of themselves, or themselves and dependents. Thirty-eight percent lived in two-earner families; the remainder pooled their earnings with two or more employed family members. The wages of working wives contributed a crucial component of family support. Among all wage-earning wives, 8.5 percent provided the sole source of family earnings and 60.7 percent had only one additional worker in their families. Widowed and divorced women—17 percent of all working women in Hill's study—had the heaviest burdens of family support. Among these family heads, 40.7 percent were the only workers in their families and an additional 33.5 percent had only one additional worker to help maintain the family.

Patterns of family support vary over time and through the life cycle of families; in the twentieth century the most dramatic changes in family economies transpired in the decades from 1950 through the 1990s. During these years men's economic roles in supporting families declined rapidly as wives shouldered increasing

Cold War propaganda of the 1950s touted the virtues of the nuclear family to Americans and foreigners alike. The number of families depending on dual earners rose as Americans reached for a comfortable family life. R. A. Payne family. United States Information Agency photograph, 1956. Courtesy National Archives

economic responsibilities and as divorce and female family headship increased sharply (see table 9.2).

FAMILY INCOME AND MARRIED WOMEN'S EMPLOYMENT

Over the course of this century, the relationship between family income and employment of wives has reversed. In the early twentieth century, only poor wives worked, and wives' earnings failed to lift their families from poverty. During the years since World War II, wives from all economic classes have participated broadly in the labor market and wives' wages have pushed the income of these families above that of male-headed, single-earner households.

Among the middle class, the transition away from father-supported families to the two-parent family economy began in the 1920s, as a few wives combined working with family care. The small number of middle-class wives who had jobs in the 1920s had trained for careers and continued to work after marriage partly for reasons of personal fulfillment. Nevertheless, college-educated working wives saw their employment largely in economic terms and rationalized their activity as born of necessity. Wives' wages supported husbands' further education or permitted a family

TABLE 9.2
Female-Headed Households, 1890–1990
(in Thousands)

	TOTAL HOUSEHOLDS	FEMALE HEADS	PERCENTAGE WITH FEMALE HEAD
1890	11,255	1,833	16.3
1900	14,064	—	—
1910	—	—	—
1920	21,826	—	—
1930	26,983	3,793	14.1
1940	31,680	5,269	16.6
1950	38,429	6,389	16.6
1960	47,868	9,151	19.1
1970	56,248	13,287	23.6
1980	78,910	21,874	27.7
1983	83,918	24,668	29.4
1985	86,789	24,097	27.8
1990	93,347	26,541	28.4

SOURCES: *U.S. Bureau of the Census,* Historical Statistics of the United States, Colonial Times to 1970, *Bicentennial ed. (Washington, D.C.: GPO, 1975), Series A 320-334;* Statistical Abstract of the United States, 1985 *(Washington, D.C.: GPO, 1984), table 58; 1991 (Washington, D.C., GPO, 1991), table 56.*

to purchase a home.[29] Winifred Wandersee argued that rising consumer expectations following World War I propelled middle-class wives into the labor force in the 1930s despite societal pressure for married women to relinquish their jobs to needy men.[30] After World War II wives enjoyed a labor market in which relatively high wages, often coupled with part-time or abbreviated work schedules, permitted them to increase family consumption without sacrificing supervision of and care for their children. By the 1960s the data collected by the Bureau of Labor Statistics and the Bureau of the Census plainly showed that families with working wives and working husbands had higher incomes than husband-supported families (see table 9.3).

As women's roles in the U.S. labor force have grown, the economic well-being of U.S. families has paradoxically improved and declined simultaneously. Overall, adult women have consistently earned more than children had in the past. Consequently, as child labor decreased and female employment rose, family well-being in two-parent households improved. On the other hand, families headed by women failed to keep pace with the rising incomes of other families. As the share of female householders under the age of 45 years increased after 1960, the wages of these

TABLE 9.3
Median Income in Current Dollars of Families and
Unrelated Individuals, 1947–89

	MALE-HEADED FAMILIES	FEMALE-HEADED FAMILIES		UNRELATED MALES	UNRELATED FEMALES
1947	3,109	2,172		1,349	792
1950	3,446	1,922		1,539	846

| | MALE-HEADED/WIFE | | FEMALE | UNRELATED | |
	IN WORK FORCE	NOT IN WORKFORCE	HEAD	MALES	FEMALES
1951	4,631	3,634	2,220	1,909	917
1955	5,622	4,326	2,471	1,831	1,054
1960	6,900	5,520	2,968	2,638	1,407
1965	8,633	6,706	3,535	3,184	1,767
1970	12,276	9,304	5,093	4,540	2,483
1975	17,237	12,752	6,844	6,612	3,978
1980	26,879	18,972	10,408	10,939	6,668
1982	30,342	21,299	11,484	12,470	8,058
1989	45,266	28,747	16,442	18,284	11,622

SOURCE: *U.S. Bureau of the Census,* Historical Statistics of the United States, Colonial Times to 1970, *Bicentennial ed. (Washington, D.C.: GPO, 1975), Series G 179-188;* Statistical Abstract of the United States, 1985, *table 747; 1991, (Washington, D.C.: GPO, 1991), table 732.*

women have had to support increasing numbers of children. The "feminization of poverty" has resulted.

Married-couple households, whether or not the wife has worked, have experienced a long-term rise in income. Since World War II households that include both a working husband and a working wife have had the greatest increase in earnings as both the number of hours worked and the hourly wages of women have grown. Economist Stanley Lebergott has estimated that the real earnings of employees, after adjustments for periods of unemployment, increased nearly fourfold between 1900 and 1960. Even with the decline in the number of workers per family, total family earnings more than doubled during the same period, because women replaced children as workers and women earned more. From 1929 through 1964, average family income in constant dollars nearly doubled, while family size decreased slightly.[31]

Family income statistics for the period since World War II demonstrate the disparate benefits derived from the overall increase in the earnings of U.S. workers. From 1951 through 1982, the median current-dollar income of women without dependents rose 878 percent, while the incomes of families with husband and wife at work rose 655 percent. In contrast, the incomes of single-worker male-headed families rose 586 percent and the income of female-headed families registered a 517 percent gain. Among female-headed families the economic consequences of socializing and educating women to stay at home or to play secondary roles as wage earners made themselves painfully apparent. Both marital instability and extramarital fertility occur more often among women with little education or low wages than among better-educated or better-paid women.

WORKING CHILDREN

Although child labor had nearly disappeared before World War II, youthful workers reappeared during the 1950s. During the first half of the century the percentage of boys ages fourteen through nineteen who participated in paid labor declined from 70 to 40, with an accompanying decline of 35 to 25 percent among girls of the same ages. The pattern of youthful employment after World War II differed markedly from earlier teenage wage earning. Through the nineteenth and early twentieth centuries, youthful employment had implied the termination of full-time schooling. During these years far more teenage boys than girls worked. Since World War II working teenagers under eighteen have held part-time jobs shaped around school attendance. The renaissance in youthful employment has involved girls almost as extensively as boys. Although markedly fewer girls than boys fourteen through seventeen worked in 1970, the two equilibrated by 1980.

With few legal work options available for children under age sixteen, this sharp rise in employment for the contemporary period has occurred primarily among sixteen- and seventeen-year-olds.[32] The Bureau of Labor Statistics reported that 44 percent of boys and 41 percent of girls ages sixteen and seventeen worked in 1980, but the author of a 1980 survey of high school students concluded that a majority of sixteen- and seventeen-year-old boys and girls worked or had worked at some time.[33]

For most of the contemporary era, teenage employment did not reflect the immediate economic needs of families. From the 1950s through the 1970s, teenage employment occurred less often among the poorest families than among those above the poverty line. Working teenagers of the 1960s and 1970s almost universally kept all of their earnings and made their own spending decisions. Teenage employment reflected the proliferation of low-paying, part-time service jobs that occurred since World War II and the absence of adult workers willing to fill these places. The escalation of consumer cravings among the young has fueled their appetite for these jobs.

Because the young after World War II kept most of their earnings, teenage employment of the 1950s and 1960s did not affect the imperative for maternal employment as directly as it did in earlier times. The coexistence of high rates of maternal employment with high rates of teen employment reinforces societal expectations that wage earning will coincide with maturity in all categories of peoples. Ellen Greenberger and Laurence Steinberg have argued that working mothers provide role models that both boys and girls imitate. As some children have watched their mothers configure part-time, low-paying service employments around domestic obligations in order to increase their consumption, they have learned to do likewise. Teenagers, the authors maintain, have also come to expect family chores and family activities to require less of their time than in earlier generations.[34] In such an environment, maternal chores in the home remain heavy despite mothers' roles as wage earners.

Sometime during the late 1970s or the 1980s, teenage employment began to take on new functions. Once again families turned to their children's earnings to make ends meet. Teenagers have traditionally used some of their part-time or summer earnings to further their own education, but current work patterns reveal trends not apparent or not noted until the 1980s. Work rates among teenagers remain higher in families in which wives work outside the home than in families with full-time homemaker/mothers. Among families with no adult workers and in the poorest U.S. families, a relatively low percentage of teenagers work. The highest percentage of working teenagers occurs in female-headed families in which the mothers work. The absence or withdrawal of adult male earnings from the support of an increasing share of the nation's families has once again increased reliance on youthful workers. While teenagers may retain a larger share of their earnings than did working children at the turn of the century, poorer families increasingly feel the need to supplement adult earnings by urging their children to find a job—thus far with modest success. The lightening of after-school assignments and the redefinition of the high school day in many cities to accommodate learning in the morning and earning in the afternoons and evenings reflect the growing tension between work and schooling among teenagers. As the necessity of career training beyond high school continues to grow, the tension between work and school increases for the nation's young women and men.

COMPOSITION OF THE LABOR FORCE

The implications of rising female work rates and declining male work rates for the support of the nation's families emerge clearly when work rates by marital status and age are considered. Regardless of marital status, the percentage of working women increased between 1960 and 1990. Among men, labor force participation increased for single, widowed, and divorced persons but declined among the married population. As age at first marriage has increased, divorce rates have risen, and fertility has declined over the past thirty years, the United States has become less and less a nation of "traditional families." "Traditional families," in which husbands work outside the home and the wives limit their activities to the home and to unpaid work, now constitute a small minority of U.S. families. No one family type represents the typical American family.[35] Through the past three decades men and women entered the labor force at increasingly younger ages. While men continue to stay in the labor force longer than women, the gap between the work rates of men and women ages forty-five and older has narrowed. Analyzed by marital status, the cycle of male and female labor force entrance and exit has changed markedly. Among single, separated, divorced, and widowed persons of both sexes the retirement age fell until the mid-1980s. Among married men retirement followed a similar pattern, but among wives the work rates of persons ages forty-five through sixty-four increased, and the work rates of persons ages sixty-five and older held steady.[36]

CONCLUSION

Changes in the economic functions of U.S. family members have followed from the maturation of industrial capitalism and the dawning of the postindustrial age. Decline in family and household size, an increase in divorce rates, and a diminution of patriarchal authority have all characterized the twentieth century, and these trends partly reflect familial adaptations to an aging capitalist economy.

The decline in family size has paralleled an even more precipitous decline in household size. The disappearance of the live-in servant, the increased tendency of single adults to establish separate households, and the rise in the number of elderly adults living alone have all contributed to the dwindling size of the U.S. household. As economic units, families and households do not function as equivalents. Historically, families unable to support themselves through the wages of their members have survived by combining one or more related family groups into extended or stem households. Patterns of family support may also stretch beyond an individual household. Increasingly in the twentieth century, the contributions of wage earners living outside the familial home played critical roles in supporting members of that household. Neither young adults nor parents leaving the family unit through separation or divorce automatically freed themselves from economic responsibility to their families. Even though income from the extended family has to some extent replaced the extended or stem households of preindustrial society, the family as an economic unit has steadily declined in size over the course of this century, increasing pressures on those who remain attached to it.

U.S. families in 1990 subsisted on the incomes of fewer wage earners than did their counterparts in 1900. By the mid-1970s child labor, as an element of family support, had all but disappeared only to resurface in the next decade. Overall, the proportion of family income provided by male workers has shrunk while women's roles as contributors to the family economy have expanded. Women have thus accepted larger responsibilities as both principal and secondary earners. As these structural reconfigurations occurred, important cultural, social, and legal changes reinforced new economic roles for women and extended the length of time during which children were exempted from contributing to family support. Industrialization and the accompanying growth of wage earning occurred amidst a long-term trend of declining fertility, generally understood by historians and demographers as a product of modernization, with couples intentionally limiting fertility through late marriage and birth control. Declining mortality, effected through advances in medicine and nutrition, also played an important role in the birthrate decline.

The large family proved incompatible with a society dependent on consumer goods and services purchased with wages, in part because each child required a sizable cash outlay over time but could not contribute much to the family's economic well-being. In addition, motherhood in industrial societies involved a conflict between nurture and productive labor. In the early twentieth century, needy families coped with this conflict by sending children into the labor market and enlarging household income by taking in boarders. Female-headed families especially often found the multiple-family household or the extended family household the only way to cope with the dual demands of employment and child care.

Through the first half of the twentieth century, societal proscriptions deterred mothers from entering the labor market when the family could manage otherwise. As the demand for female labor increased over time, women and their families paid increasing costs to keep wives and mothers at home. Rising living costs and consumer expectations encouraged couples to postpone childbearing, encouraged mothers to return to the labor force as their children grew up, and encouraged couples to have fewer children to accommodate a longer period of employment by the wife. As population growth slowed through family limitation, the demand for female workers intensified, further raising the cost of time devoted to full-time homemaking.

Although personal income in the United States has not risen over time at a constant rate, real wages have increased in the twentieth century. Contrary to the behavior of families at the turn of the century, high male wages since World War II have coincided with a transition to independent wage earning among daughters and an increased responsibility for family support among wives. In the case of daughters and sons, rising wages permitted a greater degree of autonomy among young adult workers. During the price inflation and industrial recession of the 1970s, parents bemoaned the return of adult children to their households after a twenty-year period in which the separation of young adults from the parental household had become the norm. Both mothers and child care advocates similarly lamented the absence of grandmothers with time to care for the children of their working daughters, as grandmothers, too, were drawn into the labor market.

For families and for adult women, the long-term growth in the demand for female labor signaled an attachment of women to wage earning that by the 1990s had gripped women as strongly and permanently as it has traditionally fastened upon men. For most of the twentieth century, wives and daughters clearly served as secondary workers in that their labors substituted for those of absent husbands and fathers, or their wages supplemented those of a principal male earner. The overall growth of the U.S. economy in the 1950s created unprecedented increases in male wages. Despite this, more women (and especially wives) sought work than ever before because, although male family heads brought home more money than ever, women's wages had escalated along with men's. As the range of consumer products proliferated and consumer expectations expanded, the addition of a wife's earnings could advance the family's material comfort faster than if only the husband worked.

During the 1920s, 1950s, and 1960s, some wives worked for the sake of increasing family consumption, but in the 1930s and 1970s more of them had to take permanent jobs simply to compensate for the decline in men's real earnings. The prosperity of the 1920s and the 1950s had created overall minimal expectations of family welfare in the working and middle classes that only two earners could sustain in times of depression or inflation.

Families' reliance on mothers' earnings continued to grow after the 1950s as the family economy continued to change. Between 1950 and 1990 the relative place of part-time employment in women's lives and in the support of their families declined as the full-time employment of married women climbed. After 1960 the employment of mothers of young children rose dramatically, and by the 1980s the employed mother had become the norm rather than the exception. Hard-won battles to protect married women's rights as workers accompanied the resurgence of feminism in the 1970s; however, legal protections of married women's job rights also reflected society's recognition that wives and mothers had become long-term workers and that the economy as well as families depended on them. The changes that occurred in the family economy through the century reflected the maturation of an industrial economy, but the rising importance of female wage earning also signaled dramatic changes in the female life cycle and in the composition and structure of U.S. families.

Women, Men, Work, and Families

Throughout the twentieth century women have labored to maintain themselves and their families. Over time the economy developed in ways that made employment increasingly attractive to women. Job opportunities moved away from agriculture, beyond the narrow confines of domestic work and factory labor, and into commerce, offices, the professions, and nonprofit institutions. The feminization of work increased women's commitments to the economic support of others. As daughters, as sisters, and as mothers, women saw their economic responsibilities multiply over time. Partly because of the gender gap in wages, women's financial burdens and the difficulties of balancing their domestic and work obligations mounted faster than their incomes advanced. The reality of rising costs and responsibilities encouraged women to limit fertility and postpone marriage.

The need or desire to earn wages influenced all aspects of some women's lives, from schooling and migration to marriage and childbearing. Although most female workers were native-born Americans, the strength of the labor market pulled millions of women as well as men to the shores of the United States. Throughout the century women immigrated to the United States with specific labor markets as their destinations, and once here, most twentieth-century immigrants found work in fields that required little training. For women these areas were principally domestic service and light manufacturing. Moving independently or as members of family groups, women responded not only to the growth of specific regional labor markets, but also to large-scale changes in the U.S. occupational structure. Wives who had not formerly worked for wages accepted homework or wage labor outside the home as new opportunities permitted and family needs demanded. Native-born women also sought to improve their fortunes through migration, deserting rural areas for towns and exiting the South for the Northeast and the Midwest. Although slowed by the Depression, internal migration accelerated during World War II and thereafter with urban population centers, especially in the West and the Southwest, proving especially attractive.

Educational achievement heavily determined the employment opportunities of women as well as men. Class, race, and ethnicity have all defined girls' educational options, and gender discrimination has permeated all levels of public instruction in the United States. As public education expanded in the first half of the twentieth century, girls often found themselves enrolled in secondary schools segregated by sex or following curricula different from the educational programs that boys pursued. Through the 1950s, home economics courses and typing and other business courses prepared millions of girls to enter domestic, industrial, or office work with the expectation of retiring to the home after marriage.

Through the 1950s adult-led girls' clubs sponsored by social settlements, the Girl Scouts, and other groups also prepared girls for the domestic sphere, although they encouraged employment before marriage. Schools and girls' clubs sought to instill middle-class notions of feminine deportment and family order in girls. School and club activities taught girls to take on the roles of nurturers, caretakers, and community helpers, roles that suited mothers but also described the careers of servants, waitresses, secretaries, teachers, nurses, and social workers.

Throughout this century working-class, immigrant, and African American girls have had fewer opportunities than middle-class white girls to prepare for or enter college and therefore have had less likelihood of entering the feminine professions. As the century progressed, however, post-secondary schooling gradually broadened, with teachers' colleges and nursing schools recruiting substantial numbers of working-class as well as middle-class women. During the 1950s the Cold War fueled fears that American children, especially girls, had fallen behind Soviet youth in educational achievement. Studies of U.S. secondary and higher education in the 1950s and 1960s ultimately led to the abandonment of gender-segregated curricula and encouraged collegiate training for women. Nevertheless, graduate education remained the prerogative of an elite corps of wealthy or unusually gifted women throughout most of the century.

The inclusion of women in the 1964 Civil Rights Act and other subsequent legislation opened the doors for women who wanted to pursue nontraditional professional training, but men continued to dominate the highest positions in business, politics, and the professions. The Civil Rights Act inspired middle-class women to press for additional measures encouraging gender equity. The fight for the Equal Rights Amendment (ERA) demonstrated the determination of a sizable faction of middle-class women to move public policy closer to their own needs and convictions. The failure of the ERA reflected the inability of the amendment's proponents to mobilize working-class women behind their agenda. It also exposed the potent opposition of some women and men from all social classes to the new family order that economic and social circumstances of the late-twentieth century fostered.[1]

In the nineteenth and early twentieth centuries, paid employment distinguished poor women from their more fortunate middle-class sisters. By the 1920s, however, middle-class women had moved into the labor market and many chose to pursue careers after marriage. In the 1920s the sales and clerical sectors burgeoned with new employment opportunities for women. The overall broadening of female occupations beginning in the 1920s enticed significant numbers of middle-class women out of the home and into the labor market. The clerical sector offered a clean and orderly workplace, rewarded young women who remained in school through the standard eleven or twelve years necessary to receive a secondary degree, and thus drew middle-class women into the workforce as teaching had done earlier.

Although numerically small before the Depression, the female professional sector also grew as liberal arts colleges, teacher training institutes, and nursing schools expanded. Postsecondary education prepared young women to enter the labor market as "career" women. As these women obtained secure and often satisfying employments, they postponed marriage and became less likely to terminate their employment after marriage than women had been previously. Some of these women, married or single, set examples of career accomplishment for working-class girls through their activities in schools and social settlements, even though they attempted to educate poor girls to domestic ideals. In the face of prevailing social attitudes and educational experiences that linked female moral virtue with domesticity, married career women fought for their respectability in the pages of women's magazines and through associations like the Business and Professional Women's Clubs. From the 1920s through the 1960s, married working women justified their employment decisions on the basis of financial, emotional, or intellectual needs. In the long run, middle-class advocates of married women's work largely erased the moral boundary between the home and the workplace for all working women regardless of class.

Through the remainder of the twentieth century, the growth and development of the female labor market, coupled with rising consumer costs and expectations, encouraged married women to accept paid employment and to remain on the job. Schools and gendered organizations strongly encouraged female devotion to the domestic sphere through the 1950s, but women's commitment to long-term employment nevertheless rose steadily. Working women from all backgrounds modified their goals and expectations through their work. In the workplace women learned skills and acquired perspectives that reinforced some of the formal and informal lessons of youth but undermined others. The workplace inspired some women to push for improvements in wages and working conditions through co-operative labor actions or through reform legislation. At work women acquired new skills, broadened their horizons beyond the cultural limits of their ethnic heritage, and developed self-esteem. Employment encouraged women to reevaluate their goals and expectations, sometimes driving them to seek additional job skills or fight for improvements in the workplace, but sometimes reinforcing proscriptions that bound them to the home.

Biological realities and socialization have traditionally centered women's lives on family issues that men may more easily avoid. Women not only bear children and carry the major responsibilities for their care but also disproportionally assume responsibilities for the well-being of kin other than their children. In pre-industrial societies in which women produced subsistence and market goods within the home, women's procreative and caretaking activities conflicted minimally with their economically productive roles. As industrialization evolved, women's lives grew increasingly fragmented. Wage-earning removed women's productive roles from the household circle and forced women and families to draw boundaries between procreation and production. Industrialization segregated women of the emerging middle class into the domestic sphere, but it had the opposite effect among poorer women. Industrialization segmented women's lives into phases of economically productive labor outside the home, matched with other phases dedicated to family care and subsistence home production.

A female life cycle of temporary wage earning followed by dedication to the domestic sphere worked reasonably well under specific conditions. As long as mothers remained at home to maintain household and family, daughters were free to work outside the home. As long as husbands had sufficient earnings to support their wives and young children, wives could manage home and family without engaging in wage labor. For a variety of reasons, including women's choices to forego marriage or their failure to find mates, husbands' low earnings or their untimely deaths, or fathers' abandonment of their families, women often did not have the luxury of choosing between the domestic realm and wage earning. When forced to combine family care with family support, women's lives became infinitely more complicated. Industrial homework, which persisted because of its comparatively low cost to employers, proved an unsatisfactory choice for women whose circumstances compelled them to generate income from within the home.

During the twentieth century women combined family care with wage earning somewhat more easily than formerly in that a broader range of jobs opened to women; however, paid work paradoxically increased women's financial burdens. As women, married or not married, committed more and more of their lives to market labor, families came increasingly to depend on their earnings. Women's wage work set in motion a steady escalation of the demands on women's energies. Smaller families, shorter hours of work, and the commercialization of child care moderated this trend somewhat, but the claims of the workplace and the claims of the home never achieved an equilibrium in women's lives.

While husbands of the late twentieth century have largely accepted the reality of wives' employment, their accommodation to the new economic era has remained incomplete. Husbands have had no choice but to pitch in at home occasionally, but child care and household responsibilities remain largely women's responsibilities. In this regard family life remains significantly defined by nineteenth-century ideals. Devotion to family was a male as well as a female ideal in Victorian America, but fathers did not necessarily nurture their children or care for them directly. The male ideal prescribed monogamy, financial support, defense of the family against the outside world, and patriarchal governance. Emphasis on male individualism and competition, as well as a work ethic extolling long hours in the labor market, discouraged fathers from investing time and energy in home life. In politics and in business, the greatest rewards through the twentieth century have gone to men or women for whom individual achievement was a higher priority than attention to family. Middle-class fathers who have tried to invest time in family life have often remained virtual guests in their own homes as gendered expectations and skill-based tasks acquired in youth have restrained both mothers and fathers.[2]

The conflict between male ideals and family life has existed for the working class as well as for the middle class. As working-class men strove to provide for families, child labor and wives' earnings were constant reminders of their failures. Through the labor movement working men pressed for a "family wage" that would permit them to do without the earnings of women and children. The American Federation of Labor in particular supported restrictions on women's wages and working conditions in order to minimize labor competition and thereby undermined women's claims to market labor and to wage equity. The ethos of working-class men stressed the importance of homosocial recreations as well as a homosocial world of work. Leisure, labor activism, and politics all drew working-class men away from home and family and reinforced women's ties to the home. Although gender ideals proved slow to change, family life gradually bent to the pressures of the feminization of work.

Age at marriage declined sharply, and fertility rose suddenly in the late 1940s and the 1950s as men and women chased dreams of a satisfying family life after the disruptions of the Depression and World War II. Husbands and wives enjoyed new levels of consumption, but the postwar rush to marriage and parenthood delivered new challenges. Although ordinary Americans achieved unprecedented prosperity and living standards rose as families moved to newly developed suburbs, material comfort increasingly depended on wage earning by mothers as well as fathers. Rising expectations of domestic bliss and new attitudes toward divorce encouraged the dissolution of unhappy marriages. Rates of divorce or spousal abandonment rose, with women shouldering primary financial and caretaking responsibilities for couples' children. In time marital instability, long-term employment among women, and rising costs again encouraged men and women to postpone marriage and limit fertility. By the 1970s the tension between female wage earning and family life had magnified to the point that women abandoned the personal paths their mothers had followed. The age at which women first married rose sharply, the share of women choosing never to marry increased, and the share of married women foregoing motherhood grew. By the 1990s women's median age at first marriage had risen to its highest mark in modern times and fertility had reached an all-time low.

Beneath the general trend toward later marriages and low fertility that has characterized the last three decades, striking patterns of exception also emerged. Teenage fertility and extramarital fertility began to climb notably after the 1950s. Since the 1960s the share of African American children born out of wedlock has risen from roughly one third to three fifths, and among whites extramarital fertility has increased from fewer than one in twenty to approximately four in twenty births. Teen fertility increased among African American women through the late 1970s but has since declined. While teen fertility remains much lower for whites than for African Americans, teen fertility continues to climb in the white population and is projected to rise through the turn of the century.[3] By virtue of their fertility patterns, teenage and unmarried mothers have faced crushing poverty. Their comparative lack of education doubly handicaps unwed mothers in a world where even unskilled jobs require a high school education, occupational mobility requires advanced education, and the gender gap in wages persists. While women's overall job opportunities have expanded, the competition for those jobs also has grown.

The growth and diversification in the demand for female workers enhanced women's earning potential. While women's real earnings rose, their work remained segregated by gender and underpaid relative to men's jobs. Through the twentieth century the gender gap in wages has narrowed significantly as the demand for female wage earners has driven up the price of their labor. As the feminization of labor continues, women likely will approach wage equity, but they will continue to confront major economic problems. Those who earn the lowest wages have historically carried the heaviest financial responsibilities for family support. Specific groups of Americans have failed to obtain or preserve post-Depression improvements in real earnings. Though better off than they were thirty years ago, single-earner households, regardless of the race or sex of their heads, fare worse than they did fifteen or twenty years ago.

Economic restructuring and recessions of the 1980s and the 1990s have depressed Americans' buying power. Dual-earner families and persons at the top of the earnings pyramid have managed to retain the living standards of the 1960s, but most other Americans have fallen behind. In 1959 one fifth of all persons in the United States had incomes below the poverty line. At that time, approximately 18 percent of whites and 55 percent of blacks lived in poverty. By 1978, the share of all Americans in poverty had fallen to one tenth; poverty among whites and blacks had declined to 9 percent and 31 percent, respectively. Among Hispanics (not counted separately in 1959), about 22 percent lived in poverty in 1978. After 1978 poverty resumed rising, although poverty rates remained below the 1959 levels, and poverty among women increased despite the reduction of poverty among the elderly, of whom the majority are women.[4] As the fraction of households headed by women rose, between 1959 and 1986 the proportion of poor persons who resided in households headed by women increased from 18 percent to 38 percent.[5] A decline in the real earnings of women heading households has occurred over the past decade, even though the incomes of female workers who are not sole earners has increased. The poor, male and female, cannot provide adequately for their children, resulting in high rates of neglect, poor health and nutrition, lagging educational performance, and high rates of abandonment.

The demographic, economic, and social changes in women's lives through the century redefined family governance and the internal dynamics of family life. Children lost the ability and the obligation to supplement fathers' earnings. Child-rearing costs rose simultaneously as secondary schooling increased and more parents sought to send their children on to college. Increasingly smaller families looked to children as a source of emotional enrichment rather than financial gain. With little or no competition from siblings, children expected the undivided attention of their parents. Beginning in the 1920s medical experts and child psychologists stressed the importance of parental attention to the happiness and emotional growth of children in addition to their physical health and educational development. Despite changing attitudes about child nurture, the time that parents spent with their children declined. Fathers, increasingly absent from the home during the workday, lost the ability to define their children's activities and their futures. Women also lost some control over their children, as youths devoted more time to schooling and peer-group activities and mothers accepted work outside the home.

Throughout the century changing definitions of marriage heightened women's and men's expectations of equalitarianism, companionship, and emotional fulfillment in marriage and family life. However, men failed to gain prestige as nurturers and caretakers of children in exchange for sharing authority with their wives. Whether or not men took pleasure in their domestic tasks, cooking, cleaning, and caring for sick children did not earn men respect in the world outside the home. In the contemporary era the stress of changing gender roles and the rising costs of childrearing have brought increasing numbers of couples to the breaking point, and liberalized divorce laws have given men and women the freedom to end unhappy marriages. Rising rates of divorce and abandonment of children by their fathers have increased the share of families headed by poor women. Women have assumed ultimate responsibility within families through divorce or abandonment and because of extramarital fertility. Without sufficient income to support their families, with temporary or long-term dependency on welfare, or with full-time jobs that erode their abilities to supervise their children, mothers alone may face overwhelming obstacles in exercising authority within the family.

Ethnicity and race have shaped and continued to define gender roles and family forms. Ethnic cultures have informed women's choices about home and work through the century. The distinctive family and work behaviors of the many racial and ethnic subpopulations of the United States also reflect current and past differences of opportunity. The mark of discrimination on the lives of twentieth-century women and their families has gouged especially deeply into the lives of African Americans, whose culture embodies a singular heritage of African roots, of slavery, of discrimination, of poverty, and of protest. As nonblack immigrants adapted to U.S. culture and the U.S. economy, they also developed cultural mechanisms to resist prejudice. As immigrants and their children acculturated, their economic well-being generally strengthened, but recent economic setbacks have especially handicapped some ethnic groups. Mexican Americans and African Americans, who progressed economically through the 1960s, began to fall back into poverty in the late 1970s.

Americans are a people publicly committed to the ideal that family life is the social foundation of a strong democracy. Throughout this century White House conferences on the family and numerous other public forums, from the federal to the local level, have confirmed the centrality of the family in U.S. social values. For well over a century, public policy in the form of financial aid to widowed, abandoned, or single mothers has demonstrated our commitment to the ideal of the father-headed, mother-centered family as the most viable form of social organization. Politicians have supported mothers' pensions or aid to dependent children as a temporary remediation that would allow children without paternal support to form traditional nuclear families in their adult lives. Fears that social programs have created welfare dependency over the past two generations have eroded that assumption. Rapidly rising rates of divorce and of extramarital fertility since the 1960s also cast doubt on the permanence of the "traditional" family.

Our dedication to the ideal of the patriarchal family has obscured the fact that the "traditional" family supported by a single male wage earner is much less a reality in modern America than we have presumed it to be. As our industrial economy matured, the structure of work and the changing composition of our population evolved in ways that demanded maternal participation in supporting families. The traditional or patriarchal family that we associate with middle-class Victorian ideals could not spread broadly through the working classes, and in the long run only a minority of the middle class could have maintained families on the income of a father's earnings alone.

In the 1970s fervor about the decline of patriarchy rose to new heights. Voices from Jerry Falwell to Phyllis Schlafly made the home-centered mother the focal point of a new political as well as religious agenda. Presidents Jimmy Carter and Ronald Reagan both stated publicly that the American family was in trouble and declared family well-being central to their political goals. President George Bush extolled the virtues of two-parent households, and Dan Quayle made "family values" the centerpiece of his presidential campaign. The "traditional" family has replaced the yeoman farmer in the political rhetoric of our time, but its supposed defenders ignore family history, disregard the realities of contemporary family composition and structure, and do not address marital separation as a rational response to domestic violence.

The family has also drawn renewed attention from U.S. historians. As Carl Degler and Christopher Lasch observed at the end of the 1970s, demographic and social changes have presented the nation's families with frightening challenges in the contemporary era.[6] Degler wrote that the needs of women and the needs of families have been riding a collision course with each other through this century. Indeed, the collision has occurred, leaving a substantial minority of U.S. men, women, and children with fragmented and stress-filled lives. Degler's view of the family emerged partly from his efforts to see family change within the context of women's long walk toward civil equality in the United States. In the course of the twentieth century, women gradually gained rights that enlarged their roles in politics and reduced discriminations based on gender. Woman suffrage eventually led to women's elections to public office and broadening government appointments for women. State and federal laws eased restrictions on divorce, protected women's property rights, and established women's right to U.S. citizenship regardless of their marital status. Civil rights law, implemented by legislatures and courts, moved women closer to equality in access to education and jobs. These advances helped emancipate women from nineteenth-century conventions about women's place, but they did not lessen women's responsibilities within the home.

Contrary to Degler's views, women's emancipation from patriarchy and civil disabilities did not cause the collision between women's rights and family welfare. Rather, the gender revolution stalled at a critical juncture. Women's responsibilities to maintain themselves and their children continue to march ahead of the law, gender conventions, public policy, and discrimination in the labor market. Low wages exacerbate the child care problems mothers face, and the absence of adequate publicly supported child care retards women's abilities to develop their full potential as productive workers. Single and divorced fathers, now as formerly, have difficulty sustaining their ties and their financial obligations to their children. Male liberation has hardly begun, and female family heads continue to bear condemnation for their failure to conform to anachronistic or unrealistic nineteenth-century ideals of family order.

Women continue to brave immense challenges in balancing home and family care against the demands of wage earning. With seemingly insurmountable odds against their economic success, welfare mothers and others in poverty in the 1990s can move ahead only through the mutual cooperation of friends and extended family, with the support of social and legal services, and through greater public assistance to education and child care. Additional legal steps to increase parental compliance with the child support obligations of divorce settlements will materially benefit children in single-parent homes and alleviate the stresses of single parents, most of whom are women. The expansion of low-cost social services, especially day care, will assist families in finding an equilibrium between income earning and nurture.

Further narrowing and ultimately eliminating the gender gap in wages will equip families with the resources to complete the transition to egalitarian family structures that will reflect the actual needs of families and eliminate the often unspoken tendencies of husbands and wives to measure their economic contributions to the family on the basis of men's employment advantages. When political activists from Jane Addams to Eleanor Roosevelt reached out to protect working women and their children earlier in this century, the dilemmas of the working mother were primarily class based. The protectionist measures that reformers secured for working women reinforced occupational segregation and the gender gap in wages, but gender-based workplace protections fell under legislation and litigation in the wake of the Civil Rights Revolution. In the 1990s most mothers share the dual pressures of home and work that once characterized only the poor, and equity in the labor market is the primary means by which they can secure adequate care for their children.

Gender equity in the workplace will make it easier for men and women to choose equity in marriage and in the home. Only an educational environment that recognizes all the roles that adults must fill in our society can equip women and men to meet the daily challenges of their lives. Public policies must encourage fathers as well as mothers to combine employment and education in an effort to ward off poverty and the family disintegration that accompanies poverty. Current situations in which single and divorced mothers bear the total responsibility for family welfare demand drastic measures to make room for work and job training in these women's lives. American society can move toward increasingly stable families, families headed by women, by men, and by men and women together, only if public policy finally acknowledges that a golden age of family life never existed, that the dual-earner family and the female-headed family have come to stay, and that single earners at the lower end of the income scale have never managed to support families on their wages. The eventual achievement of gender equity in the economy will not remove the necessity of dual incomes for the maintenance of most families; most families headed by single mothers or single fathers will require income from the absent parent or considerable public assistance.

Whether children are born outside of marriage or to a husband and wife, stable families depend upon the nurture and financial support of two parents, but family well-being continues to decline. Parental neglect and community violence literally maim and kill thousands of our children before adulthood. Epidemic domestic and family violence know no boundaries of race or class. Educational, employment, and social policies that support gender equity in public and private spheres can alleviate the financial stresses and sex-role crises that feed domestic violence and child neglect. Ultimately family health depends on equal opportunities for all women and men, regardless of race, to work with dignity in jobs that permit wage earners to maintain themselves and their children. Our society and the future of our families depend upon a strong economy and on social and educational conditions that discourage teenagers from bearing children and thereby jeopardizing their own futures as well as the well-being of their children. If fathers are to regain their centrality in family governance, society must recognize men's abilities to nurture just as it has come to rely on women's labor. Women, as workers and as citizens, have more influence in setting the public agenda than ever before in our history, and women of all backgrounds can join together to rescue ourselves and our children from poverty and violence. Even though past differences of perceived group interest divided working women, family welfare defines a women's agenda that can succeed where class-based and race-based feminism has faltered.

Notes

INTRODUCTION

1. Because definitions of social class in the West evolved within patriarchal institutions, women derived their status from the occupations and wealth of their fathers and husbands. Through marriage to laborers or factory workers, women became members of the working class, but middle-class men who married factory workers simply "married beneath themselves." By virtue of their pursuit of schooling or employment, twentieth-century women have frequently attained a social status different from that of their fathers or husbands. Wherever possible in the following pages, I have defined the class membership of women on the basis of their own activities or accomplishments and have defined middle-class and working-class according to educational and occupational characteristics. College education by itself or employments that require professional accreditation are attainments that convey membership in the middle class. Working-class occupations are characterized by physical labor or service tasks that do not require advanced formal training. Individual occupations such as beautician or practical nurse now require licensing after a period of training, but the level of training and skill demonstrated are lower than for the middle-class occupations of schoolteacher and registered nurse. White-collar occupations may be either working-class or middle-class pursuits. Working-class white-collar workers are generally paid by the hour, while middle-class workers are salaried employees. Women may enter working-class office work as clerks, typists, or telephone operators and rise to middle-class status as office managers. One of the long-term effects of occupational segregation has been the relegation of most working-class white-collar jobs to women, with men occupying a disproportionate share of middle-class jobs within the clerical sector.
2. Jacob Mincer, "Labor Force Participation of Married Women: A Study of Labor Supply," in National Bureau of Economic Research, H. Gregg Lewis, ed., *Aspects of Labor Economics* (Princeton: Princeton University Press, 1962), pp. 63–106.
3. Valerie Kincade Oppenheimer, *The Female Labor Force in the United States: Demographic and Economic Factors Governing Its Growth and Changing Composition* (Westport, Conn.: Greenwood, 1976).
4. *Margaret Sanger: An Autobiography* (New York: Dover, 1971), p. 45.
5. In analyzing women's work experiences through the century, this book draws on a wide range of recent women's studies scholarship that has rescued women's past from obscurity and myth, including accounts of feminist political victories that have reshaped women's roles in public and private life, and histories of female emancipation through legal and political reform. By building the record of women's public and private experiences and accomplishments, scholars have informed our understanding of gender as a cultural construct separate from but related to biological differences between the sexes. Gender more than sex has circumscribed economic roles over time. I could not have written this book

without this reservoir of feminist scholarship on politics and culture, but in this book itself the economy holds center stage as I attempt to show how structural economic changes have influenced women's work, educational experiences, and family lives.

6. For a critical assessment of the impact of automation on workplace control, see David F. Noble, *Forces of Production* (New York: Oxford University Press, 1986). For the impact of office technology, see various works by JoAnne Yates, especially *Control through Communications: The Rise of System in America* (Baltimore: Johns Hopkins University Press, 1989).

7. Claudia Goldin, *Understanding the Gender Gap: An Economic History of American Women* (New York: Oxford University Press, 1990).

8. William H. Chafe, *The Paradox of Change: American Women in the 20th Century* (New York: Oxford University Press, 1991); Claudia Goldin, *Understanding the Gender Gap*, chap. 8; Rosalind Rosenberg, *Divided Lives: American Women in the Twentieth Century* (New York: Hill and Wang, 1992).

9. Mary H. Blewett, *Men, Women, and Work: Class, Gender, and Protest in the New England Shoe Industry, 1780–1910* (Urbana: University of Illinois Press, 1990); Thomas Dublin, *Women at Work: The Transformation of Work and Community in Lowell, Massachusetts, 1826–1860*. More than half (56 percent) of all women ages 24 to 29 years were in the labor force in 1900.

CHAPTER I

1. *Historical Statistics of the United States, Colonial Times to 1970* (Washington, D.C.: GPO, 1975), Part 1, p. 140.

2. Agriculture engaged nearly as many women as manufacturing, but female farm workers did not necessarily receive wages or other income. In addition to the unpaid labor of women and girls in agriculture and in family-owned businesses, women of all ages labored at a broad variety of economically productive tasks within the home. To the extent that families reported the unpaid labor of wives and children who devoted fifteen hours per week or more to agricultural or business tasks of family enterprises, the workers were included in federal censuses of the labor force in 1900 and 1920. Changes in instructions to enumerators resulted in an undercount of female workers in the 1910 census. Women who kept boarders and lodgers, especially in the early part of this century, may not have reported themselves as workers if they suspected that their activities were in violation of urban licensing laws or health codes.

3. Jane Addams, *The Spirit of Youth and the City Streets* (New York: Macmillan, 1909), p. 5.

4. Diane Quellette, interview with Dianne Novelli, Lowell, Massachusetts, February 18, 1985, Millworkers of Lowell Collection, University of Massachusetts, Lowell.

5. The Census Bureau enumerated single mothers as widows in 1900.

6. John L. Rury, *Education and Women's Work: Female Schooling and the Division of Labor in Urban America, 1870–1930* (Albany: State University of New York Press, 1991), p. 21.

7. In professions that employed large numbers of women, such as teaching, employer policies may have precluded the employment of married women, but the marriage bar was more pervasive in the 1930s. One in 220 employed female teachers was married in 1900.

8. Hazel Stevens, interview with Karen Farmer, October 22, 1977, Millworkers of Lowell Collection.

9. Elizabeth Hamblet, interview with Rogers Hall, February 27, 1973, Millworkers of Lowell Collection.

10. Judy Barrett Litoff, ed., *The American Midwife Debate: A Sourcebook on Its Modern Origins* (Westport, Conn.: Greenwood, 1986).

11. Census polls of the birth states of internal migrants, one reliable indicator of the lower limits of migration, demonstrate that residential patterns have changed more through movement within the United States than through immigration. Immigrants, once in the United States, became important participants in the larger streams of internal population movement. For a discussion of migration trends and the difficulties in assessing internal migration, see Conrad Taeuber and Irene B. Taeuber, The Changing Population of the United States, Census Monograph Series (New York: John Wiley & Sons, 1958), pp. 94–100.

12. Elizabeth Ewen, *Immigrant Women in the Land of Dollars; Life and Culture on the Lower East Side, 1880–1925* (New York: Monthly Review Press, 1985), pp. 55–56; David Katzman, *Seven Days a Week: Women and Domestic Service in Industrializing America* (New York: Oxford University Press, 1978), pp. 204–14; Mark Reisler, *By the Sweat of Their Brow: Mexican Immigrant Labor in the United States, 1900–1940* (Westport: Greenwood Press, 1976), pp. 5, 8–12, 39, 55.

13. Diane Quellette, interview with Diane Novelli, Lowell, Massachusetts, February 18, 1985, Millworkers of Lowell Collection.

14. Delores Janiewski, *Sisterhood Denied: Race, Gender, and Class in a New South City* (Philadelphia: Temple University Press, 1985), pp. 59–60.

15. In *Immigrant Women in the Land of Dollars*, Elizabeth Ewen describes the difficulties that Italian and Jewish wives faced simply in keeping house in the tenements of New York at the turn of the century, and Donna Gabaccia has documented Sicilian women's adaptation to American homes in *From Sicily to Elizabeth Street: Housing and Social Change among Italian Immigrants* (Albany: State University of New York Press, 1984).

16. Since 1985, immigration has reached numbers that equal those of the early twentieth century, although the proportion of total U.S. population that annual arrivals represent from 1985 to the present remains far below earlier levels.

17. Hasia R. Diner, *Erin's Daughters in America: Irish Immigrant Women in the Nineteenth Century* (Baltimore: Johns Hopkins University Press, 1983); Janet A. Nolan, *Ourselves Alone: Women's Emigration from Ireland, 1885–1920* (Lexington: University Press of Kentucky, 1989), pp. 43–44.

18. Caroline Golab, *Immigrant Destinations* (Philadelphia: Temple University Press, 1977), pp. 148–49. Polish bachelors in the United States frequently married through arrangements made by the brides' and grooms' families in Poland. The young couple often had village roots in common but sometimes had never met before the prospective bride's arrival in the United States.

19. Virginia Yans-McLaughlin, "A Flexible Tradition: South Italians Confront a New Work Experience," and comment by Louise Tilly and Alice Kessler-Harris, *Journal of Social History*, 7 (Summer, 1974), 429–59; Harriet Perry, "The Metonymic Definition of the Female and the Concept of Honour among Italian Immigrant Families in Toronto," in Betty Boyd Caroli et al., eds., *The Italian Immigrant Woman in North America* (Toronto: Multicultural Society of Ontario, 1978), pp. 222–28; Judith E. Smith, "Italian Mothers, American Daughters: Changes in Work and Family Roles," in Caroli et al., pp. 206–21.

20. Edith Abbott, Immigration: Select Documents and Case Records, (New York: Arno Press, 1969), pp. 722–23.

21. Katherine Speronis, interview with Dianne Novelli, January 25, 1980, Mill Workers of Lowell Collection; Phyllis A Stromvall, "The Family History of Sophie and Teresa," in Mary H. Blewett, ed., Surviving Hard Times: The Working People of Lowell (Lowell, Mass.: Lowell Museum, 1982), pp. 149–63; Mary Podgorski, interview with Olga Spandager, November 15, 1985, Mill Workers of Lowell Collection.

22. In contrast, men dominated in movement to the Midwest and the West until the 1920s. Henry S. Shryock, Jr., Population Mobility within the United States, (Chicago: Community and Family Study Center, University of Chicago, 1964), pp. 63–69; Everett S. Lee, Net Intercensal Migration, 1870–1940, Vol. I: Introduction and Summary Tables, (Philadelphia: University of Pennsylvania Press, April 15, 1953), table C.

23. Carole Marks, Farewell—We're Good and Gone: The Great Black Migration (Bloomington: Indiana University Press, 1989), pp. 35–36, 46–47.

24. Burniece Avery, Walk Quietly Through the Night and Cry Softly (Detroit: Balamp, 1977).

25. Official work rates for black women were highest in New England and the Middle Atlantic regions.

26. Statistics of Women at Work: Based on Unpublished Information Derived from the Schedules of the Twelfth Census: 1900 (Washington: GPO, 1907), tables 12 and 13.

27. By 1944 the Boston YWCA had abandoned racial segregation, but the policy had been reaffirmed in 1921 when a representative of the Boston Urban League questioned the position of the Y. "Chronological History of Interracial Practices," folder 447, Papers of the Boston YWCA, Arthur and Elizabeth Schlesinger Library.

28. Records of the Cleveland YWCA, Cleveland, Ohio; "Field to Factory," the Smithsonian Museum of American History, Washington, D. C.

29. Mark Wischnitzer, To Dwell in Safety: The Story of Jewish Migration Since 1800 (Philadelphia: The Jewish Publication Society of America, 1948), p. 123.

30. Kate Holladay Claghorn, The Immigrant's Day in Court (New York: Harper, 1923), p. 11.

31. Faye E. Dudden, Serving Women: Household Service in Nineteenth-Century America (Middletown, Conn.: Wesleyan University Press, 1983); David M. Katzman, Seven Days a Week: Women and Domestic Service in Industrializing America (New York: Oxford University Press, 1978). pp. 100–107; Joanne Meyerowitz, Women Adrift: Independent Wage Earners in Chicago, 1880–1930 (Chicago: University of Chicago Press, 1988).

32. Claghorn, The Immigrant's Day in Court, p. 9.

33. Boston Journal, March 1, 1913.

34. U. S. Senate, Reports of the Immigration Commission, Vol. 36, Immigration and Crime (Washington, D.C.: GPO, 1911).

35. Jane Addams, A New Conscience and an Ancient Evil (New York: Macmillan, 1912), pp. 17–19.

36. Barbara Meil Hobson, Uneasy Virtue: The Politics of Prostitution and the American Reform Tradition (New York: Basic Books, 1987), pp. 141–47.

37. Records of the Women's Educational and Industrial Union, box 8, Arthur and Elizabeth Schlesinger Library.

38. Elizabeth Clark-Lewis, Living In, Living Out: African American Domestics in Washington, D.C., 1910–1940 (Washington, D.C.: Smithsonian Institution, 1994), pp. 123–73.

39. About a year after Pastrozna's baby was born, the League located Stornieczik in Pittsburgh

and encouraged him to marry Anastazia, which he did. Abbott, *Immigration*, pp. 719–21.

40. Joseph A. Hill, *Women in Gainful Occupations, 1870–1920*, Census Monograph IX (Washington, D.C.: GPO, 1929), pp. 122–56. Some lodgers were married women whose families boarded, but most lodgers and live-in employees did not have significant income beyond their own earnings. Working women who maintained their own homes or lived with relatives were much more likely to be part of a family economy. Of working women in twenty-seven cities in 1900, the majority were members of families that included workers other than themselves, and nearly two fifths of the families of wage-earning women included three or more workers. Nine in one hundred of these working women maintained their own homes and had no other workers in their families. It was then highly unlikely that a working woman, with or without dependents, was able to maintain herself in her own home.

41. Victoria Byerly, *Hard Times Cotton Mill Girls: Personal Histories of Womanhood and Poverty in the South* (Ithaca, N.Y.: ILR Press, 1986), pp. 125–27.

42. Mary Van Kleeck, *Artificial Flower Makers* (New York: Russell Sage Foundation Survey Associates, 1913), pp. 7–8.

43. The U.S. silk industry consisted of three broad categories of manufacturing: throwing mills, broad silk mills, and ribbon manufacturers. Throwing mills spin silk, while the broad silk and ribbon mills weave the silk threads. At the turn of the century, the spinning process was both the least skilled and the most labor intensive aspect of the industry. Consequently, employers first turned to female and child workers in silk throwing.

44. U. S. Senate, *Report on Condition of Woman and Child Wage-Earners in the United States, IV: The Silk Industry* (Washington, D.C.: GPO, 1911), p. 18.

45. The average fifteen-year-old girl in a New Jersey throwing mill earned nine cents per hour, while the Pennsylvania girl earned seven. Among women ages twenty-five to thirty-five, the comparison was seventeen cents to fourteen cents. The New Jersey workers were also likely to work more hours per week. In a given week at the end of 1907, 40 percent of New Jersey throwsters under age sixteen earned less than four dollars, but in the following month when a similar survey was taken in Pennsylvania, 92 percent of the Pennsylvania girls earned less than four dollars per week. Among adult female workers the comparison was similar: 9 percent versus 7 percent. U.S. Senate, *The Silk Industry*, pp. 147–59.

46. Ibid., pp. 20–21.

47. Ibid.; additional volumes of the Senate report cover the cotton, garment, glass, and metal trades as well as nonmanufacturing jobs, labor unions, and labor legislation.

48. Carole Turbin, *Working Women of Collar City: Gender, Class and Community in Troy, New York, 1864–86* (Urbana: University of Illinois Press, 1992), chap. 1; Daniel J. Walkowitz, *Worker City, Company Town* (Urbana: University of Illinois Press, 1978).

49. Anthony F. Wallace, *Rockdale: The Growth of an American Village* (New York: Norton, 1980), pp. 66–67; Tamara K. Hareven and Randolph Langenbach, *Amoskeag: Life and Work in an American Factory Village* (New York: Pantheon, 1980), pp. 21–23; U. S. Senate, *Report on Condition of Woman and Child Wage-Earners in the United States, I: The Cotton Textile Industry* (Washington, D.C.: GPO, 1910), pp. 329, 538–39, 591.

50. The Boston Associates, who planned and developed the New England mills, proceeded from an assumption that only high wages, pleasant working conditions, and a wholesome

living environment could lure female workers into the mills from their farm homes. As Thomas Dublin has documented, industrialists soon faced a glutted market and cutthroat competition that forced them to lower wages and cut overhead costs. An overall decline in the regional economy and employers' discovery of the immigrant made lower wages possible. Labor abundance replaced labor scarcity. Closing the company boarding houses and postponing repairs on company properties cut overhead costs. Since the founding of the New England textile mills, women have rarely found themselves in a highly favorable labor market. Rather, industrialists have discovered and exploited various methods for controlling female wages. Labor costs naturally concern any employer, and certainly not only women have experienced labor exploitation. However, gender has been consistently linked with wage differences.

CHAPTER 2

1. Albert H. Leake, *The Vocational Education of Girls and Women* (New York: Macmillan, 1918), p. 7.
2. Marguerite Dickson, *Vocational Guidance for Girls* (New York: Rand McNally, 1919), p. 17.
3. Leake, *The Vocational Education of Girls and Women*, p. 5.
4. U.S. Bureau of the Census, *Historical Statistics of the United States, Colonial Times to the Present*, Part 1 (Washington, D.C.: GPO, 1975), Series H 433–441, p. 370. Boys of both races were somewhat more likely to be in school than were girls of the same race in 1880, but by 1920 white boys and girls had virtually the same attendance rates and black girls had moved slightly ahead of black boys in attendance. John L. Rury, *Education and Women's Work: Female Schooling and the Division of Labor in Urban America, 1870–1930* (Albany: State University of New York Press, 1991), chaps. 1–2.
5. U.S. Bureau of the Census, *Historical Statistics*, H 598–601, p. 379.
6. Ibid., H 508–519, p. 375.
7. Ibid., H 751–765, p. 386.
8. Thomas Woody, *A History of Women's Education in the United States*, Vol. 2 (New York: Octagon Books, 1966), reprint of 1929 edition, pp. 68–73.
9. Rury, *Education and Women's Work*, p. 114.
10. "Report of the Committee on Sewing in Worcester Schools," in Massachusetts Board of Education, *Annual Report, 1878–1879*, pp. 349–50, quoted in Marvin Lazerson, *Origins of the Urban School: Public Education in Massachusetts, 1870–1915* (Cambridge, Mass.: Harvard University Press, 1977), p. 106.
11. *Union News Items*, vol 11, no. 1 (November, 1912), p. 7, Papers of the Women's Educational and Industrial Union, box 2, Arthur and Elizabeth Schlesinger Library, Radcliffe College.
12. Ibid, pp. 7, 11.
13. Louise Montgomery, *The American Girl in the Stockyards District* (Chicago: University of Chicago Press, 1913), p. 3; Louise C. Odencrantz, *Italian Women in Industry: A Study of Conditions in New York City* (New York: Russell Sage Foundation, 1919), pp. 255–56; cited by Leslie Woodcock Tentler in *Wage-Earning Women: Industrial Work and Family Life in the United States* (New York: Oxford University Press, 1979), p. 100.

14. Maxine Seller, "The Education of the Immigrant Woman, 1900–1935," *Journal of Urban History*, 4 (May, 1978), 316–19.

15. National Society for the Promotion of Industrial Education, "Synopsis of the Vocational Education Survey of the City of Richmond," unpublished report, 1914, mimeographed copy in Records of the Office of Education, National Archives, RG 12, no. 60, box 32.

16. Seller, "The Education of the Immigrant Woman," pp. 308–13.

17. Theatis Johnson Williamson, interview with Lanier Rand, February, 1977, Southern Oral History Project, Southern History Collection, University of North Carolina at Chapel Hill; Betty Brandon, "Alexander J. McKelway, Statesman of the New Order" (Ph.D. dissertation, University of North Carolina, 1969).

18. John Dewey and Evelyn Dewey, *Schools of To-Morrow* (New York: E. P. Dutton, 1915), chaps. 7–11.

19. Ibid, p. 34.

20. Diane Ravitch, *The Great School Wars, New York, 1805–1973; A History of the Public Schools as Battlefields of Social Change* (New York: Basic Books, 1974), chap. 20; Seller, "The Education of the Immigrant Woman," 317.

21. Ravitch, *Great School Wars*, pp. 273–74.

22. Dewey and Dewey, *Schools of To-Morrow*, p. 224.

23. Lillian Wald, *The House on Henry Street* (New York: Henry Holt, 1915), pp. 6–7.

24. Lillian Wald, *Windows on Henry Street* (Boston: Little, Brown, 1934), pp. 15–16. Susan A. Glenn addresses the experiences of Jewish immigrant women in *Daughters of the Shtetl: Life and Labor in the Immigrant Generation* (Ithaca, N.Y.: Cornell University Press, 1990).

25. Jane Addams, *Twenty Years at Hull-House* (New York: Macmillan, 1911), p. 355.

26. Ibid., p. 349.

27. Records of the Girls' Tomato Clubs, Winthrop College Archives and Records, Rock Hill, South Carolina.

28. *Connecticut Common School Journal* I, 10, quoted in Thomas Woody, *History of Women's Education in the United States*, Vol I (New York: Octagon Books, 1966), p. 463.

29. W. Wayne Dedman, *Cherishing This Heritage: The Centennial History of the State University College at Brockport, New York* (New York: Appleton-Century-Crofts, 1969); Daniel Putnam, *A History of the Michigan State Normal School at Ypsilanti, Michigan, 1940–1899* (Ypsilanti, Mich.: Scharf, Tag, Label & Box, 1899), pp. 36, 62–63; Clyde O. Ruggles, *Winona State Normal School, 1860–1910* (Winona, Minnesota: Jones & Kroeger, 1910), pp. 9–39, 218.

30. Rury, *Education and Women's Work*, chaps. 3–5.

31. Untitled typed manuscript, Records of South Carolina Home Economics Administration, Winthrop University (n.p., n.d.).

32. Lucy Harris, *The Harris College of Nursing: Five Decades of Struggle for a Cause* (Forth Worth: Texas Christian University Press, 1973), p. 1.

33. Darlene Clark Hine, *Black Women in White: Racial Conflict and Cooperation in the Nursing Profession, 1890–1950* (Bloomington: Indiana University Press, 1989), pp. 7–10.

34. Jeanne L. Noble, *The Negro Woman's College Education* (New York: Garland, 1987), pp. 20–30.

35. Thomas Dublin, *Women at Work: The Transformation of Work and Community in Lowell, Massachusetts, 1826–1860* (New York: Columbia University Press, 1979).

36. Glenn, *Daughters of the Shtetl*, pp. 154–55.
37. Quoted in Sharon Hartman Strom, "Italian-American Women and their Daughters in Rhode Island: The Adolescence of Two Generations, 1900–1950," in Betty Boyd Caroli, ed., *The Italian Immigrant Woman in North America: Proceedings of the Tenth Annual Conference of the American Italian Historical Association* (Toronto: Multicultural History Society of Ontario, 1978), p. 194.
38. Tentler, *Wage-Earning Women*, pp. 67–68.
39. Kathy Peiss, *Cheap Amusements* (Ithaca: Cornell University Press, 1990); Glenn, *Daughters of the Shtetl*, pp. 159–66.
40. Alice Kessler-Harris, *Out to Work: A History of Wage-Earning Women in the United States* (New York: Oxford University Press, 1982), pp. 126–27.
41. Van Kleeck, *Artificial Flower Makers*, p. 86.
42. Peiss, *Cheap Amusements*, especially chapter 3.
43. Tentler, *Wage-Earning Women*, chap. 3.
44. Barbara Mayer Wertheimer, *We Were There: The Story of Working Women in America* (New York: Pantheon, 1977), pp. 206–207, 267–69.
45. Van Kleeck, *Artificial Flower Makers*, p. 35.
46. See Roger Waldinger, "Another Look at the International Ladies' Garment Workers' Union: Women, Industry Structure and Collective Action," in Ruth Milkman, ed., *Women, Work and Protest: A Century of U.S. Women's Labor History* (London: Routledge and Keegan Paul, 1985), pp. 86–109, for an analysis of the relationship between labor protest and the division of labor in manufacturing.
47. Kessler-Harris, *Out to Work*, p. 152.
48. Kessler-Harris, *Out to Work*, pp. 180–214; Tentler, *Wage-Earning Women*, p. 44; Dorothy Sue Cobble, *Dishing It Out: Waitresses and Their Unions in the Twentieth Century* (Urbana: University of Illinois Press, 1991), pp. 61–85.
49. Delores Janiewski, *Sisterhood Denied*.
50. Susan Porter Benson, *Counter Cultures: Saleswomen, Managers, and Customers in American Department Stores, 1890–1940* (Urbana: University of Illinois Press, 1986), pp. 147–55.
51. The Lynds' studies of working mothers in Muncie, Indiana, and Glen Elder's study of children's perceptions of parental authority have demonstrated the importance of wage earning in defining authority within the family. Robert S. Lynd and Helen Merrell Lynd, *Middletown: A Study in Contemporary American Culture* (New York: Harcourt, Brace, 1929) and *Middletown in Transition: A Study of Cultural Conflicts* (New York: Harcourt, Brace, 1937); Glen Elder, *Children of the Depression: Social Change in Life Experience* (Chicago: University of Chicago Press, 1974).

CHAPTER 3

1. Rosemary Crompton, *White-Collar Proletariat: Deskilling and Gender in Clerical Work* (Urbana: University of Illinois Press, 1992); Margery W. Davies, *Woman's Place Is at the Typewriter* (Urbana: University of Illinois Press, 1992); Sharon Hartman Strom, *Beyond the Typewriter: Gender, Class, and the Origins of Modern American Office Work, 1900–1930* (Urbana: University of Illinois Press, 1992); Carole Srole, "'A Blessing to Mankind, and Especially to Womankind': The Typewriter and the Feminization of Clerical Work, Bos-

ton, 1860–1920," in Barbara Drygulski Wright et al., eds., *Women, Work, and Technology: Transformations* (Ann Arbor: University of Michigan Press, 1987), pp. 84–100.

2. Maureen Weiner Greenwald, *Women, War and Work: The Impact of World War I on Women Workers in the United States* (Westport, Conn.: Greenwood, 1980), pp. 3–45.

3. Joseph A. Hill, *Women in Gainful Occupations, 1870 to 1920*, Census Monographs 9 (Washington, D.C.: GPO, 1929), table 15, pp. 164–87; U.S. Bureau of the Census, *Fifteenth Census of the United States, Population, Vol. V, General Report on Occupations* (Washington, D.C.: GPO, 1933), table 3.

4. Notes of Daniel Starch, Vocational Counselor, February 3, 1923, in the Records of the Women's Educational and Industrial Union, Schlesinger Library.

5. Anne Jackson Williams, letters to her mother, November 5, 1920, and November 12, 1920, Anne Jackson Williams Papers, Southern History Collection, University of North Carolina.

6. Herriclia Eliades, interview with Bob Hand, November 9, 1977, Millworkers of Lowell Collection.

7. Narissa Hodges, interview with Diane Novelli, February 27, 1977, Millworkers of Lowell Collection.

8. Elizabeth Clark-Lewis, "'This Work Had A' End': African-American Women and Migration in Washington, D.C., 1910–1940," in Carol Groneman and Mary Beth Norton, eds., *"To Toil the Live-Long Day": America's Women at Work* (Ithaca: Cornell University Press, 1987), pp. 196–212; Clark-Lewis, *Living In, Living Out: African American Domestics in Washington, D. C., 1900–1940* (Washington, D.C.: Smithsonian Institution Press, 1994).

9. U.S. Bureau of the Census, *Historical Statistics of the United States, Colonial Times to 1970*, Part 1, Series C 89–119.

10. Kristina Lindberg and Charles J. Ovando, *Five Mexican-American Women in Transition: A Case of Migrants in the Southwest* (San Francisco: R & E Research Associates, 1977), pp. 9–11.

11. Recent sociological research on Mexican wives whose husbands work in the United States has documented significant alterations in familial authority and responsibility. Reynaldo Baca and Dexter Bryan studied the women of a Nayarit village whose boyfriends, husbands, and sons regularly follow the harvest season in California's Imperial Valley and then return to Mexico to plant their own crops. Baca and Bryan found that the women suffered immediate separation pain but that they also felt freedom and independence. In this village in which so many men were regularly absent, a folklore evolved that praised assertive women as the successful representatives of their husbands in a deeply patriarchal culture. Reynaldo Baca and Dexter Bryan, "Mexican Women, Migration and Sex Roles," *Migration Today*, 13 no. 3: 14–16.

12. Julia Kirk Blackwelder, *Women of the Depression: Caste and Culture in San Antonio, 1929–1939* (College Station: Texas A&M University Press, 1984), pp.92–107. The scope and persistence of homework among U.S. women is examined in Eileen Boris and Cynthia R. Daniels, eds., *Homework: Historical and Contemporary Perspectives on Paid Labor at Home* (Urbana: University of Illinois Press, 1989).

13. Blackwelder, *Women of the Depression*, pp. 1–33.

14. Edith Abbott, *The Tenements of Chicago, 1890–1935* (New York: Arno Press, 1970), p. 347.

15. Ibid., p. 341.

16. Eula Fisher, interview, April 25, 1980, Washington Women's Heritage Project, Univ. Wash.

17. Hill, *Women in Gainful Occupations*, pp. 73–74.

18. The significance of hours of work in the first half of this century has been overlooked partly because part-time employment had not yet been defined as a work week of a specific maximum number of hours and partly because employers did not finance expensive benefits packages that were withheld from part-time workers.

    Public agencies did not gather systematic statistics on part-time employment until the 1940s, but individual firms' pay schedules document a broad variety of work patterns. The Department of Labor and the Census Bureau collected little data on part-time workers before the mid-1930s. Consequently, there are few indicators of the extent of part-time employment before this period. The extant evidence shows that work hours varied among employees and from one industry to another. In manufacturing firms of seventeen states that were surveyed from December, 1908, through April, 1909, for the Senate investigation of wages and working conditions of women and children in industry, work weeks of individual firms varied from forty-five to sixty hours, and many firms adopted different work schedules in different departments of their operations.

    The statistics do not reveal whether female workplaces operated on shorter schedules than male workplaces or the female averages were depressed by the irregular schedules of some women. *Historical Statistics of the United States*, Part 1, Series D 830–844 and p. 154.

19. "Part-Time Jobs for Women," *Monthly Labor Review*, 29 (December, 1929): 1259.

20. Payroll records, Baker Chocolate Company, vols. 4–25 (1918–28), Baker Library, Harvard Business School. In the interest of privacy, the names of workers have been changed.

21. Mary Thompson, interview with Jim LeLoudis, July 19, 1979, Charlotte, N.C., Southern Oral History Project.

22. Southern Oral History Project.

23. Annelise Orleck, *Common Sense and a Little Fire: Women and Working-Class Politics in the United States, 1900–1965* (Chapel Hill: University of North Carolina Press, 1995), pp. 121–50.

24. Anne Byrd Kennon, "College Wives Who Work," (M. A. Thesis, Radcliffe College, 1927), p. 12.

25. Surveys of middle-class working mothers differed from the social surveys of conditions among the lower classes. Women of the middle class either spoke for themselves through letters or publications or responded to written surveys on equal footing with the investigators. Most survey research of the middle classes was carried out through the mails rather than in person with the respondents' thoughts unfiltered by the investigator's pen. Several of these surveys were undertaken by college alumni organizations or with the approval of such groups. Women had less reason to question the motivations of investigators than did poor working mothers who often feared that the goal of the social surveys was to eliminate their jobs.

26. *Harper's Magazine*, 151 (November, 1925): 731–38; 152 (December, 1925): 54–59; *Atlantic Monthly*, 139 (September 19, 1926): 335–43; *New Republic* (April 14, 1926): 218–20; "Six Mothers" (August 4, 1926): 304–307; "A Real Job in Passaic," (August 25, 1926): 21.

27. Kennon, "College Wives Who Work," p. 87.

28. Mary Karafelis, interview with Pamela Jane Leman, February 26, 1985; Herriclea Eliades,

interview with Bob Hand, November 15, 1985; Katherine Speronis, interview with Judith Dunning, June 25, 1980; all in the Mill Workers of Lowell Collection.

29. Arline J. Yarbrough, interview with Marcia Greenlee, August 3, 1977, in Ruth Edmonds Hill, ed., *The Black Women Oral History Project*, X, Arthur and Elizabeth Schlesinger Library (Westport: Meckler, 1991), p. 424.

30. Records of the U.S. Office of Education, Division of Home Economics, "Biennial Survey, 1926–28," National Archives, RG 12, box 107, p. 10.

31. "Report of Home Economics Survey, Swarthmore, Pennsylvania, 1923," National Archives, RG 12, Division of Home Economics, box 112, pp. 1–2.

32. Henrietta W. Calvin, "Home Economics Courses for Girls and Young Women," Education War-Service Series, No. 4, RG 12, Division of Home Economics, box 107, p. 206.

33. Ibid.

34. Pearl Idella Ellis, *Americanization through Homemaking* (Los Angeles: Wetzel Publishing, 1929), pp. 30–31.

35. Carrie Alberta Lyford, *A Study of Home-Economics Education in Teacher-Training Institutions for Negroes*, Bulletin no. 79, Home Economics Series no. 7, U.S. Office of Education, 1923, reprint ed. (New York: Negro Universities Press, 1969), pp. 2–8.

36. Jeanne L. Noble, *The Negro Woman's College Education* (New York: Garland, 1987); Elizabeth Brooks Higginbotham, *Righteous Discontent: The Women's Movement in the Black Baptist Church, 1880–1920* (Cambridge, Mass.: Harvard University Press, 1994).

37. "Projects in Home Economics for 1918–19 Year," National Archives, RG 12, Division of Home Economics, box 107, p. 24; "Survey of Mississippi, 1925," box 114, pp. 3–4.

38. Although its membership was overwhelmingly middle class, Citizen Scouts (a senior program) in New York City organized a troop for young immigrant wives and mothers in 1918. The significant ways in which local programs departed from the national agenda in scouting are documented in Elisabeth Israels Perry, "From Achievement to Happiness: Girl Scouting in Middle Tennessee, 1910s–1960s," *Journal of Women's History*, 5, no. 2 (Fall, 1993): 75–94.

39. Mary Degenhardt and Judith Kirsch, comp., *75 Years of Uniforms, Insignia, Publications and Keepsakes; Girl Scout Collector's Guide* (New York: Girl Scouts of the U.S.A., 1987), pp. 52–63.

40. Degenhardt and Kirsch, *75 Years of Girl Scouting*, p. 14; Nancy Lynn, "Juliette Gordon Low: The Eccentric Who Founded the Girl Scouts," *Ms. Magazine*, November, 1981, p. 105.

41. Degenhardt and Kirsch, *75 Years of Girl Scouting*, p. 14.

42. *The American Girl*, January, 1930, p. 3.

43. Girls Scouts of the U.S.A., *Girl Scout Leader Notebook*, n.d.

44. "The First National Training Course for Girl Scout Officers," October 12–20, 1918, Personnel Courses, Reports, 1918–1939, Girl Scouts of the U.S.A. Archives, New York, New York.

45. "Training Schools for Leaders," Personnel-Training Courses file, Girl Scouts of the U.S.A. Archives.

46. Among the many clubs that reached and influenced girls during the 1920s and 1930s were the Girls Clubs of America, Campfire Girls, the Girl Scouts, the 4-H movement, and youth programs of the YWCA. Paula Fass and John Modell discuss the emergence of peer

groups in the 1920s, but neither considers the peer groups of preadolescent and adolescent children. Paula Fass, *The Damned and the Beautiful: American Youth in the 1920's* (New York: Oxford University Press, 1977); John Modell, *Into One's Own: From Youth to Adulthood in the United States, 1920–1975* (Berkeley: University of California Press, 1989), chap. 3.

47. Pamphlets describing the leadership training programs date from 1917. Copies are in the Personnel-Training Courses files of the Girl Scouts of the U.S.A. Archives.

48. Helen Christine Hoerle and Florence B. Saltzberg, *The Girl and the Job* (New York: Henry Holt, 1919), p. v.

49. Kennon, "College Wives Who Work," pp. 11–12.

50. Lynd and Lynd, *Middletown*, footnote to p. 127.

51. Ibid., pp. 127–29.

52. *Middletown in Transition*, p. 163.

53. *Middletown*, p. 131.

54. Ruth Schwartz Cowan, *More Work for Mother: The Ironies of Household Technology from the Open Hearth to the Microwave* (London: Free Association Press, 1989).

55. Fass, *The Damned and the Beautiful*, p. 64. Middle-class Americans, largely white and largely native born, had entered the twentieth century with well-defined notions of women's places in the family and in the world outside the home. Mothers anchored morality to the home and nurtured children with the loving but firm discipline that insured productive lives. While mothers set down moral guidelines for their children in most national and racial groups, white native-born wives presumed a potential for moral purity uncommon among other women. American society remained outwardly patriarchal, but wives had gained influence in family governance through the nineteenth century by virtue of their claims to moral authority. The notion of "separate spheres" had helped middle-class women establish themselves as moral arbiters in the community through church groups, women's clubs, and voluntary societies, but the acceptable activity bumped against narrow boundaries. While wives participated in family decision making in the ideal companionate marriage, husbands remained household heads. Middle-class women's moral authority within the family did not necessarily imply economic power. In middle-class families of the early twentieth century, wives and mothers not employed outside the home exercised markedly less economic responsibility and power than working-class wives.

56. Corra Mae White Harris to "Marjorie," March 5, 1926, Harris Papers, Emory University Library.

57. Mary Thompson, interview, Southern Oral History Program Collection, #4007.

58. Fass, *The Damned and the Beautiful*; Steven Mintz and Susan Kellogg, "The Rise of the Companionate Family, 1900–1930," *Domestic Revolutions: A Social History of American Family Life* (New York: Free Press, 1988), pp. 107–31.

CHAPTER 4

1. Anonymous letter to Mildred Seydell, Seydell Collection, Woodruff Library, Emory University. Seydell wrote an advice column for the Atlanta *Georgian* during the 1930s.

2. Lois Scharf, *To Work and to Wed: Female Employment, Feminism, and the Great Depression,*

Contributions in Women's Studies, Number 15 (Westport, Conn.: Greenwood Press, 1980), pp. 46–65.

3. Letter, Records of the Women's Bureau, Box 832.

4. Goldin, *Understanding the Gender Gap*, tables 3.1 and 3.2; pp. 59–71.

5. Mabel Mangan, interview with Leslie McDonnell, October 9, 1984, Mill Workers of Lowell Collection.

6. Blackwelder, *Women of the Depression*.

7. Ibid.

8. Boris and Daniels, Introduction to *Homework*, pp. 2–6; Cynthia R. Daniels, "Between Home and Factory: Homeworkers and the State," in *Homework*, pp. 14–19; Hilary Silver, "The Demand for Homework: Evidence from the U.S. Census," in *Homework*, pp. 103–24; Sheila Allen, "Locating Homework in an Analysis of the Ideological and Material Constraints on Women's Paid Work," in *Homework*, pp. 272–90.

9. Eileen Boris, "Homework and Women's Rights: The Case of the Vermont Knitters, 1980–85," in Boris and Daniels, eds., *Homework*, pp. 238–39; Blackwelder, *Women of the Depression*, pp. 104–107.

10. Martha Hughes, interview with author, Schenectady, New York, December 28, 1986.

11. The Depression also impeded the movement of African Americans, but the gender differences in migration rates were less extreme than among whites. Ann Ratner Miller, *Net Internal Migration to Larger Areas of the United States: 1930–1940, 1940–1950, 1950–1960* (Philadelphia: University of Pennsylvania Population Studies Center, 1964), tables 3–6. Statistics are for persons ages 10 years and older.

12. Frank L. Hopkins, "Should Wives Work?" *American Mercury*, 39 (December, 1936): 414–15.

13. "Leaves from a New Amazon's Notebook," *Good Housekeeping* (June, 1935): 24.

14. "The Depression and the Negro," Atlanta *Daily World*, July 29, 1933.

15. Mrs. Franklin D. Roosevelt, "The Married Woman in Business," *Woman's Home Companion*, 60 (November, 1933): 14.

16. "A Diary Setting Out the Life of May Eckles," November 19, 1931, typed copy, Daughters of the Republic of Texas Library, San Antonio.

17. Ester S. Moore to Mary Anderson, March 28, 1935, Records of the Women's Bureau, box 832.

18. H. L. R. Emmet to Mary Anderson, April 11, 1935, Records of the Women's Bureau, box 832.

19. Dr. Helen Pearce, "The Married Woman's Right to Work: Affirmative," *The Zontian* (November, 1938): 8 & 10; Carrie Castle Dozier, "The Married Woman's Right to Work: Negative," *Ibid.*: 9–10.

20. Robert S. Lynd and Helen Merrell Lynd, *Middletown*, p. 7.

21. Lynd and Lynd, *Middletown*, pp. 126–29; Lynd and Lynd, *Middletown in Transition*, pp. 59–63, 149, 178–79, 180–86.

22. Lynd and Lynd, *Middletown in Transition*, pp. 54–63, 180–86; Winifred D. Wandersee, *Women's Work and Family Values, 1920–1940* (Cambridge, Mass.: Harvard University Press, 1981).

23. For a detailed discussion of discrimination against married women, see Lois Scharf, *To Work and to Wed*.

24. The work rate of women of Asian or Native American heritage, not reported in 1900, was 15.7 percent in 1940.

25. U.S. Bureau of the Census, Fifteenth Census of the United States, Population, 1930, *Negroes in the United States*, table 19.

26. No estimates are available for younger persons. U.S. Bureau of the Census, *Historical Statistics of the United States*, Part 1, Series D 29–41.

27. Susan Porter Benson, *Counter Cultures*.

28. James Haynes, interview with author, Atlanta, Georgia, February 14, 1992.

29. U. S. Bureau of the Census, *Historical Statistics of the United States, Colonial Times to 1970*, Part 1 (Washington, D.C.: GPO, 1975), Series H 598–601; Susan Ware, *Holding Their Own: American Women in the 1930s* (Boston: Twayne, 1982), pp. 55–60.

30. Anna Graves, interview with the author, San Antonio, May 16, 1978.

31. John A. Clausen, *American Lives: Looking Back at the Children of the Great Depression* (New York: Free Press, 1993), p. 387.

32. Jeanne L. Noble, *The Negro Woman's College Education*, pp. 20–30.

33. Emeline S. Whitcomb, "Homemaking Education," *Biennial Survey of Education in the United States, 1928–1930*, vol. 1, bulletin no. 20 (Washington, D.C.: GPO, 1931), p. 1.

34. State of Alabama, Department of Education, *Manual of Home Economics Education for Negro Schools*, bulletin 1938, no. 4 (Wetumpka, 1938), pp. 6,7, 25–26, 45.

35. Cathy Shulkin, "The Girl Scout Movement on the Rise," *Nostalgia Magazine* (New York: Girl Scouts of the U.S.A., n.d.), p 34.

36. Winona L. Morgan, *The Family Meets the Depression; A Study of a Group of Highly Selected Families* (Minneapolis: University of Minnesota Press, 1939). Although not all of the 1927 AHEA respondents participated in the 1933 study, 331 members of the 1927 study population returned the follow-up questionnaires. Nearly half of the participants' husbands in the 1933 study were professional workers, and an additional one fifth were business managers, with skilled craftsmen and small shopkeepers together accounting for fewer than one fifth of the husbands' occupations. One tenth of the women were married to farmers. The average age of the husbands was 42 years in 1933, and the mothers' average age was 39. Between the 1927 and 1933 studies, the average number of children per family rose from 2 to 2.4. The survey families overall, then, were of higher occupational status and smaller in size than most other families of the time and embodied the goals of companionate marriage with a focus on child nurture.

    In subsequent individual meetings with one third of the 1933 respondents, interviewers found that husbands and wives managed financial obligations jointly in the vast majority of households. In fewer than one tenth of the families, wives had no authority in financial decisions, and one fifth of the wives managed household expenditures from a fixed allowance paid to them by the husband. Nearly half of the couples maintained joint checking accounts, with each partner accepting responsibility for different areas of spending and major purchases being decided jointly.

37. The changes in husbands' attitudes toward wives' employment did not reflect the same relationship to the economic circumstances of the family that the Lynds found in Middletown. In contrast with the Lynds, Morgan concluded that husbands secure in the sufficiency of their own incomes were less likely to oppose mothers' employment than men with lesser earnings.

38. John Modell, *Into One's Own*, pp. 132–60.
39. U.S. Bureau of the Census, *Historical Statistics of the United States from Colonial Times to 1970*, Part 1, Series B 42–48. See Claudia Goldin, *Understanding the Gender Gap*, pp. 139–42, for a discussion of the relationship between overall fertility or childlessness and labor force participation.
40. As Claudia Goldin has pointed out, it is difficult to weigh the various social and economic forces that affect fertility, but clearly the forces are interactive rather than one-directional. *Understanding the Gender Gap*, p. 123.
41. Mary-Elizabeth Pidgeon, *Women Workers and Their Dependents*, Women's Bureau Bulletin No. 239 (Washington, D.C.: GPO, 1952), pp. 62–63, 69–91.
42. John Modell, *Into One's Own*, p. 152.
43. Glen Elder, *Children of the Depression*.
44. Lynd and Lynd, *Middletown in Transition*.
45. Richard Griswold del Castillo, *La Familia: Chicano Families in the Urban Southwest, 1848 to the Present* (Notre Dame, Ind: University of Notre Dame Press, 1984), p. 101.
46. Abraham Hoffman, *Unwanted Mexican Americans in the Great Depression: Repatriation Pressures, 1929–1930* (Tucson: University of Arizona Press, 1974); Mark Riesler, *By the Sweat of Their Brow: Mexican Immigrant Labor in the United States, 1900–1940* (Westport, Conn.: Greenwood Press, 1976), pp. 231–32; Blackwelder, *Women of the Depression*; pp. 10, 14, 100, 176–78.
47. Blackwelder, *Women of the Depression*.
48. U.S. Bureau of the Census, *Historical Statistics of the United States*, Series B 236–247.
49. *Historical Statistics of the United States*, Series B 107–115.

CHAPTER 5

1. U. S. Bureau of the Census, *Labor Force, Employment, and Unemployment in the United States, 1940 to 1946*, *Current Population Reports*, Series P-50, no. 2 (Washington, D.C.: GPO, 1947). While married women's employment rates rose especially steeply during the war, they nevertheless remained a minority of the female work force; the majority of working women were single, widowed, or divorced women without alternative means of support.
2. "Employment in War Work of Women with Young Children," *Monthly Labor Review* (December, 1942): 1184.
3. Judy Barrett Litoff and David C. Smith, "'To the Rescue of the Crops': The Women's Land Army during World War II," *Prologue*, 25 (Winter, 1993): 356–57.
4. Mary Martha Thomas, *Riveting and Rationing in Dixie: Alabama Women and the Second World War* (Tuscaloosa: University of Alabama Press, 1987), p. 53.
5. "Housewife-War Worker," *The New Republic* (October 18, 1943): 518.
6. Janie Reeves, interview with author, San Antonio, May 26, 1979; Anna Graves, interview with author, San Antonio, May 16, 1978.
7. Rhoda Pratt Hanson, "I'm Leaving Home Part-Time," *Independent Woman* 25 (December, 1946): 363, 364.
8. Modell, *Into One's Own*, pp. 170–71.
9. Mary Hardy Phifer, *Textile Voices* (n.p.: Beaumont Spartan and Startex Mills, 1943), p. 8.

10. Jeanne M. Holm, "Women in the Armed Forces," in John E. Jessup, ed., *Encyclopedia of the American Military*, Vol. 3 (New York: Charles Scribner's Sons, 1994), p. 1995.

11. Doris Weatherford, *American Women and World War II* (New York: Facts on File, 1990), pp. 28–44; Susan M. Hartmann, *The Homefront and Beyond: American Women in the 1940s* (Boston: Twayne 1982), pp. 31–48.

12. Donald Vining, ed., *American Diaries of World War II* (New York: Pepys Press, 1982), p. 93.

13. Weatherford, *American Women and World War II*, pp. 66–67.

14. Hanson, "I'm Leaving Home Part-Time," pp. 363–64.

15. Thomas, *Riveting and Rationing in Dixie*, pp. 12–15.

16. Marilynn S. Johnson, *The Second Gold Rush: Oakland and the East Bay in World War II* (Berkeley: University of California Press, 1993), p. 46.

17. College attendance and graduation rates for women continued to drop from 1947 through 1950 as returning veterans crowded higher education, frequently with economic support from their wives. After 1950 college completion rates among women rose again, passing a 1947 high of 5.8 percent of the adult female population by 1959. Women also appeared to be falling behind educationally as men made much larger gains in college completion during the 1950s. While individual women throughout the twentieth century certainly have dropped out of school in order to marry, women have also been more likely than men to return to school later if they dropped out to marry. Consequently, in terms of median years of schooling completed by adults of all ages, U.S. men and women advanced at generally the same pace through the 1950s, with men finally catching up with women's median twelve years of schooling in 1967. U.S. Bureau of the Statistics, *Historical Statistics of the United States*, Series H 602–617, Series 751–765.

18. Ibid., Series H 602–617.

19. El Marie Kirby, *Cottonwood Corner: Growing Up in Arkansas during the Great Depression* (Galesburg, Mich.: privately printed, 1994), pp. 56–64.

20. Michael E. Stevens, ed., *Women Remember the War, 1941–1945*, Voices of the Wisconsin Past (Madison: State Historical Society of Wisconsin, 1993), pp. 9–24.

21. Johnson, *The Second Gold Rush*, p. 48.

22. Ibid., p. 63.

23. Interview with author, San Antonio, May 16, 1978.

24. Martha Swain, "Mississippi Delta Goes to War," *The Journal of Mississippi History*, 57, no. 4 (Winter, 1995): 344.

25. William H. Chafe, *The Paradox of Change: American Women in the Twentieth Century* (New York: Oxford University Press, 1991), pp. 127–29; Ruth Milkman, *Gender at Work: The Dynamics of Job Segregation by Sex during World War II* (Urbana: University of Illinois Press, 1987), pp. 55–56; Thomas, *Riveting and Rationing in Dixie*, pp. 34–54, 113–20; Weatherford, *Women and World War II*, pp. 139–40.

26. William H. Chafe, *The American Woman: Her Changing Social, Economic, and Political Roles, 1920–1970* (New York: Oxford University Press, 1972), p. 144.

27. Sherna Berger Gluck, *Rosie the Riveter Revisited: Women and the World War II Work Experience* (Long Beach, Calif.: California State University, Long Beach Foundation, 1983), vol. 12., pp. 23–41; vol. 28, pp. 45–99; vol. 40, pp. 71–89.

28. Ibid., vol. 13, p. 42.

29. Ibid., vol. 40, pp. 17–21.

30. Milkman, *Gender at Work*, pp. 77–83.

31. The average weekly earnings of female production workers rose from $.50 an hour in 1940 to $.80 in 1945, but men's industrial pay rose even more, from $.75 to $1.25 an hour.

32. Mary Anderson, "Postwar Facts and Factors: The Women's Bureau Speaks," in *Newsweek's* Club Bureau, *American Women in the Postwar World: A Symposium on the Role Women Will Play in Business and Industry* (New York: Newsweek, ca. 1944) p. 4.

33. Exactly what "patriotism" meant to women themselves, as opposed to what men writing to, at, and about women assumed it meant or ought to mean deserves careful historical study. Suffice it here to say that, like such terms as "power," and "political," it had long had different implications for women than men.

34. Eleanor Ferguson Straub, "United States Government Policy toward Civilian Women during World War II" (Ph. D., Emory University, 1973); Chafe, *The American Woman*, pp. 146–49; Elaine Tyler May, *Homeward Bound: American Families in the Cold War Era* (New York: Basic Books, 1988), pp. 58–62.

35. Straub, "Government Policy toward Civilian Women during World War II," chap. 8; Kessler-Harris, *Out to Work*, pp. 297–98.

36. Straub, "Government Policy toward Civilian Working Women during World War II," pp. 260–62, 283–84; Chafe, *The American Woman*, p. 150.

37. May, *Homeward Bound*, pp. 62–75; Melissa Dabakis, "Gendered Labor: Norman Rockwell's *Rosie the Riveter* and the Discourses of Wartime Womanhood," in Barbara Melosh, ed., *Gender and American History Since 1890* (London: Routledge, 1993), pp. 182–204.

38. *Woman's Home Companion*, 70 (October, 1943): 122. For an example of the literature on wartime research and postwar consumer goods see J. D. Ratcliff, "A Home for You—Tomorrow," *Ibid.* (July, 1943), p. 21.

39. Straub, "Government Policy toward Civilian Workers during World War II," pp. 313–22.

40. "The Women in the War," Jack Goodman, ed., *While You Were Gone; A Report on Wartime Life in the United States* (New York: Simon and Schuster, 1946), pp. 173–96.

41. "The Stake of Women in Full Postwar Employment, *Ladies' Home Journal* 61 (April, 1944): pp. 6 & 183.

42. "Fade Out of the Women," *Time*, September 4, 1944, p. 78.

43. Here, as in many other instances, *Time* ignored the facts in favor of publisher Henry Luce's wishful thinking.

44. Anderson, "Postwar Facts and Factors," p. 4.

45. Rebekah S. Greathouse, "The Effect of Constitutional Equality on Working Women," *The American Economic Review*, 34, no. 1, Supplement, part 2 (March, 1944): 227.

46. Niles Trammell, "Hats Off To Them," *Ibid.*, p. 25. Trammel was president of the National Broadcasting Company when he wrote the essay.

47. Records of the Women's Bureau, National Archives, Record Group 86, box 996.

48. U.S. Women's Bureau, *Women Workers in Ten War Production Areas and Their Postwar Employment Plans*, Women's Bureau Bulletin No. 209, (Washington, D.C.: GPO, 1946), p. 23.

49. "Women Will Stay," *Business Week*, May 12, 1945, pp. 102–103.

50. U.S. Women's Bureau, *Statement to the War Labor Board in Support of Union's Request to Abolish Discrimination against Married Women* (Washington, D.C.: GPO, July, 1945), p. 3.

51. Chafe, *The American Woman*, pp. 175–80.

52. Frank Mott and Lois Shaw found that defense workers "gained a taste for work during that period, inclinations with perhaps profound effects not only for those women but also for their children's generation." "The Employment Consequences of Different Fertility Behaviors," in Lois Banfill Shaw, ed., *Midlife Women at Work: A Fifteen-Year Perspective* (Lexington, Mass.: Lexington Books, 1986), p. 23.

53. Mae Clinkscales Belk, interview with author, Atlanta, September 12, 1991; Lee Belk, interview with author, Atlanta, September 27, 1991.

54. *Proposed Resolutions and Constitutional Amendments*, United Electrical, Radio and Machine Workers of America, CIO, Twelfth International Convention, September 22–26, 1947, Boston, Mass., p. 125. I wish to thank Lisa Kannenberg for sharing with me her extensive resources and knowledge about women in the UE.

55. Agreement: "Married Women," March 31, 1948, copy in the archives of the United Electrical, Radio and Machine Workers of America, Pittsburgh, Pa., file on Westinghouse, Sharon.

56. "Report of the Investigating Committee on the Married Women's Appeal in Sharon," copy, UE Archives; Albert J. Fitzgerald to Thomas Flanagan, letter of August 26, 1948, copy in UE Archives.

57. Leonard G. Stegailov to Millie White, letter of December 17, 1948, UE Archives. As Ruth Milkman has shown, women were largely unsuccessful overall in preserving their places in skilled industrial occupations after the war. *Gender at Work*, pp. 127–52. However, women had been prominent in the electrical industry before the war and persisted in their traditional jobs thereafter.

58. "UE Guide to Fair Practices, 1950," copy in UE legal brief, *United States of America before the Equal Employment Opportunity Commission*, EEOC Charge No. TN4C-2000 and EEOC Charge No. TN4C-2002, UE Archives, Pittsburgh, pp. 401 ff.

59. Records of the Women's Bureau, box 700; editorial, Washington *Post*, May 14, 1949.

60. In 1953 Mayor Wagner wrote the Parents' Association of his "firm conviction that we must increase the City's appropriation for Day Care Centers and that we must press more vigorously for the restoration of state aid for the Day Care Center Program. Letter, Robert F. Wagner, Jr., to Mrs. Randolph Guggenheimer, October 28, 1953. Records of the Child Care Center Parents' Association of New York, Inc., Schlesinger Library.

61. Straub, "Government Policy toward Civilian Women during World War II," pp. 294–97. Although labor unions generally did not take the offensive on the day care issue, the leadership of the Union of Electrical, Radio and Machine Workers of America encouraged its locals to support day care measures. Day care appeared on the agenda at UE women's conferences. In 1953 the UE notified its branches that "every local should adopt a resolution urging the tax exemption for child care expenses of working mothers." Memorandum from Ernest Thompson to all Local Fair Practices Committees, June 24, 1953, and memorandum from Julius Emspak to UE General Vice Presidents, April 20, 1953, copies in UE legal brief in EEOC Charge No. TNP4C-2000, and EEOC Charge No. TNP4C-2002, pp. 473, 575.

62. Mimeographed report to the Interdepartmental Committee on Children and Youth from the Subcommittee on Children of Employed Mothers, March 16, 1950, Records of the Women's Bureau, box 700.

63. Letter from Ethel Erickson to Mary Elizabeth Pidgeon, Survey Materials Relating to Bulletin No. 239, Records of the Women's Bureau.

64. Gluck, *Rosie the Riveter Revisited*, vol. 28, pp. 45–66.

65. Marjorie Peto, *Women Were Not Expected* (West Englewood, N.J.: privately published, 1947), p. 158.

66. Charity Adams Earley, *One Woman's Army: A Black Officer Remembers the WAC* (College Station: Texas A&M University Press, 1989), p. 214.

67. Jeanne M. Holm, "Women in the Armed Forces," in John E. Jessup, ed., Encyclopedia of the American Military, vol. 3 (New York: Charles Scribner's Sons, 1994), 1994–2002.

68. U.S. Bureau of the Census, *Marital and Family Characteristics of the Labor Force in the United States, Current Population Reports*, Series P-50, no. 11 (Washington, D.C.: GPO, 1948).

69. Michael E. Stevens, ed., *Women Remember the War*, pp. 9–24.

70. Hanson, "I'm Leaving Home Part-Time," pp. 363, 364, 379.

71. Johnson, *The Second Gold Rush*, p. 211.

72. For a thorough discussion of propaganda and policies through the course of the war, see Straub, "United States Government Policy toward Civilian Women during World War II," 140–54; Karen Sue Anderson, *Wartime Women* (Westport, Conn.: Greenwood, 1981); D'Ann Campbell, *Women at War with America: Private Lives in a Patriotic Era* (Cambridge, Mass.: Harvard University Press, 1984), chap. 8; Hartmann, *The Home Front and Beyond*; Leila J. Rupp, *Mobilizing Women for War: German and American Propaganda, 1939–1945* (Princeton, N.J.: Princeton University Press, 1978).

CHAPTER 6

1. Stephanie Coontz, *The Way We Never Were: American Families and the Nostalgia Trap* (New York: Basic Books, 1992), pp. 76–79.

2. David Reisman, *The Lonely Crowd: A Study of the Changing American Character* (New Haven, Conn.: Yale University Press, 1950), pp. 19–23.

3. *New York Times*, September 20, 1953.

4. *Domestic Revolutions: A Social History of American Family Life* (New York: Free Press, 1988), chap. 9.

5. Mae Clinkscales Belk, interview with author, Atlanta, March 15, 1992; Ford Belk, interview with author, Atlanta, April 1, 1992.

6. "Do Women Want Outside Jobs?" *Women's Home Companion*, April, 1950, p. 8.

7. Lillian M. Gilbreth, Preface, *Working Wives and Mothers*, by Stella B. Applebaum (New York: Public Affairs Committee, 1952).

8. U.S. Women's Bureau, *Women Workers and Their Dependents*, Women's Bureau Bulletin No. 239 (Washington, D.C.: GPO, 1952).

9. U.S. Women's Bureu, *Employed Mothers and Child Care*, Women's Bureau Bulletin No. 247 (Washington, D.C.: GPO, 1953), p. 7.

10. Betty Friedan, *The Feminine Mystique* (New York: W. W. Norton, 1963), pp. 9, 194–97.

11. Historian Winifred Wandersee argued that rising expectations of an acceptable living standard also drove wives into the workforce during the Depression, a time of legislation as well as propaganda aimed at keeping married women at home. Because Wandersee

focused on a brief period in U.S. history, the long-term trends of women's work behavior did not substantially influence her findings. Winifred D. Wandersee Bolin, "The Economics of Middle-Income Family Life: Working Women during the Great Depression," *Journal of American History*, 65 (June, 1978): 60–74; Wandersee, *Women's Work and Family Values, 1920–1940*. The 1976 survey cited by Iglehart included twice as many full-time working wives as the 1957 survey. Iglehart utilized a subsample comprised of white wives with resident husbands. Virtually all of the 1976 workers said they preferred employment to full-time housework, whereas one fifth of the 1957 workers stated that they would rather be at home than in the labor force. Furthermore, proportionally more workers in 1976 than in 1957 reported that the challenges and ego satisfaction of their jobs were their primary reasons for continuing employment. Iglehart concluded that satisfaction with housework had not declined substantially during the two decades between the surveys, but the results suggested significant attitudinal change. Among women who did not work, positive satisfaction in household labor declined from 68 percent of the women in 1957 to 58 percent in 1976. Working mothers' confidence about their performance of maternal responsibilities had improved over the years.

12. Mirra Komarovsky, *Blue-Collar Marriage* (New York: Random House, 1964), pp. 49–64.

13. Several of the fifty-eight wives stated that their achievements as housewives were an important source of personal satisfaction despite the fact that the daily life of working-class mothers offered fewer opportunities for nonfamily activities outside the house than was the case among middle-class mothers.

14. Komarovsky, *Blue-Collar Marriage*, pp. 65–73.

15. For a concise analysis of the growth of married women's employment, see Lynn Y. Weiner, *From Working Girl to Working Mother: The Female Labor Force in the United States, 1820–1980* (Chapel Hill: University of North Carolina Press, 1985), pp. 83–97.

16. Mary Anderson, "Postwar Facts and Factors," p. 4.

17. *After High School What?*, Women's Bureau Leaflet 8 (Washington, D.C.: GPO, 1954), p. 1.

18. Dr. Edward Harold Litchfield, "Work and Survival," printed copy of fall, 1960, convocation address at the University of Pittsburgh, copy in vertical file Education, Schlesinger Library.

19. *Harvard Business Review*, September, 1951, p. 108.

20. Howard S. Kaltenborn, "Utilizing 'Older' Women Workers," in National Manpower Council, *Work in the Lives of Married Women; Proceedings of a Conference on Womanpower* (New York: Columbia University Press, 1958) p. 57.

21. Applebaum, *Working Wives and Mothers*, p. 4.

22. James P. Mitchell, "Coming Problems in the Labor Force," *Work in the Lives of Married Women*, pp. 15–16.

23. National Manpower Council, *Womanpower*, p. 327; National Manpower Council, *Work in the Lives of Married Women*, pp. 75–81, 88–90.

24. U.S. Women's Bureau, Bulletin No. 256 (Washington, D.C.: GPO, 1955). The bulletin covered the bureau's survey of twenty-three public and private employment training projects directed toward women ages forty-five years and older.

25. Mitchell, "Coming Problems in the Labor Force," p. 15.

26. Kaltenborn, "Utilizing 'Older' Women Workers," p. 67.

27. National Manpower Council, *Womanpower*, pp. 319–50.

28. U.S. Women's Bureau, *Part-Time Work for Women*, Women's Bureau Bulletin 273 (Washington, D.C.: GPO, 1960), pp. 5–6. While part-time jobs did draw mothers into the labor force, the increase in labor allocated to part-time workers also affected other population groups. Forty percent of part-time female workers in the 1950s were girls from fourteen to seventeen years of age, and male adolescent part-time employment also increased. Youthful wage earners helped to fuel the teen consumer market expansion of the Cold War era.

29. May, *Homeward Bound*, p. 167.

30. U.S. Women's Bureau, *Part-Time Employment of Women in Wartime*, Special Bulletin 13 (Washington, D.C.: GPO, 1943), pp. 11–12.

31. U.S. Women's Bureau, *Part-Time Jobs for Women—A Study in 10 Cities*, Bulletin 238 (Washington, D.C.: GPO, 1951), p. 1.

32. Goldin, *Understanding the Gender Gap*, pp. 179–83; census data on part-time employment.

33. U.S. Women's Bureau, *Part-Time Jobs for Women*, pp. 17–21.

34. U.S. Women's Bureau, *Part-Time Employment of Women in Wartime*, p. 11.

35. U.S. Bureau of the Census, *Current Population Reports: Labor Force*, Series P-50, No. 7 (Washington, D.C.: GPO, August 11, 1948), pp. 2 & 7.

36. A substantial proportion of workers who reported themselves as part-time workers were women, teenagers, and older persons who worked without pay in family businesses. U.S. Bureau of the Census, *Current Population Reports: Labor Force*, Series P-50, No. 12 (Washington, D.C.: GPO, December 26, 1948), table 5.

37. U.S. Bureau of the Census, *Current Population Reports: Labor Force*, Series P-50, No. 26 (Washington, D.C.: GPO, September 7, 1950), table 2.

38. U.S. Bureau of the Census, *Statistical Abstract of the United States, 1985* (Washington, D.C.: GPO, 1984), table 660.

39. Through the 1950s women displayed no greater tendency to withdraw from graduate education than from undergraduate. Through the 1940s and the 1950s, the percentage of M.A. and Ph.D. degrees awarded to women dropped, but the drop did not mean that women were less likely to pursue graduate education than they had been in the 1920s and 1930s. Rather, postgraduate education was expanding among men while it was holding steady among women. Numerically and with respect to the number of B.A. degrees granted some years earlier, women completed more advanced degrees in 1960 than in 1940, but postgraduate education was barely expanding for women while it grew rapidly among men. U.S. Bureau of the Census, *Historical Statistics of the United States*, Series H 602–617; Series H 618–647; Series H 751–765.

While women's rate of completion of both bachelor's and master's degrees did rise through the 1950s, their share of doctorates fell both relative to the number of women obtaining B.A. degrees and relative to the number of male Ph.D.s. Women earned 15 percent of U.S. Ph.D.s in 1920 and in 1930 but only 13 percent in 1940 and 10.5 percent in 1960. By 1970, when war babies were in graduate school, women had begun to return to earlier patterns, with 13 percent of Ph.D.s being awarded to women.

40. U.S. Bureau of the Census, *Historical Statistics of the United States*, Series H 602–617.

41. Phyllis A. Wallace, *Pathways to Work: Unemployment among Black Teenage Females* (Lexington, Mass.: Lexington Books, 1974).

42. Abigail Kyzer Hobson, "A Study of Values of Rural and Urban Families in Alabama with

Implications for Homemaking Education" (Ph. D. thesis, Michigan Sate University, 1962), pp. 2–3, 144–50.

43. Jean Tepperman Interview, no. 48, Jean Tepperman Interview Transcripts, Schlesinger Library.

44. Sharon Hartman Strom, "Italian-American Women and Their Daughters in Rhode Island: The Adolescence of Two Generations, 1900–1950," *The Italian Immigrant Woman in North America* (Toronto: Multicultural History Society of Toronto, 1978), p. 197.

45. Jean Tepperman Interview, no. 49.

46. National Manpower Council, *Womanpower*, pp. 31–35, 167–219.

47. Mildred Morgenroth "Ideas on the Education of Women of Significance to Home Economics Teachers," paper delivered at meeting of the Council for Home Economics Teacher Education in California, Long Beach State College, n.d., Higher Education of Women in the United States Collection, Schlesinger Library.

48. "Program in Family Relations," Earlham College, n.d.

49. Anne Moody, *Coming of Age in Mississippi* (New York: Doubleday, 1968), pp. 226–27.

50. The August, 1930, issue of *American Girl* carried a feature on Jean Norris, a New York magistrate. The article encouragingly reported that "There are a few law schools that still do not admit young women—and one by one, the number of law schools which do admit women is becoming greater." Nevertheless, *American Girl* cautioned, "Prejudice against women lawyers still exists in some communities." "Jean Norris, Magistrate," *The American Girl*, August, 1930, pp. 15, 34.

51. *Wing Scout Manual* (New York: Girl Scouts of the U.S.A., 1949), pp. 197–98.

52. "Wing Scout" Scrapbook, Girl Scouts of the U.S.A. Archives.

53. *Citizens in Action; The Girl Scout Record, 1912 . . . 1947* (New York: Girl Scouts of the U.S.A., 1947).

54. The Girl Scouts, like other voluntary associations in the United States, was a victim of the Red Scare during the earlier 1950s. Although it had always had an emphasis on internationalism, in the 1950s this emphasis came under scrutiny. Although the sources and strength of the criticisms of scouting are unclear, a number of changes in the 1954 handbook reflect the climate of fear surrounding McCarthyism. Among other changes intended to correct the impression that scouting promoted a "one world" movement, the "World Flag," which was the banner of the international scouting movement was changed to "The flag of the World Association of Girl Guides and Girl Scouts" and a reference to founder Juliette Low's concept of "one world" became "international friendship." *Changes in the Girl Scout Handbook*, Intermediate Program, 1953 ed. (New York: Girl Scouts of the U.S.A., 1954), pp. 6–11.

55. *Girl Scout Leader's Guide* (New York: Girls Scouts of the U.S.A., 1955), pp. 152–53.

56. Ibid., p. 8.

57. Lillian Moller Gilbreth, *Girl Scout Leader*, 31, no. 7 (October, 1954): 5.

58. Donald M. Hamilton, M.D., "Character Development of the Girl from Fourteen to Seventeen," part 2, *Girl Scout Leader*, 23, no. 3 (March, 1950): 5.

59. Survey Research Center, Institute for Social Research, University of Michigan, *Adolescent Girls: A Nation-Wide Study of Girls between the Ages of Eleven and Eighteen Years of Age Made for the Girl Scouts of the U.S.A.* (New York: Girl Scouts of the U.S.A., 1956).

CHAPTER 7

1. Gender divisions of various sorts, whether by choice or by discrimination, persisted as women increasingly entered male-dominated professions in the 1970s and 1980s. Currently, a disproportional share of women in medicine practice gynecology or pediatrics and a disproportionate number of women in veterinary science are small-animal rather than large-animal veterinarians.

2. Blanche Linden-Ward and Carol Hurd Green, *Changing the Future: American Women in the 1960s* (New York: Twayne, 1993), pp. 3–7.

3. Winifred D. Wandersee, *On the Move: American Women in the 1970s* (New York: Twayne, 1988), chapter 2.

4. "Roosevelt Finds Sex Discrimination Is a Major Problem; Appoints Seven Key Aides," *New York Times*, July 21, 1965; "It's Not a Man's World," *Washington Post*, October 2, 1965.

5. Valerie Quinney, "Textile Women: Three Generations in the Mill," *Southern Exposure*, 3, no. 4 (Winter, 1975): 72.

6. Tobi Lipper and Debby Warren, "Accounts Overdue," *Southern Exposure*, 9, no. 4 (Winter, 1981): 13.

7. Jean Tepperman Interview Transcripts.

8. Jean Tepperman Interview Transcripts.

9. Ellen Ross, interview with author, Ballston Spa, N.Y., July 5, 1995.

10. For a thoughtful discussion of women's education in the 1950s, see chapter 3 in Eugenia Kaledin, *Mothers and More: American Women in the 1950s* (Boston: G. K. Hall, 1984).

11. S. Alexander Rippa, *Education in a Free Society: An American History*, 6th ed. (New York: Longman, 1988), pp. 229–52.

12. William C. Bingham, "Building Bridges to Career Satisfaction," *Facilitating Career Development for Girls and Women* (New York: National Vocational Guidance Association, 1973), p. 33.

13. Bea Mayes, "Women, Equality, and the Public High School," *Education*, 97, no. 4 (Summer, 1977): 333.

14. Dan W. Dodson, "The Role of the YWCA in a Changing Era: A Study Made for the National Board in the Y.W.C.A. of the U.S.A.," ca. 1958, box 31, Papers of the Boston YWCA, Schlesinger Library.

15. Wandersee, *On the Move*, p. 119.

16. Judy Gaylin, "Exclusive: *Seventeen* Survey," *Seventeen Magazine*, March, 1980, p. 114.

17. Ibid., p. 115.

18. Sara Evans, *Personal Politics: The Roots of Women's Liberation in the Civil Rights Movement and the New Left* (New York: Random House, 1979).

19. Mary Lindenstein Walshok, *Blue-Collar Women: Pioneers on the Male Frontier* (Garden City, N.Y.: Anchor/Doubleday, 1981), pp. 43–208.

20. R. Blood and D. Wolfe, *Husbands and Wives* (New York: Free Press, 1960).

21. K. T. Dietrich, "A Reexamination of the Myth of Black Matriarchy," *Journal of Marriage and the Family*, 37 (May, 1975): 367–74; Charles Vert Willie, *Race, Ethnicity, and Socioeconomic Status* (Bayside, N.Y.: General Hall, 1983), pp. 151–77.

22. Herbert J. Gans, *The Urban Villagers: Group and Class in the Life of Italian-Americans* (New York: Free Press, 1962).

23. Carol B. Stack, *All Our Kin: Strategies for Survival in a Black Community* (New York: Harper Row, 1974).

24. In a variant of Durkheim's model of deviance, Herbert J. Gans has argued that the affluent need to stigmatize the poor in order to rationalize their own stated values of "hard work, thrift, honesty and monogamy." *More Equality* (New York: Vantage, 1974), p. 108.

25. Suzanne M. Bianchi, *Household Composition and Racial Inequality* (New Brunswick, N.J.: Rutgers University Press, 1981), p. 31.

26. *The Negro Family*, Daniel Patrick Moynihan's study, set the poverty debate in the context of race and family status. Although great criticism greeted the "Moynihan Report," its publication focused discussion of poverty more rather than less on African Americans. Despite Moynihan's attention to the low wages and high unemployment of black men and women as the explanation of their poverty, public debate about *The Negro Family* centered on Moynihan's analysis of African American family structure. In looking for differences between blacks and more economically successful whites, Moynihan observed that women disproportionately headed black families. He posited that "matriarchy" in black America bred a culture of poverty and, following the arguments of Kenneth Clark and others, traced matriarchy to slavery. Although statistical studies and generations of historians had shown Moynihan's hypothesis invalid, the debate over the sources of especially high rates of female headship among blacks remained alive even after the 1976 publication of Herbert Gutman's *The Black Family in Slavery and Freedom*, which demonstrated that two-parent families had predominated among African Americans after emancipation.

27. The percentage of women heading *households* as opposed to *families* also rose from 1950 through the 1970s as single women and widows established and maintained their own homes.

28. Niki Scott, *The Balancing Act: A Handbook for Working Mothers* (Kansas City: Sheed, Andrews, and McMeel, 1978), p. xvii.

29. *Ibid.*, p. 4.

30. Carol Kehr Tittle, *Careers and Family: Sex Roles and Adolescent Life Plans*, Sage Library of Social Research, 121 (Beverly Hills: Sage, 1981), pp. 110–15, 231–33.

31. Friedan, *The Feminine Mystique*, pp. 9, 194–97.

32. Alfreda Iglehart, *Married Women and Work, 1957 and 1976* (Lexington, Mass.: Lexington Books, 1979), pp. 14–15.

33. This finding suggests that as the employment of white mothers of young children continues to increase, a life cycle characterized by long-term work patterns with few and brief interruptions for maternity leave will characterize the working mother of the future.

34. Lois Banfill Shaw, *Midlife Women at Work*, pp. 35, 40–47, 85–97. The authors also found differences in women's retirement plans based on pension benefits, job satisfaction, marital status, and health.

35. Lois Banfill Shaw, ed., *Unplanned Careers: The Working Lives of Middle-Aged Women* (Lexington, Mass.: Lexington Books, 1983), pp. 113, 132–34.

36. Walshok, *Blue-Collar Women*, pp. 251–56.

37. Kathy Kahn, *Hillbilly Women* (New York: Doubleday, 1973), p. 98.

38. Gene B. Petersen, *Southern Newcomers to Northern Cities: Work and Social Adjustment in Cleveland.* (New York: Praeger for the Bureau of Social Science Research, 1977) p. 11.

39. U. S. Bureau of the Census, *Historical Statistics of the United States, Colonial Times to 1970*, Part I, Series C 102-114.

40. José Llamas, *Cuban-Americans: Masters of Survival* (Lexington, Mass.: Abbott Books, 1980), pp. 45–46.

41. As Vicki Ruiz has shown, many Mexican American women's first excursion into a world of varied gender roles and expectations came with employment. *Cannery Women, Cannery Lives: Mexican Women, Unionization, and the California Food Processing Industry, 1930–1950* (Albuquerque: University of New Mexico Press, 1987).

42. Thomas Kessner and Betty Boyd Caroli, *Today's Immigrants, Their Stories: A New Look at America's Newest Americans* (New York: Oxford University Press, 1981), pp. 144–47.

CHAPTER 8

1. "The Air Force's First Black Female General," *Ebony*, December, 1992, p. 66.

2. Holly Belk, interview with author, Atlanta, September 13, 1995.

3. Boris and Daniels, *Homework*.

4. AAUW Educational Foundation, *How Schools Shortchange Women: The AAUW Report: A Study of Major Findings on Girls and Education* (Washington, D.C.: National Education Association and AAUW National Educational Association, 1992).

5. Patricia O'Toole, "Thrifty, Kind—And Smart as Hell: Frances Hesselbein Teaches American Managers to Lead," *Lear's*, October, 1990, p. 26.

6. Ibid., pp. 26–30.

7. Susan D. Clayton and Faye J. Crosby, *Justice, Gender, and Affirmative Action* (Ann Arbor: University of Michigan Press, 1992), pp. 16–17.

8. Ibid., pp. 98–100.

9. Lillian B. Rubin, *Worlds of Pain: Life in the Working-Class Family*, 1992 edition (New York: Basic Books, 1992), xxii.

10. Charles Vert Willie, *Black and White Families: A Study in Complementarity* (Bayside, N.Y.: General Hall, 1985), pp. 227, 266.

11. Ibid., pp. 188–90, 154–55.

12. A. B. Hollingshead, *Elmtown's Youth* (New York: Wiley, 1949), pp. 115–18.

13. Willie, *Black and White Families*, p. 11.

14. Marian Wright Edelman, *Families in Peril: An Agenda for Social Change* (Cambridge: Harvard University Press, 1987), p. 73.

15. Ibid., p. viii.

16. Ibid., p. 3.

17. Ibid.

18. Ibid., p. 14.

19. Ibid., pp. 38–40. Edelman argues that the poor have also faced serial tax hikes since 1979, hikes partly escaped by some other Americans, that have compounded other inflationary factors.

20. Ibid., p. x.

21. U.S. Department of Commerce, *Current Population Reports*, Series P-20, no. 430, *Geographic Mobility: March 1986 to March 1987*, table 1.

22. U.S. Bureau of the Census, *Historical Statistics of the United States*, Part I, Series C 1–14.

23. Hank Whittemore, "We Can't Pay the Rent," *Parade Magazine*, January 10, 1988, p. 5.

24. Claudia Goldin, *Understanding the Gender Gap*.

25. Michael W. Horrigan and James P. Markey, "Recent Gains in Women's Earnings: Better Pay or Longer Hours?" *Monthly Labor Review*, July, 1990, pp. 11–16. Horrigan and Markey, economists with the Bureau of Labor Statistics, further claim that when adjustments are made for the average number of hours worked by women and by men, the gap in hourly wages is even smaller than general comparisons reveal.

26. Goldin, *Understanding the Gender Gap*, table 3.1.

27. Ibid., pp. 73, 117–18, 211–17.

CHAPTER 9

1. Lee Chambers-Schiller, *Liberty, A Better Husband* (New Haven: Yale University Press, 1984).

2. Lottie Lemke, interview with Paul Page, Lowell, Mass., August 13, 1985. Mill Workers of Lowell Collection.

3. Florie Hamm, interview with Suzette B. Jefferson, October 26, 1985, Mill Workers of Lowell Collection.

4. Louise A. Tilly and Joan W. Scott, *Women's Work and the Family in Nineteenth-Century Europe* (New York: Holt, Rinehart, and Winston, 1978), pp. 161–22; Charles E. Rosenberg, ed., *The Family in History* (Philadelphia: University of Pennsylvania Press, 1975).

5. For a discussion of youthful employment, see Tentler, *Wage-Earning Women*, chap. 4.

6. Quoted in Van Kleeck, *Artificial Flower Makers*, p. 86; Ewen, *Immigrant Women in the Land of Dollars*, pp. 94–101; Tentler, *Wage Earning Women*, pp. 85–114.

7. Southern Oral History Program Collection, #4007.

8. Jane Addams, *Twenty Years at Hull House* (New York: MacMillan, 1911), pp. 247–53.

9. Mary-Elizabeth Pidgeon, *Women Workers and Their Dependents*, Women's Bureau Bulletin No. 239 (Washington, D.C.: GPO, 1952), pp.62–63, 69–91.

10. Ibid., p. 85.

11. Katherine R. Allen, *Single Women/Family Ties: Life Histories of Older Women* (Newbury Park, Calif.: Sage, 1989), pp. 86–88; 127–31.

12. Pidgeon, *Women Workers and Their Dependents*, p. 79.

13. Van Kleeck, *Artificial Flower Makers*, p. 116.

14. U.S. Women's Bureau, *Home Work in Bridgeport, Connecticut, December, 1919*, Bulletin no. 9 (Washington, D.C.: GPO, 1920), pp. 14–15. Of twenty-one mill households in Atlanta in 1910, Senate investigators found that all but seven included lodgers. Wood F. Worchester and Daisy Worthington Worchester, *Report on the Condition of Woman and Child Wage-Earners*, vol. 16, *Family Budgets of Typical Cotton Mill Workers* (Washington, D.C.: GPO, 1911), pp. 1–30. Joseph Hill found that of working women in eleven cities in 1920, 14 percent were members of families that included boarders or lodgers. Lodging was an especially important source of income among sole-earner widows of whom 30 percent took in boarders and sole-earner wives of whom 28 percent rented rooms. Hill, *Women in Gainful Occupations*, pp. 154–56.

15. Gwendolyn Salisbury Hughes, *Mothers in Industry: Wage-Earning by Mothers in Philadelphia* (New York: New Republic, 1925), p. 98. See also the discussion of boarders and lodgers in chap. 3, above.

16. Edith Abbott, *Immigration: Select Documents and Case Records* (New York: Arno, 1969), p. 345.

17. Reports of the Immigration Commission, *Immigrants in Cities: A Study of the Population of Selected Districts in New York, Chicago, Philadelphia, Boston, Cleveland, Buffalo, and Milwaukee*, vol. 1, *Immigrants in Cities: Summary* (Washington, D.C.: GPO, 1911), table 42.

18. Hughes, *Mothers in Industry*, p. 111.

19. Maximal estimates compiled from U.S. Bureau of the Census, *Fifteenth Census of the United States: Families in the United States by Type and Size* (Washington, D.C.: GPO, 1940), tables 9–11.

20. Salvatore J. LaGuina, ed., *The Immigrants Speak: Italian Americans Tell Their Story* (New York: Center for Immigration Studies, 1979), p. 190.

21. Ibid., pp. 190–91.

22. *Report on the Condition of Woman and Child Wage-Earners in the United States,* vol. 1, *Cotton Textile Industry* (Washington, D.C.: GPO, 1910), p. 538; Jacqueline Dowd Hall et al., *Like a Family: The Making of a Southern Cotton Mill World* (Chapel Hill: University of North Carolina Press, 1987).

23. Martha Doherty, interview with Dianne Novelli, October 12, 1984, Mill Workers of Lowell Collection.

24. Christine Stansell, *City of Women: Sex and Class in New York, 1789–1860* (New York: Knopf, 1986).

25. Hughes, *Mothers in Industry*, pp. 22–24, 81–88.

26. Ibid., p. 90.

27. Joseph Hill also found that a considerable share of ever-married working women in 1920 did not care to maintain their own homes or were unable to do so. Thirteen percent of working wives in eleven U.S. cities and 22 percent of widows and divorcees either lodged in the homes of others or lived with their employers, as compared with 24 percent of single working women.

28. Hughes, *Mothers in Industry*, p. 101.

29. Kennon, "College Wives Who Work," pp. 11–12.

30. Wandersee, *Women's Work and Family Values.*

31. U.S. Bureau of the Census, *Historical Statistics*, Series D 722–727 and Series G 306–318.

32. The General Accounting Office estimated that 28 percent of all fifteen-year-olds were employed in 1988 and that 18 percent of these working children were employed in violation of child labor regulations. United States General Accounting Office, Human Resources Division, *Child Labor: Characteristics of Working Children* (Washington, D.C.: GPO, June, 1991), p. 1.

33. Ellen Greenberger and Laurence Steinberg, *When Teenagers Work: The Psychological and Social Costs of Adolescent Employment* (New York: Basic Books, 1986), pp. 12–41.

34. Ibid., pp. 34–37.

35. James R. Wetzel, "American Families: 75 Years of Change," *Monthly Labor Review*, 113,

no 3 (March, 1990): 4–13; Howard V. Hayghe, "Family Members in the Work Force," ibid.: 14–19.

36. U.S. Bureau of the Census, *Statistical Abstract of the United States*, 1991, table 641.

CONCLUSION

1. Winifred Wandersee has argued that the gender reform movement of the 1970s had run its course by the 1980s and that the ERA was irrelevant to the needs of working-class and minority women. Wandersee, *On the Move*, pp. 197–99. Donald Matthews and Jane De Hart maintain that opponents of the ERA understood that feminism or the failure of women to observe "traditional rules of feminine behavior" had broken down families and the amendment would further the destruction of the family. Donald G. Matthews and Jane Sherron De Hart, *Sex, Gender, and the Politics of the ERA: A State and the Nation* (New York: Oxford University Press, New York: 1990), p. 156.

2. Peter Filene, *Him/Herself: Sex Roles in Modern America*, 2nd ed. (Baltimore: Johns Hopkins University Press, 1986), pp. 78–80.

3. U.S. Bureau of the Census, *Statistical Abstract of the United States, 1991*, table 87.

4. Ibid., table 745.

5. Martin Giannaros and Demetrios Giannaros, "Would a Higher Minimum Wage Help Poor Families Headed by Women?" *Monthly Labor Review*, August, 1990, p. 33.

6. Carl N. Degler, *At Odds: Women and the Family in America from the Revolution to the Present* (New York: Oxford University Press, 1980); Christopher Lasch, *Haven in a Heartless World: The Family Besieged* (New York: Basic Books, 1977).

Bibliography

MANUSCRIPT COLLECTIONS

Anne Jackson Williams Papers. Southern History Collection. University of North Carolina, Chapel Hill.

Archives of the Girl Scouts of the U.S.A. New York.

Corra Harris Papers. Special Collections, Robert W. Woodruff Library, Emory University, Atlanta.

Records of the Baker Chocolate Company. Baker Library, Harvard University, Cambridge, Mass.

Records of the Boston Y.W.C.A. Arthur and Elizabeth Schlesinger Library. Radcliffe College, Cambridge, Mass.

Records of the Girls' Tomato Clubs. Winthrop University Archives and Records, Rock Hill, South Carolina.

Records of the R. H. Macy Company. Baker Library.

Records of the South Carolina Home Economics Administration. Winthrop University Archives and Records.

Records of the Women's Educational and Industrial Union. Arthur and Elizabeth Schlesinger Library.

Seydell Collection. Special Collections, Woodruff Library.

ORAL HISTORY COLLECTIONS

Gluck, Sherna Berger, comp. *Rosie the Riveter Revisited: Women and the World War II Work Experience.* Long Beach: California State University, Long Beach Foundation, 1983.

Hill, Ruth Edmonds, ed. *The Black Women Oral History Project.* Schlesinger Library. Westport: Meckler, 1991.

Jean Tepperman Interviews. Schlesinger Library.

Mill Workers of Lowell Collection. University of Massachusetts, Lowell.

Southern Oral History Project. Southern History Collection. University of North Carolina, Chapel Hill.

Washington Women's Heritage Project. University of Washington, Seattle.

INTERVIEWS BY THE AUTHOR

Belk, Ford. Atlanta, March 15, 1993.

Belk, Holly. Atlanta, September 13, 1995.

Belk, Mae Clinkscales. Atlanta, March 15, 1993, and September 12, 1995.

Graves, Anna. San Antonio, May 16, 1978.

Haynes, James. Atlanta, February 14, 1992.

Hughes, Martha. Schenectady, New York, December 28, 1986.
Reeves, Janie. San Antonio, May 26, 1979.
Ross, Ellen. Ballston Spa, New York, July 5, 1995.

GOVERNMENT DOCUMENTS

Hill, Joseph A. *Women in Gainful Occupations, 1870 to 1920*, Census Monographs IX. Washington: GPO, 1929.

Lyford, Carrie Alberta. *A Study of Home-Economics Education in Teacher-Training Institutions for Negroes*. Bulletin no. 79, Home Economics Series no. 7, U. S. Office of Education, 1923, reprint ed. New York: Negro Universities Press, 1969.

Massachusetts Board of Education. *Annual Report, 1878–1879*. Boston, 1879.

Moynihan, Daniel. *Negro Family, the Case for National Action*. U. S. Department of Labor. Office of Policy Planning and Research. Washington, D.C.: GPO, 1965.

Pidgeon, Mary-Elizabeth. *Women Workers and Their Dependents*. U. S. Women's Bureau Bulletin No. 239. Washington: GPO, 1952.

State of Alabama. Department of Education. *Manual of Home Economics Education for Negro Schools*, Bulletin 1938, no. 4. Wetumpka, 1938.

U. S. Department of Justice. Reports of the Immigration Commission, *Immigrants in Cities: A Study of the Population of Selected Districts in New York, Chicago, Philadelphia, Boston, Cleveland, Buffalo, and Milwaukee*, vol. 1, *Immigrants in Cities; Summary*. Washington, D.C.: GPO, 1911.

U. S. Bureau of the Census. Decennial Censuses of the United States: 1900, 1910, 1920, 1930, 1940, 1950, 1960, 1970, 1980, 1990. Washington, D.C.: GPO.

———. *Historical Statistics of the United States, Colonial Times to 1970*. Bicentennial ed. 2 vols. Washington, D.C.: GPO, 1975.

———. *Statistical Abstract of the United States*, 1975, 1978, 1980, 1985, 1988, 1990, 1991, 1995. Washington, D.C.: GPO.

———. *Statistics of Women at Work; Based on Unpublished information Derived from the Schedules of the Twelfth Census: 1900*. Washington: GPO, 1907.

U. S. Department of Commerce. *Current Population Reports*, 1948–1990. Washington, D.C.: GPO.

U. S. Department of Education. Records. Record Group 12. National Archives and Record Service, Washington, D.C.

U. S. Department of Labor. Records of the U. S. Women's Bureau. Record Group 86. National Archives and Records Service, Washington, D.C.

U. S. Senate. *Report on Condition of Woman and Child Wage-Earners in Industry*. Washington, D.C.: GPO, 1910–1913.

———. *Reports of the Immigration Commission*. v. 36. *Immigration and Crime*. Washington, D.C.: GPO, 1911.

U. S. Women's Bureau. *After High School What?*, Women's Bureau Leaflet 8. Washington, D.C.: GPO, 1954.

———. Bulletins. 1–356. Washington, D.C.: GPO.

———. *Part-Time Employment of Women in Wartime*, Special Bulletin no. 13. Washington, D.C.: GPO, 1943.

—————. *Statement to the War Labor Board in Support of Union's Request to Abolish Discrimination Against Married Women.* Washington, D.C.: GPO: July, 1945.

PUBLICATIONS OF THE GIRL SCOUTS OF THE U.S.A.

Adolescent Girls: A Nation-Wide Study of Girls Between the Ages of Eleven and Eighteen Years of Age Made for the Girl Scouts of the U.S.A. New York: Girl Scouts of the U.S.A., 1956.

The American Girl.

Changes in the Girl Scout Handbook, Intermediate Program, 1953 ed. New York: Girl Scouts of the U.S.A., 1954.

Citizens in Action: The Girl Scout Record, 1912 . . . 1947. New York: Girl Scouts of the U.S.A., 1947.

Degenhardt, Mary, and Judith Kirsch, comp. *75 Years of Uniforms, Insignia, Publications and Keepsakes: Girl Scout Collector's Guide.* New York: Girl Scouts of the U.S.A., 1987.

Girl Scout Leader.

Girl Scout Leader Notebook.

Girl Scout Leader's Guide. New York: Girls Scouts of the U.S.A., 1955.

75 Years of Girl Scouting. New York: Girl Scouts of the U.S.A., 1986.

Shulkin, Cathy. "The Girl Scout Movement on the Rise." *Nostalgia Magazine.* Girl Scouts of the U.S.A., New York, n.d., p. 33ff.

Wing Scout Manual. New York: Girl Scouts of the U.S.A., 1949.

NEWSPAPERS AND MAGAZINES

Atlantic Monthly.
Business Week.
Ebony.
Good Housekeeping.
Harper's Magazine.
Independent Woman.
Ladies' Home Journal.
Life.
New Republic.
New York Times.
Seventeen Magazine.
Time.
Washington Post.
Woman's Home Companion.

BOOKS AND OTHER PUBLISHED SOURCES

AAUW Educational Foundation. *How Schools Shortchange Women: The AAUW Report: A Study of Major Findings on Girls and Education.* Washington, D.C.: National Education Association and AAUW National Educational Association, 1992.

Abbott, Edith. *Immigration: Select Documents and Case Records.* New York: Arno, 1969.

————. *The Tenements of Chicago, 1890–1935*. New York: Arno Press, 1970.

Addams, Jane. *A New Conscience and an Ancient Evil*. New York: MacMillan Company, 1912.

————. *The Spirit of Youth and the City Streets*. New York: Macmillan, 1909.

————. *Twenty Years at Hull-House*. New York: Macmillan, 1911.

Allen, Katherine R. *Single Women/Family Ties: Life Histories of Older Women*. Newbury Park, Calif.: Sage, 1989.

Anderson, Karen Sue. *Wartime Women*. Westport, Conn.: Greenwood, 1981.

Applebaum, Stella B. *Working Wives and Mothers*. New York: Public Affairs Committee, 1952.

Avery, Burniece. *Walk Quietly Through the Night and Cry Softly*. Detroit: Balamp, 1977.

Baca, Reynaldo, and Dexter Bryan. "Mexican Women, Migration and Sex Roles," *Migration Today* 12, no. 3: 14–17.

Benson, Susan Porter. *Counter Cultures: Saleswomen, Managers, and Customers in American Department Stores, 1890–1940*. Urbana: University of Illinois Press, 1986.

Bianchi, Suzanne M. *Household Composition and Racial Inequality*. New Brunswick, N.J.: Rutgers University Press, 1981.

Bingham, William C. *Facilitating Career Development for Girls and Women*. New York: National Vocational Guidance Association, 1973.

Blackwelder, Julia Kirk. *Women of the Depression: Caste and Culture in San Antonio, 1929–1939*. College Station: Texas A&M University Press, 1984.

Blewett, Mary H. *Men, Women, and Work: Class, Gender, and Protest in the New England Shoe Industry, 1780–1910*. Urbana: University of Illinois Press, 1990.

————. ed. *Surviving Hard Times: The Working People of Lowell*. Lowell, Mass.: Lowell Museum, 1982.

Blood, R., and D. Wolfe. *Husbands and Wives*. New York: Free Press, 1960.

Boris, Eileen, and Cynthia R. Daniels. *Homework: Historical and Contemporary Perspectives on Paid Labor at Home*. Urbana: University of Illinois Press, 1989.

Brandon, Betty. "Alexander J. McKelway, Statesman of the New Order." Ph. D. diss., University of North Carolina, 1969.

Brown, Dorothy M. *Setting a Course: American Women in the 1920s*. Boston: Twayne, 1987.

Byerly, Victoria. *Hard Times Cotton Mill Girls: Personal Histories of Womanhood and Poverty in the South*. Ithaca, N.Y.: ILR Press, 1986.

Campbell, D'Ann. *Women at War with America: Private Lives in a Patriotic Era*. Cambridge, Mass.: Harvard University Press, 1984.

Caroli, Betty Boyd, ed. *The Italian Immigrant Woman in North America: Proceedings of the Tenth Annual Conference of the American Italian Historical Association*. Toronto: Multicultural History Society of Ontario, 1978.

Chafe, William H. *The American Woman: Her Changing Social, Economic, and Political Roles, 1920–1970*. New York: Oxford University Press, 1972.

————. *The Paradox of Change: American Women in the Twentieth Century*. New York: Oxford University Press, 1991.

Chambers-Schiller, Lee. *Liberty, A Better Husband*. New Haven: Yale University Press, 1984.

Claghorn, Kate Holladay. *The Immigrant's Day in Court*. New York: Harper & Bros., 1923.

Clark-Lewis, Elizabeth. *Living In, Living Out: African American Domestics in Washington, D.C., 1910–1940*. Wasington, D.C.: Smithsonian Institution, 1994.

———. "'This Work Had A' End': The Transition from Live-in to Day Work." Working Papers. Center for Research on Women, Memphis State University, 1985.

Clausen, John A. *American Lives: Looking Back at the Children of the Great Depression*. New York: Free Press, 1993.

Clayton, Susan D., and Faye J. Crosby. *Justice, Gender, and Affirmative Action*. Ann Arbor: University of Michigan Press, 1992.

Cobble, Dorthy Sue. *Dishing It Out: Waitresses and their Unions in the Twentieth Century*. Urbana: University of Illinois Press, 1991.

Cohen, Miram. *Workshop to Office: Two Generations of Italian Women in New York City, 1900–1950*. Ithaca: Cornell University Press, 1993.

Coontz, Stephanie. *The Way We Never Were: American Families and the Nostalgia Trap*. New York: Basic Books, 1997.

———. *The Way We Really Are: Coming to Terms with America's Changing Families*. New York: Basic Books, 1997.

Cowan, Ruth Schwartz. *More Work for Mother: The Ironies of Household Technology from the Open Hearth to the Microwave*. London: Free Association Press, 1989.

Crompton, Rosemary. *White-Collar Proletariat: Deskilling and Gender in Clerical Work*. Urbana: University of Illinois Press, 1992.

Davies, Margery W. *Woman's Place Is at the Typewriter: Office Work and Office Workers, 1870–1930*. Philadelphia: University of Temple Press, 1992.

Dedman, W. Wayne. *Cherishing This Heritage: The Centennial History of the State University College at Brockport, New York*. New York: Appleton-Century-Crofts, 1969.

Degler, Carl N. *At Odds: Women and the Family in America from the Revolution to the Present*. New York: Oxford University Press, 1980.

del Castillo, Richard Griswold. *La Familia: Chicano Families in the Urban Southwest, 1848 to the Present*. Notre Dame, Ind.: University of Notre Dame Press, 1984.

Deutsch, Sarah. *No Separate Refuge: Culture, Class, and Gender on an Anglo-Hispanic Frontier in the Southwest, 1880–1940*. New York: Oxford University Press, 1980.

Dewey, John, and Evelyn Dewey. *Schools of To-Morrow*. New York: E. P. Dutton, 1915.

Dickson, Marguerite. *Vocational Guidance for Girls*. New York: Rand, McNally, 1919.

Dietrich, K. T. "A Reexamination of the Myth of Black Matriarchy." *Journal of Marriage and the Family* 37 (May, 1975): 367–74.

Diner, Hasia R. *Erin's Daughters in America: Irish Immigrant Women in the Nineteenth Century*. Baltimore: Johns Hopkins University Press, 1983.

Dublin, Thomas. *Transforming Women's Work: New England Industrial Lives in the Industrial Revolution*. Ithaca: Cornell University Press, 1994.

———. *Women at Work: The Transformation of Work and Community in Lowell, Massachusetts, 1826–1860*. New York: Columbia University Press, 1979.

Dudden, Faye E. *Serving Women: Household Service in Nineteenth-Century America*. Middletown, Conn.: Wesleyan University Press, 1983.

Earley, Charity Adams. *One Woman's Army: A Black Officer Remembers the WAC*. College Station: Texas A&M University Press, 1989.

Eckles, May. "A Diary Setting Out the Life of May Eckles." Typed copy, Daughters of the Republic of Texas Library, San Antonio.

Edelman, Marian Wright. *Families in Peril: An Agenda for Social Change*. Cambridge: Harvard University Press, 1987.

Elder, Glen. *Children of the Depression: Social Change in Life Experience*. Chicago: University of Chicago Press, 1974.

Ellis, Pearl Idella. *Americanization through Homemaking*. Los Angeles: Wetzel, 1929.

Evans, Sara. *Personal Politics: The Roots of Women's Liberation in the Civil Rights Movement and the New Left*. New York: Random House, 1979.

Ewen, Elizabeth. *Immigrant Women in the Land of Dollars: Life and Culture on the Lower East Side, 1890–1930*. New York: Monthly Review Press, 1985.

Fass, Paula. *The Damned and the Beautiful: American Youth in the 1920's*. New York: Oxford University Press, 1977.

Filene, Peter. *Him/Herself: Sex Roles in Modern America*. 2nd ed. Baltimore: Johns Hopkins University Press, 1986.

Fitzpatrick, Ellen F. *Endless Crusade: Women Social Scientists and Progressive Reform*. New York: Oxford University Press, 1990.

Friedan, Betty. *The Feminine Mystique*. New York: W. W. Norton, 1963.

Gabaccia, Donna. *From Sicily to Elizabeth Street: Housing and Social Change*. Albany: State University of New York Press, 1984.

———. *From the Other Side: Women, Gender, and Immigrant Life in the U.S., 1820–1990*. Bloomington: Indiana University Press, 1994.

———. ed. *Seeking Common Ground: Multidisciplinary Studies of Immigrant Women in the United States*. Westport, Conn.: Greenwood Press, 1992.

Gans, Herbert J. *More Equality*. New York: Vantage Press, 1974.

———. *The Urban Villagers: Group and Class in the Life of Italian-Americans*. New York: Free Press, 1962.

Gatlin, Rochelle. *American Women Since 1945*. Jackson: University Press of Mississippi, 1987.

Glenn, Susan A. *Daughters of the Shtetl: Life and Labor in the Immigrant Generation*. Ithaca, N.Y.: Cornell University Press, 1990.

Gluck, Sherna B. *Rosie the Riveter Revisited: Women, the War, and Social Change*. Boston: Twayne, 1987.

Golab, Caroline. *Immigrant Destinations*. Philadelphia: Temple University Press, 1977.

Goldin, Claudia. *Understanding the Gender Gap: An Economic History of American Women*. New York: Oxford University Press, 1990.

Goodman, Jack, ed. *While You Were Gone; A Report on Wartime Life in the United States*. New York: Simon and Schuster, 1946.

Greathouse, Rebekah S. "The Effect of Constitutional Equality on Working Women." *The American Economic Review* 34, no. 1, Supplement, part 2 (March, 1944): 227ff.

Greenberger, Ellen, and Laurence Steinberg. *When Teenagers Work: The Psychological and Social Costs of Adolescent Employment*. New York: Basic Books, 1986.

Greenwald, Maureen Weiner. *Women, War and Work: The Impact of World War I on Women Workers in the United States*. Westport, Conn.: Greenwood, 1980.

Groneman, Carol, and Mary Beth Norton, eds. *"To Toil the Live-Long Day": America's Women at Work*. Ithaca, N.Y.: Cornell University Press, 1987.

Gutman, Herbert. *The Black Family in Slavery and Freedom, 1720–1925*. New York: Vintage Books, 1976.

Hagood, Margaret Jarman. *Mothers of the South: Portraiture of the White Tenant Farm Woman.* Chapel Hill: University of North Carolina Press, 1939.

Hall, Jacquelyn Dowd, et al. *Like a Family: The Making of a Southern Cotton Mill World.* Chapel Hill: University of North Carolina Press, 1987.

Hareven, Tamara K., and Randolph Langenbach. *Amoskeag: Life and Work in An American Factory Village.* New York: Pantheon, 1980.

Harris, Lucy. *The Harris College of Nursing: Five Decades of Struggle for a Cause.* Fort Worth: Texas Christian University Press, 1973.

Hartmann, Susan M. *The Homefront and Beyond: American Women in the 1940s.* Boston: Twayne, 1982.

Higginbotham, Elizabeth Brooks. *Righteous Discontent: The Women's Movement in the Black Baptist Church, 1880–1920.* Cambridge, Mass.: Harvard University Press, 1994.

Hine, Darlene Clark. *Black Women in White: Racial Conflict and Cooperation in the Nursing Profession, 1890–1950.* Bloomington: Indiana University Press, 1989.

Hobson, Abigail Kyzer. "A Study of Values of Rural and Urban Families in Alabama with Implications for Homemaking Education." Ph.D. diss., Michigan State University, 1962.

Hobson, Barbara Meil. *Uneasy Virtue: The Politics of Prostitution and the American Reform Tradition.* New York: Basic Books, 1987.

Hoerle, Helen Christine, and Florence B. Saltzberg. *The Girl and the Job.* New York: Henry Holt, 1919.

Hoffman, Abraham. *Unwanted Mexican Americans in the Great Depression: Repatriation Pressures, 1929–1939.* Tucson: University of Arizona Press, 1974.

Hollingshead, A. B. *Elmtown's Youth.* New York: Wiley, 1949.

Holm, Jeanne M. "Women in the Armed Forces." In John E, Jessup, ed., *Encyclopedia of the American Military.* vol. 3. New York: Charles Scribner's Sons, 1994.

Hopkins, Frank L. "Should Wives Work?" *American Mercury* 39 (December, 1936): 414–15.

Hughes, Gwendolyn Salisbury. *Mothers in Industry: Wage-Earning by Mothers in Philadelphia.* New York: New Republic, 1925.

Iglehart, Alfreda. *Married Women and Work, 1957 and 1976.* Lexington, Mass.: Lexington Books, 1979.

Janiewski, Delores. *Sisterhood Denied; Race, Gender, and Class in a New South Community.* Philadelphia: Temple University Press, 1985.

Johnson, Marilyn S. *The Second Gold Rush: Oakland and the East Bay in World War II.* Berkeley: University of California Press, 1993.

Jones, Jacqueline. *The Dispossessed: America's Underclass from the Civil War to the Present.* New York: Basic Books, 1992.

———. *Labor of Love, Labor of Sorrow: Black Women, Work, and Family from Slavery to the Present.* New York: Basic Books, 1985.

Kahn, Kathy. *Hillbilly Women.* New York: Doubleday, 1973.

Kaledin, Eugenia. *Mothers and More: American Women in the 1950s.* Boston: G. K. Hall, 1984.

Katzman, David M. *Seven Days a Week: Women and Domestic Service in Industrializing America.* New York: Oxford University Press, 1978.

Kennon, Anne Byrd. "College Wives Who Work." M. A. thesis, Radcliffe College, 1927.

Kessler-Harris, Alice. *Out to Work: A History of Wage-Earning Women in the United States.* New York: Oxford University Press, 1982.

Kessner, Thomas, and Betty Boyd Caroli. *Today's Immigrants, Their Stories: A New Look at America's Newest Americans*. New York: Oxford University Press, 1981.

Kirby, El Marie. *Cottonwood Corner: Growing Up in Arkansas During the Great Depression*. Galesburg, Mich.: privately printed, 1994.

Komarovsky, Mirra. *Blue-Collar Marriage*. New York: Random House, 1964.

LaGuina, Salvatore J., ed. *The Immigrants Speak: Italian Americans Tell Their Story*. New York: Center for Immigration Studies, 1979.

Lamphere, Louise. *From Working Daughters to Working Wives: Immigrant Women in a New England Industrial Commnity*. Ithaca, N.Y.: Cornell University Press, 1987.

Lasch, Christopher. *Haven in a Heartless World: The Family Besieged*. New York: Basic Books, 1977.

Lazerson, Marvin. *Origins of the Urban School; Public Education in Massachusetts, 1870–1915*. Cambridge, Mass.: Harvard University Press, 1977.

Leake, Albert H. *The Vocational Education of Girls and Women*. New York: Macmillan, 1918.

Lee, Everett S. *Net Intercensal Migration, 1870–1940*, Vol. I: *Introduction and Summary Tables*. Philadelphia: University of Pennsylvania, 1953.

Lindberg, Kristina, and Charles J. Ovando, *Five Mexican-American Women in Transition*. San Francisco: S&R Research Press, 1975.

Linden-Ward, Blanche, and Carol Hurd Green. *Changing the Future: American Women in the 1960s*. New York: Twayne, 1993.

Litoff, Judy Barrett, ed. *The American Midwife Debate; A Sourcebook on Its Modern Origins*. Westport, Conn: Greenwood, 1986.

———. *American Midwives, 1860 to the Present*. Westport, Conn.: Greenwood Press, 1978.

———. *American Women in a World at War: Contemporary Accounts from World War II*. Wilmington, Del.: Scholarly Resources Press, 1997.

Litoff, Judy Barrett, and David C. Smith. *Since You Went Away: World War II Letters from American Women on the Home Front*. Lawrence: University Press of Kansas, 1995.

———. "'To the Rescue of the Crops': The Women's Land Army during World War II," *Prologue* 25 (Winter, 1993): 356–57.

Llamas, Jose. *Cuban-Americans: Masters of Survival*. Lexington, Mass.: Abbott Books, 1980.

Lynd, Robert S., and Helen Merrell Lynd. *Middletown: A Study in Contemporary American Culture*. New York: Harcourt, Brace and Company, 1929.

———. *Middletown in Transition: A Study of Cultural Conflicts*. New York: Harcourt, Brace and Company, 1937.

Marks, Carole. *Farewell—We're Good and Gone: The Great Black Migration*. Bloomington: Indiana University Press, 1989.

Matthews, Donald G., and Jane Sherron De Hart. *Sex, Gender, and the Politics of the ERA: A State and the Nation*. New York: Oxford University Press, 1990.

May, Elaine Tyler. *Homeward Bound: American Families in the Cold War Era*. New York: Basic Books, 1988.

Mayes, Bea. "Women, Equality, and the Public High School." *Education* 97, no. 4 (Summer, 1977): 333–37.

Melosh, Barbara. ed., *Gender and American History Since 1890*. London: Routledge, 1993.

Meyerowitz, Joanne. *Women Adrift: Independent Wage Earners in Chicago, 1880–1930*. Chicago: University of Chicago Press, 1988.

Milkman, Ruth. *Gender at Work: The Dynamics of Job Segregation by Sex during World War II.* Urbana: University of Illinois Press, 1987.

Miller, Ann Ratner. *Net Internal Migration to Larger Areas of the United States: 1930–1940, 1940–1950, 1950–1960.* Philadelphia: University of Pennsylvania Population Studies Center, 1964.

Mincer, Jacob. "Labor Force Participation of Married Women: A Study of Labor Supply." In National Bureau of Economic Research, H. Gregg Lewis, ed., *Aspects of Labor Economics.* Princeton, N.J.: Princeton University Press, 1962, pp. 63–106.

Mintz, Steven, and Susan Kellogg. *Domestic Revolutions: A Social History of American Family Life.* New York: Free Press, 1988.

Modell, John. *Into One's Own: From Youth to Adulthood in the United States, 1920–1975.* Berkeley: University of California Press, 1989.

Montgomery, Louise. *The American Girl in the Stockyards District.* Chicago: University of Chicago Press, 1913.

Moody, Anne. *Coming of Age in Mississippi.* New York: Doubleday, 1968.

Morgan, Winona L. *The Family Meets the Depression: A Study of a Group of Highly Selected Families.* Minneapolis: University of Minnesota Press, 1939.

Moynihan, Daniel Patrick. *Family and Nation.* San Diego: Harcourt, Brace, Jovanich, 1986.

Muncy, Robyn. *Creating a Female Dominion in American Reform, 1890–1935.* New York: Oxford University Press, 1991.

National Manpower Council. *Womanpower in Today's World.* New York: Columbia University Press, 1957.

———. *Work in the Lives of Married Women.* New York: Columbia University Press, 1958.

Newsweek's Club Bureau. *American Women in the Postwar World: A Symposium on the Role Women Will Play in Business and Industry.* New York: Newsweek, n.d.

Noble, David F. *Forces of Production: A Social History of Industrial Automation.* New York: Oxford University Press, 1986.

Noble, Jeanne L. *The Negro Woman's College Education.* New York: Garland, 1987.

Odencrantz, Louise C. *Italian Women in Industry: A Study of Conditions in New York City.* New York: Russell Sage Foundation, 1919.

Ogden, Annegret S. *The Great American Housewife: From Helpmate to Wage Earner, 1776–1986.* Contributions in Women's Studies, No. 61. Westport, Conn.: Greenwood, 1986.

Oppenheimer, Valerie Kincade. *The Female Labor Force in the United States: Demographic and Economic Factors Governing Its Growth and Changing Composition.* Westport, Conn.: Greenwood, 1976.

Orleck, Annelise. *Common Sense and a Little Fire: Women and Working-Class Politics in the United States, 1900–1965.* Chapel Hill: University of North Carolina Press, 1995.

O'Toole, Patricia. "Thrifty, Kind—And Smart as Hell: Frances Hesselbein Teaches American Managers to Lead." *Lear's,* October, 1990, p. 26ff.

Peiss, Kathy. *Cheap Amusements.* Ithaca, N.Y.: Cornell University Press, 1990.

Perry, Elisabeth Israels. "From Achievement to Happiness: Girl Scouting in Middle Tennessee, 1910s–1960s." *Journal of Women's History* 5, no. 2 (Fall, 1993): 75–94.

Petersen, Gene B. *Southern Newcomers to Northern Cities: Work and Social Adjustment in Cleveland.* New York: Praeger for the Bureau of Social Science Research, 1977.

Peto, Marjorie. *Women Were Not Expected.* West Englewood, N.J.: privately published, 1947.

Phifer, Mary Hardy. *Textile Voices*. Beaumont Spartan and Startex Mills, n.p., n.d.

Putnam, Daniel. *A History of the Michigan State Normal School at Ypsilanti, Michigan, 1940–1899*. Ypsilanti: Scharf, Tag, Label & Box Company, 1899.

Quinney, Valerie. "Textile Women: Three Generations in the Mill." *Southern Exposure* 3, no. 4 (Winter, 1975): 70–73.

Ravitch, Diane. *The Great School Wars, New York, 1805–1973: A History of the Public Schools as Battlefields of Social Change*. New York: Basic Books, 1974.

Reisler, Mark. *By the Sweat of Their Brow: Mexican Immigrant Labor in the United States, 1900–1940*. Westport, Conn.: Greenwood Press, 1976.

Reisman, David. *The Lonely Crowd: A Study of the Changing American Character*. New Haven, Conn.: Yale University Press, 1950.

Riley, Glenda. *Divorce: An American Tradition*. New York: Oxford University Press, 1991.

———. *The Female Frontier: A Comparative View of Women on the Prairie and the Plains*. Lawrence: University Press of Kansas, 1988.

———. *Inventing the American Woman: An Inclusive History*. 2nd ed. Wheeling, Ill.: Harlan Davidson, 1995.

Rippa, S. Alexander. *Education in a Free Society: An American History*, 6th ed. New York: Longman, 1988.

Rosen, Ellen Israel. *Bitter Choices: Blue-Collar Women in and out of Work*. Chicago: University of Chicago Press, 1987.

Rosenberg, Charles E., ed. *The Family in History*. Philadelphia: University of Pennsylvania Press, 1975.

Rosenberg, Rosalind. *Divided Lives: American Women in the Twentieth Century*. New York: Hill and Wang, 1992.

Rubin, Lillian B. *Worlds of Pain: Life in the Working-Class Family*. New York: Basic Books, 1992.

Ruggles, Clyde O. *Winona State Normal School, 1860–1910*. Winona, Minn.: Jones & Kroeger Co., 1910.

Ruiz, Vicky. *Cannery Women, Cannery Lives: Mexican Women, Unionization, and the California Food Processing Industry, 1930–1950*. Albuquerque: University of New Mexico Press, 1987.

Rupp, Leila J. *Mobilizing Women for War: German and American Propaganda, 1939–1945*. Princeton, N.J.: Princeton University Press, 1978.

Rury, John L. *Education and Women's Work: Female Schooling and the Division of Labor in Urban America, 1870–1930*. Albany: State University of New York Press, 1991.

Sanger, Margaret. *Margaret Sanger, An Autobiography*. New York: Dover, 1971.

Scharf, Lois. *To Work and To Wed: Female Employment, Feminism, and the Great Depression*. Contributions in Women's Studies, Number 15. Westport, Conn.: Greenwood Press, 1980.

Scott, Niki. *The Balancing Act: A Handbook for Working Mothers*. Kansas City: Sheed, Andrews, and McMeel, 1978.

Seller, Maxine. "The Education of the Immigrant Woman, 1900–1935." *Journal of Urban History* 4 (May, 1978): 316–19.

Shaw, Lois Banfill, ed. "The Employment Consequences of Different Fertility Behaviors." *Midlife Women at Work: A Fifteen-Year Perspective*. Lexington, Mass.: Lexington Books, 1986.

————. *Unplanned Careers: The Working Lives of Middle-Aged Women*. Lexington, Mass.: Lexington Books, 1983.

Shryock, Henry S., Jr. *Population Mobility within the United States*. Chicago: Community and Family Study Center, University of Chicago, 1964.

Skolnick, Arlene S. *Embattled Paradise: The American Family in an Age of Uncertainty*. New York: Basic Books, 1991.

Stack, Carol B. *All Our Kin: Strategies for Survival in a Black Community*. New York: Harper & Row, 1974.

Stansell, Christine. *City of Women: Sex and Class in New York, 1789–1860*. New York: Knopf, 1986.

Stevens, Michael E., ed. *Women Remember the War, 1941–1945*. Voices of the Wisconsin Past. Madison: The State Historical Society of Wisconsin, 1993.

Straub, Eleanor Ferguson. "United States Government Policy toward Civilian Women During World War II." Ph. D. diss., Emory University, Atlanta, 1973.

Strom, Sharon Hartman. *Beyond the Typewriter: Gender, Class, and the Origins of Modern American Office Work, 1900–1930*. Urbana: University of Illinois Press, 1992.

Swain, Martha. "Mississippi Delta Goes to War," *The Journal of Mississippi History* 57, no. 4 (Winter, 1995): 344.

Taeuber, Conrad, and Irene B. Taeuber. *The Changing Population of the United States*. Census Monograph Series. New York: John Wiley & Sons, 1958.

Tentler, Leslie Woodcock. *Wage-Earning Women: Industrial Work and Family Life in the United States, 1900–1930*. New York: Oxford University Press, 1979.

Thomas, Mary Martha. *Riveting and Rationing in Dixie: Alabama Women and the Second World War*. Tuscaloosa: University of Alabama Press, 1987.

Tilly, Louise A., and Joan W. Scott. *Women's Work and the Family in Nineteenth-Century Europe*. New York: Holt, Rinehart, and Winston, 1978.

Tittle, Carol Kehr. *Careers and Family: Sex Roles and Adolescent Life Plans*. Sage Library of Social Research, 121. Beverly Hills, Calif.: Sage Publishers, 1981.

Turbin, Carole. *Working Women of Collar City: Gender, Class and Community in Troy, New York, 1864–86*. Urbana: University of Illinois Press, 1992.

VanKleeck, Mary. *Artificial Flower Makers*. New York: Russell Sage Foundation Survey Associates, 1913.

Vining, Donald, ed. *American Diaries of World War II*. New York: Pepys Press, 1982.

Wald, Lillian. *The House on Henry Street*. New York: Henry Holt and Company, 1915.

————. *Windows on Henry Street*. Boston: Little, Brown, and Company, 1934.

Walkowitz, Daniel J. *Worker City, Company Town*. Urbana: University of Illinois Press, 1978.

Wallace, Anthony F. *Rockdale: The Growth of an American Village*. New York: Norton, 1980.

Wallace, Phyllis A. *Pathways to Work: Unemployment Among Black Teenage Females*. Lexington, Mass.: Lexington Books, 1974.

Walshok, Mary Lindenstein. *Blue-Collar Women: Pioneers on the Male Frontier*. Garden City, N.Y.: Anchor/Doubleday, 1981.

Wandersee Bolin, Winifred D. "The Economics of Middle-Income Family Life: Working Women During the Great Depression." *Journal of American History* 65 (June, 1978): 60–74.

————. *On the Move: American Women in the 1970s*. Boston: Twayne, 1988.

———. *Women's Work and Family Values, 1920–1940*. Cambridge, Mass.: Harvard University Press, 1981.

Weatherford, Doris. *American Women and World War II*. New York: Facts on File, 1990.

Weiner, Lynn Y. *From Working Girl to Working Mother: The Female Labor Force in the United States, 1820–1980*. Chapel Hill: University of North Carolina Press, 1985.

Wertheimer, Barbara Mayer. *We Were There: The Story of Working Women in America*. New York: Pantheon, 1977.

Westwood, Sallie. *All Day, Every Day: Factory and Family in the Making of Women' Lives*. Urbana: University of Illinois Press, 1985.

Whitcomb, Emeline S. "Homemaking Education." *Biennial Survey of Education in the United States, 1928–1930*, vol. 1, Bulletin no. 20. Washington, D.C.: GPO, 1931.

Whittemore, Hank. "We Can't Pay the Rent." *Parade*, January 10, 1988, p. 5ff.

Willie, Charles Vert. *Black and White Families: A Study in Complementarity*. Bayside, N.Y.: General Hall, 1985.

———. *Race, Ethnicity, and Socioeconomic Status*. Bayside, N.Y.: General Hall, 1983.

Wischnitzer, Mark. *To Dwell in Safety: The Story of Jewish Migration Since 1800*. Philadelphia: Jewish Publication Society of America, 1948.

Woody, Thomas. *A History of Women's Education in the United States*. 2 vols. New York: Octagon Books, 1966.

Wright, Barbara Drygulski, et al., ed. *Women, Work, and Technology: Transformations*. Ann Arbor: University of Michigan Press, 1987.

Yates, JoAnne. *Control through Communications: The Rise of System in American Management*. Baltimore: Johns Hopkins University Press, 1993.

Index

Printed in the United States
65424LVS00002B/154-165

9 780890 967980